The
Media
of
Mass
communication

The Media of Mass communication

third canadian edition

160501

john vivian
winona state university

peter j. maurin
mohawk college

Toronto

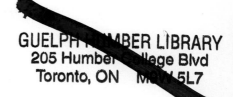

National Library of Canada Cataloguing in Publication Data

Vivian, John
    The media of mass communication

3rd Canadian ed.
Includes index.
ISBN 0-205-35925-6

1. Mass media. I. Maurin, Peter. II. Title.

P90.V58 2003   302.23   C2002-900931-6

ISBN 0-205-35925-6

Vice-President, Editorial Director: Michael J. Young
Acquisitions Editor: Marianne Minaker
Executive Marketing Manager: Christine Cozens
Developmental Editor: John Polanszky
Senior Production Editor: Joe Zingrone
Copy Editor: Valerie Adams
Senior Production Coordinator: Peggy Brown
Page Layout: Christine Velakis
Photo Research: Alene McNeill
Art Director: Mary Opper
Cover/Interior Design: Sarah Battersby, Jennifer Federico
Cover Image: Mark Johann/Photonica

1 2 3 4 5   06 05 04 03

Printed and bound in Canada.

To Harold Vivian, my father,
who sparked my curiosity about the
mass media at age five by asking what
was black and white and read all over.

And to Elaine Vivian, my mother,
who nurtured this curiosity by keeping
the house stocked with books, magazines
and reading material of every sort.

J. V.

To my soulmate Kim; thank you for all your
love, patience and understanding over the last
"twenty-something" years. To my kids, Sonja
and Joshua, who are each special in their own
way, thank you for letting me be your dad and
your friend.

P. J. M.

BRIEF CONTENTS

CONTENTS

CHAPTER 3
MUSIC   65

CHAPTER 4
RADIO   90

CHAPTER 7
NEWS 157

CHAPTER 8
PUBLIC RELATIONS 179

CHAPTER 12
MEDIA EFFECTS 274

CHAPTER 13
MASS MEDIA AND SOCIETY   300

CHAPTER 14
GLOBAL MASS MEDIA   314

PREFACE

When the first Canadian edition of *The Media of Mass Communication* was introduced in 1997, it was, to our knowledge, a new approach in mass communication education in Canada. Using the survey approach, the book was written to help students become more critical consumers of both Canadian and U.S. media. Both Canadian and American media institutions and theories were highlighted. The second edition featured more Canadian content and examples.

The Canadian media landscape has changed dramatically since the first edition was published in 1997. This is reflected in this new edition. Issues such as convergence, digital media, and globalization are given considerable examination. Noteworthy Canadian media people are spotlighted whenever possible in this new edition. Sections on evaluating media content and predicting the future of the mass media also encourage critical thinking about both the media and media content.

This edition also incorporates some organizational changes. For example, this book has three sections, each intended to examine a different aspect of the mass media:

◆ **THE MASS MEDIA:** Chapter 1, "Media in Theory" provides a foundation for understanding the mass media and the dynamics that affect the messages that they transmit. The next five chapters deal with each of the major mass media—newspapers, sound recordings, radio, television, and the web.

◆ **MASS MESSAGES:** Then come chapters on the major content forms disseminated by the media to mass audiences. These include news, public relations, and advertising. A chapter on media research is also included.

◆ **MASS MEDIA ISSUES:** The rest of the book focuses on issues, including media effects, the mass media and society, global mass media, and a chapter on media law and ethics.

Each chapter also includes the following:

◆ **MEDIA TIMELINE.** At the beginning of each chapter, a timeline will help you see the important media events at a glance.

◆ **WEBLINKS.** The margins contain hundreds of web addresses to guide your learning about the mass media beyond the textbook and the classroom.

◆ **QUESTIONS FOR REVIEW.** These questions are keyed to the major topics and themes in the chapter. Use them for a quick assessment of whether you caught the major points.

◆ **QUESTIONS FOR CRITICAL THINKING.** These questions ask you both to recall specific information and to use your imagination and critical thinking abilities to restructure the material.

◆ **FOR KEEPING UP TO DATE.** These sections list professional and trade journals, magazines, newspapers and other periodical references to help you keep current on media developments and issues. Most of these periodicals are available in college libraries.

◆ **FOR FURTHER LEARNING.** If you have a special interest in the material introduced in the chapter, you can use the end-of-chapter bibliographies to identify more detailed examinations in other sources.

◆ **KEY TERMS.** Important terms, ideas, and names are highlighted in boldface and compiled by chapter in the Glossary at the end of the book.
◆ **BOXES.** Throughout the book, you will find boxes that illustrate significant points. *Media People* boxes introduce personalities who have had a major impact on the media or whose story illustrates a major point of media history. The *Media Databank* boxes contain tables to help you see certain facts about the mass media at a glance.

Keeping Current

To you, as a student, I want to emphasize that this book is a tool to help you become a more intelligent and discerning media consumer. This book, though, is only one of many tools for staying on top of the subject for many years to come. A feature at the end of every chapter, "For Keeping Up to Date," has tips on how to keep current even when your course is over. I hope you enjoy reading the third Canadian edition of *The Media of Mass Communication.* Whether you are a student or an instructor, if you have any comments, feel free to email me at maurin@sympatico.ca

Supplements

Instructor Supplements

INSTRUCTOR'S RESOURCE MANUAL (IRM). This manual is designed to ease the time-consuming demands of instructional preparation, enhance lectures, and provide helpful suggestions to organize the course. The IRM consists of helpful teaching resources and lecture enrichment including outlines, synopses, glossaries, and an "at-a-glance" guide to the wealth of resources available in the package.

TEST BANK. The test bank includes multiple-choice, true/false, matching, fill-in-the-blank, short answer, and essay questions.

A Great Way to Learn and Instruct Online

The Pearson Education Canada Companion Website is easy to navigate and is organized to correspond to the chapters in this textbook. Whether you are a student in the classroom or a distance learner you will discover helpful resources for in-depth study and research that empower you in your quest for greater knowledge and maximize your potential for success in the course.

[www.pearsoned.ca/vivian]

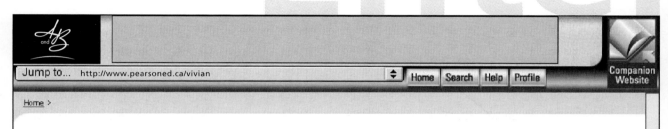

Jump to...   http://www.pearsoned.ca/vivian   Home Search Help Profile

Home >

A&B Companion Website

The Media of Mass Communication, Third Canadian Edition
by Vivian and Maurin

Student Resources

The modules in this section provide students with tools for learning course material. These modules include:

- Chapter Objectives
- Destinations
- Quizzes
- Internet Exercises
- Net Search

In the quiz modules students can send answers to the grader and receive instant feedback on their progress through the Results Reporter. Coaching comments and references to the textbook may be available to ensure that students take advantage of all available resources to enhance their learning experience.

Instructor Resources

The modules in this section provide instructors with additional teaching tools. Downloadable PowerPoint Presentations, Electronic Transparencies, and an Instructor's Manual are just some of the materials that may be available in this section. Where appropriate, this section will be password protected. To get a password, simply contact your Pearson Education Canada Representative or call Faculty Sales and Services at 1-800-850-5813.

Canada's Media Guru. Marshall McLuhan's ideas and commentaries on the role and effects of the mass media are still as popular today as they were in the 1960s. His theories make up part of the "Canadian School of Communication."

The Media of Mass Communication in Theory and Practice

MEDIA TIMELINE

Media Technology

_____ **1440s Primal Event**

Johannes Gutenberg devises movable metal type, permitting mass production of printed materials.

_____ **1455 Books**

Johannes Gutenberg prints the first of his Bibles using movable type.

_____ **1690 Newspapers**

Ben Harris prints *Publick Occurrences,* the first newspaper in the English colonies.

_____ **1741 Magazines**

Andrew Bradford prints *American Magazine* and Benjamin Franklin prints *General Magazine,* the first magazines in the English colonies.

_____ **1877 Recording**

Thomas Edison, with help from Montreal's Emile Berliner, introduces the phonograph, which can record and play back sound.

_____ **1888 Movies**

William Dickson devises the motion-picture camera.

_____ **1906 Radio**

Canada's Reginald Fessenden broadcasts to ships at sea.

_____ **1927 Television**

Philo Farnsworth invents the tube that picks up moving images for live transmission.

_____ **1969 Web**

The U.S. Defense Department establishes the computer network that would become the Internet.

_____ **2001**

Convergence becomes a key media issue.

MEDIA IN THEORY

Two Canadian Theories on Communication

Media scholars have devised several ways to dissect and analyze the mass media. This chapter is about these theoretical approaches to **communication**. These include the ideas of the so-called "Canadian School" of communication, which embodies the ideas of Harold Innis and Marshall McLuhan. Both men were determinists; they argued that the physical form of communication would determine the psychological and social outcome. Innis was interested in the economics of communication, while McLuhan looked at how the form of the medium influenced our perception of the message.

Marshall McLuhan

While the phrase has become something of a cliché, McLuhan developed the theory that the "medium is the message." McLuhan examined how we perceive media messages: not only looking at the content of the message but also the form of the message. He used the metaphor of a lightbulb to explain his idea.

He argued that while everyone notices the content of the lightbulb (the light it provides), no one notices the form, that is, the bulb itself. The same holds true for content in the context of the media. People notice the content of the media (a speech on radio, a comedy on television) but not the medium that transmits the message. McLuhan came to believe that the characteristics of the medium influence how we perceive the message.

McLuhan developed an innovative model to help explain the mass media. To McLuhan's thinking, books, magazines, and newspapers were **hot media** because they require a high degree of thinking to use. To read a book, for example, you must immerse yourself to derive anything from it. The relationship between medium and user is intimate. The same is true with magazines and newspapers. McLuhan also considered movies a hot medium because they involve viewers so completely. Huge screens command the viewers' full attention, and sealed, darkened viewing rooms shut out distractions.

In contrast, McLuhan classified television as a **cool medium** because it can be used with less intellectual involvement and hardly any effort. Although television has many of the sensory appeals of movies, including sight, motion, and sound, it does not overwhelm viewers to the point that all else is pushed out of their immediate consciousness. When radio is heard merely as background noise, it does not require any listener involvement at all, and McLuhan would call it a hot medium.

Although confusing and sometimes contradictory, McLuhan's basic argument here deals with how active or passive we are when we consume media messages. McLuhan's point is underscored by research that has found that people remember much more from reading a newspaper or magazine than from watching television or listening to the radio. The harder you work to receive a message from the media, the more you remember.

Hot and Cool. Canadian scholar Marshall McLuhan, whose work is often associated with the "Toronto School," developed the idea of *hot* and *cool* media. The more the audience is immersed in the message, the warmer McLuhan considered the medium. He saw movies as very warm because they can engage so many human senses simultaneously with a darkened environment and huge screen keeping out competing stimuli.

Harold Innis

McLuhan developed many of his ideas based on the work of another Canadian, Harold Innis. Innis was interested in communication as it applied to how people or groups in power remained in power. Innis was a political economist at the University of Toronto whose communication model was based on what he referred to as **bias in communication**. This bias had effects in both time and space.

This analysis of time and space bias was examined in some detail in *Empire and Communication*, a book he published in 1950. This book included a historical look at forms of communication that have helped in the rise and fall of civilizations. His study reported on life from ancient Egypt up to and including North American society in the 1940s. His hypothesis was that the type of social organization in all these different societies was signified by the type of media that each used to communicate important information. In turn, that media was directly related to how those in power kept power through their "monopolies of knowledge."

By Innis's way of thinking, this communication bias is linked to the media of choice during each historical period and by each civilization. For example, stone and clay have a bias for time; that is they can last a long time due to their material composition and therefore can be passed down from generation to generation. Societies using these "time-based" media, according to Innis, were hierarchical and decentralized and based on tradition. On the other hand, paper has a bias for space; it's light and can be passed around from person to person. Cultures using this medium were less hierarchical and more centralized and more commercial than earlier civilizations. In short, media that were light and fast favoured control over space, while heavy, slow, and face-to-face media were better suited to keeping cultures stable over time.

In his article "The Office of the Future: Weber and Innis Revisited," Canadian James R. Taylor begins to elaborate on these ideas of communication bias in contemporary terms. The use of computers in contemporary society, combined with the use of telephones, has given communication a "lightness" that it never had in the past. Memos, phone calls, faxes, and e-mails are biased toward rapid, efficient communication through space. Modern Canadian society has seen corporate downsizing in terms of massive layoffs of employees, many of them middle-managers. This is what Innis meant when he said that societies became less hierarchical when using media that favour space. New technologies have also helped centralize power and control, but they don't do much to maintain cultural traditions. Needless to say, the implications are significant.

The works of Innis and McLuhan, while at times confusing for students, should not be overlooked. Both men made "The 100 Most Important Canadians in History" list published by *Maclean's* in 1998.

Importance of Mass Media

PERVASIVENESS

Mass media are pervasive in modern life. Every morning Canadians wake up to clock radios, the morning paper, or morning TV news programs. Political candidates spend most of their campaign dollars on television to woo voters. The economy is dependent on advertising to create mass markets. Children see 30 000 to 40 000 commercial messages a year. With mass media so influential, we need to know as much as we can about how they work. Consider the following:

- The mass media are our window on the world. Canadian media interpret the world for us through Canadian eyes.
- An informed and involved citizenry is possible in modern democracy only when the mass media work well.
- People need the mass media to express their ideas widely. Without mass media, your expression would be limited to people within earshot and to whom you write letters.

Media History Project: Investigates trends in historical media, the scope of media development, and the integration of the media with political, economic, social, cultural, and moral institutions.

www.mediahistory.com/ histhome.html

Media People

Marshall McLuhan

Marshall McLuhan

Born in Edmonton in 1911, Canadian communication theorist Marshall McLuhan taught at Assumption College in Windsor (now the University of Windsor) and at St. Michael's College at the University of Toronto. In 1954 he founded *Explorations*, a journal devoted to the analysis of popular media and culture. His ideas in the 1960s and 1970s took popular culture by storm. He was a frequent guest on talk shows in both Canada and the United States. He even appeared in a cameo role in the 1977 Woody Allen movie *Annie Hall*. McLuhan is also the patron saint of *Wired* magazine.

While the phrase "the medium is the message" is the most popular "McLuhanism," he did have some other attention-grabbing things to say on various aspects of mass media. For example:

- "Television is a serious medium, it's an inner oriented medium, you are the vanishing point, it goes inside you, you go on an inner trip, it is the prelude, the vestibule to LSD."
- "All news is fake. It's pseudo-event. It's created by the medium that is employed. Newspaper news has nothing to do with TV news."
- "Advertising is a service industry that provides its satisfactions quite independent of the product, and that people are increasingly tending to get their satisfactions from the ad rather than the product."

Friends of Canadian Broadcasting: This group supports indigenous broadcasters.

Friendscb.org

- Powerful forces use the mass media to influence us with their ideologies and for their commercial purposes. The mass media are the main tools of propagandists, advertisers, and other persuaders.
- How does American media shape Canadian culture? Consider that with the exception of news programming, the average Canadian watches more American television than Canadian television. The same is true of movies. The majority of movies playing in Canadian movie houses are American.

Due to the pervasiveness of American media on Canadian airwaves, the government formed an independent body to supervise and regulate broadcasting. The CRTC is the Canadian Radio-Television Telecommunications Commission, whose roots go back to the early days of broadcasting in Canada. As Canada enters the 21st century, the CRTC has the tenuous job of balancing the economic realities of broadcasting with the cultural goals of ensuring that Canadians are seen and heard on Canadian media.

How pervasive is American media in Canada? In their Broadcast Policy Monitoring Report, the CRTC points out that, on average, 65 percent of all TV programs watched by Canadians are foreign (mostly American) in nature. This echoes comments made by former Prime Minister Kim Campbell, in a speech to the American Film Market in 1997. In that address she pointed out that:

- Ninety-five percent of movies shown in Canada are American.

- Over 80 percent of non-news programming on Canadian television is foreign, mostly from the U.S.
- Sixty percent of the books sold in Canadian bookstores are American, as are 85 percent of magazines sold.
- The majority of music heard on Canadian radio stations is American.

More often than not, English-Canadians choose American popular culture over home-grown popular culture. Does this mean that Canadian media content is inferior to American media? Not necessarily. The issue might also be one of availability. The above statistics also suggest we simply have more American than Canadian choices.

INFORMATION SOURCE

The importance of the media as an information source was obvious in the days following the September 11, 2001, attacks on the World Trade Center and the Pentagon. People around the world turned to the media for updates. The heart of the media's informing function lies in messages called **news**. Journalists themselves are hard pressed to agree on a definition of news. One useful definition is that news is reports on things that people want or need to know. Reporters try to tell the news without taking sides. Advertising also is part of the mass media's information function. The media, especially newspapers, are bulletin boards for business. People look to grocery advertisements for specials. Classified advertisements also provide useful information.

ENTERTAINMENT SOURCE

The mass media can be wonderful entertainers, bringing together audiences not otherwise possible. The Molson Canadian "I Am Canadian" advertising campaign, including "Joe's Rant" and "No Doot Aboot It," likely did more to promote patriotism in Canada than government commissions into media content. While its content is clearly satiric, many Canadians get their sense of Canadian politics from shows such as *This Hour Has 22 Minutes* and *The Royal Canadian Air Farce* on the CBC.

Almost all mass media have an entertainment component. The thrust of the American movie industry is almost wholly entertainment, although there can be a strong informational and persuasive element. Even the most serious newspaper has an occasional humour column. Most mass media are a mix of information and entertainment—and also persuasion.

Pervasiveness of Media. In the last few years, Harry Potter has become a huge part of pop culture. Books, movies, websites, and other merchandising of the J.K. Rolwing character show how pervasive a media message can be.

PERSUASION FORUM

People form opinions from the information and interpretations to which they are exposed, which means that even news coverage has an element of persuasion. The media's attempts to persuade, however, are usually in editorials and

MEDIA DATABANK 1.1

Media Consumption

People average 40 percent of their day and 60 percent of their waking hours with the mass media. These data, extracted from 2000 research from Veronis Suhler, show slight shifts over the years. Most notable are growth in time spent with the web and recorded music and shrinkage in time spent with television and radio.

	1997	2001	2003
Television	4.3 hours	4.4 hours	4.4 hours
Radio	3.0 hours	2.8 hours	2.7 hours
Records	0.7 hour	0.8 hour	0.9 hour
Newspapers	0.4 hour	0.4 hour	0.4 hour
Books	0.3 hour	0.3 hour	0.3 hour
Movies (including home video)	0.2 hour	0.2 hour	0.2 hour
Magazines	0.2 hour	0.2 hour	0.2 hour

commentaries whose purposes are obvious. Most news media separate material designed to persuade from news. Newspapers package their opinion articles in an editorial section. Commentary on television is introduced as opinion.

The most obvious of the media messages designed to persuade are advertising. **Advertisements** exhort the audience to action—to go out and buy toothpaste, cornflakes, and automobiles. **Public relations** is subtler, seeking to persuade but usually not to induce immediate action. Public relations tries to shape attitudes, usually by persuading mass media audiences to see an institution or activity in a particular light.

BINDING INFLUENCE

The mass media bind communities together by giving messages that become a shared experience. A rural newspaper editor scrambling to get out an issue may not be thinking about how her work creates a common identity among readers, but it does. The town newspaper is something everyone in town has in common. In the same way, what Metro riders in Montreal read on their way to work in the morning gives them something in common. A shared knowledge and a shared experience are created by mass media, and thus they create a base for community. The same phenomenon occurs on a national level. The coverage of the funeral of former Prime Minister Trudeau in the fall of 2000 brought Canadians together at a time of mourning.

Primary Mass Media

PRINT MEDIA

Books, **magazines**, and **newspapers**, the primary **print media**, can generally be distinguished in the following four categories: binding, regularity, content, and timeliness:

	Books	*Magazines*	*Newspapers*
Binding	Stitched or glued	Staples	Unbound
Regularity	Single issue	At least quarterly	At least weekly
Content	Single topic	diverse topics	diverse topics
Timeliness	Generally not timely	Timeliness not an issue	Timeliness important

Although these distinctions are helpful, they cannot be applied rigidly. For example, timeliness is critical to *Time* and *Maclean's*. Over the past 20 years, book publishers have found ways to produce "instant books" on major news events within a couple of weeks so that their topics can be timely.

The technological basis of books, magazines, and newspapers (as well as that of lesser print media such as brochures, pamphlets, and billboards) is the printing press, which for practical purposes dates back to the 1440s. Print media messages are in tangible form. They can be picked up physically and laid down, stacked, and filed and stored for later reference. Even though newspapers may be used to wrap up the leftovers from dinner for tomorrow's garbage, there is also a permanency about the print media.

ELECTRONIC MEDIA

Television, radio, and sound recordings flash their messages electronically. Pioneer work on **electronic media** began in the late 1800s, but they are mostly a 20th-century development. Unlike print messages, television and radio messages disappear as soon as they are transmitted. Messages can be stored on tape and other means, but usually they reach listeners and viewers in a nonconcrete form. Television is especially distinctive because it engages several senses at once with sound, sight, and movement.

PHOTOGRAPHIC MEDIA

The technology of movies is based on the chemistry of photography. Movies, however, may not be with us much longer as a chemical medium. While Hollywood still makes movies on film that is pulled "through the soup," a lot of video production, including some prime-time television, is shot on tape and stored digitally. Photography itself is moving from chemistry to digital technology, which means production and editing occur on computer screens rather than in darkrooms. Eventually, as digital technology improves and costs come down, movies will shift entirely from chemical to electronic technology.

DIGITIZATION AND MELDING

The primary mass media as we know them today are in a technological transition, a **melding** that is blurring the old distinctions that once clearly separated them. For example, newspapers are experimenting with electronic delivery via cable and telephone lines—"no paper" newspapers. Through personal computers thousands of people have access to databanks to choose the news coverage they want. This is called **digitization,** a process that compresses, stores, and transmits data, including text, sound, and video, in extremely compact and efficient ways.

Economics of Mass Media

ECONOMIC FOUNDATION

The mass media are expensive to set up and operate. The equipment and facilities require major investment. Meeting the payroll requires a bankroll, print media must buy paper by the ton, and broadcasters have gigantic electricity bills to pump their messages through the ether.

To meet their expenses, the mass media sell their product in two ways. Either they derive their income from selling a product directly to mass audiences, as do the movie, record, and book industries, or they derive their income from advertisers who pay for the access to mass audiences that the media provide, as do newspapers, magazines, radio, and television. In short, the mass media operate in a capitalistic environment, and with few exceptions, they are in business to make money.

ADVERTISING REVENUE.   Advertisers pay the mass media for access to potential customers. From print media, advertisers buy space. From broadcasters, they buy time.

The more potential customers a media company can deliver to advertisers, the more advertisers are charged for time or space.

Book publishers once relied solely on readers for revenue, but that has changed. Today, book publishers charge for film rights whenever Hollywood turns a book into a movie or a television program. The result is that publishing houses now profit indirectly from the advertising revenue that television networks pull in from broadcasting movies.

Movies too have come to benefit from advertising. Until the 1950s, movies relied entirely on box-office receipts for profits, but moviemakers now calculate what profits they can realize not only from movie-house traffic but also from recycling their movies through home videos, pay per view on Viewer's Choice Canada, on discretionary services such as TMN and Moviepix, and finally on advertising-supported television.

CIRCULATION REVENUE.   While some advertising-supported mass media, such as network television, do not charge their audiences, others do. When income is derived from the audience, it's called **circulation** revenue. *Globe and Mail* readers pay 75 cents a copy at the corner store. *Maclean's* costs $4.50. Little if any of the newsrack charge or even subscription revenue ends up with the *Globe* or *Maclean's*. Distribution is costly, and distributors all along the way take their cut. For some publications, however, subscription income makes the difference between profit and loss.

Direct audience payments have emerged in recent years in broadcasting. Cable subscribers pay a monthly fee. Audience support is the basis of Canadian Specialty Channels such as Outdoor Life Network, Teletoon, Prime, and HGTV. Non-commercial broadcasting, including provincial broadcasters like B.C.'s Knowledge Network, Saskatchewan's SCN, and Ontario's TVO, rely heavily on viewer contributions. Record makers, moviemakers, and book publishers depend on direct sales to the consumer.

GOVERNMENT SUBSIDIES.   While the idea of government support for the mass media might seem to some a waste of public money, both the U.S. and Canadian governments support some form of public broadcasting. In Canada, the **Canadian Broadcasting Corporation (CBC)** is mandated by the government to promote Canadian culture to Canadians. The cost of the CBC is roughly one dollar per week for each Canadian adult. This money helps to fund national radio and television networks in both French and English. Due to belt tightening since the 1990s, government support for public broadcasting seems to be dropping off, as both Canadian and U.S. government funds for public broadcasting have been cut drastically in the last few years.

ECONOMIC IMPERATIVE

Economics figures into which messages make it to print or the airwaves. To realize their profit potential, the media that seek large audiences choose to deal with subjects of wide appeal and to present them in ways that attract great numbers of people. A subject interesting only to a small number of people does not make it into *Canadian Living*. CTV drops programs that do not do well in the television ratings. This is a function of economics for those media that depend on advertising revenue to stay in business. The larger the audience, the more advertisers are willing to pay for time and space to pitch their goods and services.

Even media that seek narrow segments of the population need to reach as many people within their segments as possible to attract advertisers. A jazz radio station that attracts 90 percent of the jazz fans in a city will be more successful with advertisers than a competing jazz station that attracts only 10 percent.

Media that do not depend on advertising also are geared to finding large audiences. For example, a novel that flops does not go into a second printing, and only successful movies generate sequels.

Guide to Federal Programs for the Film and Video Sector: Available for download from the Cultural Industries Branch of the Ministry of Canadian Heritage.

www.pch.gc.ca/culture/ cult_ind/fp/fptoc_e.htm

MEDIA DATABANK 1.2

Media Costs

Here is a sampler of rates for time and space in major media for one-time placements. Major advertisers pay less because they are given discounts as repeat customers.

CBS, Super Bowl XXXV	30-second spot	US$ 2 500 000
NBC, *ER*	30-second spot	US$ 545 000
ABC, *Monday Night Football*	30-second spot	US$ 380 000
CTV, *The West Wing*	30-second spot	$35 000
CTV, *The Associates*	30-second spot	$7 000
Globe and Mail	Full page	$49 375
Maclean's	Full page	$31 960
TV Guide (Canadian National Edition)	Full page	$19 775

Upside and Downside

The drive to attract advertising can affect media messages in sinister ways. For example, the television station that overplays the ribbon-cutting ceremony at a new store is usually motivated more by pleasing an advertiser than by telling news. The economic dependence of the mass media on advertising income gives considerable clout to advertisers who threaten to yank advertising out of a publication if a certain negative story appears. Such threats occur, although not frequently. At a subtler level, during the 1950s, as racial injustice was emerging as an issue that would rip apart the nation a decade later, American television avoided documentaries on the subject. No advertisers were interested.

The quest for audience also affects how messages are put together. The effect is relatively benign, although real, when many high school science textbooks have danced gingerly around the subject of evolution rather than become embroiled with creationists and lose sales.

Mass Media Trends

Conglomeration

The trend toward **conglomeration**, sometimes referred to as "concentration of ownership" by Canadian writers, involves a process of mergers, acquisitions, and buyouts that consolidates the ownership of the media into fewer and fewer companies. The deep pockets of a wealthy corporate parent can see a financially troubled media unit, such as a radio station, through a rough period, but there is a price. In time, the corporate parent wants a financial return on its investment, and pressure builds on the station to generate more and more profit. This would not be so bad if the people running the radio station loved radio and had a sense of public service, but the process of conglomeration often doesn't work out that way. Parent corporations tend to replace media people with career-climbing, bottom-line managers whose motivation is looking good to their superiors in faraway cities who are under serious pressure to increase profits. Management experts, not radio people, end up running the station, and often the quality of media content suffers.

Convergence

The other media trend is **convergence**. This term is used to describe media cross ownership. This refers to the practice of one company with interests in publishing, broadcasting, and the Internet. Ted Rogers defined convergence in two different ways: "The computer and the TV set are coming together. You're putting together different media through one instrument. That's technological convergence. And then there's the convergence we might call marketing convergence, where you're packaging together people's needs in a way to make it easier for them. In Rogers's case it be all the services—telephony, long distance, high speed Internet, low speed Internet, cable, paging, etc...." It's interesting to note that Rogers made these comments in *Maclean's*—a magazine he owns.

Ted Rogers is correct—part of the process of convergence is made possible with changes in technology. Due to both advances in technology and the convergence process, the traditional mass media as we know them today are in a technological transition that is blurring the old distinctions that once clearly separated them.

Gannett: Links to corporate profile, shareholder services, dividend information, corporate annual reports, and Gannett newspapers, including *USA Today;* television stations; outdoor advertising subsidiary.

www.gannett.com

Hearst: Links to individual Hearst properties, including book houses, broadcasters, television production, magazines, newspapers, and new media subsidiaries.

www.hearstcorp.com

Thomson: Links to company news releases.

www.thomson.com

Viacom: Links to subsidiaries, including Paramount movie studio, MTV, Nickelodeon and VH1 cable networks, Blockbuster video stores, and Simon & Schuster books.

www.viacom.com

Izzy Asper. The actions of both Izzy Asper and Ted Rogers have recently raised concerns in Canadian media circles about who owns how much of the media and the ethics of having so few people controlling so much media and media content. *Maclean's* named Izzy Asper, Jean Monty (BCE), and Ted Rogers as three of the most influential Canadians.

Through personal computers, thousands of people have the ability to choose the news coverage they want. Major Canadian Internet news websites, like globaltv.com or globeandmail.com, allow surfers to pick and choose the stories that are most important to them. An individual sitting at a computer screen could control the editing by passing unwanted portions and focusing on what was most valuable to him or her. These websites also offer video clips of recent news stories to be viewed at the person's leisure.

Technological convergence isn't just for TV and newspapers. Many Canadian radio stations are now available through streaming on the Internet or on satellite using StarChoice or Bell ExpressVu. This means that someone in St. John's can listen to Vancouver stations such as CFOX on a satellite system.

CONVERGENCE IN CANADA

How extensive is convergence in Canada? Consider the information on the five media rivals that have established themselves as the major players in Canada, as of early 2002:

- Bell Canada Enterprises (BCE), through Bell GlobeMedia, owns several media platforms, including CTV, CTVNewsNet, TSN, RDS, Talk!TV, the Discovery Channel, and the Comedy Network. It also has interests in media distribution with Bell ExpressVu Satellite Systems and Sympatico-Lycos.
- CanWest Global is another Canadian media powerhouse with interests in radio and television broadcasting. It is also 50 percent owner of the *National Post* and 26 other daily Canadian newspapers. Its Internet holdings include canada.com, and it also has media holdings around the world.
- Quebecor owns TVA (the largest television network in Quebec), Sun Media (the second largest Canadian newspaper group), and the CANOE websites. The company also has interests in 12 publishing houses and Videotron, a chain of video rental stores.

- Rogers Media not only has interests in cable TV distribution but also in programming with Sportsnet. In publishing, they own *Maclean's*, *Chatelaine*, and *Flare* magazines. Their Internet division includes excite.ca, and Rogers owns radio and television stations in British Columbia, Alberta, Manitoba, and Ontario. In addition to all of this, Rogers also has a strong presence in wireless communication and is the owner of the Toronto Blue Jays.
- Shaw Communications is second only to Rogers in cable television distribution. Its holdings include interests in radio, TV specialty channels, and Star Choice satellite television.
- Emerging as a major player in 2001 was Torstar. In addition to owning the *Toronto Star* and other daily newspapers, it also has interests in publishing and applied for broadcasting licences in late 2001.

How significant is convergence? CRTC Commissioner Martha Wilson feels that "it is a big deal from at least two standpoints. As a result of convergence, some very big companies are being created. And in order to get as big as they are getting, these companies have paid very big prices for perceived value when it really remains to be seen whether or not successful business strategies can be developed around these resulting organizations." Dwayne Winseck, a journalism professor at Carleton University, says that while convergence and consolidation make sense from a business standpoint, "it is not good for journalism or democracy, where citizens continue to look to the media to reflect, extend and amplify public life."

Others also see the results of convergence in vague and uncertain terms. In his speech to the International Institute of Communications, CRTC Chairperson David Colville said "industry leaders and watchers have been musing publicly about the difficulty of making convergence pay off over the next few years. In fact, Jean Monty (Chair of BCE) himself said, "no one knows what services will work at the end of the day." To use a business cliché, the bottom line is this: While technologically possible, the economics of it have yet to be worked out. The effects of convergence are just being felt. Even Matthew Fraser, media columnist for the *National Post*, writes, "convergence, it seems, will take some time to prove itself as a business model." The real impact of convergence for everyone—people working in the media, consumers, and media moguls—won't be felt for years.

DUBIOUS EFFECTS OF CONGLOMERATION AND CONVERGENCE

Critics such as **Ben Bagdikian** say that conglomeration affects the diversity of messages offered by the mass media. Speaking at the Madison Institute, Bagdikian portrayed conglomeration in bleak terms:

> They are trying to buy control or market domination not just in one medium but in all the media. The aim is to control the entire process from an original manuscript or new series to its use in as many forms as possible. A magazine article owned by *the company* becomes a book owned by *the company*. That becomes a television program owned by *the company*, which then becomes a movie owned by *the company*. It is shown in theaters owned by *the company*, and the movie sound track is issued on a record label owned by *the company*, featuring the vocalist on the cover of one of *the company* magazines. It does not take an angel from heaven to tell us that *the company* will be less enthusiastic about outside ideas and production that it does not own, and more and more we will be dealing with closed circuits to control access to most of the public.

Nobody begrudges a company making a profit. The difficulty comes when the recycling displaces creative new entries in the mass media marketplace. NBC executive Don Ohlmeyer concedes that a vertically integrated network is disinclined "in even considering projects in which they don't own a financial interest." Independent Hollywood producers, who once competed to produce network shows, are finding themselves out of the loop. The result, says Gary Goldberg, creator of *Spin City* on ABC: "You see this blandness and similarity to the shows. Consumers are the ones who get hurt."

One of the negative effects of conglomeration occurs when a parent company looks to its subsidiaries only to enrich conglomerate coffers as quickly as possible and by any means possible, regardless of the quality of products that are produced. This is especially a problem when a conglomerate's subsidiaries include, for example, widget factories, cherry orchards, funeral homes and, by the way, also some book companies. The top management of such diverse conglomerates is inclined to take a cookie-cutter approach that de-emphasizes or even ignores important traditions in book publishing, including a sense of social responsibility. Many of these conglomerates focus on profits alone. One result, according to many literary critics, has been a decline in quality.

QUALITY.   Headquarters push subsidiaries to cut costs to increase profits, a trend that has devastated the quality of writing and editing. Fewer people do more work. At newspapers, for example, a reporter's story once went through several hands—editor, copy editor, headline writer, typesetter, and proofreader. At every stage, the story could be improved. In today's streamlined newsrooms, proofreaders have been replaced by spell-check software, which not only introduces its own problems but also lacks the intelligence and judgment of a good proofreader. The jobs of the reporter and the typesetter have been consolidated. In many newsrooms, so have the jobs of copy editors and headline writers.

SAMENESS.   You can fly from the east to the west coast on the same day and read the same Associated Press stories word for word. Newspaper publishers learned long ago that sharing stories could reduce costs. The resulting economics came at the cost of less diversity in content.

Cultural sociologists fret about the sameness. In recorded music, for example, major record companies often encourage artists to imitate what is already popular. The result is that derivative music squeezes original artists and material out of the marketplace—or at least makes it more difficult for these artists to find an audience. Sociologists think that this process slows the movement of culture in new directions.

CORPORATE INSTABILITY.   Conglomeration also has introduced instability. Profit-driven corporate parents are quick to sell subsidiaries that fall short of profit expectations even for a short term or just to raise cash. An alarming example of the cash problem unfolded in 1991 after media magnate **Robert Maxwell** died, apparently of suicide. Within days of his death, it was discovered that Maxwell had been illegally shuffling vast amounts of money around his subsidiaries to cover loans he had taken out to expand his empire, which included Macmillan, the prestigious book-publishing company. Maxwell was not alone among conglomerate builders who found themselves in deep trouble after overextending themselves financially. The problem was not only in the instability wrought by their miscalculations and recklessness, but also in the products that their media subsidiaries produced. Michael Lennie, a San Diego textbook author attorney, put the problem this way: "The industry continues to grow more and more concentrated with large debt-ridden publishers too preoccupied with serving crippling debt to pay attention to the publishing of quality texts."

POSITIVE EFFECTS OF CONGLOMERATION AND CONVERGENCE

At the end of World War II, family-run publishing houses dominated the mainline book-publishing business, and all were relatively small by today's standards. Although there are still hundreds of small publishers in the United States today, consolidation has reduced the industry to six giants. Depending on whom you ask, the conglomeration has been a godsend or a disaster. Looking at the effects positively, the book industry is financially stronger today.

In the Canadian television industry, both CTV and Global have promised the CRTC that they will spend more money developing Canadian content for their new companies. This should mean more employment for media professionals and better Canadian programming for audiences. Ken McDonald, vice president of news for CanWest Global, says that convergence has become a way of life at CanWest: "We don't talk about the 'C' word much anymore. We're past that now. We're just doing it every day." McDonald is optimistic about convergence. He says that being able to make use of print, broadcast, and Internet resources is "value added journalism. I think it means new opportunities. I've seen that and I see it every day."

DEMASSIFICATION

Another contemporary economic phenomenon is **demassification.** The mass media are capable of reaching tremendous numbers of people, but most media today no longer try to reach the largest possible audience. They are demassifying—going after narrower and narrower segments of the mass audience. The first wave of digital channels introduced in late 2001 are prime examples of this trend. WTSN, PrideVision, and BookTV each have their specific "niche" programming market that they target for advertisers who are keen to have access to these markets.

The effects of the demassification process, the result of technological breakthroughs and economic pressures, are only beginning to emerge. At first, advertisers welcomed demassification because they could target their pitches to groups of their likeliest customers. Although demassification dramatically changed the mass media—network radio went into a decline, for example—the economic base of the mass media remained advertising. Local radio stations found new profitability from advertisers anxious to support demassified formats. Direct mail catalogues and flyers to selected addresses, television commercials at the point of purchase (such as screens in grocery store shopping carts), and place-based media (such as magazines designed for distribution only in physicians' waiting rooms) are all examples of how specific demassification has become.

The Process of Mass Communication

MYSTERY OF MASS COMMUNICATION

The mass communication process is full of mystery. Major corporations commit millions of dollars to advertising a new product and then anxiously hope the promotional campaign works. Sometimes it does. Sometimes it doesn't. Even experts at

Alternative Media. With advertising spending at record levels in 2000, traditional media were filled up. Advertisers accelerated their search for alternative media. Car owners were paid to turn their vehicles into rolling billboards. One company, Hardwear International, introduced wearable video. The phenomenon was called "ad nauseum" by the trade journal *Advertising Age*.

mass communication, such as the people at advertising agencies, haven't unlocked the mysteries of the process, nor have scholars who try to understand the influence of mass communication on society and individuals.

Despite the mystery and the uncertainties, there is no alternative to mass communication in modern society. Therefore, it is important for people who create or consume mass media messages to learn all that can be known about the process. It is no less important that people who receive the messages have a sense of the process that is being used to inform, entertain, and persuade them.

FOUR BASIC COMPONENTS

The mass media are a relatively recent arrival in human experience. The oldest mass medium, the printed book, has been around more than 500 years, and the newest medium, television, only 50 years. These media affect us in many ways, but we know much less than we should about how they work. One way to understand how the mass media work is to define the following four different but related terms.

MASS MESSAGES.   A news item is a message, as are a movie, a novel, a recorded song, and a billboard advertisement. The message is the most apparent part of our relationship to the mass media. The people who create **mass messages** include journalists, lyricists, scriptwriters, television anchors, radio disc jockeys, public relations practitioners, and advertising copywriters.

MASS MEDIA.   The **mass media** are the vehicles that carry messages. The primary mass media, as we have discussed, are books, magazines, newspapers, television, radio, sound recordings, and movies. Most theorists view media as neutral carriers of messages. The people who are experts at media include technicians who keep the presses running and who keep the television transmitters on the air. Media experts are also the tinkerers and inventors who come up with technical improvements, such as compact discs, AM stereo radio, and newspaper presses that can produce high-quality colour.

MASS COMMUNICATION.   The process through which messages reach the audience via the mass media is called **mass communication**. This is a mysterious process about which we know far less than we should. Researchers and scholars have unravelled some of the mystery, but most of how it works remains a matter of wonderment. For example: Why do people pay more attention to some messages than to others? How does one advertisement generate more sales than another? Is behaviour, including violent behaviour, triggered through the mass communication process? There is reason to believe that mass communication affects voting behaviour, but how does this work? Which is most correct—to say that people can be controlled, manipulated, or influenced by mass communication? Nobody has the answer.

MASS AUDIENCES.   The size and diversity of mass audiences add complexity to mass communication. Only indirectly do **mass communicators** learn whether their messages have been received. Mass communicators are never exactly sure of the size of audiences, let alone of the effect of their messages. **Mass audiences** are fickle. What attracts great attention one day, may not the next. The challenge of trying to communicate to a mass audience is even more complex because people are tuning in and tuning out all the time, and when they are tuned in, it is with varying degrees of attentiveness.

COMMUNICATION TYPES

The communication in which the mass media engage is only one form of communication. One way to begin understanding the process of mass communication is to differentiate it from other forms of communication.

INTRAPERSONAL COMMUNICATION.   We engage in **intrapersonal communication** when we talk to ourselves to develop our thoughts and ideas. This intrapersonal communication precedes our speaking or acting.

INTERPERSONAL COMMUNICATION.   When people talk to each other, they are engaging in **interpersonal communication.** In its simplest form, interpersonal communication is between two persons physically located in the same place. It can occur, however, if they are physically separated but emotionally connected, like lovers over the telephone.

The difference between the prefixes *intra-* and *inter-* is the key difference between intrapersonal and interpersonal communication. Just as intrasquad athletic games are within a team, intrapersonal communication is within one's self. Just as intercollegiate games are between schools, interpersonal communication is between individuals.

GROUP COMMUNICATION.   There comes a point when the number of people involved reduces the intimacy of the communication process. That's when the situation becomes **group communication.** A club meeting is an example. So is a speech to an audience in an auditorium.

MASS COMMUNICATION. Capable of reaching thousands or even millions of people is **mass communication,** which is accomplished through a mass medium like television or newspapers. Mass communication can be defined as the process of using a mass medium to send messages to large audiences for the purpose of informing, entertaining, or persuading.

In many respects, the process of mass communication and other communication forms is the same: Someone conceives a message, essentially an intrapersonal act. The message then is encoded into a common code, such as language. Then it's transmitted. Another person receives the message, decodes it, and internalizes it. Internalizing a message is also an intrapersonal act.

In other respects, mass communication is distinctive. Crafting an effective message for thousands of people of diverse backgrounds and interests requires different skills than chatting with a friend across the table. **Encoding** the message is more complex because a device is always used—for example, a printing press, a camera, or a recorder.

One aspect of mass communication that should not be a mystery is spelling the often-misused word "communication." The word takes no "s" if you are using it to refer to a process. If you are referring to a communication as a thing, such as a letter, a movie, a telegram, or a television program, rather than a process, the word is "communication" in singular form and "communications" in plural. The term "mass communication" refers to a process, so it is spelled without the "s."

Models of Mass Communication

THE PROCESS SCHOOL

Many ways have been devised to display the communication process to help explain how it works. One model was laid out in 1948 by two Bell telephone engineers, **Claude Shannon** and **Warren Weaver**, who were working on advanced computer applications in telephone systems. Shannon and Weaver needed a reference point for their research, so they devised a model that has become a standard baseline for describing the communication process.

STIMULATION.   In the Shannon-Weaver model, communication begins with a source who is stimulated internally to want to communicate a message. The **stimulation** can result from many things. Emotions can be stimuli, as can something that is sensed— seeing a beautiful panorama, feeling a cold draft, or hearing a child cry.

ENCODING.   The second step is encoding. The source puts thoughts into symbols that can be understood by whomever is destined to receive the message. The symbols take many forms—for example, the written word, smoke signals, or pictographs.

TRANSMISSION.   The message is the representation of the thought. In interpersonal communication, the message is almost always delivered face to face. In mass communication, however, the message is encoded so that it is suitable for the equipment being used for **transmission.** Shannon and Weaver, being telephone engineers, offered the example of the sound pressure of a voice being changed into proportional electrical current for transmission over telephone lines. In technical terms, telephone lines were channels for Shannon and Weaver's messages. On a more conceptual basis, the telephone lines were the media, in the same way that the printed page or a broadcast signal is.

Internalization. A consumer who has seen and heard ads for a product retrieves those messages from memory to weigh whether to make a purchase. Those retrieved messages are considered with packaging messages, which also are a form of mass communication.

DECODING.   The receiver picks up signals sent by the transmitter. In interpersonal communication, the receiver is a person who hears the message or sees it, or both. An angry message encoded as a fist banging a table is heard and perhaps felt. An insulting message encoded as a puff of cigar smoke in the face is smelled. In mass communication, the first receiver of the message is not a person but the equipment that picks up and then reconstructs the message from the signal. This mechanical **decoding** is necessary so that the human receiver of the message can understand it. As Shannon and Weaver put it, "the receiver ordinarily performs the inverse operation that was done by the transmitter."

INTERNALIZATION.   In mass communication, a second kind of decoding occurs with the person who receives the message from the receiving equipment. This is an intrapersonal act, **internalizing** the message. For this second kind of decoding to work, the receiver must understand the communication form chosen by the source in encoding. Someone who reads only English will not be able to decode a message in Greek. Someone whose sensibility is limited to punk rock will not understand Handel's "Water Music." In other words, the source and the receiver must have enough in common for communication to occur. This common experience, which can be as simple as speaking the same tongue, is called **homophyly**. In mass communication, the encoder must know the audience well enough to shape messages that can be decoded accurately and with the intended effect.

NOISE.   If speakers slur their words, the effectiveness of their messages is jeopardized. Slurring and other impediments in the communication process are called **noise**. In mass communication, which is based on complex mechanical and electronic equipment, the opportunities for noise interference are countless because so many things can go wrong. Noise occurs in three forms. **Channel noise,** such as transmission static, faulty microphones, and smudged pages, occurs in the transmission of messages. **Environmental noise**—a doorbell that interrupts someone reading an article or shouting kids who distract a viewer from the six o'clock news—interferes with the decoding process. **Semantic noise,** such as sloppy wording, involves problems in crafting messages.

Mass communicators go to special lengths to guard against noise interfering with their messages. For example, in encoding, broadcast scriptwriters avoid "s" sounds as much as possible because they can hiss gratingly if listeners are not tuned precisely on the frequency.

To keep noise at a minimum, technicians strive to keep their equipment in top-notch condition. Even so, things can go wrong. Also, mass communicators cannot control noise that affects individual members of their audience—such as the siren of a passing fire truck, a migraine headache, or the distraction of a pot boiling over on the stove. Clear enunciation, whether sharp writing in a magazine or clear pronunciation on the radio, can minimize such interference, but noise is mostly beyond the communicator's control.

Repetition is the mass communicator's best antidote against noise. If the message does not get through the first time, it is repeated. Rare is an advertisement that plays only once. Radio newscasters repeat the same major news stories every hour, although they rehash the scripts so they will not bore people who heard the stories earlier.

FEEDBACK.   Because mass communication is not the one-way street that the Shannon-Weaver model indicated, later theorists embellished the model by looping the process back on itself. The recipient of a message, after decoding, responds. The original

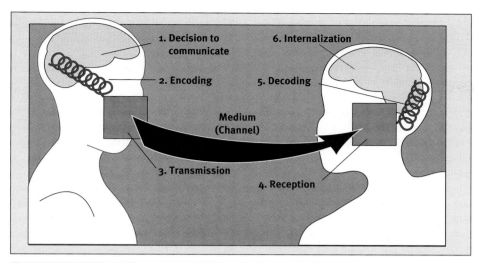

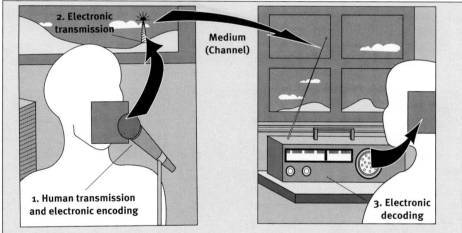

Claude Shannon

Wilbur Schramm

Classic Communication Model.
This is the classic communication model to which people like Claude Shannon and Warren Weaver began adding the mechanical and electronic components of mass communications in the 1940s. In mass communication, the transmitter is not the human voice or a writing utensil but, in the case of a radio, a transmitter. The receiver is not a human ear but a radio receiver. The conception of a message by a sender and the internalization by the receiver remain human functions in mass communication. The terms encoder and decoder were added by scholar Wilbur Schramm.

recipient then becomes the sender, encoding a response and sending it via a medium back to the original sender, who becomes the new destination and decodes the response. This reverse process is called **feedback.**

In interpersonal communication, you know if your listener does not understand. If you hear "Uhh?" or see a puzzled look, you restate your point. In mass communication, feedback is delayed. It might be a week after an article is published before a reader's letter arrives in the newsroom. Because feedback is delayed and because there usually is not very much of it, precise expression in mass communication is especially important. There is little chance to restate the point immediately if the television viewer does not understand. A mass communicator cannot hear the "Uhh?"

Semantic Noise. In every issue, the *Columbia Journalism Review* delights in reproducing bad headlines and other newspaper gaffes as a reminder to journalists to be more careful. These gaffes are examples of semantic noise, in which ambiguous wording and other poor word choices interfere with clear communication.

The Lower case

"Some sort of post Supreme Court decision quote or reaction information should go in this slot right about here."

AL GORE
Reacts to Supreme Court decision

The Morning Call (Allentown, Pa.) 11/22/00

Copy editors find headline workshops irresistible

ACES September 2000

The importance of bondage between voter and government

The Fairfax (Va.) Journal 10/18/00

Last week for faulty art display

Central Florida Future 10/4/00

Egg plant must pay damages for fly problem

Star Tribune (Minneapolis, Minn.) 3/11/00

Need to breed spurs bird call from queen

The Des Moines Register 11/14/00

The two-headed management team is typical for Belo Interactive properties, the pair said.

The Press-Enterprise (Riverside, Calif.) 8/24/00

Faite R-P. Mack Jr., 56, a professor in the graduate education program at Grand Valley State University, said he has been frustrated by voters' take on Bush's debate performances.

"I'm mystified at how dumb Americans are in thinking Bush won those debates," said the Grand Rapids resident, who declined to give his age.

The Grand Rapids (Mich.) Press 10/17/00

Talks end in killing of black motorist

Lexington (Ky.) Herald-Leader 11/21/00

Young supports hitting coach

Pittsburgh Post Gazette 9/20/00

Drug firms urged to stop selling medicines

The Indiana (Pa.) Gazette 11/7/00

Steven Gartner, *one of the sexist U.S. bachelors*

The Seattle Times 9/28/00

Doughnut hole, nude dancing on council table

Redlands (Calif.) Daily Facts 4/3/00

CJR offers $25 for items published in The Lower case. Please send only original, unmutilated clippings suitable for reproduction, together with name and date of publication, and include your social security number for payment.

OTHER IMPORTANT COMMUNICATION TERMS

INFORMATION.   The content of the message that is being sent is important to communication researchers. Content can include photographs, words, and song lyrics. In the process of mass communication, information is usually coded and transmitted through at least one channel.

CHANNEL.   This refers to the way the message (information) is sent: radio uses sound waves, television can use co-axial cables to carry a combination of audio and video signals, and telephones and the Internet use telephone wires.

MEDIUM.   A medium is the way the message is transformed in order to be sent through a channel. As McLuhan observed, which medium is used to communicate a message has important implications.

REDUNDANCY.   In the context of communication, redundancy is beneficial; it helps the process of communication. A redundant message is easily decoded by the receiver; there is little room for error. The term is used by communication theorists to explain how predictable a message is. A catchy slogan or jingle needs to be redundant to be effective. Can any Canadian hockey fan hear the theme music from *Hockey Night in Canada* and not know what it is? A redundant message only needs a passive receiver in order to be understood. A redundant message may also be called a conventional message.

ENTROPY.   This is the opposite of redundancy. An entropic message is not easy to decode and is clearly not conventional. An entropic message may need a more active receiver in order to be understood. This is usually seen as a problem in the process of communication, particularly in mass communication, where the aim is to appeal to a large audience.

CONCENTRIC CIRCLE MODEL

The Shannon-Weaver model can be applied to all communication, but it misses some things unique to mass communication. In 1974 scholars Ray Hiebert, Donald Ungurait, and **Thomas Bohn** presented an important new model—a series of concentric circles with the encoding source at the centre. In the **concentric circle model,** one of the outer rings was the receiving audience. In between were several elements that are important in the mass communication process but less so in other communication processes.

GATEKEEPERS.   Mass communication is not a solo endeavour. Dozens, sometimes hundreds, of individuals are involved. A Margaret Atwood novel passes through several editors before being published. When it's adapted as a screenplay, substantial modifications are made by many other individuals, all expert in the medium of the movie. Later, when it is adapted for television, experts in television as a mass medium make further changes, and so might the network program standards office. Anyone who can stop or alter a message en route to the audience is a **gatekeeper.** Newscast producers are gatekeepers because they decide what is aired and what is not. They make decisions about what to emphasize and what to de-emphasize. Magazine and newspaper editors do the same, sorting through hundreds of stories to choose the relatively few that will fit in their publications. When gatekeepers make a mistake, however, the communication process and the message suffer.

Gatekeeping. Despite favourable reviews as a gentle sitcom, *God, the Devil and Bob* worried some NBC affiliates. God, in the starring role, liked toaster pastries and occasionally sipped a light beer. Seven affiliates declined to carry the program—in Boise, Idaho; Pocatello, Idaho; Salt Lake City, Utah; Shreveport, Louisiana; South Bend, Indiana; Tupelo, Mississippi; and Twin Falls, Idaho.

REGULATORS.   The concentric circle model also recognizes **regulators** as a force that shapes and reshapes mass-communicated messages before they reach the mass audience. Regulators are non-media institutions that influence media content. Canadian Broadcasters must follow the rules set down by the CRTC. Peer pressure is institutionalized in trade and professional organizations. In Canada, there are self-regulatory bodies for all forms of media. Broadcasting has the Canadian Broadcast Standards Council, while Canadian advertisers have Advertising Standards Canada.

FILTERS.   Hiebert, Ungurait, and Bohn note that receivers are affected by a variety of **filters** in decoding a message. They call the language or symbols used for a message **informational filters.** If the sender and receiver are not in tune with the same symbols, the communication process is flawed. If you did not know how to read, an informational filter would be interfering right now with your understanding this sentence. **Physical filters** exist when a receiver's mind is dimmed by fatigue.

   If a receiver is a zealous animal rights activist, **psychological filters** likely will affect the reception of news on medical research involving animals. Being on a different wavelength can be a filter. Imagine two women friends going to the movie *Fatal Attraction* together. One woman is married and monogamous, the other is involved with a married man. Having different ideas on and experiences with marital fidelity, which is at the heart of the movie, the women hear the same words and see the same images, but they see two "different" movies.

EFFECTS.

A decoded message can do more than prompt verbal feedback. It can also affect how someone votes or even provoke a riot. The outermost ring of the concentric circle model, the **effects** of a message, goes beyond the Shannon-Weaver model to include this important point.

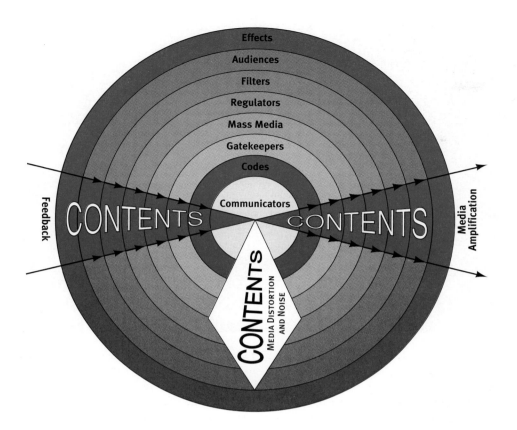

Concentric Circle Model. The scholars who designed the concentric circle model suggest thinking of it as a pebble being dropped into still water. The ripples emanating outward from the communicator go through many barriers before reaching the audience or having any effect. The model takes note of feedback, media amplification, noise, and distortion introduced by the media.

AMPLIFICATION.   An outgoing arrow in the concentric circle model points out that mass media have the ability to amplify, which is related to gatekeepers. **Amplification** is a process by which mass communication confers status to issues and personalities merely by covering them.

Status conferral can work positively and negatively. For example, some scholars claim that the U.S. government overreacted in 1980 to the 444-day Iran hostage situation because media coverage kept fuelling public reaction. Oliver North's name would not have become a household word had it not been for saturation media coverage of the Iran-Contra issue.

Status conferral is not limited to the news media. Ballads and music, amplified through the mass media, can capture the public's imagination and keep an issue alive and even enlarge it. In World War I, catchy songs such as "Over There" helped rally support for the cause. Fifty years later, the "Ballad of the Green Berets" lent legitimacy to the hawkish position on Vietnam. Bob Dylan's 1975 song "Hurricane" reopened the investigation into the murder conviction of Reuben "Hurricane" Carter. Movies also have the power to move people and sustain issues. For example, the movie *Philadelphia*, starring Tom Hanks, brought the issues of AIDS home for many North Americans.

NARRATIVE MODEL

Yale professor **Harold Lasswell,** an early mass communication theorist, developed a useful yet simple mass communication model, the **narrative model**. The Lasswell model is not diagrammed. Instead, it is in narrative form and poses four questions: Who says what? In which channel? To whom? With what effect?

You can easily apply the model. Pick any bylined story from the front page of a newspaper:

- Who says what? The newspaper reporter tells a story, often quoting someone who is especially knowledgeable on the subject.
- In which channel? In this case, the story is told through the newspaper, a mass medium.
- To whom? The story is told to a newspaper reader.
- With what effect? The reader decides to vote for Candidate A or B, or perhaps readers just add the information to their reservoir of knowledge.

Semiotics for Beginners: This website offers newbies to semiotics an excellent overview of signs and codes.
www.aber.ac.uk/dgc/ semiotic.html

THE SEMIOTIC SCHOOL

The semiotic school of thought looks at the creation of meaning in communication.

What are some of the differences between the semiotic and process schools? Let's take the example of a particular program, say, *Hockey Night in Canada*. The semiotic school would be interested in how viewers find and create meaning while watching the program. For example, during a game between the Ottawa Senators and Vancouver Canucks, how would fans of each team decode the messages being communicated? How would each find pleasure in watching the hockey game? What meaning does each fan find in the broadcast? On the other hand, the process school would be interested in how this program gets transmitted from point A to point B, how the show is produced, who produces it, and who it is aimed at.

This approach to communication theory draws on the work of French cultural theorist **Roland Barthes** and the idea of signs, what they refer to, and the influence of culture on those references.

To understand what semiotics is and what signs are, it is important to see how Barthes expanded on the work of Swiss linguist Ferdinand de Saussure. For de Saussure, the sign is composed of a signifier and a signified, as shown in the figure below.

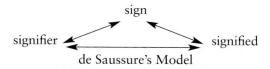

de Saussure's Model

For example, the words "maple leaf" constitute a sign. This sign is composed of a signifier, the letters in the words "m-a-p-l-e-l-e-a-f," and its signified, the mental concept of leaves from a maple tree that accompanies the words. Together, the signifier and signified form the sign of the "maple leaf." The relation between the signifier and its signified is entirely arbitrary. The words "maple leaf" denote what they do solely because of the linguistic conventions of the English language.

DENOTATION AND CONNOTATION

Barthes took this idea of signification one step further. For Barthes, there is not only one level of signification (the mental concept of "maple leaf"), but two: first- and second-order signified. He called these levels of meaning **denotation** and **connotation** respectively. Barthes's conceptualization of signs is shown in the figure below.

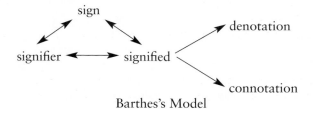

Barthes's Model

Denotation is the same as de Saussure's idea of the signified. It is what Barthes calls the simple, everyday meaning in the sign. For example, "maple leaf" signifies, or denotes, a type of leaf from a particular tree. But, it can also mean many other things. There is a difference in its connotation, which deals with an additional level of meaning. For example, a maple leaf can signify Canada, or an NHL team, as well as signifying a leaf from a maple tree. For Barthes, this second-level meaning is a vehicle for cultural ideology. It's only because we are Canadians that the maple leaf signifies Canada to us. Hockey fans will interpret a maple leaf as signifying the team from Toronto. The multitude of meanings that can be associated with a sign is also arbitrary and depends largely on cultural conventions. That's what semiotics looks at—the many different types of meanings that are created by cultural influences.

By analyzing the relationship between denotation and connotation in popular culture, Barthes believed that hidden ideologies (or what he called "mythologies") could be uncovered. A myth can also be defined as a culture's belief system. In Barthes's view, these myths "naturalized" (or established) the interests and values of the dominant class in society. By exposing these bourgeois mythologies as arbitrary, Barthes believed they could be eliminated.

Not all signs are created equal. Communication theorist C.S. Pierce designed a way to classify signs according to their level of connotation or denotation. Pierce divided signs into three categories: icons, indexes, and symbols.

- Icons are signs that resemble what they represent because the signifier looks like what is signified. For example, a map of Canada is an icon of Canada because it looks like the geographic layout of the country. A picture of Nelly Furtado is an icon of the Canadian singer. If the sign is denotative and not connotative, it is an icon.

- An index is directly related to what it represents. A popular example of an index is smoke, which usually indicates there is a fire. Smoke is an index of fire because smoke has a connection with fire. An index is a mixture of connotation and denotation. Smoke by itself is largely denotative, but it connotes something else: fire. A Mountie's hat is also an index; it is not only a hat but has come to represent an RCMP officer. The late Prime Minister Pierre Trudeau always wore a rose on his lapel. The rose became an index of Trudeau.

- A symbol is a sign that is entirely connotative because there is no clear connection between the signifier and the signified. Words are symbolic of what they represent. The Canadian flag, the fleur-de-lis, and the beaver are all Canadian

The Royal Canadian Air Farce. Is this comedy team's portrayal of life in a dough-nut shop an example of what Barthes might call "Canadi-anness?" What Canadian sig-nifiers would you argue are present in this photo?

symbols. They don't look like Canada but they have all become symbolic of various aspects of our culture. Symbols develop their meaning over time through convention. The meaning given to symbols is arbitrary and can change.

Looking for Canadian Signs and Myths

In a book called *Mythologies*, Roland Barthes looked at various forms of popular culture and subjected them to semiotic analysis. In one of the essays, entitled "Wine and Milk," the two drinks carry the following connotations:

- "Wine: high class, French, good for the soul."
- "Milk: pure, innocent."

The "Newfie" is a well-known Canadian signifier. The Newfoundland government took aim at the negative mythology surrounding the province with an ad campaign to sell its Economic Diversification and Growth Enterprises program in 1996. The ads, showing pictures of fish, stated, "If you think this is all Newfoundland and Labrador exports ... think again."

In *National Dreams: Myth, Memory and Canadian History* (1997), Daniel Francis looked at some popular Canadian myths, past and present. These included "the last spike," used for years to signify the building of Canadian railroads, and the red serge outfit of the Royal Canadian Mounted Police. The television show *Due South* played with the Canadian myth of the Mountie. A series of Labatt's beer commercials in 1998 that featured a street hockey game being interrupted by a "streetcar," and declared that anything can happen "Out of the Blue," is a classic example of Canadian mythology at work. The series of Heritage Minutes, featuring Canadian historical moments, is another example of how the mass media can use myths to convey its messages. So are the Comedy Network's "Sacrilege Moments," only with a comic twist.

Using Barthes's ideas, think of some mythical Canadian signifiers; try to get beyond Mounties and beavers. What Canadian icons, indexes, and symbols can you think of?

Entertainment and Information

Many people find it helpful to define media by whether the thrust of their content is entertainment or information. By this definition, newspapers almost always are considered an information medium, and audio recordings and movies are considered entertainment. As a medium, books both inform and entertain. So do television and radio, although some networks, stations, and programs do more of one than the other. The same is true with magazines, with some titles geared more for informing, some for entertaining.

Although widely used, the entertainment–information dichotomy has limitations. Nothing inherent in newspapers, for example, precludes them from being entertaining. Consider the *National Enquirer* and other supermarket tabloids, which are newspapers but which hardly anybody takes seriously as an information source. The neatness of the entertainment–information dichotomy doesn't work well with mainstream newspapers either. Most daily newspapers have dozens of items intended to entertain. Open a paper and start counting with "Calvin and Hobbes," "Garfield," and the astrology column.

The entertainment–information dichotomy has other weaknesses. It misses the potential of all mass media to do more than entertain and inform. The dichotomy misses the persuasion function, which you read about earlier in this chapter. People may consider most movies as entertainment, but there is no question that Steven Spielberg has broad social messages even in his most rollicking adventure sagas. In the same sense, just about every television sitcom is a morality tale wrapped up in an entertaining package. The ideology may be soft-pedalled, but it's everywhere.

Dividing mass media into entertainment and information categories is becoming increasingly difficult as newspapers, usually considered the leading information medium, back off from hard-hitting content to woo readers with softer, entertaining stuff. For better or worse, this same shift is also taking place at *Time* and *Maclean's*. This melding even has a name that's come into fashion: **infotainment**.

ELITIST VERSUS POPULIST

An ongoing tension in the mass media exists between advancing social and cultural interests and giving broad segments of the population what they want. This tension, between extremes on a continuum, takes many forms. At one end of the continuum is serious media content that appeals to people who can be called **elitists** because they feel the mass media have a responsibility to contribute to a better society and a refinement of the culture, regardless of whether the media attract large audiences. At the other end of the continuum are **populists**, who are entirely oriented to the marketplace. Populists feel the mass media are at their best when they give people what they want.

Most mass media in Canada are somewhere in the middle of the elitist–populist continuum. CBC offers some serious fare, but also offers Don Cherry on *Coach's Corner* and Red Green's hints on duct tape use.

CONTENT-DISTRIBUTION MODEL

Many dynamics in mass media behaviour today can be visualized in a model that divides media functions into message creation and message distribution. It's the **content-distribution model.** Some companies are heavily into creating content, like producing movies, publishing books, and putting out magazines. Other companies are heavily into distribution, like operating movie houses, bookstore chains, and cable systems. Some even own major league baseball teams. The heaviest players, including AOL Time Warner, Bell Globe Media, Rogers, TVA, CanWest Global, and the like, are building stakes in both content creation and distribution.

mass media

Dynamics are at work that are changing the mass media as we know them. With digitization the media are converging into new forms. Old distinctions are fading. Is a book still a book if it's not on paper and bound but instead is available on an e-tablet? As well, it's not always easy to distinguish television from the web any more.

Digitization is furthering demassification because it's easier to identify segments of the mass audience and tailor messages to narrow interests. Some web news sites, for example, can be programmed to send coverage only on subjects you choose. What this means to the generalist is unclear. We do know, though, that it is increasingly possible to use the mass media to focus on your interests so narrowly that you are blind to other things happening in the world.

The long-term effect of concentration of media ownership is difficult to predict. Although technology has made it possible for a great diversity of media products to exist, the fact is that the major mass media products are controlled by fewer and fewer corporations. For most of us, relatively few corporations control the media to which we expose ourselves. The economic imperative of these companies—to increase profits—worries elitists. Their concern is that the traditional media commitment to enriching and bettering the society is being lost in the drive for profits.

The upside of this is that if we as media consumers are aware of the dynamics at work; we can have a better understanding of why the media do what they do. That understanding can help us cope with the changes ahead.

CHAPTER WRAP-UP

The mass media are the vehicles that carry messages to large audiences. These media—books, magazines, newspapers, records, movies, radio, television, and the web—are so pervasive in modern life that many people do not even notice their influence. Because of that influence, however, we should take time to understand the mass media so that we can better assess whether they are affecting us for better or worse.

Mass communication is a mysterious process. Many scholars have developed theories and models to help us understand some aspects of mass communication, but the process is so complex that we will never master it to the point of being able to predict reliably the outcome of the process. There are just too many variables. This does not mean, however, that the quest for understanding is pointless. The more we know about how mass communication works, the better mass communicators can use the process for good effects and the better media consumers can intelligently assess media messages before using them as a basis for action.

QUESTIONS FOR REVIEW

1. How are the mass media pervasive in our everyday lives?

2. What are the three technologies on which the primary mass media are built?

3. Explain the models that scholars have devised to explain the mass media.

4. How do mass media organizations make money to stay in business?

5. Define demassification. Describe demassification that has occurred in radio, magazines, and television.

6. Define convergence. Is it good for Canadian mass media consumers?

7. Why are Innis and McLuhan important figures in Canadian communications?

QUESTIONS FOR CRITICAL THINKING

1. Some people are confused by the terms *cool media* and *hot media* because, in their experience, radios and television sets heat up and newspapers are always at room temperature. What is the other way of looking at hot and cool media according to Marshall McLuhan?

2. The effectiveness of messages communicated through the mass media is shaped by the technical limitations of each medium. A limitation of radio is that it cannot accommodate pictures. Can you provide examples of content limitations of certain media? What are the audience limitations that are inherent in all mass media?

3. Which mass media perform the informing purpose best? The entertaining purpose? The persuading purpose? Which of these purposes does the advertising industry serve? Public relations?

4. What purpose do media models serve?

5. Which is more important to the mass media: profits or doing social good?

6. Can you create a sentence that uses the "Five Ms": mass communication, mass messages, mass media, mass audiences, and mass communicators?

7. Are any types of mass media not dependent on advertising or consumer purchases?

8. Do we need a CRTC in Canada, given the changes brought about by convergence?

9. Take any pop song and analyze its lyrics in terms of both denotation and connotation. Look for first- and second-order signifieds. Here are some songs to get you started: "Stan" by Eminem, "At the 100th Meridian" by The Tragically Hip, "Prairie Town" by Randy Bachman, "Insensitive" by Jann Arden, or "With Arms Wide Open" by Creed.

FOR KEEPING UP TO DATE

Media trade publications, such as *Broadcaster, Marketing Magazine,* and *Broadcast Dialogue* offer an excellent look at the ever-changing Canadian media landscape.

Scholarly discussion on the communication process can be found in *Communication Yearbook,* published since 1977, and *Mass Communication Review Yearbook,* published since 1986. *The Journal of Communication* is a quarterly scholarly publication from Oxford University Press. From a Canadian perspective, *The*

Canadian Journal of Communication is published quarterly by Wilfrid Laurier Press.

Newsmagazines including *Time* and *Maclean's* cover major mass media issues more or less regularly, as do *The Globe and Mail, The National Post,* and other major newspapers.

The monthly *Brill's Content,* launched in 1998, offers enterprise coverage of the news and information media, often with a critical edge.

FOR FURTHER LEARNING

Ken Auletta. Three Blind Mice: How the TV Networks Lost Their Way (Random House, 1991).

Ben H. Bagdikian. "Special Issue: The Lords of the Global Village." *The Nation* 248 (June 12, 1989): 23, 805–20.

Roland Barthes. *Mythologies* (Paladin, 1973).

Paul Benedetti and Nancy DeHart. *On McLuhan: Forward Through the Rear View Mirror* (Prentice Hall, 1996).

Arthur Asa Berger. *Media USA: Process and Effect* (Longman, 1988).

John Fiske. *Introduction to Communication Studies* (Routledge, 1990).

Matthew Fraser. "Iron Law Brought us Convergence, Heaven's Gate." *The National Post* (June 11, 2001). A look at the business implications of convergence in the Canadian media.

Matthew Fraser. "How Much Con in Convergence?" *The National Post* (July 30, 2001).

Laurel Hyatt. "Letting the Genie out of the Bottle." *Broadcaster Magazine* (March 2001).

Harold Innis. *Empire and Communications* (Oxford Press, 1950).

Daphne Lavers. "deKerckhove." *Broadcast Dialogue* (September 1999).

Stephen W. Littlejohn. *Theories of Human Communication,* 3rd ed. (Wadsworth, 1989).

Michelle Martin. *Mainstream Models in Mass Communication Research* from *Communication and Mass Media: Culture, Domination and Opposition* (Prentice Hall Canada, 1997).

Eric McLuhan and Frank Zingrone. *Essential McLuhan* (Anansi, 1995).

Marshall McLuhan. *Understanding Media* (Signet, 1964).

Denis McQuail. *Mass Communication Theory* (Sage, 1987).

Denis McQuail and Sven Windahl. *Communication Models for the Study of Mass Communication* (Longman, 1981).

Barbara Shecter. "Alliance, Atlantis Forge $750 Million Giant." *The Financial Post* (July 21, 1998).

Anthony Smith. *The Age of the Behemoths: The Globalization of Mass Media Firms* (Priority Press, 1991).

Bohdan Szuchewycz and Jeannette Sloniowski, eds. *Canadian Communications,* 2nd ed. (Prentice Hall Canada, 2001).

Alexis S. Tan. *Mass Communication Theories and Research* (Macmillan, 1986).

James R. Taylor. "The Office of the Future: Weber and Innis Revisited." *Communications in Canadian Society,* Benjamin Singer, ed. (Addison-Wesley, 1983).

Antonia Zerbisias. "Ready or Not, CRTC Takes on Media Convergence." *Toronto Star* (April 14, 2001).

Wordless Society Ahead? No, says futurist George Gilder, not even the generation raised on MTV can communicate effectively without words. Visuals can enhance but not replace them, he says.

Print

MEDIA IN THEORY

Wordless Society Ahead? Not Likely

Do newspapers and other word-based print media have a future? In a variation of Canadian Marshall McLuhan's "medium is the message" theory, media seer **George Gilder** puts his money on word-based media over television, which relies on visuals to tell stories.

As Gilder sees it, people who see the communication of the future as primarily video have missed the fact that video works better than words for only an extremely narrow range of messages:

"Video is most effective in conveying shocks and sensations and appealing to prurient interests of large miscellaneous audiences. Images easily excel in blasting through to the glandular substances of the human community; there's nothing like a body naked or bloody or both to arrest the eye." However, human communication goes far beyond shock scenes and sensual appeals, he says, noting that people communicate mostly through words.

The printed product you receive on your doorstep every morning may seem like a technological dinosaur from Johannes Gutenberg's time. The fact, however, is that newspapers are well into the digital age. Reporters dip into digitized data for source material and write stories on computers. Editors edit stories and lay out pages electronically. It is in final production that old technology reigns, with multimillion-dollar presses that consume tons and tons of newsprint and barrels and barrels of ink. In delivery too, with minimum-wage carriers entrusted to get the product to readers, newspapers lag.

That is changing. In the vanguard of changing to electronic production, rather than printing, and to **electronic delivery,** rather than "paperboys and the local newsstand," are newspapers ranging from modest circulation weeklies in small rural communities to the lofty *Toronto Star.* Some online editions offer only word-for-word versions of what is in the print editions or just selected stories, but some newspapers are repackaging stories to take advantage of opportunities that electronic delivery offers. Still, true to their tradition, the online newspapers remain word-based. Visuals are a useful accoutrement but seldom the heart of the message.

Even as newspaper circulation withers, as it has in recent years, newspaper companies will survive. They are well positioned to dominate the future of news because, in almost every community, they have the largest, most sophisticated staffs for gathering and telling local news. That resource is unmatched by even the largest television networks or other news operations.

Books, Gutenberg, and Movable Type

The introduction of mass-produced books in the 15th century marked a turning point in human history. Before then, most books were handwritten, usually by scribist monks who copied existing books onto blank sheets of paper letter by letter, one page at a time. These scribists could turn out only a few hand-lettered books in a lifetime of tedium. In the mid-1400s, Johannes Gutenberg, a metallurgist in what is now Germany, devised an innovation that made it possible to print pages using metal letters.

Johannes Gutenberg was eccentric—a secretive tinkerer with a passion for beauty, detail, and craftsmanship. By trade he was a metallurgist, but he never made much money at it. Like most of his fellow 15th-century Rhinelanders, he pressed his own grapes for wine. As a businessman he was not very successful, and he died penniless. Despite this unpromising combination of traits, quirks, and habits—perhaps because of them—Johannes Gutenberg wrought the most significant change in history: the mass-produced written word. He invented movable metal type.

Printing itself was nothing new. Artisans in ancient China had been printing with a process that is still an art form:

- Impressions are carved in page-size wooden blocks.
- The blocks are laid on a flat surface and inked.
- A sheet of paper is carefully laid on the blocks.
- Pressure is brought down on the inked blocks.
- The carved-out niches in the block remain uninked, and the surface of the block becomes inked figures impressed on the paper.

Gutenberg's revolutionary contribution was in applying metallurgy to the process. The idea occurred to Gutenberg in the mid-1430s. Instead of wood, which often cracked in the pressing process, he experimented with casting individual letters in a lead-based alloy. He built a frame the size of a book's page and then arranged the metal letters into words. Once a page was filled—with letters and words and sentences—he put the frame into a modified wine press, applied ink, laid paper, and pressed. The process made it possible to produce dozens, even hundreds and thousands, of copies.

First Mass-Produced Written Word. Johannes Gutenberg and his assistants could produce 50 to 60 imprints an hour with their modified wind press, but Gutenberg's real contribution was movable metal type. His movable type expedited the putting together of pages and opened the age of mass communication.

Despite the significance of his invention, there is much we do not know about Gutenberg. Even to friends, he seldom mentioned his experiments, and when he did he referred to them mysteriously as his "secret art." When he ran out of money, Gutenberg quietly sought investors, luring them partly by the mystique he attached to his work. What we know about Gutenberg's "secret art" was recorded only because Gutenberg's main backer didn't realize the quick financial return he expected on his investment and sued. The litigation left a record from which historians have pieced together the origins of modern printing.

The date that Johannes Gutenberg printed his first page with movable type is unknown, but historians usually settle on 1446. Gutenberg's printing process was widely copied—and quickly. By 1500, presses all over western Europe had published almost 40 000 books.

Gutenberg's impact cannot be overstated. The duplicative power of movable type put the written word into wide circulation and fuelled quantum increases in literacy. One hundred years after Gutenberg, the state of communication in Europe had undergone a revolution. Elaborate postal systems were in place. Standardized maps produced by printing presses replaced hand-copied maps, with all their inaccuracies and idiosyncrasies. People began writing open letters to be distributed far and wide. Newspapers followed.

Marshall McLuhan once said, "Gutenberg's invention of moveable type forced man to comprehend in a linear, uniform, connected, continuous fashion." The invention of the printing press also made sight more important than sound in the communications process. This made print a cool medium. The importance of Gutenberg was evident in A&E's Biography of the 100 most important people of the second millennium. Gutenberg topped the list.

Importance of Newspapers

NEWSPAPER INDUSTRY DIMENSIONS

The newspaper industry dwarfs other news media by almost every measure. In the U.S., about 1570 daily newspapers put out 60 million copies a day. While smaller by

The Canadian Newspaper Association's 1998 advertising campaign seems to be saying something about the value of reading a newspaper. Referring to the ideas of McLuhan in Chapter 1, are newspapers a "hot" or "cool" medium?

comparison, Canadian newspapers are equally as important. According to data from the Canadian Newspaper Association:

- In Canada, 104 dailies publish about 5.1 million copies each day. This means that about 1 in 5 Canadians reads a daily newspaper. That's one of the highest ratios in the world.
- Two-thirds of Canadians read a weekend newspaper.
- Community weeklies in Canada publish over 10 million copies and are read by 1.6 people per household.

(Source: The Canadian Newspaper Association and the Canadian Community Newspapers Association.)

What makes a newspaper Canadian? Changes to the 1988 Income Tax Act state that a newspaper is Canadian if:

- the type is set in Canada (excluding ads or feature stories);
- it is wholly printed in Canada (excluding comics); and
- it is edited and published by people living in Canada.

(Source: Canadian Income Tax Act with income tax regulations consolidated to 22 September 1988.)

The Canadian Newspaper Association: This organization represents 101 Canadian English and French daily newspapers.

www.cna-acj.ca

CONTENT DIVERSITY AND DEPTH

In most communities, newspapers cover more news at greater depth than competing media. A metropolitan daily like the *Hamilton Spectator* typically may carry hundreds of items—more than any television or radio station and at greater length. Magazines, for example, offer more depth on selected stories, but the magazines are published relatively infrequently and run relatively few articles.

Newspapers have a rich mix of content—news, advice, comics, opinion, puzzles, and data. It's all there to tap into at will. Some people go right for the stock market tables; others to sports or a favourite columnist. Unlike radio and television, you don't have to wait for what you want.

People like newspapers. Some talk affectionately of cuddling up in bed on a leisurely Sunday morning with their paper. The news and features give people something in common to talk about. Newspapers are important in people's lives, and as a medium they adapt to changing lifestyles. Ads in weekend papers are often their guide for shopping excursions.

All this does not mean that the newspaper industry is not facing problems from competing media, new technology, and ongoing lifestyle shifts. But to date, newspapers have reacted to change with surprising effectiveness. To offset television's inroads, newspapers put new emphasis on being a visual medium and shed their drab graphics for colour and aesthetics. To accommodate the work schedule transition over recent years from factory jobs starting at 7 a.m. to service jobs starting at 9 a.m., newspapers have emphasized morning editions and phased out afternoon editions. Knowing that the days of ink-on-paper technology are limited, the newspaper industry is examining electronic delivery methods for the 21st century.

Some problems are truly daunting, like the aversion of many young people to newspapers. Also, chain ownership has raised fundamental questions about how well newspapers can do their work and still meet the profit expectations of distant shareholders.

Chain Ownership, Convergence, and Newspapers

TREND TOWARD CHAINS

Knight-Ridder Newspapers: All in one place.
www.nmc.infi.net/kri/newsstand/pp

Reasoning that he could multiply profits by owning multiple newspapers, American magnate **William Randolph Hearst** put together a chain of big-city newspapers in the late 1880s. Although Hearst's chain was not the first, his empire became the model in the public's mind for much that was both good and bad about **newspaper chains.** Like other chains, Hearst also expanded into magazines, radio, and television. The trend toward chain ownership continues, and today chains own the majority of dailies in the United States and Canada. Chain ownership is also coming to dominate weeklies, which had long been a bastion of independent ownership.

Newspaper profitability skyrocketed in the 1970s and 1980s, which prompted chains to buy up locally owned newspapers. Single-newspaper cities were especially attractive because no competing media could match a local newspaper's large audience. It was possible for new owners to push ad rates up rapidly, and local retailers had to go along. The profit potential was enhanced because production costs were falling dramatically with less labour-intensive back-shop procedures, computerized typesetting, and other automation. Profits were dramatic. Only soft drink companies did better.

ASSESSING CHAIN OWNERSHIP

Is chain ownership good for newspapers? The question raised in Hearst's time was whether diverse points of view were as likely to get into print if ownership were concentrated in fewer and fewer hands. The corporate focus on profits raises a dark new question: Are chains so concerned about profits that they forget good journalism? These are the types of questions that were the basis of two Royal Commissions in Canada.

In 1970 a special Senate Committee on the status of the mass media in Canada, headed by Senator Keith Davey, released its report about the state of Canadian newspapers. Part of the rationale for this committee was the growing concern regarding concentration of newspaper ownership in Canada. In its report, the committee noted that "the media is passing into fewer and fewer hands, and that the experts agree that this trend is likely to continue." In terms of newspaper ownership, at the time of its publication, the **Davey Commission** noted that genuine competition existed in only five Canadian cities; that at the turn of the last century, 35 Canadian cities and towns were multi-newspaper towns (meaning they had two or more newspapers), but by 1970, there were only 15. In five of those 15 cities, both papers were published by the same owner. In 1930 116 daily newspapers were owned by 99 publishers, but by 1970 three newspaper chains—Southam, Thomson, and F.P.—had a controlling interest in three-quarters of newspaper circulation in Canada.

The Davey Report made many recommendations. Among them was the creation of a press ownership review board. The role of the board would be to monitor ownership changes and proposed mergers between newspapers in order to control the trend toward concentration of ownership. The board would have the power to veto any sale of a newspaper if it meant an increase in concentration of ownership. The government's response to the recommendations was lukewarm at best and such a board was never created.

A little more than 10 years later the situation had not improved. Ownership of Canada's newspapers, particularly in Quebec, had fallen into fewer and fewer hands. The 1981 **Kent Commission** into newspaper ownership in Canada, headed by Tom Kent, came about following an incident that was too convenient to be coincidental. On the same day in August of 1980, the *Ottawa Journal*, which had been publishing for 94 years and was owned by Thomson, and the 90-year-old *Winnipeg Tribune*, owned by Southam, closed their doors and ceased publication, leaving Winnipeg and Ottawa as one-newspaper towns. Each city still had a daily newspaper—the *Winnipeg Free Press*, owned by Thomson, and the *Ottawa Citizen*, owned by Southam. Within a week, the Kent Commission was born. Its mandate was to look into the state of newspapers in Canada and to propose a course of action for the government. Its mandate was considerably broader than its predecessor's. A multi-volume report, the Kent Commission made recommendations not only on concentration of ownership but on editorial expression and the quality of journalism in Canada. The goal of the commission was to establish legislation governing the newspaper industry in Canada. Among those recommendations it was stated that:

- No owner could control more than 5 percent of Canada's total newspaper circulation.
- No owner could own more than five newspapers.
- No owner could own more than one newspaper within a radius of 500 kilometres.
- To stop the trend towards chains, several papers, including Thomson, would be ordered to "divest" themselves of some of their newspaper holdings.

As was the case with the Davey Commission, the Kent Commission's suggestions died before becoming law. In 1984 while the Newspaper Act was being debated in Parliament, an election was held. When Parliament reconvened, the bill died.

Southam: A listing of all Southam's Canadian newspapers.

www.southam.com

CURRENT STATE OF THE NEWSPAPER INDUSTRY IN CANADA

The landscape has changed dramatically since the Kent Commission in 1981. It has changed in terms of who the players are but not in terms of the fears of either Kent or Davey. The major players in the Canadian newspaper industry are owned by conglomerates. Hollinger (owned by CanWest Global) controls 27 of Canadian daily newspapers, while Southam (owned by Hollinger) owns 26 dailies, and SunMedia (owned by Quebecor) controls 15. By 2002, only five of Canada's daily newspapers were considered "independent." The other 99 were owned by a corporation. Maude Barlow of the Council of Canadians says that Canadians should be more concerned with the concentration of media ownership. Says Barlow, "there is a potential in that situation to have a homogeneity of news."

Why all the concern about concentration of ownership in Canada? After all, in a capitalist society, one should be able to venture into any enterprise one wants to. One might also argue that since Montreal and Toronto each have several daily newspapers there is competition for readers. While the players have changed in the last 25 years, both the Davey and Kent Commissions leave us with these points to think about when discussing the effects of concentration of ownership:

- News is a product; it needs a variety of voices to be produced. Without this variety, newspapers "become more alike, less individual, less distinctive." In short, concentration of ownership limits choice on the part of the reader.
- As newspapers become part of a large corporation, the people who run them won't likely have a background in journalism, but a background in business or management. Given this scenario, profits become more important than editorial content and the whole news-gathering and writing process.

MEDIA DATABANK 2.1

Top Newspapers in Canada

Here are the top newspapers in Canada. Note the impact of conglomeration and convergence in terms of the ownership groups.

Newspaper	Weekly Circulation	Ownership Group
Toronto Star	3 469 255	Torstar
Globe and Mail	2 003 935	BCE
Le Journal de Montreal	1 949 429	Quebecor
Toronto Sun	1 785 626	Quebecor
National Post	1 763 934	CanWest Global/Southam
La Presse	1 419 204	Power
Vancouver Sun	1 199 776	CanWest
Ottawa Citizen	1 026 662	CanWest
Montreal Gazette	1 026 278	CanWest
Vancouver Province	999 716	CanWest

Source: The Ultimate Guide to Newspapers, Canadian Newspaper Association, 2001.

- Too much power in too few hands contradicts the role of the press in a democracy. Concentration of press ownership in Canada may mean power without accountability.

- While it's true that newspapers have competition from radio and television, it's newspapers that have traditionally been used to record history. Radio and television newscasts are not archived in the same manner as newspapers. This has serious implications for future historical research.

National Dailies

THE *Globe and Mail*

The *Globe* was founded in 1844 in Toronto by Scottish immigrant **George Brown**. Although labelled as politically conservative, Brown was also somewhat of a publishing

Media People

Roy Thomson

The Thomsons

Mass media companies, like other companies, go where the money is.

The fact that the mass media are economic creatures can be illustrated no better than with the story of Thomson newspapers. At its peak as a newspaper company, Canada-based Thomson owned 233 dailies and weeklies in the United States and Canada and 151 in Britain. It was a profitable business. Then profits slipped and Thomson began looking elsewhere to make the returns it had come to expect. The answer was online publishing.

In the early 1990s Thomson began unloading newspapers. By 1999 it was down to 50 dailies in the United States and eight in Canada. In that same period, Thomson paid US$3.4 billion for West Publishing of St. Paul, Minnesota, the leading publisher of law reference books, and its online Westlaw legal information service. Then Thomson bought Beta Systems, Computer Language Research, Creative Solutions, digiTrack, Nelson Information, and Technimetrics—all companies that generate and sell data. The revenue from these new enterprises was US $4.8 billion in 1998 with profits of 26.6 percent. Profits at the remaining Thomson newspapers continued their drop and were running at 17.6 percent. In 2000,

Thomson began unloading the rest of its newspapers, with the lone exception being the flagship *Globe and Mail*, based in Toronto.

A barber's son, Roy Thomson quit school at 13. When he grew up, he became a travelling salesman in northern Ontario, hawking auto parts and washing machines. One day in 1932 somebody mentioned that a radio station was for sale. Things weren't going that well on the road, so Thomson scraped together a down payment. Years later, Thomson said his favourite radio music was "the sound of radio commercials at $10 a whack." Two years later, for $200 down, he bought the run-down Timmins, Ontario, *Weekly Press*. There, Thomson applied a two-part principle that would make him one of the richest people in the world. First, keep expenses minimal. Second, boost income by charging advertisers and subscribers as much as the market will bear. Eventually the paper went daily.

Before he died in 1976 at age 82, Roy Thomson owned more than 200 newspapers in Canada and the United States. The *Globe and Mail* was the prestige flagship, but most Thomson newspapers were distinguished only as low-budget money machines. Thomson, known for quips, once was asked to define news: "The stuff you separate the ads with."

When Lord Thomson died, he was worth almost US$1 billion. His son, Ken Thomson, of Toronto, still runs the company in the money-machine style of his father. In 1981 he sold the London *Sunday Times* and *Times*. "Just a drag on profits," he said. Ken Thomson was ranked the seventh richest person in the world in 1998 by *Forbes* magazine, his net worth estimated at US$14.4 billion.

innovator. He expanded the format of the paper and the *Globe* began publishing daily in 1853. He also published a weekly edition for readers living outside of Toronto. He was rewarded for his efforts; by 1872, circulation had almost tripled to 45 000. By the turn of the last century, it had increased to 80 000. The *Globe* merged with the *Mail and Empire* in November of 1936.

True to George Brown's innovations, the *Globe* was the first Canadian newspaper to offer electronic services. In 1980 it created InfoGlobe, an electronic information and research tool. An online version of the paper became available in 1984. Due to the competition in the Canadian newspaper industry in the mid-1980s, it became clear that the paper needed to look beyond its traditional southern Ontario market. Thanks to satellite distribution, it was possible for readers in Vancouver and Halifax to get the *Globe* in the morning. The *Globe* had previously been distributed using airplanes. *Globe* readers in Edmonton, Whitehorse, and Montreal had been able to get the paper delivered the same day, but it didn't hit the newsstands until the afternoon. In the mid-1980s the *Globe* also began to publish *Report on Business Magazine* and other glossy magazines on a regular basis in the hope of broadening national circulation and increasing advertising revenue. In 2001, the *Globe and Mail* became part of the multimedia platform owned by BCE, owners of the CTV network. It's still a widely read and respected paper, with circulation of about 2 million readers

USA Today

A strict format, snappy visuals, and crisp writing give **USA Today** an air of confidence and the trappings of success, and the newspaper has its strengths. In less than a decade, circulation has reached 1.6 million, behind only the *Wall Street Journal*, and **Gannett** executives exude sureness about long-term prospects. The optimism is underscored by the confident if not brash Page 1 motto: "The Nation's Newspaper."

Graphics Innovator. Since its founding in 1981, *USA Today* has had a profound impact on many other newspapers. The most obvious influence has been to establish newspapers as a strong visual medium with colour and graphics integrated with words. The newspaper's weather coverage and high story counts also have been widely imitated. *USA Today* is designed for travellers and as a "second buy" for people who already have read their hometown daily. Subscriptions are only a small part of *USA Today*'s circulation. Most sales are in distinctive TV-shaped newsracks and in airports, hotels, and places where travellers pick it up for a fix on the news.

Stories strain to be lively and upbeat to make the experience of reading the paper a positive one. The brevity and crispness of *USA Today*, combined with the enticing graphics, has led some critics to liken the newspaper to fast food and dub it "McNewspaper"—not bad for you but not very nourishing.

The introduction of *USA Today* came at a time when most newspapers were trying to distinguish themselves from television news with longer, exploratory, and interpretive stories. While some major newspapers were unswayed by *USA Today's* snappy, quick-to-read format, many other newspapers moved to shorter, easily digested stories, infographics, and more data lists, and colour has become standard. *USA Today* has clearly influenced today's newspaper style and format.

THE *National Post*

Nineteen ninety-eight was a busy year for **Conrad Black.** In July, Southam newspapers sold its interest in the *Hamilton Spectator*, *Kitchener-Waterloo Record*, the *Guelph Daily Mercury*, and the *Cambridge Reporter* to Sun Media for 80 percent of the *Financial Post* and $150 million. However, the real significance of Conrad Black in Canadian newspaper publishing increased dramatically on October 27, 1998. Black's Southam entered the national newspaper sweepstakes when it began publishing the *National Post*. As the *Post's* website trumpets, "Canadian news has changed in a big way with the *National Post*. Canada's first truly national daily newspaper is a lively source of information that speaks with a contemporary voice. A national voice."

The *National Post*. In 1998, Canada had its first "National" newspaper when Conrad Black launched the *National Post*. In 2000, Black sold 50 percent of the *Post* to CanWest Global. In 2001, he sold the paper outright to CanWest Global.

National Post: Canada's newest national daily newspaper.

www.nationalpost.com

Boston Globe: Read a story, then send it to a friend.

www.boston.com/globe/ap/glahome.htm

Chicago Tribune: Winner of the 1998 Best Online Newspaper award from the trade journal *Editor & Publisher*.

www.chicago.tribune.com

Los Angeles Times–Washington Post: This site includes *Times* and *Post* stories from the combined syndicated news service they operate. This includes coverage from the papers' Washington and foreign staffs. There is a charge for access, but you can sample free for a month.

www.newsservice.com

New York Times: The web edition, called the New York Times on the Web, has won awards for its design and strong news content. Distinctive features include links to Page One headlines, a digest of Page One stories, and a scanned look at the print edition of Page One.

www.nytimes.com

This new paper became a notable presence in the lucrative Southern Ontario market. For example, in Toronto, it is competing with the *Globe and Mail*, the *Toronto Star*, and the *Toronto Sun*. The *National Post* is a broadsheet that publishes six times a week. It initially hired many respected Canadian journalists, such as Christie Blatchford, Linda Frum, Anne Marie Owens, Scott Burnside, and the late Mordecai Richler, to their *National Post* team.

In the summer of 2000, Canadian media history was made when CanWest Global Communications, a broadcast media giant, paid $3.5 billion for Hollinger International. The sale included not only a 50 percent interest in the *National Post*, but also 13 Canadian daily newspapers and 136 smaller newspapers. In the fall of 2001, CanWest purchased the remaining 50 percent interest in the *National Post*. Conrad Black was no longer a Canadian media baron. That title now belongs to Izzy Asper of CanWest Global.

Although only in existence a few short years, the *National Post* has clearly established itself as an industry leader. Within three years of its launch, the *Post* was a top-five national paper, with a circulation of 1.7 million.

Hometown Newspapers

METROPOLITAN DAILIES

In every region of the United States and Canada, there is a newspaper whose name is a household word. These are metropolitan dailies with extensive regional circulation. In New England, for example, the *Boston Globe* covers Boston but also prides itself on extensive coverage of Massachusetts state government, as well as coverage of neighbouring states.

Following is a snapshot of Canada's leading metro daily.

THE *TORONTO STAR*. The *Toronto Star* is not only a metropolitan daily, it also has the largest daily circulation of any newspaper in Canada: almost half a million copies. The *Star* was founded in 1892 as the Toronto Star and Publishing Company. Its founding fathers were 21 printers who were on strike (or were locked out, depending on who you listen to). They had worked for the *Toronto News* until a new typesetting process threatened their jobs. Within days of losing their jobs, they borrowed old printing presses and, with each printer assuming the roles of writer, reporter, ad salesperson, and proofreader, the first *Evening Star* was printed on November 3, 1892. The masthead proclaimed "A paper for the people." It's this incident that gave rise to the *Star* being identified as a "liberal" paper for many years.

Today the *Star* employs more than 4500 people, including almost 400 people in its newsroom. The *Star*'s press centre produces almost 4 million newspapers each week, and the *Saturday Star* has a circulation of almost three-quarters of a million.

The *Star* is owned by Torstar Corporation, which publishes community newspapers, distributes mail-order catalogues, and also publishes the successful Harlequin romance series.

HOMETOWN DAILIES

With their aggressive reporting on national and regional issues, the metro dailies receive more attention than smaller dailies, but most people read **hometown dailies**. By and large, these locally oriented newspapers, most of them chain-owned, have been incredibly profitable while making significant journalistic progress since World War II.

Hometown Coverage. The *Toronto Star* has the highest circulation of any Canadian daily. It began publishing in 1892. In 2001, the Star's parent company, Torstar, entered the convengence sweepstakes by applying for TV licences in selected markets.

Fifty years ago, people in small towns generally bought both a metropolitan daily and a local newspaper. Hometown dailies were thin and coverage was hardly comprehensive. Editorial pages tended to offer only a single perspective. Readers had few alternative sources of information. Since then, these smaller dailies have hired better-prepared journalists, acquired new technology, and strengthened their local advertising base.

Hometown dailies have grown larger and more comprehensive. The years between 1970 and 1980 were especially important for quantum increases in news coverage. The space available for news, called the news hole, increased. Many hometown dailies also gave much of their large news holes to bigger and more diverse opinion sections. Most editorial sections today are smorgasbords of perspectives. Vancouver, Montreal, and Toronto feature strong metropolitan newspapers.

Challenges for Daily Newspapers

CIRCULATION PATTERNS

The circulation decline has been heaviest among evening newspapers, and television is largely responsible. The decline in evening newspapers, called PMs, has been especially severe in blue-collar towns, where most families once built their lifestyle around 7 a.m. to 3 p.m. factory shifts. Today, as we shift from an industrial to a service economy, more people work 9-to-5 jobs and have less discretionary time in the afternoon and evening to read a newspaper. Predictably, advertisers have followed readers from evenings to mornings, and one by one afternoon newspapers in two-newspaper cities folded. In many places, afternoon newspapers have followed their readers' lifestyle changes and converted to the morning publication cycle.

ADVERTISING PATTERNS

Even morning papers are having advertising problems. The heady days when newspapers could count on more advertising every year seem over. Projections indicate that newspaper advertising will be lucky to hold its own. Television's growth is a factor, but other media, including ads distributed by mail, are eating into the historic dominance of the newspaper as an advertising medium. Local advertising is still the backbone of Canadian newspapers. The Canadian Newspaper Association says that local ads account for 53 percent of ad revenues, while revenue from classified ads is worth 28 percent, and national ads are worth 19 percent of a newspaper's profits from ads.

Besides television, daily newspaper advertising revenue has taken a hit from the **consolidation** of retailing into fewer, albeit bigger, companies. Grocery, discount, and department store mergers cut down on advertising revenue, and fewer competing retail chains meant fewer ads. This was a major loss because the grocery, discount, and department stores were newspapers' largest source of income.

PROSPECTS FOR THE DAILY PRESS

While daily newspapers, both metros and smaller dailies, face problems, they are hardly on the verge of extinction. While competing media have taken away some newspaper retail advertising, the want ads, formally called **classified advertising**, may not be glamorous to anybody except newspaper owners. At some newspapers, classifieds generate more than half of the revenue. Television and radio have not found a way to offer a competing service, and not even free-distribution papers devoted to classified advertising have reversed the growth in daily newspaper classified revenue.

Also, the newspaper remains the dominant advertising medium for most major local advertisers: grocery stores, department stores, automobile dealerships, and discount stores.

On the downside, daily newspapers have suffered major losses over the years in national advertising, mostly to magazines and network television. Despite the losses, newspapers have not given up on national advertising. Every newspaper has a broker, called a **national representative**, whose business is to line up national advertising for its client newspapers.

Daily newspapers, however, do have several inherent advantages that competing media cannot match, at least not now.

PORTABILITY. Newspapers are a portable medium. People can pick up a newspaper any time and take it with them, which is hardly possible with newspaper's biggest rival for advertisers—television. In the long term, as television sets are installed in more places and with the arrival of miniaturized, battery-operated television receivers, this newspaper advantage may erode.

VARIETY. A newspaper has more room to cover a greater variety of events and provide a greater variety of features than competing media units. The entire script for a 30-minute television newscast can fit on a fraction of a single newspaper page. This advantage may dissipate as people have greater access to new specialized television services and zip and zap among them: The Weather Channel, CTV NewsNet, Headline Sports, information channels, ticker-tape streamers on cable. Also, 900-number telephone services offer scores, game details, and sports news on demand, although they are more expensive than buying a newspaper.

INDEXED CONTENT.   Newspapers remain quick sources of information, ideas, and entertainment. Readers can quickly find items that interest them by using headlines as an indexing device. With television, people have to wait for the items they want.

DEPTH COVERAGE.   Newspapers have room for lengthy, in-depth treatments, which most contemporary broadcast formats preclude. Rare are radio newscasts with stories longer than 120 words, and most television news focuses only on highlights.

These traditional advantages that accrue to the newspaper as a medium are being eroded, but the newspaper remains the only package that has them all. In general, newspaper companies are in a good position to survive because of an asset that competing media lack: the largest, most skilled newsroom staffs in their communities. Television stations have relatively minuscule news-gathering staffs, and they lack the tradition and experience to match the ongoing, thorough coverage of newspapers. The strength of newspaper companies is their news-gathering capability, not their means of delivery. Since the 1970s newspapers have experimented with facsimile and television text delivery, gaining familiarity with alternate technology for disseminating their main product—which is news, not newsprint.

NEWSPAPER WEBSITES.   Today almost every daily newspaper runs a website. The people who run news organizations sense profits from the web at some future point, and they want to be on the ground floor. But how long will the wait be for these news sites to turn a profit? Hoag Levins, editor of *mediainfo.com*, published by the newspaper trade journal *Editor & Publisher*, expects advertisers will flock to the web when penetration reaches 50 percent of a city's households.

Weekly Newspapers

COMMUNITY WEEKLIES

Weekly community newspapers have been making strong circulation gains since the 1990s. In Canada, weekly newspapers can lay claim to combined circulation of almost 11 million copies. Some weeklies, particularly those in upscale suburbs, offer sophisticated coverage of community issues. Others feature a homey mix of reports on local social events. The success of these weeklies is sometimes called **telephone book journalism** because of the emphasis on local names and events, the somewhat overdrawn theory being that people buy papers to see their names in print. Weeklies tend to cover their communities with a detail that metro dailies have neither the staff nor the space to match. There is no alternative to

Community News. Suburban weeklies are thriving: readers like the detailed local coverage and advertisers like the target market and the relatively low cost of ads.

keeping up with local news. The Canadian Community Newspapers Association says that focus on local content "provides readers with a sense of identity and belonging. While reading their community newspaper, they are highly involved, interested and engaged."

This emphasis on local content and creating a sense of community among its readers makes community weeklies a useful vehicle for advertisers. The Canadian Community Newspapers Association claims that "it is through this process that community newspapers enable you to effectively forge strong customer relationships—the ultimate communications objective in today's highly competitive climate." Advertisers have also found that they can buy space in weeklies for less and reach their most likely customers.

Shoppers

Free-distribution papers that carry only advertisements have become increasingly important as vehicles for classified advertising. In recent years, **shoppers** have attracted display advertising that earlier would have gone to regular newspapers. Almost all shoppers undercut daily newspapers on advertising rates. The number of shoppers has grown, and they no longer are merely an ignorable competitor for daily newspapers for advertising.

By definition, shoppers are strictly advertising sheets, but beginning in the 1970s some shoppers added editorial content, usually material that came free over the transom, such as publicity and occasional self-serving columns from legislators. Some shoppers have added staff members to compile calendars and provide a modicum of news coverage. Most of these papers, however, remain ad sheets with little that is journalistic. Still, their news-gathering efforts and expenses are minuscule compared to those of a daily newspaper.

Alternative and Minority Newspapers

Counterculture Newspapers

Village Voice: Out of New York and in your face.

www.villagevoice.com

A group of friends in the Greenwich Village neighbourhood of New York, including novelist **Norman Mailer** and Don Wolf, decided to start a newspaper. Thus in 1955 was born the *Village Voice*, a free-wheeling weekly that became a prototype for a 1960s phenomenon called the **alternative press** and that has continued to thrive.

In its early days, the *Village Voice* was a haven for bohemian writers of diverse competence who volunteered occasional pieces, some lengthy, many rambling. Many articles purported to be investigative examinations of hypocritical people and institutions, but, as *Voice* veteran Nat Hentoff has noted, nobody ever bothered to check "noisome facts," let alone the "self-righteous author." The *Voice* seemed to scorn traditional, detached, neutral reporting. Despite its flaws, the amateurism gave the *Voice* a charm, and it picked up readership.

The *Voice* today is more polished and journalistically serious. The characteristics that made it distinctive in its early history, and which were picked up by other **counterculture newspapers**, include:

- anti-establishment political coverage with a strong anti-military slant;
- cultural coverage that emphasizes contrarian music and art and exalts sex and drugs;

- interpretive coverage focusing more on issues of special concern to alienated young people;
- extensive entertainment coverage and listings of events;
- a conversational, sometimes crude style that includes four-letter words and gratuitous expletives for their shock value; and
- extensive personals for dating and sex liaisons.

By delivering a loyal readership that was hard to reach through mainstream media, many counter culture newspapers became fat with advertising. Today, about 100 alternative newspapers are published in the United States, and many are prospering. With a circulation of 172 000, the *Village Voice* is widely available in big-city news racks and by mail throughout the country.

Canada has its share of alternative newspapers, mostly distributed free at bus stops, bars, restaurants, and malls. These publications are typically regional in nature, with each metropolitan centre boasting at least one such newspaper. Examples include the *Georgia Straight* in Vancouver, *Now* in Toronto, and *The Coast* in Halifax.

GAY NEWSPAPERS

Jim Michaels began publishing the first gay newspaper, the Los Angeles *Advocate*, out of his living room in 1967. Today, gay newspapers in North America have a total circulation of more than 1 million. Most are free papers distributed at gay bars, nightclubs, and businesses. However, mainstream advertisers are beginning to take notice of the loyalty of gay readers to their newspapers. In 1990 the Columbia CD Club tested a membership ad offering eight discs for $1 in 12 gay newspapers. The response rate was so high that the club began placing the ad in 70 gay papers within a year. Other advertisers followed Columbia into the gay press.

Pink Triangle Press is a leading publisher of gay and lesbian newspapers in Canada. Their mandate is "committed to the struggle of lesbians and gay men for sexual liberation and human fulfillment." They began publishing in Toronto in 1971 as *The Body Politic*. In 1984, *Xtra* began publishing weekly. Their newspapers also include *Xtra West* in Vancouver, and *Capital Xtra* in Ottawa. Both have been published since 1993. Combined circulation is around 90 000 copies. They also have an online presence at xtra.ca.

ETHNIC NEWSPAPERS

Research on the ethnic press in Canada and the U.S. reflects ideological differences between the two countries. In America, the model is assimilation; in Canada it's accommodation. One of the earliest studies on the role of the U.S. ethnic press was done by Robert Park in the early 1920s. He found that most immigrants said they only planned to live in America temporarily and would return to their native country once they had earned enough money. On the other hand, in their study of the Portuguese community in Quebec, Alpalhao and Da Rosa (1990) found that in some areas of Quebec the existence of an ethnic means of mass communication, as well as other ethnic institutions (social services, churches, etc.), "permit a large percentage of the community to live as if they were still in the milieu of origin."

Canada has been officially multicultural since 1971. The Canadian Multiculturalism Act passed in 1988 supports the idea that Canada is pluralist and that all

Ethnic Newspapers. As the percentage of Chinese-speaking people in Canada has increased, so has the circulation of Chinese-language newspapers. Whether this growth will be sustained depends on the assimilation process. Earlier foreign-language newspapers went through explosive growth that accompanied immigration patterns and then withered as immigrants eased into the mainstream language and lifestyles. The largest Canadian Chinese-language newspaper is *Sing Tao*, published in Vancouver.

cultures should be encouraged to maintain their heritage and traditions while living in Canada. Given this status as a multicultural country, it's not surprising that ethnic newspapers have existed in Canada since the early 20th century. According to Canada's Information Office, more than 40 different cultures make up Canada's ethnic press. Most of those publications are local in nature; Toronto features more than 100 ethnic publications alone. The National Library of Canada lists well over 150 ethnic newspapers that circulate in Canada.

Evaluating Newspapers

Quantitative measures of a newspaper's success include circulation and penetration, but how can we judge quality? Rankings and awards are indicators, although they are imperfect. You yourself can evaluate whether the newspaper you read gives adequate resources to coverage.

CIRCULATION AND PENETRATION

Once upon a time, measuring a newspaper's marketplace success against its competition was simple. The paper with the largest circulation won. Today, though, many cities don't have competing dailies. Even so, numbers count. Is circulation growing? Declining? Because almost every newspaper reports its circulation to an auditing agency, you can track circulation year to year, even quarter to quarter.

Even more significant comparative data come from comparing **penetration**. Penetration is the percentage of people or households that get the paper. The ABC circulation auditing agency doesn't collect penetration data, but fairly reliable penetration is easy to calculate: Divide the population by the circulation. Seeking precise penetration data can get tricky. How you measure the circulation area, for example, can make a difference. There are other variables too. Even so, simple math can give you a good indicator of whether a newspaper's acceptance in the marketplace is improving.

QUALITY INDICATORS

While the Canadian Daily Newspaper Association and the Canadian Community Newspaper Association both hold annual awards for excellence in newspaper publishing, there are some quality indicators that you can generically use to evaluate your local paper. These are described below.

NEWS HOLE.   What percentage of the space in the newspaper goes to news? This is called the **news hole.** From a reader's perspective the bigger the news hole, the better. Discount postal rates are available only to newspapers that cap advertising at 70 percent. Many publications push the limit to maximize revenue, sometimes shorting readers on news coverage, commentary, and other non-ad content.

CONTENT.   Because local coverage is more costly than stories from news agencies, a good measure of quality is whether a newspaper has extensive local coverage or loads up with wire stories. Is local coverage thorough? Is it accurate? Does the newspaper have its own reporter in Ottawa? Its own provincial affairs reporter?

STAFF.   What kind of professionals report and edit the newspaper? Seasoned reporters who know the community well? Or beginners? Does the newspaper offer competitive salaries for the best talent? Salary scales generally are available on request at newspapers with collective-bargaining agreements.

MANAGEMENT.   Does top management have a permanent stake in the community? Or does leadership rotate in and out, with individuals focusing on making a name in order to move up in the corporate structure?

The Influence of Magazines

A NATIONAL ADVERTISING MEDIUM

Advertisers used magazines through the 1800s to build national markets for their products, which was an important factor in transforming North America from an agricultural economy into a modern economy. This also contributed to a sense of nationhood. The other mass media could not do that as effectively. Few books carried advertisements, and newspapers, with few exceptions, delivered only local readership to advertisers. Today, advertising is still an important concern to Canadian magazine publishers. Approximately 70 percent of their total revenue is generated by advertisers.

MAGAZINE INDUSTRY DIMENSIONS

The Canadian magazine industry has grown dramatically since the 1956 O'Leary Commission. That commission was set up to investigate ways to make Canadian magazines stronger. At that time, there were 661 Canadian magazines. By the 1990s, there were 1440 Canadian periodicals available to readers. There is a Canadian magazine for almost every city and region of the country and for almost any interest.

Canadian Magazine Publishers Association: Lists over 250 magazines and has an online newsletter.

www.CMPA.CA/ maghome.html

MASSIVE MAGAZINE AUDIENCE

Canada has a healthy magazine industry. According to the Canadian Magazine Publisher's Association:

- Over 1300 magazines are published in Canada.
- Forty percent of magazines purchased by Canadians were Canadian.
- Over 90 percent of the content of Canadian magazines, including illustration and photography, was produced by Canadians.

In short, magazines are a pervasive mass medium. Magazines, however, are not only for the upper crust. Many magazines are edited for "downscale" audiences, which means the medium's role in society is spread across almost the whole range of people with literacy skills. Even illiterates can derive some pleasure and value from magazines, which by and large are visual and colourful.

The massiveness of the audience makes the magazine an exceptionally competitive medium. About 12 000 publications vie for readers, ranging from general-interest publications like *Reader's Digest* to such specialized publications as *Winetidings*, for people interested in wine, and *Canadian Thoroughbred*, for racehorse aficionados. In recent years, new titles have been launched annually, although only one in five survives into its third year. Even among major magazines, a huge following at the moment is no guarantee of survival. Magazine publishing is a risky business.

PROTECTING CANADIAN MAGAZINES

June Callwood calls Canadian magazines "the only ones that will tell you how complex this country is, how interesting, how beautiful, where the troubled places are, they find our rascals and our heroes and they have become the fabric of our ordinary lives. We can look in a magazine and see ourselves." The Canadian government agrees with Callwood. They see magazines as playing a "significant role in the cultural life of Canadians" by reflecting our own distinctive people, places, and lives. For over a hundred years, the government has helped foster the growth and development of magazines with many different initiatives. Today, the Ministry of Canadian Heritage helps Canadian magazines in several ways:

- The Foreign Publishers Advertising Services Act, Bill C-55, assists Canadian magazines by channelling advertising money away from American publications. American magazines can only sell 18 percent of their ad space to Canadian advertisers.
- Amendments to the Income Tax Act in 2000 allow for advertisers to deduct the cost of advertising in magazines available in Canada. Fifty percent of the cost of the ad will be tax deductible if the magazine features more than 20 percent foreign content; 100 percent is tax deductible if the magazine has more than 80 percent Canadian content.
- Foreign purchase of Canadian publishing firms is not allowed.
- New Canadian magazines, with foreign ownership and control, must be reviewed under the Investment Canada Act to see what the benefits to Canadians will be.
- The **Postal Assistance Program (PAP)** helps Canadian magazine publishers offset the cost of distributing their periodicals by mail. This is particularly significant because the majority of Canadian magazines rely heavily on mail subscriptions.
- The Canadian Magazine Fund supports Canadian magazines with marketing, distribution, and professional development.

The reason for government help with the magazine industry is simple: competition from U.S. magazines.

Magazines as Media Innovators

INVESTIGATIVE REPORTING

Muckraking, usually called "investigative reporting" today, was honed by magazines as a journalistic approach in the first years of the 20th century. Magazines ran lengthy explorations of abusive institutions in society. It was **Theodore Roosevelt,** the reform U.S. president, who coined the term "muckraking." Roosevelt generally enjoyed investigative journalism, but one day in 1906, when the digging got too close to home, he likened it to the work of a character in a 17th-century novel who focused so much on raking muck that he missed the good news. The president meant the term derisively, but it came to be a badge of honour among journalists.

PERSONALITY PROFILES

The in-depth **personality profile** was a magazine invention. In the 1920s Harold Ross of the *New Yorker* began pushing writers to a thoroughness that was new in journalism. They used multiple interviews with a range of sources—talking not only with the subject of the profile but with just about everyone and anyone who could comment on the subject, including the subject's friends and enemies. Such depth required weeks, sometimes months, of journalistic digging. It's not uncommon now in newspapers, broadcasting, or magazines, but before Harold Ross, it didn't exist.

Under Hugh Hefner, *Playboy* took the interview in new directions in 1962 with in-depth profiles developed from a highly structured question-and-answer format. The *Playboy* Q-A format became widely imitated.

PHOTOJOURNALISM

Magazines brought visuals to the mass media in a way books never had. *Harper's Weekly* sent artists to Civil War battles, leading the way to journalism that went beyond words.

The young editor of the *National Geographic,* Gilbert Grosvenor, drew a map proposing a route to the South Pole for an 1899 issue, putting the *Geographic* on the road to being a visually oriented magazine. For subsequent issues, Grosvenor borrowed government plates to reproduce photos, and he encouraged travellers to submit their photographs to the magazine. This was at a time when most magazines scorned photographs. However, Grosvenor was undeterred as an advocate for documentary photography, and membership in the National Geographic Society, a prerequisite for receiving the magazine, swelled. Eventually the magazine assembled its own staff of photographers and gradually became a model for other publications that discovered they needed to play catch-up.

Aided by technological advances involving smaller, more portable cameras and faster film capable of recording images under extreme conditions, photographers working for the *Geographic* opened a whole new world of documentary coverage to their readers. Among *Geographic* accomplishments included these:

■ A photo of a bare-breasted Filipino woman field-worker shocked some *Geographic* readers in 1903, but Grosvenor persisted against Victorian sensitivities to show the peoples of the world as they lived.

National Geographic: The original coffee table magazine is now interactive.
www.nationalgeographic. com

Life: Once too big for your lap, now fits nicely on your screen.
www.lifemag.com

Life **Defined America.** The giant general-interest magazines like *Life* gave meaning to the word "photojournalism." The grisliness of war was indelible in George Strock's shot of G.I.s felled in their steps in New Guinea in World War II. After the war, *Life* chronicled the suburbanization of America with photo and text coverage of Leavittown.

- The first photographs from Tibet, by Russian explorers, appeared in 1905 in an 11-page spread, extraordinary visual coverage for the time that confirmed photography's role in journalism.
- A 17-page, 2.5 m foldout panorama of the Canadian Rockies in 1911 showed that photojournalism need not be limited by format.
- The magazine's 100th anniversary cover in 1988 was the first hologram (a three-dimensional photograph) ever published in a mass-audience magazine. It was a significant production accomplishment.

Life magazine brought photojournalism to new importance in the 1930s. The oversize pages of the magazine gave new intensity to photographs, and the magazine, a weekly, demonstrated that newsworthy events could be covered consistently by camera. *Life* captured the spirit of the times photographically and demonstrated that the whole range of human experience could be recorded visually. Both real life and *Life* could be shocking. A 1938 *Life* spread on human birth was so shocking for the time that censors succeeded in banning the issue in 33 cities.

Consumer Magazines

NEWSMAGAZINES

Although it is often compared to *Time*, **Maclean's,** "Canada's Weekly News magazine," was founded in 1905 by John Bayne Maclean, almost 20 years before *Time* first appeared. However, the magazine we now know as *Maclean's* was called *Busy Man's Magazine* until 1911. Originally, it was a large-format magazine, about the

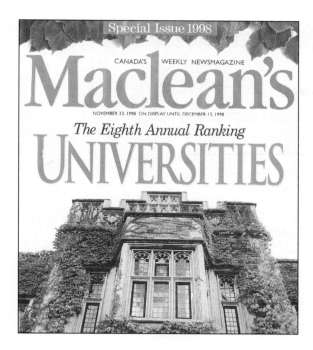

Special Issue 1998

CANADA'S • WEEKLY • NEWSMAGAZINE

Maclean's

NOVEMBER 23, 1998 ON DISPLAY UNTIL DECEMBER 13, 1998

The Eighth Annual Ranking

UNIVERSITIES

Newsmagazines. Canada's counterpart to *Time* magazine is *Maclean's* magazine. It brings the Canadian journalism tradition of analysis to the newsstands.

size of *Life*, but in 1969 it was reduced to a standard size. In content, *Maclean's* is similar to *Time*, with an emphasis on in-depth coverage of national and international stories. Columnists like Peter C. Newman (a former editor of *Maclean's*), Barbara Amiel, and Allan Fotheringham have offered their various perspectives to Canadians in the pages of this magazine. *Maclean's* even issues a national edition written in Chinese.

Fresh out of Yale in 1923, classmates **Henry Luce** and Briton Hadden begged and borrowed $86 000 from friends and relatives and launched a new kind of magazine: *Time*. The magazine provided summaries of news by categories such as national affairs, sports, and business. It took four years for *Time* to turn a profit, and some people doubted that the magazine would ever make money, noting that it merely rehashed what daily newspapers had already reported. Readers, however, came to like the handy compilation and the sprightly, often irreverent writing style that set *Time* apart. The Canadian edition of *Time*, published in Toronto, has a circulation of 300 000.

In 1974 Time-Life created the **consumer magazine** *People*, aimed at the same supermarket checkout-line customers as the *National Enquirer*. *People*, however, concentrates on celebrities and avoids much of the *National Enquirer's* blatant rumour mongering and sensationalism. *People* proved a quick success and also spawned a slew of imitators. Even the New York Times Company joined the bandwagon with *Us*. Together the celebrity-focused magazines robbed circulation from the sensationalistic **tabloids**.

WOMEN'S MAGAZINES

The first magazine edited to interest only a portion of the mass audience, but otherwise to be of general interest, was *Godey's Lady's Book*. It was started by Sarah

Maclean's: Canada's national weekly newsmagazine.
www.macleans.ca

Electronic Newsstand: Links to 2000 online magazines.
www.enews.com

MEDIA DATABANK   2.2

Magazine Circulation Leaders: Canada

According to the Print Measurement Bureau, here are the top magazines in Canada. Data were compiled using the "recent reading" method, which asks respondents when they last read an issue of a Canadian magazine.

Magazine	Readers
Health Watch	4 949 000
Chatelaine	4 792 000
Canadian Living	4 498 000
TV Guide	4 284 000
Maclean's	3 090 000
Time (Canadian Edition)	3 074 000
Canadian Gardening	2 842 000
Canadian House and Home	2 447 000
National Post Business	1 620 000
Report on Business	1 326 000

Source: Print Measurement Bureau, 2001.

Josepha Hale in 1830 to uplift and glorify womanhood. Its advice on fashions, morals, taste, sewing, and cooking developed a following, which peaked with a circulation of 150 000. The *Godey's* tradition is maintained today in competing magazines: *Better Homes & Gardens*, *Family Circle*, *Good Housekeeping*, *Ladies' Home Journal*, *McCall's*, *Redbook*, and *Woman's Day*. While each can be distinguished from her siblings, there is a thematic connection: concern for home, family, and quality living from a traditional woman's perspective. Canadian offerings like *Homemakers*, *Chatelaine*, and *Canadian Living* also fit the mould.

Another women's magazine is *Cosmopolitan*. Under Helen Gurley Brown, *Cosmopolitan* has geared itself to a subcategory of women readers—young, unmarried, and working. Gurley Brown retired in 1997, and Canadian editor Bonnie Fuller briefly took charge before moving on to *Glamour*, until she resigned in 2001. *Cosmopolitan* remains the most successful in a large group of women's magazines seeking narrow audiences. Other women's magazines include *Elle*, focusing on fashion; *Playgirl*, with its soft pornography; *Mirabella*, which mixes fashion and social issues; *Essence*, for black women; *Seventeen*, for teenage girls; and *Self*, for women of the "me generation." In Canada, *Flare*, *Images*, and *Focus on Women* are also geared toward narrow audiences.

Cosmopolitan: While not an elaborate site or an online edition of the magazine, the mission of *Cosmo* and some history is available here.

www.hearstcorp.com/mag2.html

MEN'S MAGAZINES

Founded in 1933, **Esquire** was the first classy men's magazine. It was as famous for its pin-ups as its literary content, which over the years has included articles from

Ernest Hemingway, John Dos Passos, and Gay Talese. Fashion has also been a cornerstone in the *Esquire* content mix.

Hugh Hefner learned about magazines as an *Esquire* staff member, and he applied those lessons when he created *Playboy* in 1953. With its lustier tone, *Playboy* quickly overtook *Esquire* in circulation. At its peak, *Playboy* sold 7 million copies a month. The magazine emphasized female nudity but also carried journalistic and literary pieces whose merit attracted many readers. Readers embarrassed by their carnal curiosity could claim they bought the magazine for its articles. Critics sniped, however, that *Playboy* published the worst stuff of the best writers.

Playboy imitators added raunch—some a little, some a lot. The most successful, Bob Guccione's *Penthouse*, has never attracted as many readers or advertisers as *Playboy*, but it has been a success.

Not all men's magazines dwell on sex. The outdoor life is exalted in *Field & Stream*, whose circulation tops 2 million, and fix-it magazines, led by *Popular Science* and *Popular Mechanics*, also have a steady following.

SPONSORED MAGAZINES

The founders of the National Geographic Society decided in 1888 to put out a magazine to promote the society and build membership. The idea was to entice people to join by bundling a subscription with membership and then to use the dues to finance the society's research and expeditions. Within a few years, the *National Geographic* had become a phenomenal success both in generating membership and as a profit centre for the National Geographic Society. Today, more than 100 years old and with circulation near 10 million, the *National Geographic* is the most widely recognized **sponsored magazine** in the U.S. Other sponsored magazines include *CARP News*, published by the Canadian Association of Retired People for its members. Also in Canada, *Legion* has a circulation of 446 000.

Many sponsored magazines carry advertising and are financially self-sufficient. In fact, the most successful sponsored magazines compete aggressively with consumer magazines for advertising. In 1991 *National Geographic*'s advertising staff put together an elaborate pitch to the Ford Motor Company for more of its ads. Impressed with the *Geographic*'s readership data, Ford increased its *Geographic* advertising for 1992 models by 250 percent—at a time when Ford was cutting back overall in magazine advertising.

Many sponsored magazines do not seek advertising. These include many university magazines, which are considered something that a university should publish as an institutional expense to disseminate information about research and scholarly activities and, not incidentally, to promote itself. Other sponsored magazines that typically do not carry advertising include publications for union members, in-house publications for employees, and company publications for customers. These publications do not have the public recognition of consumer magazines, but many are as slick and professional as consumer magazines. All together, they employ more editors, photographers, and writers than consumer magazines.

TRADE JOURNALS

Everyone in a profession or trade has at least one magazine for keeping abreast of what is happening in the field. In entertainment, the **trade journal** *Billboard* provides a solid journalistic coverage on a broad range of subjects in music—new recording releases, new acts, new technology, new merger deals, and so forth. *Billboard* is essential reading for people in the industry. About 4000 trade journals cover a mind-boggling range of businesses and trades. Consider the diversity in these titles: *Rock and Dirt, Progressive Grocer, Canadian Plastics, Hogs Today,* and *Hardware Age.*

Like consumer magazines, the "trades" rely mostly on advertising for their income and profits. Some charge for subscriptions, but many are sent free to a carefully culled list of readers whom advertisers want to reach. Trade magazines covering the Canadian and American mass media include *Marketing Magazine* for advertising and marketing, *The Publisher* for the newspaper industry, and *Broadcaster* and *Broadcast Dialogue* for the Canadian radio and television industries.

Many trade magazine companies have reputations for honest, hard-hitting reporting of the industries they cover, but the trades have a mixed reputation. Some trade magazines are loaded with puffery exalting their advertisers and industries. At some trades, the employees who solicit ads write news stories that echo the ads. These trades tend to be no more than boosters of the industries they pretend to cover. Kent MacDougall, writing in the *Wall Street Journal,* offered this especially egregious example: *America's Textile Reporter,* which promoted the textile industry from a management perspective, once dismissed the hazard of textile workers' contracting brown lung disease by inhaling cotton dust as "a thing brought up by venal doctors" at an international labour meeting in Africa, "where inferior races are bound to be afflicted by new diseases more superior people defeated years ago." At the time, in 1972, 100 000 U.S. textile workers were afflicted with brown lung. Responsible trade journals are embarrassed by some of their brethren, many of which are upstarts put out by people with no journalistic experience or instincts. Because of this, and also because it takes relatively little capital to start a trade magazine, many bad trade magazines thrive. Several trade magazine professional organizations, including the American Business Press and the Society of Business Press Editors, work to improve both their industry and its image. Even so, as former ABP president Charles Mill said, trades continue to be plagued "by fleabag outfits published in somebody's garage."

WEB MAGAZINES

Consumer and trade magazines adapted quickly to digital delivery in the late 1990s with web editions. Time Warner created a massive website, Pathfinder, for *Time, Sports Illustrated, People,* and its other magazines. With substantial original content, Pathfinder wasn't merely an online version of Time Warner magazines but a distinctive product. There were hopes that advertisers would flock to online magazine sites and make them profitable, but ad revenue only trickled in. In 1998 Pathfinder went to subscriptions to supplement the meagre advertising revenues. An access code was issued to *Entertainment Weekly* subscribers for an extra $30 a year. For the *Money* site the fare was $30 to subscribers and $50 to everybody else. All in all, the Pathfinder exercise was not a success. Time Warner gave up on Web subscriptions, dismantled Pathfinder, and set up individual sites for its brand-name magazines. The Canoe website in Canada offers readers links to magazines owned by Sun Media, while the Rogers site can connect you to *Maclean's, Chatelaine,* and other Rogers-owned publications. Meanwhile, the number of websites offering magazine-type content continues to grow. The proliferation includes thousands of hand-crafted zines, as they're called, on the Web.

Canoe: Canada's largest news and information portal.

www.canoe.ca

Rogers: Homepage for all of Rogers Communications Inc.'s media and corporate assets. Provides links to the online versions of Rogers's media publications including *Maclean's, Chatelaine,* and *Flare.*

www.rogers.com

Hissyfit: A highly successful online "zine" that celebrates and critiques pop culture.

www.hissyfit.com

Magazine Demassfication

A Narrower Focus

With the demise of many general-interest magazines, doomsayers predicted that magazines were a dying breed of media. The fact, however, was that advertisers withdrew only from magazines with broad readerships. What advertisers discovered was that although it was less expensive to use television to peddle universally used products like detergents, grooming aids, and packaged foods, television, geared at the time for mass audiences, was too expensive for products appealing to narrow groups. Today, relatively few magazines seek a truly mass audience.

Special-interest magazines, whose content focused on limited subjects and whose advertising rates were lower, fit the bill better than either television or the giant mass-audience magazines for reaching customers with special interests. For manufacturers of $3000 video systems, for example, it made sense to advertise in a narrowly focused videophile magazine like *Video News and Reviews*. In the same way, neither mass-audience magazines nor television was a medium of choice for top-of-the-line racing skis, but ski magazines were ideal. For hockey cards, *Canadian Sportscard Collector* made sense.

Among new magazines that emerged with the demassification in the 1960s were regional and city magazines, offering a geographically defined audience to advertisers. Some of these magazines, which usually bore the name of their city or region, including *Voilà Québec*, *Vancouver Magazine*, *Cityscope* (Calgary), and *Hamilton Magazine*, offered hard-hitting journalistic coverage of local issues. Many, however, focused on soft lifestyle subjects rather than antagonize powerful local interests and risk losing advertisers. Indeed, hypersensitivity to advertisers is a criticism of today's demassified magazines.

Critics of Demassification

Norman Cousins, once editor of the highbrow *Saturday Review of Literature*, criticized demassified magazines for betraying their traditional role of enriching the culture. Cousins said specialization had diluted the intellectual role of magazines in the society. Advertisers, he said, were shaping magazines' journalistic content for their commercial purposes—in contrast to magazine editors independently deciding content with loftier purposes in mind.

Calvin and Hobbes   by Bill Watterson

Magazine Demassification. Advertisers favour magazines that are edited to specific audience interests that coincide with the advertisers' products. Fewer and fewer magazines geared to a general audience remain in business today. Communication theorists refer to the process of demassification as narrowcasting.

Scholar Dennis Holder put this "unholy alliance" of advertisers and readers this way:

> The readers see themselves as members of small, and in some sense, elite groups—joggers, for example, or cat lovers—and they want to be told that they are terribly neat people for being in those groups. Advertisers, of course, want to reinforce the so-called positive self-image too, because joggers who feel good about themselves tend to buy those ridiculous suits and cat lovers who believe lavishing affection on their felines is a sign of warmth and sincerity are the ones who purchase cute little cat sweaters, or are they cat's pajamas?

Magazine editors and writers, Holder said, are caught in the symbiotic advertiser–reader alliance and have no choice but to go along.

Norman Cousins and Dennis Holder were right that most consumer magazines today tend to a frothy mix of light, upbeat features, with little that is thoughtful or hard-hitting. However, most readers want to know about other people, particularly celebrities, and a great many trendy topics, and advertisers want to reach those readers, avoiding controversies that might hurt sales. So profitability for most magazines and their advertisers is locked into providing information their target audiences are interested in rather than serving an undefinable "public interest." The emphasis on profits and demassification saddens a number of people who believe that magazines have a higher calling than a cash register. These critics would agree with Cousins, who warned that emphasizing the superficial just because it sells magazines is a betrayal of the social trust that magazine publishers once held. "The purpose of a magazine," he said, "is not to tell you how to fix a leaky faucet, but to tell you what the world is about."

There is no question that demassification works against giving readers any kind of global view. In demassified magazines for auto enthusiasts, as an example, road test articles typically wax as enthusiastically as the advertisements about new cars.

Future for Magazines? Convergence and demassification have also affected the magazine industry. This Canoe webzine is an example of technological convergence with the blending of print and Internet technology. This also makes further demassification within the magazine industry possible.

These demassified magazines, edited to target selected audiences and thereby attract advertisers, make no pretence of broadening their readers' understanding of substantive issues by exploring diverse perspectives. The narrowing of magazine editorial content appears destined to continue, not only because it is profitable but also because new technologies, like Time Warner's geodemographic TargetSelect program, make it possible for magazine publishers to identify narrower and narrower segments of the mass audience, and then to gear their publications to those narrower and narrower interests.

On the other hand, it could be argued that magazines with broad readerships never truly gave a "global view," and in fact gave a narrow and/or parochial view a global reach. Consider *National Geographic:* Its view is global in terms of what it looks at, but its viewpoint is that of a select group of American editors and researchers.

Magazine Challenges

HAZARDS OF DEMASSIFICATION

While many magazines have prospered through demassification by catering to special interests, serving a niche of readers has its hazards. One problem is that a narrow audience may turn out to be transitory. Citizen's band radios were the rage in the 1970s, and CB magazines suddenly cropped up, only to die as public interest in CBs waned.

A second problem stems from the fact that, in coming years, specialized magazines may feel competition from other media, which are going through their own belated demassification. Radio is already demographically divided, with stations using formats designed for narrow audiences, and the narrowing is continuing. At the start of the 1990s, major cities had stations that aired only comedy, only financial news, and only motivational talk. Specialized magazines were losing their monopoly on narrow audience segments.

NEW COMPETITION

Another ominous sign for magazines is the cable television industry, which is eating into magazine advertising with an array of demassified channels, such as HGTV, WTN, and Discovery. The demassified cable channels are picking up advertisers that once used magazines almost exclusively to reach narrow slices of the mass audience with a presumed interest in their products and services.

Another drain on magazine revenue is the growth of **direct mail** advertising. Using sophisticated analysis of potential customer groups, advertisers can mail brochures, catalogues, fliers, and other material, including video pitches, directly to potential customers at their homes or places of business. Every dollar that goes into direct-mail campaigns is a dollar that in an earlier period went into magazines and other traditional advertising media.

NEWSRACKS OR SUBSCRIPTIONS

A magazine's financial health can hinge on finding the right balance between single-copy sales at newsracks and subscriptions. Subscriptions represent long-term reader commitment, but they are sold at deep discounts. Newsrack sales generate more revenue. In Canada, for every magazine sold on a newsrack, another 7.5 are sold through subscription. Finding the right balance is complicated because advertisers have different points of view on which delivery system is better for reaching potential customers. Some advertisers reason that readers who pay cash for individual issues are more attentive to the content than people who routinely receive every issue via mail. Other advertisers are impressed by the loyalty implicit in subscriptions.

To find the right balance, magazines manipulate their subscription rates and newsrack prices. When its advertisers shifted to a newsstand preference, *Cosmopolitan* lowered its single-copy price and hiked subscription rates until 95 percent of its circulation was through newsracks. The shift helped make the magazine attractive to advertisers.

Single sales benefit magazines in another way. They are more profitable than subscriptions, which means that magazines can keep their advertising rates down because readers pick up more of the bills. In general, the shift through the 1970s and 1980s was toward single-copy sales. The shift helped magazines improve their competitive stance against television.

Evaluating Magazines

Circulation and advertising revenue are measures of a magazine's populist success. More difficult is finding magazines that regularly fulfill their potential to examine significant issues and make an enduring contribution to a better society.

POPULIST MEASURES

Measures of commercial success in the magazine industry are easy to find. Circulation is one measure. *Time*, *Maclean's*, and *Reader's Digest* all score well by that measure. Even more telling as a populist gauge of success is advertising revenue. Advertisers use all kinds of sophisticated research and analysis to determine where their ad dollars are most effectively spent. *People* draws more advertising revenue than any other magazine—US $627 million a year.

QUALITY MEASURES

Critics say that commercial measures recognize magazines that pander to consumerism. Certainly, many magazines today work hard at being magnets for audience niches and for advertisers that seek access to those niches. *Canadian Living*, for example, offers a lot of predictable content on homemaking that a certain segment of consumers want, and advertisers are lined up to place ads in that magazine to reach those consumers. But is *Canadian Living* a magazine that makes people think? Or that offers insights into fundamental issues of human existence? Or that contributes to a better world in a broad and enduring sense? Elitists would fault it on all those scores.

What, then, are measures of excellence that would meet the standards of elitists?

Cerebral magazines with long records of commentary and analysis, often in the vanguard of thinking on enduring issues, include *Harper's* and *Atlantic*. Sometimes called **highbrow slicks**, these magazines steer an editorial course that's not beholden to narrow consumer niches or advertisers. The thrust is on social, economic, political, and artistic and cultural issues, often analyzed at great length by leading authorities. It should be no surprise that Vannevar Bush's thoughts on possibilities for a worldwide web appeared in the *Atlantic* in 1945—almost 50 years ahead of Tim Berners-Lee's invention of the web. The *New Yorker*, a weekly, prides itself on regularly breaking ground on significant issues in articles that run as long as the editors think is necessary, sometimes the length of a small book.

Outside of highbrow slicks, significant articles sprout occasionally in commercially oriented magazines. *Time* and *Newsweek* excerpt important new books from time to time. *Wired*, which focuses on future issues, gives cutting-edge thinkers all the space they need to explore their thoughts. Serious journalism appears occasionally in *Esquire*, *Outside*, and other magazines amid all the advertiser-friendly pap but hardly as a staple.

The ideological magazines, like *New Republic, National Review,* and *Nation*, frequently are cerebral, but partisanship often clouds their focus.

Newspapers and Magazines

Convergence is seen clearly as newspapers and magazines merge with broadcast companies to create multimedia-platform companies. Critics see the trend as a cost-cutting move to crank more mileage out of news staffs. In Chicago a labour union representing journalists at WGN television has objected to the station's newspaper partner, the *Tribune*, asking a television reporter to write a column at no extra compensation. Some reporters at converged news operations have felt overworked. In covering an out-of-town trial, Jackie Barron of WFLA found herself doing a TBO.com roundup of the previous day's testimony story before breakfast, phoning updates to WFLA ahead of newscasts during the day, then after dinner writing up all the day's events in a summary story for the *Tampa Tribune*. "My brain was mush by the end," she told Joe Strupp for an article in the trade journal *Editor & Publisher*. Media General executives say that getting triple mileage out of reporters is not the routine.

What about diversity? Do combination newsrooms reduce the number of interpretations of community news that are available? No, says Gil Thelen, executive editor at the *Tampa Tribune*, "This multimedia effort does not serve the community if it turns into homogenized mediocrity." Whether tight-budget multimedia conglomerates, especially those in small markets, see it that way, or as a means to maximize profits by putting fewer total resources into reporting, remains to be seen. This is also a concern of many here in Canada, including the CRTC, which, in 2001, asked the big media conglomerates, including Bell Globe Media and CanWest Global, to keep their print and broadcast newsroom management separate and distinct.

The future for magazines as a distinct mass medium is not clear. Hundreds of magazines have established websites, where people can call up digital versions that physically bear no resemblance to the slick paper and stitching that we normally associate with magazines. Furthermore, the traditional content distinction between magazines and other media is vaporizing. Newspapers are offering more and more coverage of specialized issues and events that once were the province of magazines. Conglomeration-driven convergence is also undermining magazines as a distinct medium.

CHAPTER WRAP-UP

Can newspapers survive? Even if people were to stop buying newspapers tomorrow, newspaper organizations would survive because they have an asset that competing media lack: the largest, most skilled newsroom staffs in their communities. The presses and the ink-on-newsprint medium for carrying the message may not have a long future, but newspapers' news-gathering capability will endure.

The magazine industry once was defined by giant general interest magazines, epitomized by *Life*, that offered something for everybody. Advertisers soured on these oversized giants when television offered more potential customers per advertising dollar. Magazines then shifted to more specialized packages. This focused approach worked. Magazines found advertisers who were seeking readers with narrow interests. Now, as other media—particularly television—are demassifying, magazines stand to lose advertisers, which poses new challenges.

QUESTIONS FOR REVIEW

1. How did the mass production of the written word change society?

2. Describe the rise of newspaper chains and the trend toward conglomeration in Canada.

3. Why are most newspapers morning editions now?

4. Why are community newspapers booming?

5. Why have alternative publications experienced increased readership?

6. Are magazines losing their influence as a shaper of the culture? Explain your answer.

7. How have magazines been innovative as a journalistic and a visual medium?

8. How has demassification affected both newspapers and magazines?

QUESTIONS FOR CRITICAL THINKING

1. Did the Davey Committee and Kent Commission leave any legacies that we can learn from?

2. When U.S. magazines came into their own in the 1820s, they represented a mass medium that was distinct from the existing book and newspaper media. How were magazines different?

3. Is demassification good or bad for readers?

4. What will the affect of convergence be on newsroom staff?

5. Discuss the role of these innovators in contributing to magazines as a visual medium: Gilbert Grosvenor, Margaret Bourke-White, and Henry Luce.

6. The late Norman Cousins, a veteran social commentator and magazine editor, worried that trends in the magazine industry were undermining the historic role that magazines have had in enriching the culture. What is your response to Cousins's concerns?

7. There are no laws protecting Canadian newspapers, yet there are many government initiatives in place for magazines. Is this fair?

FOR KEEPING UP TO DATE

CARD (Canadian Advertising Rates and Data) is a listing of newspapers and magazines published in Canada. It includes circulation data and current ad rates.

Editor & Publisher is a weekly trade journal for the newspaper industry.

Folio is a trade journal on magazine management. Among major newspapers that track magazine issues in a fairly consistent way are the *New York Times*, the *Wall Street Journal*, and *USA Today*.

NewsInc. is a monthly trade journal on newspaper management.

Newspaper Research Journal is a quarterly dealing mostly with applied research.

Presstime is published monthly by the American Newspaper Publisher's Association.

The Publisher covers community newspapers across Canada.

Many general interest magazines, like *Maclean's*, cover print media issues on a regular basis.

FOR FURTHER LEARNING

J. Antonio Alpalhao and Victor Da Rosa. *A Minority in a Changing Society: The Portuguese Communities of Quebec* (University of Ottawa Press, 1980).

Roland Barthes. "The Photographic Message." In *Image-Music-Text* (Fontana, 1973).

James L. Baughman. *Henry R. Luce and the Rise of the American News Media* (Tawyne, 1987).

Bill Bishop. "A Warning from Smithville: Owning Your Own Weekly." *Washington Journalism Review* 10 (May 1988): 4, 25–32.

Leo Bogart. *Preserving the Press: How Daily Newspapers Mobilized to Keep Their Readers* (Columbia University Press, 1991).

Reginald Bragonier, Jr., and David J. Fisher. *The Mechanics of a Magazine* (Hearst, 1984).

Walter M. Brasch. *Forerunners of Revolution: Muckrakers and the American Social Conscience* (University of America Press, 1990).

Robert Brehl. "Conrad Black Takes on Toronto." *Globe and Mail* (June 13, 1998).

Canada. Royal Commission on Newspapers, 1981.

Canada. Senate Special Committee on the Mass Media, *Report*. 3 vols. (Ottawa, 1970).

J. William Click and Russell N. Baird. *Magazine Editing and Production*, 5th ed. (Wm. C. Brown, 1990).

Ellis Cose. *The Press* (Morrow, 1989).

Jonathan Curiel. "Gay Newspapers." *Editor & Publisher* 224 (August 3, 1991): 32, 14–19.

Keith Damsell. "Magazine Numbers Unravelled." *Globe and Mail*, July 6, 2001.

Francis X. Dealy. *The Power and the Money: Inside the Wall Street Journal* (Birch Lane Press, 1993).

Peter Desbarats. *Guide to the Canadian News Media* (Harcourt, Brace, Jovanovich, 1990).

Edwin Diamond. *Behind the Times: Inside the New York Times* (Villard Books, 1994).

Robert Draper. *Rolling Stone Magazine: The Uncensored History* (Doubleday, 1990).

Elizabeth L. Eisenstein. *The Printing Press as an Agent of Change: Communications and Cultural Transformation in Early-Modern Europe*, 2 vols. (Cambridge University Press, 1980).

Bob Ferguson. "Critics Crank Up Pressure Over Black's Newspaper Play." *Toronto Star* (May 23, 1998).

Douglas Fetherling. *The Rise of the Canadian Newspaper* (Oxford University Press, 1990).

Otto Friedrich. *Decline and Fall* (Harper & Row, 1969).

Geddes, John. "The Izzy and Leonard Show." *Maclean's* (August 14, 2000).

Douglas H. George. *The Smart Magazines: 50 Years of Literary Revelry and High Jinks at Vanity Fair, the New Yorker, Life, Esquire and the Smart Set* (Archon Books, 1991).

The *Globe and Mail: 150 Years in Canada*. 1994.

Dennis Holder, Robert Love, Bill Meyers, and Roger Piantadosi, contributors. "Magazines in the 1980s." *Washington Journalism Review* 3 (November 1981): 3, 28–41.

Ernest C. Hynds. *American Newspapers in the 1980s* (Hastings House, 1980).

M. Thomas Inge, ed. *Handbook of American Popular Culture*, 2nd ed. (Greenwood, 1989).

Amy Janello and Brennon Jones. *The American Magazine* (Harry N. Abrams, 1991).

Lauren Kessler. *Against the Grain: The Dissident Press in America* (Sage, 1984).

Wilfred Kesterton. *A History of Journalism in Canada.* (McClelland and Stewart, 1967).

Wilfred Kesterton, "The Growth of the Newspaper in Canada, 1981." In *Communications in Canadian Society*, edited by Benjamin Singer (Addison-Wesley, 1983).

Michael Leapman. *Arrogant Aussie: The Rupert Murdoch Story* (Lyle Stuart, 1985).

Kent MacDougall. *The Press: A Critical Look from the Inside* (Dow Jones Books, 1972).

Ted Magder. "Franchising the Candy Store." Canadian American Public Policy Centre, April 1998.

Casey Mahood. "Black Daily Marks Sector's Boom." *Globe and Mail* (April 9, 1998).

Barbara Matusow. "Allen H. Neuharth Today." *Washington Journalism Review* 8 (August 1986): 8, 18–24.

Marshall McLuhan. *The Gutenberg Galaxy* (University of Toronto Press, 1962).

Richmond M. McClure. *To the End of Time: The Seduction and Conquest of a Media Empire* (Simon & Schuster, 1992).

Minister of Supply and Services Canada. *A Question of Balance: Report of the Task Force on the Canadian Magazine Industry* (1994).

Al Neuharth. *Confessions of an S.O.B.* (Doubleday, 1989).

Alan and Barbara Nourie. *American Mass-Market Magazines* (Greenwood, 1990).

Andrew M. Osler, "From Vincent Massey to Thomas Kent: The Evolution of National Press Policy in Canada, 1981." In *Communications in Canadian Society*, edited by Benjamin Singer (Addison-Wesley, 1983).

Theodore Peterson. *Magazines in the Twentieth Century* (University of Illinois Press, 1964).

Sam G. Riley, ed. *Corporate Magazines in the United States* (Greenwood Press, 1992).

Sam G. Riley and Gary W. Selnow, eds. *Regional Interest Magazines of the United States* (Greenwood Press, 1991).

Edward E. Scharfe. *Worldly Power: The Making of the Wall Street Journal* (Beaufort, 1986).

William Shawcross. *Murdoch* (Simon & Schuster, 1993).

Ted Curtis Smythe. "Special Interest Magazines: Wave of the Future or Undertow." In Michael Emery and Smythe, *Readings in Mass Communication*, 6th ed. (Wm. C. Brown, 1986).

James D. Squires. *Read All About It! The Corporate Takeover of America's Newspapers* (Times Books, 1993).

Jim Strader. "Black on Black." *Washington Journalism Review* 14 (March 1992): 2, 33–36.

W. A. Swanberg. *Luce and His Empire* (Scribners, 1972).

William H. Taft. *American Magazines for the 1980s* (Hastings House, 1982).

John Tebbel. *A History of Book Publishing in the United States*, Vols. 1–3 (R. R. Bowker, 1972–1977).

John Tebbel and Mary Ellen Zuckerman. *The Magazine in America*, 1741–1990 (Oxford University Press, 1991).

Times Mirror Center for The People and The Press. *The Age of Indifference* (Times Mirror Company, 1990).

Eric Utne. "Tina's New Yorker." *Columbia Journalism Review* 31 (March/April 1993): 6, 31–37.

Jennifer Wells. "Assessing Black's Toronto Plan." *Maclean's* (October 13, 1997).

Anthony Wilson-Smith. "The Scoop on Black." *Maclean's* (March 30, 1998).

Canadian Icon. For many years retailers such as Sam the Record Man sold music to Canadians. But technology is changing that. Web ordering and delivery are more efficient. People can order CDs online; they can share MP3 files. What will the record store of the future look like? Read on to find out.

Music

MEDIA TIMELINE

Development of the Record Industry

1877	Thomas Edison introduces a recording-playback device, the Phonograph.
1887	Montreal's Emile Berliner introduces technology to record discs simultaneously.
1920s	Joseph Maxwell introduces electrical microphones and recording system.
1948	Peter Goldmark introduces long-play microgroove vinyl 33 1/3-rpm records.
1950s	Rock 'n' roll, a new musical genre, shakes up the record industry.
1960	Stereo recordings and playback equipment are introduced.
1970	CRTC introduces CanCon guidelines to Canadian radio.
1983	Digital recording on CDs is introduced.
1998	Streaming technology makes downloading from the web possible.
1999	Shawn Fanning's Napster shakes up the record industry.

MEDIA IN THEORY

Analysis of Canadian Content

Since 1970 the Canadian Radio-Television and Telecommunications Commission (CRTC) has required that Canadian radio stations play a certain amount of Canadian content (known as **CanCon**) between the hours of 6 a.m. and midnight. However, this system was not without its problems. At first, when the quota was 30 percent, there was not much Canadian content to play. Canadian production houses and distribution networks simply did not exist. The Canadian musical talent might have been there, but it was hard to fight the machinery of large U.S. record distributors. While some good Canadian singers and groups emerged in the early 1970s, Canadian music was difficult to find at the time. As a result, some Canadian recordings were compared unfavourably with American ones. This was true even in the 1960s. In his autobiography, *Taking Care of Business*, Randy Bachman of the Guess Who and Bachman Turner Overdrive said that quite often Canadian radio wouldn't play a Canadian song until it became a "hit" in the U.S. The resulting myth that Canadian music wasn't as good as American music

plagued this country's artists for several years. Canadian music has only recently been able to escape this negative mythology.

Adding to this negative myth about Canadian music, certain broadcasters played little Canadian content during the day, instead choosing to "bury" it after 10 p.m. on weeknights and early in the morning on weekends, when fewer people listened to the radio. This practice was also reported in 1994, following a two-year study of FM radio stations sponsored by SOCAN (the Society of Composers, Authors and Music Publishers of Canada) and CIRPA (the Canadian Independent Record Production Association). In its report, the task force found that during morning drive times only 18 percent of music was Canadian, while Canadian music accounted for 26 percent of the music played during the corresponding afternoon period. Nancy Lanthier, in *Music Scene* magazine, has referred to this as the "CanCon Ghetto."

Most of these issues were dealt with by the CRTC in its 1998 decision regarding radio broadcasting in Canada. Now, English-language radio stations are required to play 35 percent Canadian content on a consistent basis through the day. In other words, this decision marked the end of "the ghettoization of Canadian music and Canadian talent," according to Michael McCarty, who is president of EMI Music Publishing in Canada.

What Is Canadian about Canadian Content?

As for promoting Canadian culture, since music and lyrics (as signs) signify something other than themselves, one might ask, "What does the lyrical content of 'CanCon' say about Canadian culture?"

An examination of songs that reached number one on the CHUM chart for a 13-year period before and a 13-year period after the implementation of the CanCon regulations might help answer these questions. CHUM was a Top 40 powerhouse in Toronto during the heyday of Top 40 radio (late 1950s to 1980). The survey reveals that 13 Canadian songs reached number one between 1957 and 1969, while between 1970 and 1982, there were 19 number-one Canadian songs. On the surface, this seems to show that the regulations were successful in promoting Canadian talent and the music industry as six more Canadian songs reached number one. But a closer analysis of the songs shows that these songs had few Canadian signifiers in the lyrics.

During the period before the regulations, 1957 to 1969, at least four of the Canadian songs that reached number one were recorded by Americans. They included "It Doesn't Matter Anymore," written by Paul Anka and recorded by Buddy Holly; "Love Child," co-written by Canadian R. Dean Taylor and recorded by Diana Ross and the Supremes; "Aquarius" and "Let the Sun Shine In," co-written by a songwriter from Montreal and recorded by the Fifth Dimension; and "Sugar, Sugar," co-written by Andy Kim and sung by the Archies. These songs undoubtedly helped Canadian songwriters to make money, but their lyrics say little, if anything, about Canada. In essence they are American songs, written for the U.S. market. In addition, two of the number-one Canadian songs were included on American movie soundtracks. For example, "Born to Be Wild" by Steppenwolf was featured in the film *Easy Rider*, while "One Tin Soldier" by The Original Caste was used in the movie *Billy Jack*.

Several other songs written by Canadians reflected American or British values instead of mirroring Canadian culture. Examples include "Diana" by Paul Anka, "My True Love" by Jack Scott, "Which Way You Goin' Billy?" by the Poppy Family, and "Charlena" by Richie Knight and the Mid-Knights. The only Canadian song to reach number one that was explicitly about Canada was the novelty song "Clear the Track, Here Comes Shack" by Douglas Rankine and the Secrets. The song was a tribute to Eddie Shack, a hockey player for the Toronto Maple Leafs.

After the Canadian content regulations came into effect in 1970, the number of Canadian number-one singles on the CHUM charts increased from 13 to 19. However, the same patterns that had existed before the CanCon regulations came into effect were still evident: American artists continued to record songs written by Canadians. For example, "Puppy Love," recorded by Donny Osmond, and "She's a Lady," sung by Tom Jones, were written by Paul Anka. "Woodstock," which was about the mythic American music festival, was written by Joni Mitchell and recorded by Crosby, Stills, Nash and Young. Meanwhile, the "Theme from S.W.A.T.," by the T.H.P. Orchestra, was the theme music to the American television program of the same name. Perhaps only two number-one Canadian singles in Canada during this period were openly nationalistic. The first was "American Woman" (which also reached number one in the United States) by The Guess Who. Appropriately, the band had dubbed itself The Guess Who in 1965 to avoid facing prejudice against Canadian artists by Canadian radio stations. The song's lyrics made clear distinctions between Canadian and American culture. The other uniquely Canadian number-one single was "Take Off" by Bob and Doug Mackenzie (*SCTV* comics Rick Moranis and Dave Thomas). However, like "Clear the Track, Here Comes Shack," this brand of nationalism was humorous in nature and perhaps reached number-one status due to its novelty.

Have the Canadian content regulations worked? The regulations had two general objectives: to promote Canadian culture and to help strengthen the Canadian music industry. Given the recent rise in popularity of Canadian artists and songs, one could easily argue that the music industry is stronger today than it was in 1970. Canadian music certainly doesn't have the same negative myth it did in the 1970s and 1980s. A Goldfarb poll conducted in 2000 claims that 90 percent of us consider Canadian music as good or better than music by foreign artists. CanCon is a success.

Music and Society

MUSIC AND POPULAR CULTURE

Released in 1984, "We Are the World" was the fastest-climbing record of the decade. Four million copies were sold within six weeks. Profits from the record, produced by big-name entertainers who volunteered, went to the USA for Africa project. The marketplace success paled, however, next to the social impact. The record's message of the oneness of humankind inspired one of the most massive outpourings of donations in history. Within six months, US$50 million in medical and financial support was en route to drought-stricken parts of Africa. "We Are the World," a single song, had directly saved lives. Canadian artists formed Northern Lights and recorded "Tears Are Not Enough" in the spring of 1985.

The 2001 Juno Hall of Fame nominee Bruce Cockburn has always used his music to bring about awareness of many different causes, including OXFAM. Incensed and enraged after seeing firsthand some of the cruelty during a trip to Central America in 1983, he wrote "If I Had a Rocket Launcher." Other Canadian musicians who help raise social issues on smaller but still significant levels through their music include Diana Krall, whose annual fundraiser helps raise money for Bone Marrow Transplants at Vancouver General Hospital, Deborah Cox travelling to Uganda with World Vision, and Terri Clark and The Guess Who performing in Walkerton, Ontario, raising awareness about the safety of drinking water. Kim Mitchell's "Go For Soda" became a rallying cry against drinking and driving.

The power of recorded music is not a recent phenomenon. In World War I, "Over There" and other records reflected an enthusiasm for American involvement in the war. Composers who felt strongly about the Vietnam War wrote songs that put their views on vinyl. "The Ballad of the Green Berets" cast American soldiers in a heroic vein, "An Okie From Muskogee" glorified blind patriotism, and there were antiwar songs, dozens of them. "American Woman" by The Guess Who symbolized Canada's stormy relationship with the U.S., while Joni Mitchell's "Big Yellow Taxi" was environmentally conscious long before that became the norm.

Advertisers also know the value of tapping into popular music. Beer companies often use popular music to sell suds. Remember Labatt's Blue using Blur's "Song 2" in a beer commercial? Also, Revlon used Shania Twain's "Man, I Feel Like a Woman" in a series of ads, while Microsoft used Tom Cochrane and Red Rider's "Lunatic Fringe" to promote its XP software.

Recording Industry

INDUSTRY SCOPE

When urban sophisticates in earlier eras wanted music, they arranged to attend a concert. If wealthy enough, they went to the parlour and sat at the piano. Rural folks had their music too—a fiddle on the front porch in the evening, a harmonica at the campfire. Music was a special event, something to be arranged. To those folks, life today would seem one big party—music everywhere all the time. Yes, we arrange for concerts and major musical events, but we also wake to music, shop to music, and drive to music. Many of us work to music and study to music. In fact, the recording industry has products in so many parts of our lives that many people take most of them for granted.

Polygram: Links to music and (no surprise) film and video.

www.polygram.com

Sony Online: Music from the media monolith.

www.sonymusic.com

Warner Records: Another media giant that is a big player in the recording industry.

www.wbr.com

Indie Labels: Tom Wicks maintains a web list of independent record labels, complete with his own flavoured commentary.

mailto:twicks@cs.ucl.ac.uk

MCA: Music is just one of this media monster's interests.

www.mca.com

Music is a big business in Canada. The Ministry of Canadian Heritage says that in 1999, sales of music in Canada were worth $1.3 billion, with $144 million being spent on Canadian recordings alone. Those totals don't include the value of black-market music that the industry estimates at an additional third. Nor do the totals include symbiotic industries like fan magazines, music television, and radio. Then there are concerts, performers' merchandise, sponsorships, and a miscellany of other related enterprises.

In addition to these economic facts, research released by Canadian Heritage says that 82 percent of us say that music is a big part of our lives and over half of us (54 percent) say that we are heavy music buyers.

THE BIG FIVE

Canada is the seventh largest music market in the world. The worldwide record industry is concentrated in five major companies, known as the **Big Five**, with 84 percent of the market. Each of these major companies is, in turn, part of a larger media conglomerate:

- *Paramount.* After the late 1990s mergers, nobody else was larger. The parent company is Vivendi of France. Labels include Decca, Geffen, Kapp, MCA, and UNI.
- *Warner.* Warner, a company owned by AOL Time Warner, includes the labels Atco, Atlantic, East West, Elektra, Giant, Interscope, Nonesuch, Reprise, Sire, and Warner.
- *Sony.* This Japanese company bought Columbia Records from CBS in 1988. Labels include Columbia, Epic, and WTG.
- *BMG.* Bertelsmann Music Group is named for the German media conglomerate that owns the company. Labels include RCA and Arista.
- *EMI.* This London-based company is part of the Philips conglomerate in the Netherlands. Labels include PolyGram, Motown, Mercury, Island, Deutsche Grammophon, and ATM.

INDIES

About 10 percent of the U.S. record market is held by independent companies. Although many indies are financially marginal, they are not to be written off. A Seattle indie, Sub Pop, did Nirvana's rough-edged first album *Bleach* in 1988. Some indies prosper in market niches. Windham Hill succeeded with high-tech jazz recordings in the 1980s, as did 415 Records with its own brand of rock. The Ministry of Canadian Heritage says that over 250 independent labels are responsible for roughly 90 percent of CanCon produced here at home. Most of the companies are in Ontario, but Quebec and British Columbia are also responsible for much of our independent music. Some major Canadian independent labels include Nettwerk, Aquarius, and Justin Time.

Evaluating Record Companies

COMMERCIAL SUCCESS

The measure of success in the record-making business is the **gold record.** Once a single sells 1 million or an album sells 500 000 copies, the **Recording Industry Association of**

Nelly Furtado. The singer is one of many recent Canadian artists to win both a Juno Award and a Grammy Award. Others include Celine Dion, Alanis Morrisette, and Shania Twain.

America confers a gold-record award. A **platinum record** is awarded for 2 million singles sold or 1 million albums. In Canada, the **Canadian Recording Industry Association** awards a **gold seal** for sales of 50 000, a **platinum seal** for sales of 100 000, and a **diamond seal** for recordings that sell 1 million copies in Canada.

QUALITY MEASURES

Your evaluation of record companies will flow from your own values. For many rap fans and free-expression advocates, Gerald Levin assumed heroic dimensions at Time Warner for his eloquent defence of artistic liberties in a controversy over Ice T's *Cop Killer* album. Police groups and others calling for a ban were less impressed with Levin. Months later, Levin waffled on the issue and called for Warner artists to begin a dialogue on standards. The fervid support of free-expressionists waned.

A key qualitative measure of record companies is their support of new artistic directions. The majors once played it mostly safe, regurgitating already popular styles rather encouraging fresh material and new genres that could help define the human condition in new and telling ways. Elitists, who believe that the mass media should use their influence to advance culture, would be especially critical of toning down cutting-edge work to avoid confronting tough social issues and to sidestep controversy. This is less a problem than it was at one time, but a lot of safe pap is still issued.

A question worth asking: From a record company's products and rhetoric, what seems to be its commitment to the potential of the music to examine issues, both personal and social, to advance our understanding and our ability to live fulfilling lives?

EVALUATING MUSIC

While the popularity of records is measurable, quality is not. As with all art, beauty is in the eye of the beholder—and people have a great range of tastes. What is it, then, that elitists would identify as music that's important? Which music most improves our sense and understanding of our world, our existence, and our relationships? These questions are difficult because many people are so emotionally tied up with their music that intelligent dialogue is impossible. Someone who is wound up in the incessant beat of rave culture might have little feel for the intricate elegance of a lullaby or the sophisticated interplay of a 132-piece orchestra's horn section performance of Jan Sibelius's "Symphony No. 2 in D, Opus 43."

Also, people change. Music that excites a 13-year-old who has just discovered pop on the radio might have no appeal to the same person 10 years later. Tastes change.

Developing a sense for excellence in recorded music, something transcending a visceral response, means joining the best dialogue. Finding music critics on your wavelength is an excellent starting point. Then stretch out to include other critics. Where to tap into the dialogue? Some genres receive continued and excellent comment in music magazines, including *Rolling Stone*. Major newspapers, notably the *New York Times* and *Wall Street Journal*, approach a wide range of recorded music seriously. Jurgen Gothe's *Disc Drive*, heard every afternoon on CBC Radio, spends a lot of time on music.

Among yardsticks that people apply in evaluating music are:

- *Originality.* Nobody sees much artistic merit in imitative music. A toned-down cover version of a song, recorded merely to sell copies, clutters the marketplace with more of the same. This isn't to say that all remakes are artistic dead-ends. New renditions can be significant, fresh interpretations. But music that merely regurgitates doesn't score high on any kind of qualitative scale.
- *Commercial appeal.* Music that is recorded for commercial reasons, nothing more, cannot score well qualitatively. Many people derive pleasure from listening, but artistic significance is lacking.
- *Lyrics.* Lyrics are like poetry and can be scored in the same kinds of ways. In fact, some of our time's best poetry is from songwriters.
- *Composition.* Like lyrics, the score and the arrangement are indicators of a recording's value.
- *Sophistication.* An appreciation of some music requires sophistication. Someone versed in Italian cultural history is likely to derive more from a fresh interpretation of Ottorino Respighi's Renaissance dance music than will someone who can't find Italy on a map. Some art, recorded music included, requires listeners to bring their special knowledge, intelligence, and sensitivity to the table.
- *Body of work.* The genius of a particular recording sometimes is best understood and appreciated in terms of its context. Does a song fit into a significant larger theme in Ricky Martin's latest album? Has Joni Mitchell moved into a new phase of her exploration of the human condition?

Sound Recording Technology

VIBRATION-SENSITIVE RECORDING

For years scientific journals had speculated on ways to reproduce sound, but not until 1877 did anyone build a machine that could do it. That was when inventor **Thomas Edison** applied for a patent for a talking machine. He used the trade name **Phonograph**, which was taken from Greek words meaning "to write sound."

The heart of Edison's invention was a cylinder wrapped in tin foil. The cylinder was rotated as a singer shouted into a large metal funnel. The funnel channelled the voice against a diaphragm, which fluttered to the vibrations. A stylus, which most people called a "needle," was connected to the diaphragm and cut a groove in the foil, the depth of the groove reflecting the vibrations. To listen to a recording, you put the cylinder on a player and set a needle in the groove that had been created in the recording process. Then you placed your ear to a megaphone-like horn and rotated the cylinder. The needle tracked the groove, and the vibrations created by the varying depths of the groove were fed through the horn.

Edison's system contained a major impediment to commercial success: a recording could not be duplicated. In 1887 **Emile Berliner** introduced a breakthrough in Montreal. Rather than recording on a cylinder covered with flimsy foil, as Edison did, Berliner used a sturdy metal disc. From the metal disc, Berliner made a mould and then poured a thermoplastic material into the mould. When the material hardened, Berliner had a near-perfect copy of the original disc—and he could make

Edison National Historic Site: Information about Edison and photos and sound recordings online.

www.nps.gov/edis/list.htm

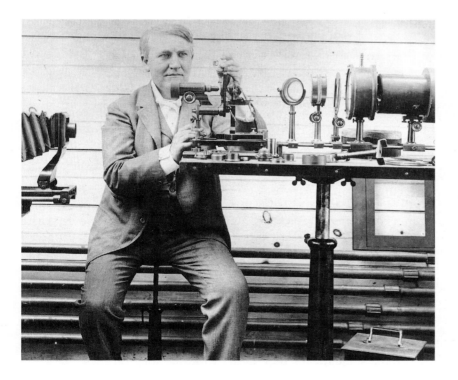

Thomas Edison. Prolific inventor Thomas Edison devised a machine that took sound waves and etched them into grooves on a foil drum. When the drum was put on a replacing mechanism and rotated, you could hear the recorded sound. Edison's Phonograph, as he called it, was never a commercial success because his recordings could not be duplicated. It was a later inventor, Emile Berliner, who found a way to mass-produce recorded music in Montreal.

hundreds of them. Berliner's system, called the gramophone, led to mass production. His company, the Berliner Gramophone Company, began to produce and market sound recordings in Canada.

ELECTROMAGNETIC RECORDING

In the 1920s, the Columbia and Victor record companies introduced records based on an electrical system perfected by **Joseph Maxwell** of Bell Laboratories. Metal funnels were replaced by microphones, which had superior sensitivity. For listening, it was no longer a matter of putting an ear to a mechanical amplifying horn that had only a narrow frequency response. Instead, loudspeakers amplified the sound electromagnetically.

Magnetic tape was developed in Germany and used to broadcast propaganda in World War II. In 1945 American troops brought the German technology home with them. Ampex began building recording and playback machines. The 3M Company perfected tape, and recording companies shifted from discs to magnetic tape to record master discs. An advantage of tape was that bobbles could be edited out. Creative editing also became possible.

While magnetic tape suggested the possibility of long-playing records, the industry continued to use brittle shellac discs that revolved 78 times a minute. One problem with the 10-inch **78-rpm** disc was that it could accommodate only three to four minutes of sound on a side.

VINYL RECORDS AND MICROGROOVES

One day **Peter Goldmark,** chief engineer at Columbia Records, was listening to a 78-rpm recording of Brahms's Second Piano Concerto, with Arturo Toscanini conducting. The concerto was divided onto six discs, 12 sides. Fed up with flipping discs, Goldmark got out his pencil and calculated whether a slower spin and narrower grooves could get the whole concerto on one disc. It was possible, although it would take both sides. At least the break could come between movements.

In 1948 Goldmark's long-playing record was introduced. Each side had 240 **microgrooves** per inch and contained up to 25 minutes of music. Offering several advantages, **LPs** soon replaced the 78-rpm record. Not only did each record have more music, but also the sound was better. The records were of vinyl plastic, which meant less hissing and scratching than shellac records. Also, vinyl discs were harder to break than the brittle 78s.

Refusing to be upstaged, RCA, which earlier had dabbled unsuccessfully with 33 1/3-rpm records, introduced extended-play records called EPs. They were small 45-rpm discs with a large spindle. Thus was launched the battle of the speeds, which pitted RCA and Columbia against each other. RCA, which manufactured phonographs, included only 78-rpm and 45-rpm speeds on its machines—no 33 1/3-rpm speed. The battle was costly. Unsure which would prevail, the public hesitated to buy phonographs and records. Record sales slumped.

A truce came, finally, when conductor Arturo Toscanini took RCA boss David Sarnoff aside and pointed out the obvious—that Brahms's Second Piano Concerto could not fit even on two sides of an RCA 45-rpm disc. Toscanini convinced Sarnoff to add a 33 1/3-rpm speed to RCA phonographs for classical music. The 45-rpm disc, meanwhile, became the standard for pop music, with one song on each side—and the Rock and Roll era was born.

THE STEREO REVOLUTION

Technical progress until the late 1970s produced nothing as revolutionary as the microgroove, but the improvements, taken all together, made for dramatically better sound. Anyone who has grown up with the production values of Canadians David Foster and Daniel Lanois would hardly believe that record-buyers accepted the sound quality of Bill Haley records only 30 years earlier. Better fidelity, called high fidelity, or hi-fi, was introduced in the early 1950s. The full audio range of the human ear could be delivered to listeners exactly as it was recording. **Stereo** came in 1961, with multiple microphones recording on separate tracks. Records played the sound back through two speakers, simulating the way people hear—through their left and their right ears. Consumers went for the new quality. FM stereo radio was introduced at about the same time.

Except for tapes, Edison's 1877 technology, refined by Maxwell half a century later, was at the heart of sound recording for 101 years. The technology was called **analogue recording** because it converted the waves that were physically engraved in the grooves of the record into electrical pulses that coincided analogously with the waves in the grooves.

Digital Technology

Record-makers developed a technological revolution in 1978: the **digital recording**. No longer were continuous sound waves inscribed physically on a disc. Instead, sound waves were sampled at millisecond intervals, and each sample was logged in computer language as an isolated on-off binary number. When discs were played back, the digits were translated back to the sound at the same millisecond intervals they were recorded. The intervals would be replayed so fast that the sound would

MEDIA DATABANK 3.1

Megadeals

Big-star megadeals have returned to fashion after almost ruining the U.S. record industry in 1979. The question, again, is whether the industry may be overextending itself financially. Recent deals surpass any of those of the 1970s. Many are multi-year packages, sometimes including more than records. Both Madonna and Michael Jackson's deals, for example, include movies. Here, according to industry insiders, are among the best deals of recent years. All figures are given in U.S. dollars.

Artist	Label	Deal
Prince	Warner	$108 million
Madonna	Warner	$75 million
Michael Jackson	Sony	$65 million
ZZ Top	BMG	$50 million
Aerosmith	Sony	$50 million
Janet Jackson	Virgin	$40 million

seem continuous, just as the individual frames in a motion picture become a moving blur that is perceived by the eye as continuous motion.

By 1983 digital recordings were available to consumers in the form of **compact discs,** silvery 4.7-inch platters. The binary numbers were tiny pits on the disc that were read by a laser light in the latest version of the phonograph: the **CD** player. The player itself converted the numbers to sound.

Each disc could carry 70 minutes of uninterrupted sound, more than Peter Goldmark dared to dream. Consumers raved about the purity. Some critics argued, however, that there was a sterility in digital recording. The sound was too perfect, they said. Instead of reproducing performances, said the critics, compact discs produced a quality that was more perfect than a performance. Traditional audiophiles had sought to reproduce live music perfectly, not to create a perfection that could never be heard in a live performance.

STREAMING

When the web burst into existence in the 1990s, everybody saw the potential, at least in theory, for the web to move sound and animation. One practical problem: The wires on which web messages moved were far short of the capacity, called **bandwidth,** to accommodate the massive digital files needed for re-creating sound

Media People

Shawn Fanning

Shawn Fanning

Shawn Fanning's freshman year at Northeastern in Boston was an academic disaster. Bored, he partied his time away. One day, his roommates complained that they couldn't find the music they wanted to download from the web, so Fanning decided to write a program to help. He obsessed over the project, writing code day and night until he had a system that would allow people to tap into each other's hard drives for MP3 downloads.

That was in 1998. The rest is history. Fanning dropped out of college, found a venture capitalist, moved to Silicon Valley, and went into business. His program, called Napster after his childhood nickname, almost instantly attracted thousands of music fans who began trading millions of songs online. Napster did it all automatically, listing every song every participant had on a hard drive.

At age 19, to many, Shawn Fanning was a cyberhero. He was also in trouble. The record industry watched sales tumble at campus-area record shops. Alarmed, the Recording Industry Association of America sued Fanning's company, charging that Napster enabled people to undermine the whole intellectual property legal apparatus that allowed music creators and owners to profit from their work.

Napster's popularity also created campus problems. At some colleges, half the computer resources were being consumed by Napster traffic in the spring 1999 semester. Several colleges barred Napster, not only to clear the way for other web traffic but also because the colleges were being sued as accomplices.

In Canada, three-quarters of 18- to 24-year-olds download music from the Internet, according to Ipsos-Reid, ranking them at the top of the list worldwide. Music sales dropped by 6 percent in 2000 and many attributed that drop to music sharing over the Internet.

Fanning responded to critics that Napster was nothing more than an electronic way for people to swap records—an age-old practice. The court decisions went against Napster in 2001. Although the company's future was in doubt, Shawn Fanning's technology had prompted a fundamental rethinking of intellectual property rights. The issue is far from settled.

and video. E-mail messages were tidy little packets that were easily handled. Web pages with illustrations and photos were fatter but manageable. But sound and animation? In 1997 it required 21.4 hours to move 18 minutes of animation.

Then came **compression** software that trimmed excess coding for digitized messages before transmission. With music, extreme sounds, generally beyond the range of human hearing, were dropped. In other ways too, the software trimmed the digital files. People still couldn't hear transmissions live, but if they waited a few minutes for a download to be completed, they could use the web for music and even video. **Streaming** technology went a step further, allowing earlier parts of a transmission to be seen or heard while later parts of the file were still being downloaded.

CRITICS OF MUSIC DOWNLOADING

From the mainstream record industry's perspective, digital technology seemed to have gotten wildly out of control in the late 1990s. **MP3** compression technology and streaming technology made it possible for fans to swap music on an unprecedented scale. Fans were exchanging for free what they once had to buy through retail outlets and record clubs. Doomsayers forecasted the end of the industry or at least a devastating restructuring.

Denise Donlon, president of Sony Canada, says downloading music for free is wrong and is the same as walking into a music store and walking out with a CD in your pocket. Says Donlon, "having creators compensated for the work they do is an issue we need to champion. We have to have an actual conversation about intellectual copyright and how we're all shareholders in this."

The record companies fuelled the gloomy forecasts with frantic suits against Napster, MP3.com, Gnutella, and other companies whose software made web swapping possible. When the decision came down in 2001 that effectively shut down the Napster site that Shawn Fanning had developed, Brian Robertson, president of the Canadian Recording Industry Association (CRIA), said that he and other members of CRIA welcomed the decision against Napster. According to Robertson, "all elements of the Canadian recording industry welcome the decision. The court clearly established that the principle of copyright law has to be respected."

However, some argue that record companies were far less desperate than it appeared. The lawsuits were designed to slow web inroads into sales while the companies created their own web marketing vehicles. The companies held some trump cards:

- Most major artists were contractually bound to major record-makers in long-term deals. With only a few exceptions, the popular talent wasn't leaving.
- The record companies had the marketing expertise and muscle—large budgets too—to create big hits. Odds were still against artists succeeding by going it alone on the web.

The major labels recognized the impossibility of wiping out illegal downloading but figured that aggressive court actions could minimize the threat. The majors were willing to leave free downloading to niche music and new performers seeking any exposure they could get. To the consternation of record-store chains and independent record shops, the record companies set up online sales channels. In the fall of 2001, MusicNet, owned by AOL Time Warner, Bertelsmann AG, and EMI, and PressPlay, owned by Sony and Vivendi, were the first to offer downloading of music for a monthly fee in Canada.

MP3.com: This company, owned by Vivendi-Universal (also the parent company of Paramount) is "dedicated to growing the digital music space"—within the confines of copyright law, naturally.

www.mp3.com

Meanwhile, most business analysts project that the record industry will sustain the steady, though unspectacular, 3 to 6 percent growth rate of recent years. Recording technology had come a long way since Edison. Stay tuned.

Evolution of Music

FOLK MUSIC

Most music historians trace contemporary popular music to two roots in distinctive folk music, both of which emerged in the American South.

BLACK MUSIC.   Black slaves who were brought to the colonies used music to soothe their difficult lives. Much of the music reflected their oppression and hopeless poverty. Known as **black music,** it was distinctive in that it carried strains of slaves' African roots and at the same time reflected the black American experience. This music also included strong religious themes, expressing the slaves' indefatigable faith in a glorious afterlife. Flowing from the heart and the soul, this was folk music of the most authentic sort.

After the U.S. Civil War, black musicians found a white audience on riverboats and in saloons and pleasure palaces of various sorts. That introduced a commercial component into black music and fuelled numerous variations, including jazz. Even with the growing white following, the creation of these latter-day forms of black music remained almost entirely with African-American musicians. White musicians who picked up on the growing popularity of black music drew heavily on black songwriters. Much of Benny Goodman's swing music, for example, came from black arranger Fletcher Henderson.

In the 1930s and 1940s, a distinctive new form of black music—rhythm and blues—emerged. The people who enjoyed this music were all over the United States, and these fans included both blacks and whites. Mainstream American music had come to include a firm African-American presence.

HILLBILLY MUSIC.   Another authentic American folk music form, **hillbilly music,** flowed from the lives of Appalachian and southern whites. Early hillbilly music had a strong colonial heritage in English ballads and ditties, but over time hillbilly music evolved into a genre in its own right. Hillbilly fiddles and twangy lyrics reflected, like black music, the poverty and hopelessness of rural folk, "hillbillies" as they called themselves. Also like black music, hillbilly music reflected the joys, frustrations, and sorrows of love and family. Hillbilly music, however, failed to develop more than a regional following—that is, until the 1950s, when a great confluence of the black and hillbilly traditions occurred. This distinctive new form of American music, called **rockabilly** early on, became rock 'n' roll.

EARLY ROCK 'N' ROLL.   Music aficionados quibble about who invented the term rock 'n' roll. There is no doubt, though, that Memphis disc jockey **Sam Phillips** was a key figure. From his job at WREC, Phillips found an extra $75 a month to rent a 20-foot by 35-foot storefront, the paint peeling from the ceiling, to go into business recording, as he put it, "anything, anywhere, anytime." His first jobs, in 1949, were weddings and bar mitzvahs, but in 1951 Phillips put out his first record, "Gotta Let You Go," by one-man blues singer Joe Hill Louis, who played his own guitar, harmonica, and drums for accompaniment. In 1951 he recorded B.B. King and then **Jackie Brenston's** "Rocket 88," which many musicologists call the first rock 'n' roll record. Phillips sold his early recordings, all by black musicians, mostly in the blues tradition, to other labels.

In 1952, Phillips began his own Sun Records label and a quest to broaden the appeal of the black music he loved to a wide audience. "If I could find a white man who had the Negro sound and the Negro feel, I could make a billion dollars," he said. In a group he recorded in 1954, the Starlight Wranglers, Sam Phillips found **Elvis Presley.**

Elvis's first Sun recording, "That's All Right," with Scotty Moore and Bill Black, found only moderate success on country radio stations, but Sam Phillips knew he was on to something. It wasn't quite country or quite blues, but it was a sound that could move both white country fans and black blues fans. Elvis moved on to RCA, a major label, and by 1956 had two of the U.S.'s best-selling records, the flip-side hits "Don't Be Cruel" and "Hound Dog," plus three others among the year's top 16. Meanwhile, Sam Phillips was recording Carl Perkins, Roy Orbison, Johnny Cash, and Jerry Lee Lewis, adding to the distinctively American country-blues hybrid: wild, thrashing, sometimes reckless rock 'n' roll.

A Premier Indie. Memphis music promoter Sam Phillips was the visionary who saw a mass audience for a hybrid of hillbilly music and black soul music. Looking for "a white boy who can sing colored," Phillips found Elvis Presley in a threesome that put out four singles, beginning with "That's All Right" in 1954, on Phillips's Sun label. Sun became a major indie.

Elvis: A fan maintains this elaborate Elvis site, with links to dozens of Elvis pages. These include a tour of Graceland (Elvis's home in Memphis), poetry about Elvis, and lyrics to Elvis songs.
sunsite.unc.edu/elvis/ elvishom.html

Music Central Online: Sure Microsoft is everywhere, but the content is good.
www.musiccentral.msn. com/Home.htm

Vibe: Funky and hip happenings in music.
metaverse.com/vibe

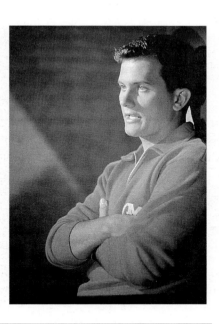

Covering. When Little Richard's 1955 recording "Tutti Frutti" picked up a following, there were white parents who didn't want the kids listening to "black music." That racist phobia contributed to the practice of covering, in which major labels issued the same music, sometimes toned down, with white artists. Pat Boone, for example, covered "Tutti Frutti." The kids, though, both black and white, wanted the real thing, and that's how rock 'n' roll furthered the cultural integration of American society. Looking back, Little Richard is amused: "Pat Boone was on the dresser, but I was in the drawer. At least I was in the same house."

The new music found a following on radio stations that picked up on the music mix that Cleveland disc jockey **Alan Freed** had pioneered as early as 1951—occasional rhythm 'n' blues amid the mainstream Frank Sinatra and Peggy Lee. By 1955, Freed was in New York and clearly on a roll. Freed helped propel Bill Haley and the Comets' "Rock Around the Clock" to number one. Rock's future was cemented when "Rock Around the Clock" was the musical bed under the credits for the 1955 movie *Blackboard Jungle*. Young people flocked to the movie not only for its theme on teen disenchantment and rebellion but also for the music.

ROCK 'N' ROLL IN CANADA

While rock 'n' roll is an American musical genre, many Canadians have been successful rock 'n' rollers. Paul Anka is the most obvious Canadian success story. His good looks, combined with his singing and songwriting abilities, brought him success—not only at home, but in the United States. "Diana," "Lonely Boy," "Put Your Head on my Shoulder," and "Puppy Love" all reached the Top 10 in both countries. Other artists also recorded Anka's material, including Buddy Holly, who recorded "It Doesn't Matter Anymore," and Elvis, whose "My Way" was cowritten by Anka.

Anka wasn't alone in having success south of the border. The Guess Who, led by Burton Cummings and Randy Bachman, reached the top of the charts in both countries with "These Eyes," "Undun," and, of course, "American Woman." Bachman's success in the United States continued when he left The Guess Who and formed Bachman Turner Overdrive, which reached number one with "You Ain't Seen Nothin' Yet." Throughout the 60s, 70s, and 80s, Canadians like Anne Murray, Gordon Lightfoot, Rush, Neil Young, Blood, Sweat and Tears (led by Canadian David Clayton Thomas), The Four Lads, Joni Mitchell, The Diamonds, The Crew Cuts, and others became pop music stars in the U.S. In the 90s, Bryan Adams, Shania Twain, Celine Dion, and Alanis Morrisette continued the Canadian assault across the border.

Within Canada, there have been other success stories. While not achieving much fame in the U.S., several singers and groups were popular in Canada. For example, Thunder Bay, Ontario's Bobby Curtola, who never reached Billboard's Top 40, had nine Top-10 records and 16 Top-40 records in Canada. Pretty amazing when you realize that Curtola wasn't with a major record label. While on tour, he used to sell records and memorabilia out of the trunk of his car. He was also the first Canadian artist to record a commercial jingle (it was for Coca-Cola). Other artists who succeeded at home during this period include The Beau-Marks, The Five-Man Electrical Band, Trooper, Kim Mitchell, Lighthouse, The Bells, Chilliwack, Ian Thomas, and Murray McLauchlan. During the 1990s, Jann Arden, Our Lady Peace, Sloan, I Mother Earth, Leahy, Treble Charger, and The Tragically Hip developed loyal followings in Canada, but had limited success in the U.S.

Canada's musical landscape is, like the country, a wide and diverse assortment of

Alanis Morissette. No single formula exists for breaking into the big time. Edgy Canadian Alanis Morissette and her producer, Glen Ballard, were turned down by both Geffen and Sony records when they were pitching themselves around Hollywood. By chance, a young associate of Madonna's manager, Freddy DeMann, heard the tape, liked it, and recommended it. DeMann liked it too and signed up Morissette and Ballard for Madonna's Maverick label. The album, *Jagged Little Pill,* sold 19 million copies.

many musical styles. The sounds of Nelly Furtado, the boy band sound of the Moffats or Soul Decision, the classical guitar based Jesse Cook, the basic rock 'n' roll sound of Treble Charger, and the humour of Barenaked Ladies are all different, yet distinctively Canadian. Writing the liner notes for the *Oh What a Feeling 2* box set, rock writer Larry Leblanc says that today "Canadian music is a sprawling, raucous, big family with its share of triumphs and griefs. Canada's artists and songwriters are a collection of minstrels, vagabonds and visionaries."

The Juno Awards. The Junos have signified excellence in the Canadian music industry since 1971.

THE JUNO AWARDS

The **Juno Awards** were named after Pierre Juneau, who was head of the CRTC when the Canadian content regulations were implemented. The idea of honouring the Canadian music industry came from Walt Grealis and Stan Klees, who published *RPM*, a music industry trade journal. The Junos have been televised by the CBC since 1975.

Jam! Music's Canadian Music Encyclopedia: Created by Toronto-based music writers Jaimie and Sharon Vernon, this site provides information on over 1200 Canadian music artists from the 1950s to the present.

www.canoe.ca/JamMusic PopEncycloPages/ home.html.

The Junos: The official website of the Juno Awards, presented each year by the Canadian Academy of Recording Arts and Sciences.

www.junoawards.ca

MEDIA DATABANK 3.2

Best of the CanCon Crop

The Juno Hall of Fame honours those artists who have made a significant contribution to music in Canada. Here is a list of those honoured by the Junos that have been inducted into the Canadian Music Hall of Fame:

Daniel Lanois	Anne Murray
Michael Cohl	Ian and Sylvia Tyson
Bruce Cockburn	Leonard Cohen
Bruce Fairbairn	Maureen Forrester
Luc Plamondon	The Band
David Foster	The Guess Who
Moe Koffman	Gordon Lightfoot
Gil Evans	Wilf Carter
Lenny Breau	Crew Cuts
Rob McConnell	Diamonds
David Clayton Thomas (Blood, Sweat and Tears)	Four Lads
	Glen Gould
Denny Doherty (The Mamas and Papas)	Joni Mitchell
John Kay (Steppenwolf)	Paul Anka
Domenic Triano	Hank Snow
Zal Yanovsky (Lovin Spoonful)	Guy Lombardo
Buffy Sainte Marie	Oscar Peterson
Rush	

Every year in October, nomination forms are sent to members of the Canadian Association of Recording Arts and Sciences (CARAS) asking for nominations. In January of each year, the nominees are announced and ballots are sent to CARAS members. The firm KPMG Peat Marwick Thorne tabulates the results and keeps them confidential until the Junos are presented in the spring.

Changes in the Music Business

MUSIC DEMASSIFICATION

Although company-dictated homogenization is a factor in popular music, performers won't put up with corporate people choosing everything from their music to their wardrobe. The South Carolina quartet Hootie and the Blowfish, for example, started by making the rounds at college bars and frat houses in the late 1980s and, along the way, found the cash to produce the album *kootchypop*. It was a distinctive work, hardly something manufactured by corporate marketing people, and Hootie gradually built a following. In fact, the group self-marketed an astounding 50 000 copies of *Kootchypop*, which headed them to the big time. Their 1994 album *Cracked Rear View*, on the major Atlantic label, sold 3 million the first year out, 2 million the next.

Technology has put sophisticated low-cost recording and mixing equipment within the means of a lot of **garage bands.** As little as $15 000 can buy 16-track recorders and 24-channel mixing boards, plus remodelling, to do what only a major studio could a few years ago. Back then, only big-name artists could afford their own studios. Now almost everyone can. Home recording studios in North America now number more than 100 000. Since 1980, commercial studios in North America have dwindled from 10 000 to 1000. Dan Daley, an editor at the trade journal *Mix,* calls this the democratization of the recording industry, which has returned an independent attitude among artists that record companies have been forced to recognize.

The widespread availability of **mini-studios** is contributing to a **demassification** in recorded music that, in some respects, should please elitists. Music that flows from the soul and heart of the musicians, reflecting the life experiences of the artists without strong commercial imperatives, is being recorded. And some of this music moves the culture in new directions. Early rap and hip-hop, for example, had authenticity. So did early Seattle grunge. Elitists note, though, that breakthroughs are always subsumed by derivative artists who try to pick up on a new sound that's become popular. The result, at worst, is a cultural setback and, at best, the cultural stagnation that comes from homogenization.

Across-the-Board Musical Tastes. Although known for his salsa, Ricky Martin has a broad range of musical interests that he attributes to his mother. Fed up with the kids playing rock all day, she pulled them by their ears to a Celia Cruz concert. Now, says Martin, "I listen to everything. I'm like a sponge."

Marketing Records

RADIO AIRPLAY

Record companies ship new releases to radio stations in the hope of **airplay.** Few make it. Stations are inundated with more records than they can possibly audition. Also, most stations stick to a playlist of already-popular music rather than risk losing listeners by playing untried records. To minimize the risk and yet offer some fresh sounds, most radio station music directors rely heavily on charts of what music is selling and being played elsewhere. The most-followed charts appear in the trade journal *Billboard.* In Canada, besides *Billboard*, the Canadian Music Network publishes a weekly trade journal offering Canadian radio a snapshot of the music business in this country.

MARKETING CANADIAN MUSIC

The radio and record industries are intimately connected. This was the main reason for the Canadian content regulations for radio that were introduced in 1970. But what makes a song "Canadian?" In 1970 Stan Klees of *RPM* magazine developed the "CanCon MAPL" to help the industry define Canadian content. To be categorized as CanCon, a song must generally fulfill two of the following four conditions:

- M: The *music* must be written by a Canadian (citizen or landed immigrant).
- A: The music or lyrics must be principally performed by a Canadian *artist*.
- P: The recording must have been either *produced* in Canada or *performed* and broadcast live in Canada.
- L: The *lyrics* must be written by a Canadian.

Since its introduction in 1970, Canadian content has been a hotly debated topic in Canadian radio circles. Since 1970 the CRTC regulations have required radio stations in Canada to play a certain level of Canadian content. One of the reasons for this policy was to help strengthen the Canadian music industry by encouraging radio to support Canadian singers, songwriters, performers, and others involved in the production of Canadian music. Prior to the 1970 regulations, it's estimated that Canadian music made up about 4 percent of all music heard on Canadian radio.

While the system seems to favour Canadian artists, it can also discriminate against Canadian singers. A controversy involving Bryan Adams is a good example of discrimination against Canadian singers. His song from *Robin Hood: Prince of Thieves*, "Everything I Do, I Do It For You," and other songs on his album *Waking Up the Neighbours* were not considered Canadian content because he co-wrote them with a British songwriter. Due to the controversy that ensued from this classification, the CRTC amended the MAPL formula (the criteria of music, artist, produced/performed, lyrics) to allow for Canadian songwriters collaborating with foreigners. This amendment only applied to songs recorded after September 1991.

In the future, the CRTC hopes to raise the level of Canadian music to 40 percent. Broadcasters don't like playing that much Canadian music. They ask why they should play 35 percent CanCon when it only accounts for about 14.5 percent of total record sales in Canada. Some broadcasters even argue that Canadian audiences don't want to hear more Canadian content on the radio. They say Canadian music makes people "tune out." This is not a new argument. According to Nicholas Jennings in *Before the Goldrush*, when they began debating the issue of Canadian content on radio in the late 1960s, radio stations were against it. Jennings explains that the Canadian Association of Broadcasters claimed that imposing Canadian content regulations on radio would "lower the attractiveness of stations to the listener."

Debate on the issue rages on. Even today, some say that CanCon reduces the credibility of Canadian music by "forcing" radio stations to play Canadian artists. When Bryan Adams was asked for advice on how to succeed in Canadian music, he

CRTC: The Canadian Radio-Television and Telecommunications Commission.

www.crtc.gc.ca

CIRPA: The Canadian Independent Record Production Association represents the independent sector of the Canadian music and sound recording industry.

www.cirpa.ca

SOCAN: The Society of Composers, Authors and Music Publishers of Canada's site has information on performing rights, copyright, licensing, and distribution.

www.socan.ca

MEDIA DATABANK 3.3

CanCon?

The fact is that most of the most popular Canadian songs are hybrids of American music. In *Canada's Top 1000 Singles* by Nanda Lwin, the Top 10 Canadian songs are:

1. "Macarena" by Los Del Mar (1995)
2. "Never Surrender" by Corey Hart (1985)
3. "Sometimes When We Touch" by Dan Hill (1977)
4. "Hot Child in the City" by Nick Gilder (1978)
5. "Building a Mystery" by Sarah McLachlan (1997)
6. "Don't Forget Me When I'm Gone" by Glass Tiger (1986)
7. "Sweet Surrender" by Sarah McLachlan (1998)
8. "Pop Goes the World" by Men Without Hats (1988)
9. "Ahead by a Century" by The Tragically Hip (1996)
10. "Life Is a Highway" by Tom Cochrane (1991)

said, "Stay away from the Canadian music business. It's full of politics and bureaucracy. It's trouble. Don't sign to a Canadian publisher. Go south of the border, you'll get a better deal."

Playing Canadian songs isn't the only way radio helps out the Canadian music industry. Michael McCabe, past president and CEO of the Canadian Association of Broadcasters (CAB), claims that the development of the Canadian Radio Music Awards is an excellent way of showcasing new Canadian talent. The live awards show spotlights the best new Canadian talent in four categories: Contemporary Hit Radio, Country, Pop Adult, and Rock.

Under its new radio policy, the CRTC has legislated that when a radio station is sold, 6 percent of the value of the radio station be paid to help develop Canadian talent. The CRTC has determined that the 6 percent be divided up as follows: 3 percent to a Canadian music promotion fund, 2 percent to FACTOR or MusicAction (two nonprofit groups that help new Canadian musicians), and a further 1 percent to other enterprises committed to boosting Canadian musical talent.

While CanCon certainly has its opponents, it has its fair share of supporters too. Bernie Finkelstein of True North Records and the Canadian Independent Record Production Association says, "Canadian music is good for business. If you don't believe me, talk to Amanda Marshall, Shania Twain and Celine Dion." He also disputes radio's claim that Canadian music doesn't sell well. He claims Canadian music accounts for well over 20 percent of record sales in Canada. Laura Bartlett, the vice-president of marketing for HMV Music, supports his theory. She claims that, in 1997, Canadian albums accounted for about 23 percent of total sales at HMV, Canada's largest music chain.

The relationship between the radio and record industries was a two-way street. Not only did radio stations need records, but record-makers needed jockeys to air their products. Records that won airplay were almost assured success. Record companies scrambled to curry favour with leading disc jockeys. This interdependence expanded to television in the 1980s, when cable television services, like MTV and MuchMusic, built their programming on video versions of popular music. Today, between cable channels, digital television channels, and music via satellite on Star-Choice and Bell ExpressVu, Canadian music is enjoying even greater exposure and is less reliant on radio.

PAYOLA

The relationship between the radio and record industries has had problems, notably **payola**. In 1958 the grapevine was full of stories about record companies' bribes to disc jockeys to play certain records. One audit found that US$263 000 in "consulting fees" had been paid to radio announcers in 23 cities. The U.S. **Federal Trade Commission (FTC)** filed unfair competition complaints against record companies. Radio station managers, ever conscious that their licences from the Federal Communications Commission (FCC) could be yanked for improprieties, began demanding signed statements from disc jockeys that they had not accepted payola. Dozens of disc jockeys in major markets quietly left town.

Payola scandals did not end with the 1950s. Competition for airplay has continued to tempt record promoters to "buy" airtime under the table. There were indictments again in the 1970s. And in 1988 two independent promoters were charged with paying US$270 000 to program directors at nine widely imitated radio stations to place records on their playlists. One station executive was charged with receiving US$100 000 over two years. Some payola bribery involved drugs.

Celine Dion. Although she is among the elite in popular music worldwide, CanCon regulations don't recognize much of Dion's music as "Canadian."

TRACKING SALES

A lot of the mystery about popularity lists for recorded music has disappeared. In 1991, amid growing concern that using lists based on calls to record shops wasn't working, Soundscan Inc. launched a new system for *Billboard* magazine. Soundscan arranged with record shops to record sales by dragging CDs over a bar-code scanner. From the resulting data, Soundscan provided *Billboard* with information for its influential weekly lists.

One problem with the earlier system, which involved calling up record shops and talking to whichever clerk answered, was that the clerks, who were usually young people, were more inclined to notice the pop stuff. As a result, country and middle-of-the-road music was slighted.

That the old system had problems was illustrated the first week of *Billboard*'s Soundscan lists. New, alternative music, such as that of Jesus Jones and Fishbone, plummeted. Jesus Jones dropped from fifth to 29th, Fishbone from 133rd to 182nd. Country singer Garth Brooks suddenly had two albums in the Top 30. The *Pretty Woman* soundtrack rose from 127th to 75th.

Heisting Music

HOME-DUBBING REVENUE DRAIN

The lopsidedness of the relationship between the radio and record industries became obvious in another way in the 1970s. Instead of buying albums, people began sharing records and dubbing them onto relatively inexpensive blank tapes. Phonograph manufacturers offered machines that not only could dub tapes from records but also could record from the air at the flick of a toggle. Many FM stereo radio stations catered to home dubbers by announcing when they would play uninterrupted albums.

The economic effect of **home dubbing** on the record industry is hard to measure precisely, but the CRIA (Canadian Recording Industry Association) estimates the industry loses over $300 million each year because of home taping and the illegal burning of CDs. The CRIA says that in 1999, 45 million blank CDs were sold in Canada. By 2001, 130 million were sold. In 1999, the Copyright Board of Canada added a levy to the cost of blank cassettes at the point of purchase. The tax was later applied to blank CDs bought for dubbing. Proceeds from the tax are to go to artists and songwriters, to compensate for revenue lost to home-dubbing.

AUDIO AND VIDEO PIRACY

Criminal **piracy** involves dubbing records and videos and selling the dubs. An estimated 18 percent of the records and tapes sold are from shadowy pirate sources, mostly in Asia but also in other countries, including Saudi Arabia. These pirate operations have no A & R, royalty, or promotion expenses. They dub tapes produced by legitimate companies and sell them through black-market channels. Their costs are low, and their profits are high.

Recording Piracy. Seeking visibility for their occasional crackdowns, Thai officials steamroll seized pirated videotapes. Still, Bangkok is a major pirating centre on the Pacific Rim. So is China, where Beijing vendors accost tourists for surreptitious street transactions. Illegal tapes often find their way into the black market ahead of their release through legal channels.

These pirate operations are well financed and organized. It is not uncommon for a Bangkok pirate operation to have 100 "slave" tape-copying machines going simultaneously 24 hours a day and even to ship illegal copies before the official release by the distributor. Local authorities have other priorities, and antipiracy laws are weak. In an interview with *Fortune* magazine, Frank Knight, a Bangkok investigator who specializes in these cases, said: "Anybody who's been involved in past mischief, such as drug exports, finds this to be a highly lucrative crime that's easier and less punishable." Knight has tracked exports of illegal tapes to South Africa, to the Indian subcontinent, throughout the Asian Rim, and to the United States.

Bootleg recordings are also a concern of the Canadian recording industry. A bootleg is an illegal recording of a performer in concert. As of January 1, 1996, the Antibootleg amendment to the Canadian Copyright Act became law. It is now illegal to record a performance and sell it. Anyone caught can be sued by the performer under the Criminal Code of Canada. The maximum penalty for this form of copyright infringement is a $1 million fine or imprisonment for up to five years, or both penalties.

Music Industry Issues

OBJECTIONABLE MUSIC

Campaigns to ban records are nothing new. In the Roaring 20s, some people saw jazz as morally loose. White racists of the 1950s called Bill Haley's rock "nigger music." War protest songs of the Vietnam period angered many Americans.

Government attempts to censor records have been rare, yet they indirectly keep some records off the market. The CRTC and FCC can take a dim view of stations that air objectionable music, which guides broadcasters toward caution. Stations do not want to risk their licences. Because the record industry is so dependent on airplay, hardly any music that might seriously offend makes it to market. In recent years, objectionable music has been brought to the attention of the Canadian Broadcast Standards Council. Formal complaints were filed for two songs in particular, "Boyz in the Hood" by Dynamite Hack and "The Bad Touch" by the Bloodhound Gang. Both complaints dealt with language used in each song. The song "Boyz in the Hood" was the more problematic of the two, as the CBSC wrote in its decision:

> The juxtaposition of lyrics such as "Gotta get my girl to rock that body" with such violent imagery as "I reached back like a pimp and I slapped the ho" clearly perpetuates the link between women in a sexual context and women as victims of violence. The lyrics portray the woman in question as a "stupid bitch" and a "ho," whose "talkin' shit" warranted the violent reaction by her partner. Whether the intention of the song is serious or satirical, the Council finds that the lyrics, in their sanctioning, promotion or glamorizing of violence against women, constitute abusive commentary on the basis of gender and are insensitive to the dangers of stereotyping generally and to the exploitative linking of sexual and violent elements in dealing with women.

Eminem. Concern about the lyrical content of songs is nothing new. Parents have always found the music of the younger generation somewhat "objectionable." However, the recent use of explicit lyrical content has also sparked debate about how much further lyrics can push the envelope.

Rap Dictionary: Decodes the lingo, identifies the artists, and locates the places they talk about.

www.sci.kun.nl/thalia/rapdict

BMI.com: Nonprofit organization representing more than 180 000 songwriters, composers, and music publishers.

www.bmi.com

Hit Music: This award-winning website includes links to radio playlists around the United States and the world, including Raadio2 in Estonia and FM957 in Reykjavik, Iceland. You also will find links to mini-reviews of current hits.

www.hitsworld.com

imusic.com: Regular music features.

www.imusic.com

RECORD LABELLING

In the 1980s complaints about lyrics narrowed to drugs, sexual promiscuity, and. In the U.S., **Parents' Music Resource Center,** a group led by Tipper Gore and wives of several other influential members of Congress, claimed there were links between explicit rock music and teen suicide, teen pregnancy, abusive parents, broken homes, and other social ills. The group objected to lyrics like Prince's "Sister," which extolls incest; Mötley Crüe's "Live Wire," with its psychopathic enthusiasm for strangulation; Guns 'n' Roses' white racism; and Ice-T and other rap artists' hate music.

The Parents' Music Resource Center argued that consumer protection laws should be invoked to require that records with offensive lyrics be labelled as dangerous, like cigarette warning labels or the movie industry's rating system. Record companies began labelling potentially offensive records: "Explicit Lyrics—Parental Advisory." In some cases, the companies printed lyrics on album covers as a warning.

LYRICS AND YOUNG PEOPLE

Despite countless studies, it is unclear whether mores are affected by lyrics. Two scholars from California State University at Fullerton found that most high school students are hazy on the meaning of their favourite songs. Asked to explain Bruce Springsteen's "Born in the U.S.A.," about the hopelessness of being born in a blue-collar environment, many teenagers were simplistically literal. "It's about the town Bruce Springsteen lives in," said one. Led Zeppelin's "Stairway to Heaven" has been criticized for glorifying drug or sexual rushes, but many teenagers in the study were incredibly literal, saying the song was about climbing steps into the sky. What does this mean? Professor Lorraine Prinsky of the Fullerton study concluded that teenagers use rock music as background noise. At most 3 percent, she said, are fully attentive to the lyrics.

Critics, however, see an insidious subliminal effect. Some songs repeat their simple and explicitly sexual messages over and over, as many as 15 to 30 times in one song. Said a spokesperson from the Parents' Music Resource Center: "I can't believe it's not getting through. It's getting into the subconscious, even if they can't recite the lyrics."

media future

MUSIC

Now reduced to five major players, the record industry might not see further conglomeration on a grand scale. The majors can be expected, however, to gobble up indies that score big. Indies probably will proliferate with new technology that has dramatically cut the expense of studio equipment. It has become an easy business to get into.

As the majors join upstarts in distributing music on the web, the corner record store and even massive chain stores may become relics of the past. Web delivery is far more efficient than manufacturing, warehousing, and shipping discs. Record companies probably will try a mixture of single sales and subscription sales on the web.

The record industry will continue its battle against piracy, pressing especially hard on China through the World Trade Organization to enforce international copyright agreements. Crackdowns will never eradicate all piracy, however. It will be the same with bootleg music on the web. Record companies can discourage and reduce illegal activity but will never eliminate it.

CHAPTER WRAP-UP

For most of the 20th century, recorded music had been a banner that successive generations have used to identify themselves and their values: jazz, rock 'n' roll, bebop, disco, hip-hop, grunge. The record industry's continuing success depends on how well it can help each new generation set itself apart from mom and dad. The generational differences, however, are a two-edged issue for record-makers. Through most of the 20th century, record-makers had to deal with critics, generally older people and authorities, who believe that pop music is undermining traditional social values.

QUESTIONS FOR REVIEW

1. Why is recorded music important?
2. Can you name the conglomerate owners of the major record companies?
3. Trace the technology of sound recording from Edison on.
4. What were the innovations of Thomas Edison, Emile Berliner, Joseph Maxwell, Peter Goldmark, and Shawn Fanning?
5. How is digital reproduction different?
6. What are the roots of U.S. popular music? Canadian popular music?
7. What is the relationship of the record and radio industries?
8. How has the recording industry addressed losses through home-dubbing and piracy?
9. What are the Junos?
10. What makes a record "Canadian?"

QUESTIONS FOR CRITICAL THINKING

1. In recent months, how has new recorded music shaped significant human events? Consider music that is inspiring human actions. This might be war music. It might be music that's flowing from a generation or subculture and giving it an identity. It might be a new love song that has become standard at weddings.
2. What has been the effect of global conglomeration in the record industry on the music you like?
3. Look into your crystal ball to assess how technological changes in the record business will play out in the future.
4. While rock 'n' roll has roots in hillbilly and black slave music, that music has even earlier roots. Trace the music to precolonial times. Also discuss what additional streams of music have fed into modern popular music. For example, is there a "Canadian sound"?

5. How has the relationship between artists and recording companies changed since World War II? Why has the change occurred?

6. How are measures of commercial and artistic success different in the recorded music business?

7. Why is airplay important to a recording becoming a commercial success? Explain the exceptions.

8. What do you see as a solution to the revenue drain created by MP3 technology on the record industry? If there is no solution, what will happen?

9. Discuss the effect of moralists and others who would like to change the content of some recorded music. How do these people go about trying to accomplish their goals? What common threads have there been to their criticism throughout the 20th century?

10. Given the phenomenal success of Canadian music in recent years, do we still need CanCon regulations for radio?

FOR KEEPING UP TO DATE

The weekly *Billboard* is the recording industry's leading trade journal. In Canada, check out The Canadian Music Network or Jam Music at the Canoe website.

Consumer magazines that track popular music and report on the record industry include *Rolling Stone* and *Spin*.

Entertainment Weekly and *Maclean's* both have regular sections on music, as do many daily papers, such as the *Globe and Mail* and the *National Post*.

FOR FURTHER LEARNING

Paul Audley. Canada's Cultural Industries (Lorimer and Company, 1983).

Randy Bachman and John Einarson. *Taking Care of Business* (McArthur and Company, 2000).

Robert Brehl. "CRTC Causes Static Among Radio Bosses," *Globe and Mail* (June 9, 1998).

Iain Chambers. *Urban Rhythms: Pop Music and Popular Culture* (St. Martin's, 1985).

Steve Chapple and Reebee Garofalo. *Rock 'n' Roll Is Here to Pay: The History and Politics of the Music Industry* (Nelson-Hall, 1977).

R. Serge Denisoff with William Schurk. *Tarnished Gold: The Record Industry Revisited* (Transaction Books, 1986).

Peter Fornatale and Joshua E. Mills. *Radio in the Television Age* (Overlook Press, 1980).

Roland Gelatt. *The Fabulous Phonograph: From Tin Foil to High Fidelity* (J.B. Lippincott, 1955).

Peter Goddard and Phillip Kamin, editors. *Shakin' All Over: The Rock and Roll Years in Canada* (McGraw-Hill Ryerson, 1989).

Hugh Graham. "Rule Changes May See Rebirth of Top 40 Radio," *Globe and Mail* (July 19, 1997).

Ron Hall. *The CHUM Chart Book* (Stardust Publications, 1984).

Laurel Hyatt. "Back in the Black," *Broadcaster* (February, 1998).

Nicholas Jennings. *Before the Gold Rush: Flashbacks to the Dawn of the Canadian Sound* (Viking, 1997).

Nicholas Jennings. "Canadian Rock Explodes," *Maclean's* (March 27, 1995).

Ted Kennedy. *Oh! Canada Cuts* (Canadian Chart Research, 1989).

Nancy Lathier. "The CanCon Ghetto," *Music Scene* (May/June 1989).

Daphne Lavers. "The Canadian Music Industry," *Broadcast Dialogue* (April 2000).

Nanda Lwin. *Canada's Top Hits of the Year, 1975–1996* (Music Data Canada, 1998).

Steve Maclean. "HMV Analysis reveals 23% Canadian Sales," *The Record* (May 25, 1998).

Katherine Macklem. "Turn Up the Music," *Maclean's* (July 30, 2001).

Michael McCabe. "CANCON Not the only Measure of Radio's Contribution," *Broadcaster* (February, 1998).

Martin Melhuish. *Heart of Gold: 30 Years of Canadian Pop Music* (CBC Enterprises, 1983).

Mike Roberts. "Finger on the Pulse: MuchMusic Still Strong after 10 Years," *Montreal Gazette* (January 22, 1995).

Heather Schoffield and Robert Brehl. "Radio Stations Told To Turn Up the Volume" and "CRTC Opens Radio Markets," *Globe and Mail* (May 1, 1998).

Barry L. Sherman and Joseph R. Dominick. "Violence and Sex in Music Videos: TV and Rock 'n' Roll." *Journal of Communication* 36 (Winter 1986): 1, 79–93.

Justin Smallbridge. "Think Global: Act Local," *Canadian Business* (June 1996).

Dick Weissman. *The Music Business: Career Opportunities and Self-Defense* (Crown Publishers, 1979).

Chapter 4

Stalwart Reporter. At right at a recent Michener Awards ceremony is long serving CBC radio reporter Curt Petrovich—whose voice we've heard countless times on the air, but whose visage may be less recognizable.

Radio

MEDIA TIMELINE

Radio Technology and Regulation

1901 Guglielmo Marconi receives a message by radio from Signal Hill, Newfoundland, to England.

1906 Reginald Fessenden broadcasts to ships at sea on Christmas Eve.

1906 Lee De Forest creates the audion tube that allows voice transmission.

1912 David Sarnoff uses radio to learn news of the *Titanic* disaster, putting radio in the public eye.

1920 XWA in Montreal begins broadcasting in Canada.

1927 Canada's Diamond Jubilee is broadcast.

1929 Aird Commission releases its report on radio broadcasting in Canada.

1936 CBC begins broadcasting.

1939 Edwin Armstrong puts the first FM station on air.

1998 CRTC relaxes regulations on radio ownership.

1999 DAB, digital audio broadcasting, begins in Canada.

MEDIA IN THEORY

What Makes Radio Different?

What makes radio different from other media? **Andrew Crissell**, a cultural theorist, refers to radio as a blind medium: you can't see it with your eyes, like you can television, a movie, or a newspaper. You can only see the pictures in your mind. Radio broadcasters use time, not space, as their canvas to communicate their messages. Building on the ideas of Barthes, radio uses four signs to create its imagery: words, sounds, music, and silence.

As discussed earlier, words can be symbolic in that they represent something other than themselves: The phrase "maple leaf" isn't a real maple leaf, it is only a label that our culture attaches to the physical object of a maple leaf. This naming process is entirely arbitrary. However, words in radio differ from words in print. Why? Because they are spoken. It's not so much what you say, but how you say it. The way in which an announcer or radio performer speaks also communicates meaning. Words end up working on two levels; not only do the words themselves stand for something else, but the way in which they are spoken signifies something as well. For example, the announcer can say "great!" and mean it in two different ways—one positive, one negative.

Sounds or sound effects are indexical signs. The sound of a creaking door is an index of a creaking door. To someone listening to Tom Cheek and Jerry Howarth broadcast a Blue Jays game, the loud crack of a bat and the cheering of a crowd signify a home run has been hit. Like the words that help us decode the meanings of a press photograph, sounds anchor the meaning or image created by radio; this is important due to the invisible nature of radio. Sounds let us know where we are and what's going on.

The third sign of radio, music, works on several levels. The music you hear on a radio station helps you to identify the station. When you hear Julian Austin or Beverly Mahood, you know you're listening to a country station; if you're listening to Nelly Furtado or Baby Blue Sound Crew, you know the station is not country. Music can also act as a bridge between segments of a radio show, newsmagazine, or play, or it can be used to create a mood in a radio play.

An absence of any of the three signs signifies something in itself. As a sign, silence works to communicate meaning two ways. First, it can be symbolic. A minute of silence on Remembrance Day symbolizes respect and honour for soldiers who died in war. But silence can also be an index that something's wrong with the broadcast—a power outage, a faulty microphone, or radio transmitter problems can all cause what is known as "dead air."

Significance of Radio

RADIO AS A MOTIVATOR

Radio can motivate people to action. When Rafe Mair, a B.C. talk show host on CKNW 98, talks about politics, people in British Columbia listen. A former politician, Mair's views on Canadian political issues have aggravated and stimulated radio listeners for years. Former Reform Party leader Preston Manning once said, "Rafe Mair is B.C." The late Peter Gzowski moved people with his *Morningside* program on CBC Radio.

Record companies also know the power of radio. Without radio stations playing new music, a new CD is almost certainly doomed. Airplay spurs people to go out and buy a record. Advertisers value radio to reach buyers. Only newspapers, television, and direct mail have a larger share of the advertising dollars spent, and radio's share is growing. In Canada, radio accounts for about 14 percent of all advertising revenue spent.

UBIQUITY OF RADIO

Radio is everywhere. Hardly a place in the world is beyond the reach of radio. In spite of this, radio is often a forgotten medium. Imagine this scenario: scores of media academics driving to school or to a conference to discuss the evils and perils of the modern mass media. Topics like sexism in advertising, the impact of viewing television violence on children, convergence, and how Canadian culture is being smothered by U.S. media conglomerates are at the top of their research lists. The scholars ponder these important questions en route while listening to CBC Radio in their Volvos. Many of them overlook what may be the most pervasive medium of all, radio.

MEDIA DATABANK 4.1

Top Five Radio Chains by Hours Tuned, 1999

In its 2000 Broadcast Policy Monitoring Report, the CRTC lists the top radio operations in Canada based on total hours tuned. In simpler terms, these are the top radio chains in Canada based on how long people listen to stations owned by that corporation. It offers an interesting perspective on how omnipresent radio is in Canada.

Corporation	Total Listening Hours
Rogers Communications	46 662 000
Standard Broadcasting	43 275 000
CHUM Limited	40 663 000
Telemedia	38 401 000
WIC	38 293 000

Radio Marketing Bureau: The authoritative source for information on radio advertising in Canada, representing over 80 percent of all radio revenue in the country.

www.rmb.com

The general public, not just academics, overlook radio for numerous reasons. The main reason is this: While radio is a medium of mass communication, it is also a medium of interpersonal communication. It acts as a friend. We usually listen to a radio station that reflects our taste in music, our political orientation, and our overall ideology. We listen to what we are in the mood for. Radio is so personal that we often do not see it as a mass medium.

But it is a mass medium. Here are some interesting facts on the ubiquity of radio from Canada's Radio Marketing Bureau:

- Radio is accessible anytime and anywhere; 99 percent of homes have radios and 90 percent of cars do too.
- People use radio while doing other things: exercising, doing the dishes, or eating.
- The average Canadian listens to about 22 hours of radio each week.
- Eighty percent of Canadians listen to the radio every day.

Technical Development

ELECTROMAGNETIC SPECTRUM

Radio waves are part of the physical universe. They have existed forever, moving through the air and the ether. Like light waves, they are silent—a part of a continuing spectrum of energies, the **electromagnetic spectrum.** As early as 1873, physicists speculated that the electromagnetic spectrum existed, but it was a young Italian nobleman, **Guglielmo Marconi,** who made practical application of the physicists' theories while in Canada.

Young Marconi became obsessed with the possibilities of the electromagnetic spectrum and built equipment that could ring a bell by remote control—no strings, no wires. The Marconi device shaped a radio wave in such a way that another device could intercept it and decipher a message from the wave's shape. In 1895, when he was 21, Marconi used his wireless method to transmit codes for more than a mile on his father's Bologna estate.

On December 12, 1901, Marconi stood on Signal Hill, Newfoundland, and received the Morse code signal for the letter "S" from Cornwall, England. This day has been well documented as a significant date in the study of broadcasting. However, Canadian **Reginald Fessenden** played an equally important role in the early days of radio. He constantly vied with Marconi for both funding and fame. On Christmas Eve 1906, he broadcast music and voices to ships at sea. The broadcast took place from Brant Rock, Massachusetts. Fessenden played the violin for his listeners as a Christmas present. He also played an Ediphone recording of Handel's *Largo*. It is significant that the first radio musical broadcast also featured one of the world's first musical recordings. But history has not been kind to Fessenden. In spite of his contributions, Marconi is the one who is remembered as the father of radio. Others also experimented with the transmission of electromagnetic waves in the late 1800s. Many, however, feel that Marconi is the father of telegraphy, while Fessenden is the father of radio.

Marconi patented his invention in England, and his mother, a well-connected Irish woman, arranged British financing to set up the Marconi Wireless Telegraph Co. Soon ocean-going ships were equipped with Marconi radiotelegraphy equipment to communicate at sea, even when they were beyond the horizon, something never possible before.

Guglielmo Marconi, The Father of Telegraphy: An informative site on the BBC's online education network providing a good deal of information on Marconi's role in the development of radio. However, was Marconi really the father of radio? **www.bbc.co.uk/education/ archive/making_waves/ history.shtml**

Reginald Fessenden. Canadian Reginald Fessenden competed with Marconi in the early days of radio technology.

Who Invented Radio? Numerous theorists conceived of wireless transmission ahead of the Irish-Italian inventor Guglielmo Marconi. A dentist, Mahlon Loomis, detected signals between two mountains in Virginia in 1866 and won a patent for wireless telegraphy in 1872. Scottish mathematician James Maxwell and German physicist Heinrich Hertz did important theorizing. Who, then, invented radio? Marconi became interested in radio in 1894 and succeeded in a wireless transmission in 1895, and he aggressively exploited the potential of his experiments into a commercial success that tightly linked his name with the invention of radio in the public's mind. But admirers of a reclusive but brilliant Croatian-born American scientist, Nikola Tesla, have mounted a campaign for him to be recognized as the inventor of radio. Among their evidence is a 1943 U.S. Supreme Court decision recognizing that Tesla had transmitted on the electromagnetic spectrum before Marconi. The debate remains open, however, whether Tesla really conceived of the electromagnetic spectrum as a vehicle for transmitting messages. Tesla's focus at the time was wireless transmission of electricity.

TRANSMITTING VOICES

Breakthroughs came quickly. In 1906 **Lee De Forest** created the **audion tube,** which made voice transmissions possible. Technical development stalled during World War I. Military and civilian research concentrated on other things, and work on the newfangled wireless was put off. After the war, Americans were wary as never before about the dangers of dependence on foreign goods. They worried about being cut off if another war disrupted transoceanic commerce. The worry extended to patents, even those in friendly countries, like Marconi's British wireless patent. At the urging of the federal government, three American companies, General Electric, Westinghouse, and American Telephone & Telegraph, pooled their resources in 1919 and bought Marconi's American subsidiary and patents. Although the consortium broke up within a few years, it helped to refine the technology further. In this same period, physics department experiments at many universities added to the technology, which gave further impetus to radio's development.

Static-free transmission was developed by **Edwin Armstrong**, a Columbia University researcher. In 1939 Armstrong built an experimental station in New Jersey using a new system called **frequency modulation,** or FM for short. FM's system, piggy backing sound on airwaves, was different from the older **amplitude modulation,** or AM, method. In time, Armstrong developed FM stereo with two soundtracks, one for each ear, duplicating the sensation of hearing a performance live. FM radio wasn't fully utilized as a medium until the 1950s and 1960s in North America. CHFI in Toronto, owned by Rogers, was Canada's first FM station. It began broadcasting in 1961. The CBC developed its network of FM stations in the early 1960s.

Characteristics of Radio

HISTORY OF CANADIAN RADIO

In 1918, the Montreal-based radio station **XWA** (now CIQC) was the first station to get a broadcasting licence, under the Radiotelegraph Act of 1913, from the federal government. Its first broadcast took place in May 1920, under the supervision of Marconi. XWA was the first station to have regularly scheduled programs, the first of

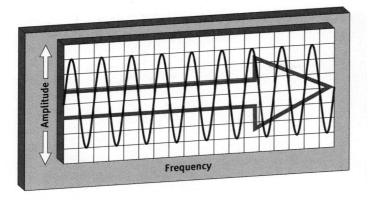

Gugliemo Marconi

Unmodulated Wave. If you could see electromagnetic waves, they would look like the cross-section of a ripple moving across a pond, except they would be steady and unending. Guglielmo Marconi figured out how to hitch a ride on these waves to send messages from Signal Hill, Newfoundland, in 1901.

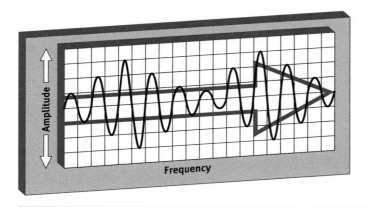

Lee De Forest

Amplitude-Modulated Wave. Lee De Forest discovered how to adjust the height of electromagnetic waves to coincide with the human voice and other sounds. De Forest's audion tube made voice transmission possible, including an Enrico Caruso concert in 1910.

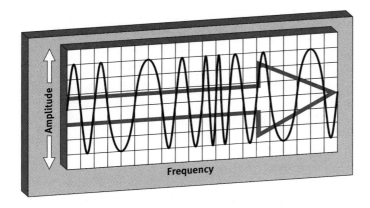

Edwin Armstrong

Frequency-Modulated Wave. FM radio transmissions squeeze and expand electromagnetic waves without changing their height. Edwin Armstrong introduced this form of broadcasting, which had superior clarity and fidelity, in the 1930s. Not even lightning interferes with transmission.

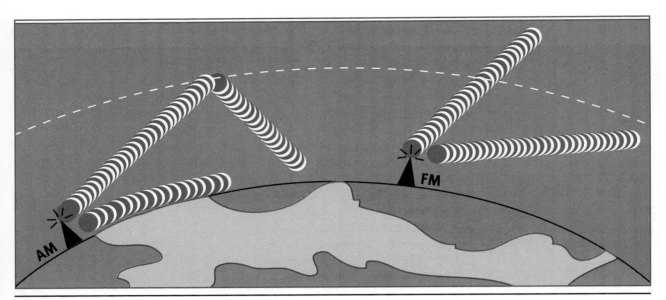

Bounce-Back Effect. When AM electromagnetic waves are transmitted, many of them follow the contour of the earth, which extends their range beyond the line-of-sight from the transmitter. Some AM waves go upward, and many of these are bounced back to earth by reflective layers in the ionosphere, which further extends the station's range. The bounce-back effect is weaker during the day when the sun warms the ionosphere and reduces its reflective properties. FM transmissions have a shorter range than AM because the signals move in straight lines and tend not to adhere to the earth's contours. Also, upward-moving FM waves pass through the ionosphere rather than being reflected back.

which was a musical program, a Dorothy Lutton concert, to the Royal Society of Canada in Montreal. This was not only the first radio broadcast in Canada but also in North America, contrary to what KDKA in Pittsburgh claims. The first broadcast licence for radio was issued to CJCG in Winnipeg in May of 1922. It was on the air for only one year. All in all, 33 radio licences were issued in 1922. Some of those stations are still on the air today. They include CKOC in Hamilton and CKCK in Regina.

During the 1920s, radios became an integral part of Canadians' living rooms. These were big radios, some as large as today's home entertainment units. People listened to the radio then in much the same way we watch television: after supper, with or without the family. A radio was considered a status symbol and much of the programming reflected this: broadcasts included concerts, political commentary, dramas, and comedies.

Another place where Canadians listened to radio in the 1920s was on the **Canadian National Railway** (CNR). Like many entrepreneurs at the time, the president of the CNR thought that radio was the ideal medium for promoting Canada and train travel. You could travel from Ottawa to Toronto and be entertained by radio music and other radio programs. Most of this programming was highbrow: it featured singers, orchestras, and dramas. By the end of the decade, the CNR had established a sizable private network, with radio stations in Ottawa, Montreal, and Moncton; it was also leasing stations from coast to coast. By 1932, 20 radio stations made up the CNR's regional and national network.

An interesting phenomenon occurred in the 1920s, one that is still with us: Canadians were listening to more American programming than domestic programming. This was partly due to geography and the availability of many U.S. radio signals. Canadians also claimed American radio offered them more choice. And why not? A number of U.S. radio stars were also Broadway or vaudeville celebrities.

RADIO'S EARLY ROLE IN UNIFYING CANADA

Unlike American radio, Canadian politicians saw radio not only as a way to promote entertainment but also as a tool to unite the country. In its early days, Canadian radio succeeded in uniting the country in a way that had never been done before. On July 1, 1927, on Canada's 50th birthday, the CNR's network of telephone and telegraph lines joined orchestras in several Canadian cities from Halifax to Vancouver through its 23 private radio stations across the nation. About 5 million people in Canada and the U.S. tuned into the **Diamond Jubilee Broadcast**, which originated in Ottawa. The program was also broadcast on short-wave radio. It must have been an interesting sight; people gathered in the streets to listen to it on speakers and on telephone party lines. In Montreal, an estimated 20 000 people congregated at Fletcher's Field to listen to the performance of "The Maple Leaf Forever." For the first time in history, Canadians were linked from coast to coast via a mass medium.

YOU'RE "ON THE AIRD": CANADA'S FIRST ROYAL COMMISSION ON BROADCASTING

The idea that radio could help build a country was one of the factors behind the first Royal Commission on Broadcasting. The fact that Canadians were listening to more American than Canadian programming worried Ottawa, especially combined with the fact that there were 400 000 radios in Canada. For the first time (and certainly not the last time) in Canadian media history, politicians began to worry about the domination of Canada by American mass media. To solve this problem, they set up the first of many Royal Commissions on broadcasting in Canada. The **Aird Commission** (named after Sir John Aird) was created to examine the danger that American programming posed to Canadian culture. The verdict it reached in 1929 wasn't surprising: American networks were a threat to our airwaves and our culture.

The commission recommended that Canada set up and fund a public broadcasting network like the BBC in England. This network would produce and broadcast Canadian programs for and by Canadians. This recommendation caused quite a conflict between the owners of private radio stations, who were making a tidy profit, and those who preferred the public system. By 1932 Prime Minister Bennett laid out the government's official position on radio broadcasting in Canada. Canada would have both public and private radio stations. The government's proposal regarding public broadcasting revolved around three issues, issues that were very different from those relating to the American system:

- National sovereignty was to be preserved.
- Broadcasting services were to be made available to anyone in Canada, no matter where they lived.
- Broadcasting was not to be exploited by private interests.

In 1932 the Canadian Radio Broadcasting Act was passed, resulting in the creation of the Canadian Radio Broadcasting Commission, which began broadcasting in 1933. The CRBC was a direct product of the Aird Commission. Initially it broadcast for only one hour a day. By the time it was replaced by the CBC in 1936, it was reaching just under half the Canadian population. By 1936 the Canadian Broadcasting Corporation (CBC) was formed. In addition to being a national radio network, it was responsible for granting licences to private radio broadcasters, even though the government did not officially recognize private broadcasting—an ideal position

BBC Online: An extensive site featuring links to all the BBC's services, including show information, listings, news, and sport.

www.bbc.co.uk/home/today/

CBC Radio: Listings for CBC Radio One, Radio Two, and RadioCanada International, and links to other CBC websites.

www.cbc.ca/onair

for the government to be in. In 1957 the Fowler Commission changed the name of the CBC's board of governors to the Board of Broadcast Governors (BBG) to emphasize their power, and, in the Broadcast Act of 1958, the BBG was given the power to regulate broadcasting in Canada. The CBC was now simply a broadcasting network with no control over private broadcasting. In 1968, the BBG became the Canada Radio-Television Commission (CRTC). It had the power to license radio and television stations in Canada and was the forerunner of today's CRTC.

U.S. RADIO IN THE PRIVATE SECTOR

A Pittsburgh engineer, **Frank Conrad**, fiddled with radiotelegraphy in his home garage, playing music as he experimented. People with homemade receivers liked what they heard from Conrad's transmitter, and soon he had a following. When Conrad's Westinghouse bosses learned that he had become a local celebrity, they saw profit in building receivers that consumers could buy at $10 a set and take home to listen to. To encourage sales of the receivers, Westinghouse built a station to provide regular programming of news, sports, and music—mostly music. That station, **KDKA**, became America's first licensed commercial station in 1920.

"Radio" Becomes a Household Word. When the Titanic sank in 1912, newspapers relied on young radio operator David Sarnoff for information on what was happening in the mid-Atlantic. For 72 hours Sarnoff sat at his primitive receiver, which happened to be on exhibit in a department store, to pick up details from rescue ships. The newspaper coverage of the disaster made "radio" a household word, which paved the way for consumer acceptance over the next few years.

The licensing of KDKA was important because it demonstrated the United States' commitment to placing radio in the private sector. In Europe, broadcasting was a government monopoly. KDKA's entertainment programming also sent American broadcasting in a certain direction. In many other countries, radio was used mostly for education and high culture, not mass entertainment.

ROLE OF ADVERTISING

Like the CNR, Westinghouse never expected radio itself to make money, only to spur sales of their $10 home receivers. The economic base of KDKA and the rest of American broadcasting changed in 1922 when **WEAF** in New York accepted $50 from a real estate developer and allowed him 10 minutes to pitch his new Long Island apartments. Then the Gimbel's department store tried radio advertising. Within months, companies were clamouring for airtime. The Lucky Strike Orchestra produced programs, as did the Taystee Loafers from the Taystee bread company, and the A&P Gypsies, the Goodrich Silvertown Orchestra, and the Interwoven Pair from the sock company.

Unlike Canadian radio in those first years of the 1920s and 1930s, American radio took on these distinctive traits:

- Private rather than state ownership of the broadcasting systems.
- An entertainment thrust to programming that emphasized popular culture.
- An economic foundation based on selling time to advertisers who needed to reach a mass audience of consumers.

Radio as Entertainment

EARLY MASS PROGRAMMING

In the early days, most stations were on the air at night with hotel teatime music. It was pleasant programming, offensive to no one. Sandwiched among the **potted-palm music,** as it was called, were occasional soloists, poets, and public speakers. As broadcasting expanded into the daytime, stations used more recordings, which introduced a bit more variety. In the late 1920s, evening programming became more varied. Potted-palm music gave way to symphonies and big bands. Guy Lombardo, the Dorsey Brothers, and Benny Goodman all found that radio helped to promote their record sales. In Nashville, WSM built a country music program on the Saturday night Southern tradition of picking, singing, and gossiping with your neighbours on the front porch or the courthouse lawn. In 1928 the program was named the *Grand Ole Opry.*

Broadcasts of hockey games, sponsored by General Motors, were the most popular radio programs of the early days of the medium, beginning in 1923. Within 10 years, hockey broadcasts were heard on 20 Canadian radio stations from coast to coast. This sponsorship also marked the beginning of "commercial" radio in Canada.

With more varied programs, radio attracted a true mass audience in the 1930s. Fred Waring and His Pennsylvanians demonstrated that variety shows could attract large audiences. Jack Benny, Milton Berle, and Bob Hope did the same with comedy. Drama series were introduced—murder mysteries, soap operas, Westerns, thrillers. Quiz shows became part of the mix. *Woodhouse and Hawkins* was a popular Canadian radio show. In 1940 Texaco began sponsoring the Saturday matinees of the Metropolitan Opera from New York, which had been airing since 1931. The opera broadcasts remain the longest continuously sponsored program on radio.

Old Time Radio: A site filled with many entertaining and educational topics for fans of nostalgic and old-time radio shows.

www.old-time.com

During this time, the CBC also established itself as a first-rate producer of radio. One drama of note was *The Investigator*, a play written by Rueben Ship and directed by Andrew Allan in 1954. It poked fun at the Communist hunt in America spearheaded by Joseph McCarthy. It was so controversial that it was banned in the U.S.

The early radio programming, geared to attract large audiences, was a culturally unifying factor. Almost everyone had a common experience in the radio programs of the time. But then television came along, and radio had to change.

FORMATS FOR SPECIFIC AUDIENCES

Comedies, dramas, and quiz shows moved to television beginning in the late 1940s, and so did the huge audience that radio had cultivated. The radio networks, losing advertisers to television, scaled back what they offered stations. As the number of listeners dropped, local stations played more recorded music, which was far cheaper than producing programs.

Although most stations in the pre-television period offered diversity, a few stations emphasized certain kinds of programming. Some stations carried only religious programs. In the 1950s, **Alan Freed** introduced rock 'n' roll, which became the fare at hundreds of stations and began wide-scale fragmentation in radio programming. Today, hardly any station tries to offer something for everyone, but everyone can find something on the radio to like. There is a format for everyone.

After Freed came the **Top 40** format, in which the day's top songs were repeated in rotation, and then the wizard of radio formatting, **Gordon McLendon**, developed the format by mixing fast-paced newscasts, disc jockey chatter, lively commercials and promotional jingles, and hype with the music. It was catchy, almost hypnotizing—and widely imitated. McLendon designed beautiful music as a format in 1959, all-news in 1961, and all-classified ads in 1967. In all of his innovations, McLendon was firm about a strict structure. Top 40, for example, had no deviations from music in rotation, news every 20 minutes, the station call letters named twice between songs, upbeat jingles, and no dead-pan commercials. McLendon's classified-ad format bombed, but the others have survived in both Canada and the U.S.

Below are terms used to distinguish radio's major music formats for private radio in Canada. Due to demassification, many formats have become fragmented.

ADULT CONTEMPORARY (A/C). Many advertisers like the A/C format because so many people in the big-spending 25-to-40 age group listen. Some of the formats with A/C include Hot AC (Mix 96 in Edmonton), Soft AC (CHFI in Toronto), and Mainstream A/C (KISS-FM in Vancouver).

TOP 40. Top 40, also called "CHR" (short for "Contemporary Hits Radio") emphasizes current rock but not as strictly as McLendon insisted. These stations target teenagers. Some of the variations within this format include Rhythmic Top 40 and Adult Top 40.

NEWS AND TALK. As FM stations drew listeners away from AM with their superior sound for music, many AM stations switched to news and talk programming. Talk radio is becoming a dominant format. There is at least one talk radio station in every major market in Canada, including Vancouver, where talk radio has been popular since the 1960s. The variations on this format include Mojo Radio 640 (talk radio for guys) in Toronto and The Team, CHUM's all sports network across Canada. In fact, the fastest-growing niche in talk radio programming is sports. Why?

CAB: Facts and the latest news about the private broadcasting industry from the Canadian Association of Broadcasters.

www.cab-acr.ca

CBSC: The Canadian Broadcast Standards Council monitors media compliance with the standards developed by the Canadian Association of Broadcasters, and mediates listener and viewer complaints.

www.cbsc.ca

MEDIA DATABANK 4.2

Radio Formats

The CRTC and BBM offer us a look at the diversity of radio formats in Canada.

Format	*Percentage*
Adult contemporary	23%
Country	11%
Contemporary hits	10%
News/talk	9%
Album-oriented rock	5%

Source: 2001 Broadcast Policy Monitoring Report.

Because advertisers find that sports stations are good for reaching male potential customers, an elusive group that is outnumbered by women in many other media.

COUNTRY.   Once called "country and western," or "CW" for short, this format goes back to WSM's *Grand Ole Opry* program from Nashville. The music varies significantly from twangy western ballads to what's called "urban country." In Canada, "young country" and "new country" have become two popular music formats. By abandoning Loretta Lynn and George Jones for Shania Twain and Michelle Wright, new country radio stations have been able to attract younger listeners. Traditional country fans are older males; fans of the new formats are a mix of younger males and females, making it easier to attract listeners and advertisers. Some diversification has occurred in this format, including the emergence of "Classic Country" on stations such as CFDR-FM in Halifax.

ALBUM-ORIENTED ROCK (AOR).   AOR formats offer songs from the 100 best-selling albums. A casual listener might confuse AOR with Top 40, but album stations go back a couple of years for wider variety. Audiences tend to be aged 18 to 24. This is one of the most diversified formats, with Classic Rock available on CIRK-FM (Edmonton), Mainstream Rock (The Bear in Ottawa), and New Music with CFNY (Toronto).

OLDIES.   Oldies stations play music that the 45-to-64-year-old demographic grew up with, mostly music of the 1960s and 1970s. Sometimes it's called "classic hits."

ETHNIC.   More than 9 million Canadians belong to ethnic groups other than First Nations, French, or British. These people represent over 70 different cultures. Given this fact and Canada's official status as a multicultural country, it's not surprising that full-time, ethnic radio stations have taken root in many of Canada's urban centres. Vancouver has CJVB and CHMB, Edmonton has CKER, and Toronto has CHIN. All in all, Canada is home to 13 ethnic radio stations. Many other radio stations feature ethnic programming on a part-time basis, during the evenings and on weekends.

Casey's Hits. Casey Kasem has been a popular mainstay on U.S. and Canadian radio since the early 1970s. His American Top 40 is heard, via satellite, all over the world.

Spanning Generations.
Newscaster and commentator Paul Harvey, reportedly the highest-paid person in radio, survived the change from radio's heyday to today's specialized programming with his touch for the ironic. His clipped delivery and signature items, like his drawn-out "good day," have made his ABC programs a fixture in the lives of millions of people. Canadian stations can pick up satellite feeds of Harvey's commentary and other U.S. programming. This trend has the CRTC worried about the demise of Canadian culture.

CLASSICAL.   This format offers the basic repertoire of enduring music since the Baroque era, although some classical stations also play experimental symphonies, operas, and contemporary composers. Because highbrow music has a limited following, most classical stations are supported not by advertising but by listener donations, universities, and government funding. CBC Radio Two broadcasts classical music on a national basis. CFMX, located in Cobourg, Ontario, has achieved significant ratings in the Toronto area.

RELIGIOUS.   Inspirational music is the programming core of religious stations. The music is interspersed with sermons from evangelists who buy time for their programs, seeking both to proselytize and to raise funds to support ministries.

OTHER FORMATS.   The CRTC has recently issued licences to some new formats in Canada. They include "Smooth Jazz" in Calgary and Hamilton, and "Urban" music stations in Vancouver, Calgary, and Toronto.

PROGRAMMING ISSUES

Like most mass media, radio is imitative. When major programming innovations occur, which is rare, the cloning begins. In the 1980s, when audiences glommed onto talk radio, for example, hundreds of stations copied the format. The coast-to-coast sameness of radio formats—and even the on-air voices and personalities—have been reinforced by the growth of chain ownership. Chain managers prefer tried-and-true routes to profits. They avoid the risks attendant on striking out in fresh directions.

On the other hand, while some argue that radio programming has become more populist and formulaic, some stations set themselves apart with local and distinctive content. Newcap Broadcasting's "Radio Newfoundland" features nothing but East Coast artists. Country stations in the west continue to serve their largely agricultural listeners well, while CHWO in Oakville calls itself "Prime Time Radio," with the emphasis on older listeners.

A CANADIAN ALTERNATIVE: CBC

As Canada's public broadcaster, CBC Radio brought Canadian programming home to Canadians. Today CBC Radio is known as either Radio One or Radio Two. Radio One features a mix of information, talk, and Canadian music, while Radio Two's programming is more "highbrow," with an emphasis on classical music and opera. CBC radio is commercial free, funded through taxpayer money. Much of their programming, as mandated by the Broadcasting Act, is regional. Over 85 percent of CBC English Radio is produced at the local level, with much of that broadcast nationally. CBC Radio also spotlights Canadian talent. Over 60 hours of performance programming on both networks focuses on Canadian performers. The listenership for CBC radio has remained fairly steady in recent years, as 3.5 million Canadians tune in each week to either CBC Radio One or Radio Two.

Some recent programming highlights of CBC Radio include:

- *Pianists of the 20th Century*. This show was so popular it eventually aired on National Public Radio in the U.S.
- *From Naked Ape to Superspecies* with David Suzuki.
- *Alice in Cyberspace*, which had both web and broadcast elements.

Gordon McLendon. The views of radio programming guru Gordon McLendon were widely sought in the 1950s. It was McLendon who created the Top 40 and all-news formats that enabled radio to survive massive audience losses to television.

Talk Radio

TALK FORMATS

Call-in formats were greeted enthusiastically at first because of their potential as forums for discussion of the public issues, but there was a downside. Many stations with music-based formats used the advent of news and talk stations to reduce their news programming. In effect, many music stations were saying, "Let those guys do news and talk, and we'll do music." While some might lament the lack of news on all-music stations, in these days of demassification and diversification, people who tune in to a music station are tuning in for music; they don't want much in the way of news and information programming.

Disturbing too was that talk formats failed to live up to expectations that they would be serious forums on public policy. While talk shows provided opportunities for immediate listener feedback, many of the most popular ones degenerated into advice programs on hemorrhoids, psoriasis, face-lifts, and psychoses. Sports trivia went over big. Talk shows gave an illusion of being news, but in fact they were low-brow entertainment. The call-in shows that focused on public issues, mostly late at night, attracted many screwballs and hate-mongers who diminished the quality of public dialogue on important issues. The shows were vulnerable to people who tried to divide communities. A Denver talk show host, Alan Berg, who was Jewish, was shot to death by an anti-Semite who became fired up over what he heard on the radio. In Houston, talk shows encouraged the airing of a rash of antigay sentiments. Talk shows, by their nature, lend themselves to misinformation—even disinformation—from crackpots, fanatics, and ignoramuses.

Also, the influence of talk radio may be overrated. A 1996 Media Studies Centre survey of people who listen to political talk shows found that they are hardly representative of the mainstream.

Media People

Steve Jones

Steve Jones

Steve Jones loves radio. He was hooked from his earliest years, and began his career as a 13-year-old board operator at small-market CFNO-FM in Marathon, Ontario. Today he is the national director of programming for Newcap Broadcasting as well as program director of MIX 96 and K-Rock, Newcap's Edmonton properties. In his 19 years in radio, Steve has worked on the air and in programming in almost every format, including rock, Top 40, country, A/C, and oldies. In his current position, he oversees the programming initiatives and branding of all of Newcap's stations operating in six provinces and all market sizes.

Steve has seen changes in radio in Canada. Two significant changes have occurred in radio station formats and in radio station ownership. In terms of formats, he says:

> While Canadian cities have significantly fewer radio stations than comparable American cities, the trend toward format fragmentation impacted Canada in the early 1990s. By 2001, most major Canadian cities were served by variations of the various formats. For example, the standard Top 40 as envisioned by pioneers like McLendon segmented into Rhythmic Top 40, Adult Top 40 and other long and short-lived variations of the format. Instead of one Adult Contemporary station in each market, by the early 1990s most markets were home to "Soft A/C," "Hot A/C," and "Adult A/C."

Changes by the CRTC to the Radio Regulations impacted the ownership structure in Canadian radio. "Companies like Corus, Rogers, CHUM and Standard have become Canada's largest broadcasters," Steve says. "In many markets, these and other companies operate multiple stations in a consolidated environment that did not exist even five years ago. This trend toward consolidation is likely to continue."

While Steve will admit that Canada does have its share of homogenized radio, he also feels strongly that Canadian radio is in better shape than U.S. radio. Says Jones, "there are very few major market stations that use extensive multi-station voice tracking. Whereas in the U.S., the mid-day host in Los Angeles may hypothetically also voice the evening show in Denver and the overnight show in Pittsburgh."

As for the impact of satellites, Jones says, "the danger for the young broadcaster is in the smaller markets, where only a decade ago there was a need for announcers around the clock. Now, with satellite and automated programming, a skeleton staff can handle the same workload. The result is a rapidly depleting farm team for medium and large market broadcasters."

While the DAB bandwagon may have lost a few people over the past few years, the growth of DAB in some form is almost inevitable. However, with a variety of DAB platforms proposed, its growth is limited. Furthermore, it will launch in an extremely competitive market, where terrestrial radio alternatives will already exist in the form of satellite radio and high-bandwidth Internet radio. The success or failure of satellite radio may be a key in how quickly terrestrial broadcasters move to adopt DAB technology. If satellite radio is a success, traditional broadcasters may push harder for DAB roll out.

Jones says the most important thing for the CRTC to recognize is that a strong and healthy radio industry accomplishes many of the CRTC's goals. When healthy as a business, radio can become more creative, diverse, and more relevant to the everyday lives of Canadians.

Talk radio may offer access to the "commoners," or so it would seem; Paul Rutherford, a communication professor at the University of Toronto, says that talk radio is "providing a voice for people who otherwise wouldn't have one."

This was especially true during the late 1980s and early 1990s, a time when the government was dealing with issues such as the GST, the Meech Lake Accord, and free trade. At the time, many Canadians felt a sense of alienation; they believed that their politicians simply weren't listening to them. To vent their frustrations, many turned to talk radio. This gave listeners a sense that they were finally being heard.

How is Canadian talk radio different from American talk radio? Many differences exist, according to those who claim that Canadians are "kindler, gentler" talk show participants. Rutherford claims that there are two types of talk show hosts: warriors and father figures. The warrior is clearly American: confrontational and in your face. Male Canadian talk show hosts tend to be father figures, with a few exceptions—namely, Rafe Mair in British Columbia, Gilles Proulx in Quebec, and John Michael in Ontario. Bill Rowe in Newfoundland and Andy Barrie in Toronto offer more thought-provoking and well-researched fare and belong to neither category.

Perhaps one of the reasons talk radio is different in Canada is the regional or local nature of talk shows. Compared to the United States, which boasts numerous national talk show hosts, Canadian talk show hosts are generally local in character. Gary Slaight of Standard Broadcasting says there's only one real issue in the U.S., "and that's whether you're left-wing or right-wing. Whether you're in New York or Seattle, it's the same question. Not in Canada, where we're defined so many ways: English/French, East/West."

HOWARD STERN

No wonder they call **Howard Stern** a **"shock jock."** The New York disc jockey is outrageous, cynical, and vulgar. But people listen to his bathroom-wall jokes and his topless female studio guests. Not surprisingly, the Canadian Broadcast Standards Council didn't cotton well to Stern's brand of humour. That didn't bother Stern much. During his first Canadian broadcast, he thanked CHOM-FM for "opening up the sewer gate for me to pollute yet another country." To those Canadians who don't like his approach to morning radio, Stern replied that the show was "just entertainment. Jokes, laughter and whatever's on our minds."

Shock Jock. Blunt and uninhibited on the air, radio personality Howard Stern is the epitome of the "shock jock." Although his New York-based program has strong listenership, Stern's crude humour is not universally popular. His morning show, which was carried for a while on two Canadian radio stations, resulted in an avalanche of complaints filed with the Canadian Broadcast Standards Council.

CHOM-FM in Montreal carried the show briefly, but bowed to pressure from various groups and dropped the show in 1998, while Q-107 in Toronto dropped Stern late in 2001 due to poor ratings.

Howard Stern has known controversy a long time. At Boston College, he worked at the campus radio station—until they fired him for a show on Godzilla going to Harlem. Later at WNBC in New York, a bit called "Bestiality Dial-a-Porn" got him fired again.

At WXRK in New York, Stern proved he could draw listeners. The station shot from number 21 to number 1 in morning ratings after he signed on in 1985. At his current Infinity home, the blue humour, as well as his racism, sexism, homophobia, misogyny, and bad taste, continue to attract a large, profitable audience.

Rules for Radio

THE CRTC AND RADIO BROADCASTING LEGISLATION IN CANADA

In the 1998 overhaul of its policy regarding commercial radio in Canada, the CRTC stated that its policy mirrors the basic objectives of Section 3 of the Broadcasting Act. Basically, the CRTC stated that:

- Programming on Canadian radio should be Canadian in nature.
- Radio should present listeners with a wide variety of programming from a variety of sources, particularly new voices.
- On matters of public concern, programming should provide a balanced analysis.
- Radio service should be relevant to its community.
- Programming, when possible, should reflect the bilingual nature of Canada.
- Programming should also reflect Canada's multicultural diversity, including Aboriginal peoples.

In addition to the changes in Canadian content discussed in Chapter 3, the biggest changes the CRTC made were regarding ownership. Prior to 1998, a person or corporation could only own one AM and one FM station in any market. Now, in markets with fewer than eight (commercial) radio stations, one person may be allowed to own up to three radio stations. In larger markets of more than eight radio stations, an individual may own two AM and two FM stations. The rationale for this decision is economic. The battle between AM and FM radio in Canada isn't even a close one. According to the CRTC and the Canadian Association of Broadcasters, audiences on AM radio are tuning out. Generally speaking, AM broadcasters didn't make a profit between 1991 and 1998.

Radio stations have had a hard time making money in the 1990s. The Canadian Association of Broadcasters reports that Canadian radio stations, particularly AM radio, have collectively lost $180 million since the early 1990s. This fact is one reason that the CRTC was forced to make some legislative changes in 1998. The CRTC feels that mergers may be one way to make radio a more attractive investment and make radio more competitive with other media in Canada. This in turn, it hopes, will result in an increase in competition and a growth in the number of diverse voices heard.

The CRTC has also withdrawn its Radio Market Policy. Under that policy, each market in Canada was allocated a certain number of frequencies, based on several factors, including population. Now, the CRTC will entertain applications for new stations in all markets and is prepared to issue new licences for any market if the new station fills a particular void in the marketplace. In its 2001 review of its Ethnic Broadcasting Policy, the CRTC would like to see more radio stations on the air directed at minorities here in Canada, namely Aboriginal and ethnic groups.

While the debate on levels of Canadian music on the radio was addressed in Chapter 3, a new discussion has emerged regarding Canadian content. It seems that radio policy in Canada has come full circle from the days of the original Aird Commission, which looked at the influx of American programming into Canadian radios. Due to economic factors, many Canadian radio stations rely on foreign-produced (read American) satellite programming to help fill their broadcast day. A CRTC survey of English-language broadcasters indicated that around 50 percent of the stations had some form of foreign-based programming. Currently, despite the mention in the Broadcasting Act that Canadian radio programming be predominantly Canadian, the CRTC has no specific legislation regarding the amount of foreign programming a radio station may carry. However, it is warning private broadcasters to be wary, as they will have to explain and justify their (over) use of foreign programming when their licences come up for renewal. In addition to Howard Stern, some Canadian stations air programs by Art Bell, Dr. Laura Schlesinger, and Dr. Gabe Mirkin to fill airtime.

QUALITY ON THE AIR

Quality is in the beholder's eye—or ear. If wall-to-wall music is the measure of quality, then a lot of superb stations are on the air. Recorded music, though, is a low-overhead format that's so formulaic that stations have a hard time distinguishing themselves from each other. There are, however, other measures.

The Broadcasting Act says that Canadian radio should reflect a Canadian way of life. The idea was for radio to play the local community back to itself. How well do stations do this? By this standard, a station would get high marks for programming indigenous culture—performances by local musicians, coverage of local news, discussion of local issues, and play-by-plays of local athletic events. Radio can have a role in creating a distinctive local culture. However, some Canadian stations, particularly at night, are opting for U.S. satellite programming and are devoid of community content except for local weather forecasts and advertising. Some stations are conduits for programming services from far away, nothing more. Even the disc jockey is in a remote city, the music being transmitted to multiple stations simultaneously.

A station can be evaluated by the size and quality of its programming staff. How talented are on-air personalities? Is theirs mindless chatter? Or is it comedic genius? How many news reporters are on the street, on top of news? Or is news a rehash from the wires or piped in from networks? If the station runs public service announcements, are they geared to local causes?

Broadcasting Act: The full text of the Broadcasting Act.

www.crtc.gc.ca/eng/ legal/broad.htm

radio

World Digital Audio Broadcasting Forum: This organization promotes international cooperation between sound and data broadcasters, network providers, manufacturers, and governments.

www.worlddab.org

The future of radio is digital and web-based. In the late 1980s, when radio stations tore out their turntables and began playing CDs, many proclaimed a giant step forward in broadcasting. It was hollow hype. While CDs have superior sound to old analogue records, stations still transmitted in the same old analogue way—and still do.

When digital audio broadcasting, or **DAB**, was introduced in the 1990s, few could really experience all that it had to offer. Technically it is possible for stations to upgrade to digital transmission, using Eureka 147 wide-band technology, picking up the long chain of binary 0s and 1s from CDs, with the transmission corresponding precisely to the binary encoding on the CD. The hitch was that the receivers most people own today—in their cars, at home, at work, wherever—cannot pick up digital signals. However, in late 2001, the cost of the chip used to make digital radio receivers came down in price dramatically. This was encouraging news for those pushing for the deployment of DAB in Canada.

Many Canadian radio stations, mostly in Toronto, Montréal, and Vancouver, began broadcasting in digital in 1999. According to David Bray, senior VP of Hennessy and Bray Communications:

> DAB delivers a variety of fundamental benefits. It has numerous advantages over both current analogue transmission and the current streaming via the World Wide Web. Digital offers both outstanding CD quality sound and portability. It will lead to a host of display services for the consumer, including geographic positioning, traffic and weather information, advertising supplements, song credits and a good deal more. All the while the listener is treated to interference-free reception.

Many radio stations have established music sites on the World Wide Web. Theoretically, the quality of sound, being digital, should be excellent, but for the time being, the web's bandwidth limitations can't handle enough digital data for smooth delivery. Until bandwidth is expanded to accommodate real-time listening, there is software available that picks up web music and stores it for playback. Also, technology is finding ways to compress digital signals so more and more data, including the binary 0 and 1 code that underlies digital music, can be squeezed through the bottlenecks on the Internet pipelines.

In these days of convergence, the web and radio may be perfect partners, says John Harding of the Canadian Radio Marketing Bureau. Harding says that "as radio content evolves onto the Internet, radio will excel in its ability to attract and maintain ears and eyes, that being radio's forte. Radio knows how to hold an audience. The skill sets are transferable from terrestrial radio to Internet radio to build and maintain audience loyalty."

CHAPTER WRAP-UP

The proliferation in radio programming can be expected to continue with stations narrowcasting into more and more specialized niches. Broadcast industry commentator Erik Zorn predicts hundreds of formats, some as narrow as Czech-language stations and full-time stations for the blind. With on-demand programming, listeners will be able to choose among literally hundreds of programs at any time—a far cry from pre-television days when mainstream radio was truly a mass medium and sought the whole audience with every program.

QUESTIONS FOR REVIEW

1. Why is radio called a ubiquitous and influential medium?
2. How does radio move invisibly through the air on electromagnetic waves?
3. What are characteristics of the radio industry in Canada?
4. Why did the government begin broadcast regulation in 1932? What has happened since?
5. What forces contribute to a sameness in radio programming? Will technology affect programming in the future?
6. Who "invented" radio—Fessenden or Marconi?
7. How will DAB or the web change radio?

QUESTIONS FOR CRITICAL THINKING

1. Guglielmo Marconi introduced radio wireless telegraphy, while Fessenden was responsible for the first radio broadcast. What was the difference?
2. Lee De Forest was a technical and programming innovator. Explain the significance of his audion tube and his 1916 broadcast of election returns.
3. A new way of transmitting radio was developed by Edwin Armstrong in the 1930s, and by the 1980s it had left the original AM broadcast system in economic peril. Discuss Armstrong's invention and how it has reshaped U.S. radio.
4. Radio was reshaped by the advent of television in the 1950s. Explain these influences, and be sure to cite radio's transition from literal broadcasting toward narrowcasting. What about the influence of Gordon McLendon? What of the future?
5. Explain the significance of XWA of Montreal.
6. How does programming today differ from the potted-palm music of early radio?
7. Is there a role for CBC Radio in the future? Explain.

FOR KEEPING UP TO DATE

The trade journals *Broadcaster* and *Broadcast Dialogue* keep abreast of news and issues.

Other news coverage can be found in the *National Post*, the *Globe and Mail*, and other major daily newspapers.

Scholarly articles can be found in the *Canadian Journal of Communication, Journal of Broadcasting, Electronic Media, Journal of Communication, and Journalism Quarterly.*

R&R, a weekly trade journal published by Radio & Records, carries charts and playlists that not only reflect what's getting airtime but also shape what will be getting airtime.

FOR FURTHER LEARNING

Erik Barnouw. *A Tower in Babel, A History of Broadcasting in the United States to 1933* (Oxford, 1966).

Erik Barnouw. *The Golden Web, A History of Broadcasting in the United States, 1933–1953* (Oxford, 1968).

Erik Barnouw. *The Image Empire, A History of Broadcasting in the United States, 1953–On* (Oxford, 1970).

John R. Bittner. *Broadcast Law and Regulation* (Prentice Hall, 1982).

David Bray. "Digital Radio: A Numbers Game." *Broadcaster* (September 2000).

David Bray. "Radio Revs Up for the Internet." *Broadcaster* (March, 1996).

Robert Brehl. "CRTC Causes Static Among Radio Bosses." *Globe and Mail* (June 9, 1998).

John Bugailiskis. "Stern's Show Slim on Canadian Content." *Broadcaster* (September, 1997).

"CAB Fires Back at Music Industry Radio Content Claims." *Broadcaster Industry News* (April 1996).

Canadian Association of Broadcasters. *A Broadcaster's Guide to Canada's Cultural Mosaic*, 1988.

Gerald Carson. *The Roguish World of Dr. Brinkley* (Holt, Rinehart & Winston, 1960).

CBC Enterprises. *Fifty Years of Radio: A Celebration of CBC Radio 1936–1986.*

Ray Conlogue. "Radio Shock Jock Strikes a Nerve." *Globe and Mail* (September 3, 1997).

Andrew Coyne. "Cracking Down on Howard." *St. Catharines Standard* (September 20, 1997).

Andrew Crissell. *Understanding Radio* (Methuen, 1990).

Philip Fine. "Radio Stations Ponder Fate of Stern's Show." *Globe and Mail* (November 22, 1997).

"The Fowler Years: A Chairman Who Marches to His Own Drummer." *Broadcasting* 112 (March 23, 1987): 12, 51–54.

Peter Goddard. "It's Talk, Talk, Talk All Over the Radio." *Toronto Star* (October 29, 1995).

Lynne Schafer Gross. *Telecommunications: An Introduction to Radio, Television and Other Electronic Media*, 2nd ed. (Wm. C. Brown, 1986).

John Harding. "Radio—The Momentum Continues." *Broadcast Dialogue* (January 2001).

Laurel Hyatt. "Back in the Black." *Broadcaster* (February. 1998).

Laurel Hyatt. "Radio's Recipe for Success." *Broadcaster* (April 1996), 12–15.

Donald Jack. *Sinc, Betty and the Morning Man* (Macmillan, 1977).

Daphne Lavers. "DAB Launch." *Broadcast Dialogue* (August 1999).

Murray B. Levin. *Talk Radio and the American Dream* (D.C. Heath, 1987).

Kirk Makin. "Brrrrring....brrrrring: You're on the Air." *Globe and Mail* (July 16, 1994).

Michael McCabe. "CANCON Not the Only Measure of Radio's Contribution." *Broadcaster* (February 1998).

Doug Saunders. "AM Listeners Tuning Out." *Globe and Mail* (October 20, 1997).

Heather Schoffield and Robert Brehl. "Radio Stations Told To Turn Up the Volume" and "CRTC Opens Radio Markets." *Globe and Mail* (May 1, 1998).

Sandy Stewart. *A Pictorial History of Radio in Canada* (Gage, 1975).

Erik Zorn. "Radio Lives!" *Esquire 101* (March 1984): 3, 45–54; "The Specialized Signals of Radio News." *Washington Journalism Review* 8 (June 1986): 6, 31–33.

First Telecast. A production still from the CBC's first *Hockey Night in Canada* telecast. The program has been a staple of Canadian television programming for more than 40 years.

Television and the Moving Image

MEDIA IN THEORY

Cultural Impact of Television

Scholars and broadcasters may have different views on the potency of television's effect on society, but they all agree that there is some degree of influence. The role of television in riveting attention on serious matters was demonstrated in the fall of 2001 when terrorists launched attacks on the World Trade Center and on the Pentagon. For months, people were tuned in to CNN or CBC Newsworld to hear about the latest developments in the war on terrorism.

Fictional television characters can capture the imagination of the public. Perry Mason did wonders for the reputation of the law profession. Mary Tyler Moore's role as a television news writer showed that women could succeed in male-dominated industries. Roles played by Alan Alda were the counter-macho models for the bright, gentle man of the 1970s. In this same vein, however, Bart Simpson's bratty irreverence toward authority figures sent quivers through parents and teachers in the 1990s. Then came the alarm that Beavis and Butt-Head's fun with matches might lead kids all over the world to set everything in sight on fire.

Although television can be effective in creating short-term impressions, there also are long-term effects. A whole generation of children grew up with

Teenage Mutant Ninja Turtles as part of their generational identity. Later came *Pokémon* and *South Park.* The long-term effects exist at both a superficial level, as with *Teenage Mutant Ninja Turtles,* and at a serious level. Social critic **Michael Novak** puts the effect of television in broad terms: "Television is a molder of the soul's geography. It builds up incrementally a psychic structure of expectations. It does so in much the same way that school lessons slowly, over the years, tutor the unformed mind and teach it how to think."

What are the lessons to which Novak refers? Scholars **Linda and Robert Lichter** and **Stanley Rothman,** who have surveyed the television creative community, make a case that the creators of television programs are social reformers who build their political ideas into their scripts. The Lichters and Rothman identify the television creative community as largely secular and politically liberal.

Scholars have different views on the potency of television's effect on society, but they all agree that there is some degree of influence. Media scholar George Comstock, in his book *Television in America,* wrote, "Television has become an unavoidable and unremitting factor in shaping what we are and what we will become."

But what of American TV's influence on Canadian culture? Canadian broadcaster Moses Znaimer claims that "as transmitter of information and entertainment, television is the acknowledged king. It's also very effective as a reflector of values and teacher of ideals, often in ways you don't notice." If Comstock, Novak, and Canadian actor, writer, and producer Steve Smith are correct (see the Media People box on page 113), then the need for Canadian television is obvious. Without Canadian television, Smith says that Canadians "would be like North Dakota with more interesting currency."

Television in Canada

MASS MEDIA SHAKE-UP

Since its introduction in the early 1950s, the presence of television has reshaped the other media. Consider the following areas of impact:

BOOKS. The discretionary time people spend on television today is time that once went to other activities, including reading, for diversion and information. To stem the decline in reading, book publishers have responded with more extravagant promotions to draw attention to their products. A major consideration with fiction manuscripts at publishing houses is their potential as screenplays, many of which end up on television. Also, in deciding which manuscripts to accept, some publishers even consider how well an author will come across in television interviews when the book is published.

NEWSPAPERS. Evening television newscasts have been a major factor in the steady decline of afternoon newspapers, many of which have ceased publication or switched to mornings. Also, newspapers have lost almost all of their national advertisers, primarily to television. Most newspaper redesigns attempt to be visual in ways that newspapers never were before television. In 1998, the *Globe and Mail* added colour photos to its look.

MAGAZINES. Television took advertisers from the big mass-circulation magazines, forcing magazine companies to shift to magazines that catered to smaller segments of the mass audience that television could not serve.

Media People

Steve Smith

Steve Smith

Is there a cultural impact of U.S. television on Canadians? Are Canadians being taught to "think American?" **Steve Smith** thinks so. Smith is the actor behind the successful *Red Green Show*. Smith is more than the duct tape and Possum Lodge persona he depicts on television. He is also an accomplished writer, director, and producer of Canadian television programs. Canadian television has an important role as a vehicle for Canadian culture. Smith claims that with "Canadians being constantly exposed and bombarded with American culture, there's a natural tendency to assimilate and with Canadians, if all they're exposed to all is American media, they will become more and more like Americans and less and less like Canadians. For some people, that doesn't bother them. For me I think that would be a terrible tragedy."

Smith has been on the air in Canada since 1978. At first, Smith focused on acting and writing, but he's turned his attention to producing Canadian programs. His company, S and S Productions, is responsible for producing many programs for Canadian networks, including the CBC, WTN, and the Comedy Network. It also produced the movie *Red Green: Duct Tape Forever* in 2002.

Smith feels very passionately about Canadian television. He says it's unfair to categorize all American TV shows as better than all Canadian shows. "There are some great Canadian shows. If you look at the ratings book

people would be surprised that a lot of Canadian shows out rate a lot of the American shows." Some of Smith's favourite Canadian programs include comedies like *Made in Canada, This Hour Has 22 Minutes,* and *The Royal Canadian Air Farce.* In terms of drama, *DaVinci's Inquest* and *The Associates* are at the top of his list. In addition, Smith says that Canadian sports broadcasts are among the best.

What Smith dislikes about Canadian TV is "the philosophy behind some of the broadcast outlets in that they really aren't in the business of making Canadian television good or popular. They are really in the business of importing American shows. That bothers me. Canadian broadcasters should be judged on the Canadian shows that they offer to the public, not on how many American shows that they run. If Canadian networks lived or died by the success of their Canadian programming, they would find a way to make them great." For many broadcasters in Canada, the production and scheduling of Canadian programming is an afterthought.

The key to becoming successful in Canadian television, according to Smith, isn't to try and emulate what someone else is already doing. He feels that people working in any of the cultural industries, including television, should take their ideas and see if they work on a small scale. According to Smith, the initial goal isn't to become a big fish in a big pond, but to be a big fish in a little pond and then make the pond bigger. It's hard to disagree with that philosophy; it's that philosophy that made *Red Green* and S and S Productions the success they have become. The show currently airs in a dozen countries, including the U.S., where it is seen on the majority of PBS affiliates.

MUSIC. The success of recorded music today hinges in many cases on the airplay that music videos receive on television on MTV, MuchMusic, or YTV's *Hit List.*

MOVIES. Just as magazines demassified after television took away many of their advertisers, Hollywood demassified after television stole its audience. Today, savvy moviemakers plan their projects for both the big screen and for reissuing to be shown on television (via the networks) and for home video rental. These aftermarkets, in fact, have come to account for far more revenue to major studios than their moviemaking. Canadian television has also proven to be an excellent outlet for showcasing Canadian films.

RADIO. Radio also demassified with the arrival of television. The television networks first took radio's most successful programs and moved them to television. After losing its traditional programming strengths, radio then lost both the mass audience and advertisers it had built up since the 1920s. For survival, individual radio stations shifted almost entirely to recorded music and geared the music to narrower and narrower audience segments.

THE EARLY DAYS OF CANADIAN TV

While there were several experimental television broadcasts in Canada through the 1930s and 1940s, Canadians were first exposed to American television signals. The first television broadcast signal received in Canada was in 1947. Engineers at General Electric in Windsor picked up the transmission of WWDT in Detroit. This set the trend for television viewing in the early years of television in Canada. If you lived close enough to the border and had access to a television, you probably watched some American programming.

Television officially arrived in Canada in 1952. As had been the case with the first radio station 30 years earlier, the first television station was in Montreal. **CBFT**, a public station, began broadcasting on September 6, 1952, with CBLT Toronto broadcasting two days later. In 1953 stations began broadcasting in Vancouver, Sudbury, and Ottawa; by 1954, Winnipeg and Halifax had television stations. At first programming was a mix of Canadian and American fare. Early Canadian programming also reflected its roots in radio. *Wayne and Schuster* was a staple of Canadian television during the 1960s and 1970s, while *Hockey Night in Canada*, which began on radio in the 1920s, continues to draw a huge audience for the CBC on Saturday nights. A microwave link between Buffalo and Toronto made it possible to carry American programs live. There was no doubt about it; television was a hit in Canada. A million television sets had been purchased in Canada by 1954. By 1958, the CBC television network stretched from Victoria to Halifax. In 1961, CTV began as Canada's first private broadcaster.

MEDIA DATABANK 5.1

Canadians and TV

Research by the TV Bureau of Canada indicates just how popular a medium television has become for Canadians. TV ranked as the number one choice for entertainment, excitement, information, education, and believability. It was a close second behind radio for relaxation. The CRTC and BBM (Bureau of Measurement) offer us this snapshot of television viewing in Canada:

- Ninety-eight percent of Canadian homes have at least one television; 60 percent have two or more.
- The average Canadian watches 22.6 hours of television per week.
- Women watch the most TV: 26.5 hours each week, men watch about 22 hours.
- Canadians are watching more Canadian television programs, particularly English-language pay and specialty services. In 1994, the total hours tuned during prime time to a Canadian specialty or pay service was 30 million. By 1999 that figure had almost tripled to 85 million hours.

Source: Broadcast Policy Monitoring Report, 2000.

Technological Development

Electronic Scanning

In the 1920s, an Idaho farm boy, **Philo Farnsworth**, came up with the idea for using a vacuum tube to pick up moving images and then display them electronically on a screen. He found financial backers to build a lab, and in 1927, the first live moving image was transmitted. Farnsworth's tube, called the **image dissector**, was an incredible feat, considering that some of the world's greatest research labs, including RCA's, were trying to accomplish the same thing.

Not wanting to be upstaged, RCA claimed that **Vladimir Zworykin** devised a vacuum tube, the **iconoscope**, that could pick up moving images and then display them electronically on a screen first. That would have meant that RCA could reap a fortune from the patent rights. In the patent trail, however, it was learned that both Zworykin and his boss, RCA chief David Sarnoff, had visited Farnsworth's lab and had the opportunity to pirate his invention. Zworykin claimed to have the idea for the iconoscope as early as 1923, but his evidence was not as forthcoming. RCA ended up paying Farnsworth a licence fee to use his technology.

In retrospect, the technology seems simple. A camera picks up light reflected off a moving subject and converts the light to electrons. The electrons are zapped one at a time across stacked horizontal lines on a screen. The electrons follow each other back and forth so fast that they seem to show the movement picked up by the camera. This process creates an illusion of movement—the **persistence of vision** phenomenon.

However, this wasn't the only technology that television was experimenting with. In 1926, John Logie Baird was able to successfully transmit an image using mechanical technology that featured a metal disc with holes. As the disc revolved, the eyes were tricked into "seeing" a televised image through the holes in the disc. By 1931, VE9EC in Montreal was Canada's first television station using mechanical technology. In 1933, Eaton's sponsored a tour of mechanical television at its stores in Montreal, Toronto, and Winnipeg. In 1935, William Hoyt Peck conducted a month of experimental mechanical broadcasts in Montreal.

However, to the dismay of Baird and Peck, the image supplied by electronic television was superior to the mechanical image and became the industry standard in the U.S. and Canada. Westinghouse, RCA, and General Electric pooled their television research and Zworykin was put in charge of a team of engineers to develop a television system. In 1939 RCA flamboyantly displayed the Zworykin invention at the New York World's Fair. Soon, 10 American commercial stations were licensed and several companies were manufacturing home receivers. Electronic television was also featured at the Canadian National Exhibition in 1939. Then

Watching TV: A look at a previous exhibition examining the past, present, and future of television at the Canadian Museum of Civilization.

www.civilization.ca/hist/ tv/tv00eng.html#menu

Philo T. Farnsworth: The Farnsworth Archives.

www.philotfarnsworth.com

Vladimir Zworykin: Exposition about the work of Zworykin.

www.invent.org/book/ book-text/111.html

Farm Boy Invention. While harvesting an Idaho potato field in 1921, the 13-year-old Philo Farnsworth came up with the idea to transmit moving pictures live on a magnetically deflected electron beam. Crafting his own materials, including hand-blown tubes, Farnsworth completed his first image dissector while barely in his 20s. Later, RCA used the technology for its flamboyant public introduction of television.

came World War II, and the companies that were developing commercial television diverted their research and other energies to the war effort.

INTEGRATED STANDARDIZATION

Even after the war, there were delays. The U.S. Federal Communications Commission (FCC), wanting to head off topsy-turvy expansion that might create problems later, halted further station licensing in 1948. Not until 1952 did the FCC settle on a comprehensive licensing and frequency allocation system and lift the freeze. The freeze gave the FCC time to settle on a uniform system for the next step in television's evolution: colour. RCA wanted a system that could transmit to both existing black-and-white and new colour sets. CBS favoured a system that had superior clarity, but people would have to buy new sets to pick it up, and even then they would not be able to receive black-and-white programs. Finally, in 1953, the FCC settled on the RCA system. The Canadian government soon followed the American lead. Colour TV arrived in Canada in 1966, shortly after its arrival in the U.S.

DIGITAL TELEVISION

Digital television, or DTV for short, is a technical improvement over traditional analogue television. This means that programs are produced, not on tape, but using digital equipment, broadcast using digital transmitters, and best viewed on a digital television. The signal is stored as pieces of binary information. These bits of data become pixels, which are really little dots, on your television. When combined, these dots make up the television picture. Digital television can receive about 10 times as many pixels as a conventional television set. What makes digital television better, according to Canadian Digital Television Incorporated (CDTV), is:

- A better, clearer colour picture that eliminates "ghosting."
- An improved aspect ratio. Digital television sets feature an aspect ratio of 16:9 instead of the conventional 4:3. This makes for what is called "widescreen format."
- Dolby digital audio.

The CRTC reports that roughly two-thirds of customers with digital television receive their signals via satellite with Star Choice or Bell ExpressVu.

HIGH-DEFINITION TELEVISION

There are two digital television formats—SDTV, which is standard definition television, and HDTV, or high-definition television. SDTV can receive either analogue (traditional) television signals or basic digital signals. On the other hand, HDTV features higher resolution and better digital sound. Canadian Jim Bray of *Technofile* magazine says there are two HDTV formats available: "the 720p format uses 720 scan lines, progressively displayed the same way your computer monitor works. The other format, 1080I, uses more lines, but interlaces them. This means the odd scan lines are displayed first, then the even ones." Unlike earlier races for one technology to become the dominant format, Bray says that for the time being, these two formats are coexisting.

Converting to digital isn't cheap and, therefore, expense is an issue for broadcasters. In order to broadcast in HDTV, they need new equipment, including transmitters. Alan Morris, CTV's vice-president of engineering, claims, "it's a very costly proposition. It's not a matter of converting all production to HD, the question then is how do you transmit your signal. If you do it over the air, then you need new transmitters and new antennas. I'm not sure the business base is there right now to do that." Terry Horbatiuk of Panasonic Canada agrees: "It's not a matter of whether HDTV is coming, but rather when and how broadcasters are going to get there. You don't have to do everything at once. But you have to do something."

Cost is also a concern for the public. By early 2001, HDTV was available in Canada through digital cable or through either Star Choice or Bell ExpressVu satellite systems. To receive HDTV signals, the consumer must have a special receiver to decode the signal. When HDTV was first introduced, the cost of these receivers was expensive; they could cost around $1000. These receivers can also be rented from cable companies for around $10 a month, but many Canadians don't want to pay more than they have to for cable. As a result, HDTV is progressing at a slower rate in Canada than the early pundits had forecast. As of 2002, there was no clear mandate from the CRTC for Canadian broadcasters for the implementation of HDTV.

However, the CRTC and the television industry are trying to make digital and HDTV more appealing to consumers. Starting in 2001, digital specialty channels were offered by direct-to-home and cable companies. These specialty channels offered a mixed bag of niche programs. Some of the initial channels included WTSN, Pride Vision, LoneStar, and Book TV. These channels were only available via digital boxes. If consumers wanted access to these channels, they had to rent or purchase the appropriate technology to subscribe.

STREAMING

Broadcasters see the web as an additional delivery system, despite wobbly technology. The cables that make up the connections of the web lack the capacity to carry all the data that underlie video. A technique called **streaming** is used to move video on the web. In streaming, signals are broken up into packets for transmission and then accumulated in a viewer's computer for replay once it's downloaded. It's not live, and the video often has a jerky quality.

Even so, the networks and stations regard the web as a way to supplement their existing audience, especially for daytime newscasts that people can call up at work, where they may have computers but not television sets. Considering the jerkiness of streaming and the delay in delivery, short segments, such as news accounts, work best. Said Forrester Research analyst Mark Hardie, "Online audiences have a couple minutes' worth of attention span. You're forcing them to sit for several minutes to watch poor quality video."

Also working against the web for television delivery any time soon is that many people have creaky, old computers that are maxing out their potential with simple word-processing. Just as serious, computers crash. As technology writer Walter Mossberg put it: "If you watch television on a PC, you've traded a very stable, inexpensive platform for a costly and erratic one. In effect, you've just brought into your family room the first television set that crashes."

Theoretically, the transition to digital television will help facilitate the convergence of television and the Internet. Whether the full potential of this convergence will be realized is still up in the air. The conglomeration frenzy of the late 20th and early 21st century with BCE, Rogers, Shaw, and CanWest all becoming companies with various media platforms was based on the idea of convergence. Cost is a huge issue.

Personal Television. A hot consumer item beginning in 2000 was the PTV, short for "personal television," marketed under names such as TiVo and Replay TV. The devices store incoming programs digitally so people can play back programs in unreal time. Although designed as input devices, capable only of receiving programs, television networks and other content providers are uneasy that manufacturers might add output functions. That would enable people to use their PTVs like a PC to download programs from each other's devices. The result would be MP3-type legal issues about short-circuiting the usual suppliers of programming in a snub at copyright ownership. In Canada, Bell ExpressVu began offering PTV in 2001.

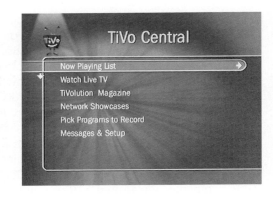

Interactive TV Today:
Founded in 1998 by Tracy Swedlow, InteractiveTV Today [itvt] is the leading source of information on the rapidly emerging interactive television (ITV) industry.

www.itvt.com

INTERACTIVE TELEVISION

Almost as soon as the web took root as a new mass medium, futurists saw television and the web melding into a single interactive medium. Their crystal ball had people watching television with hand-held keyboards that would let them simultaneously send and receive messages. The media hybrid was dubbed **interactive television.** Although technologically feasible, the concept took off slowly.

Microsoft acquired WebTV, an early interactive company, in 1997. In Canada, Rogers signed a deal with Microsoft in 1999 to bring interactive TV to Canadians. Interactive TV makes many things possible, including:

- Sending and receiving e-mails during television commercials.
- Clicking to the web for more details on a television news story.
- Zapping messages to friends that a great baseball game is tied in the ninth inning: "Better tune in."
- While you're watching *Made in Canada*, receiving on-screen news flashes from web sources that you've programmed to keep you abreast on subjects of your choice.
- Buying an item that you see advertised on television online—even as the advertisement is playing.
- Going to a continually updated program directory on-screen rather than leafing through the pages of *TV Guide*.

The full impact of interactive TV won't be felt for a few years. At the present time, customers with Star Choice, Bell ExpressVu, and digital cable are able to experiment with some of the choices offered by interactive TV.

Delivery Systems

At the present time, Canadians have plenty of choices regarding how to receive television signals. There are legal dishes, grey-market dishes, black-market dishes, cable, digital cable, and—even in the 21st century—antennas.

OVER-THE-AIR SYSTEMS

The people who conceived television really thought in terms of **radio with pictures.** That's not surprising when you consider that Sarnoff and Zworykin were radio people. The systems they built used towers, just like radio, to transmit their signals. Even early radio programming in the U.S. and Canada drew heavily from radio stars. The early days of broadcast regulation in Canada also followed the precedents set by radio.

American and Canadian networks thwarted localism and diversity to an extent by creating popular national programs for local stations in the early days. Just like radio, this created a two-tier television system. Stations were local and offered local programming, but the most popular programs tended to be national.

CABLE SYSTEMS

Ironically, cable TV arrived in Canada before the first Canadian television station, perhaps reflecting our desire for American programming. An experiment with redistributing U.S. antenna signals in 1952 in London, Ontario, marked the start of cable TV in Canada. Later that year, cable companies were also established in Vancouver and Montreal. Research by BBM indicates that Canadians love cable television, as 76 percent of Canadians are wired for cable. Major cable companies in Canada include Shaw, Cogeco, and Rogers.

Initially, cable companies used to tack their cables on utility poles, but **coaxial cable** was in fact better than telephone wire because it had to carry more sophisticated signals. Today, both cable and phone companies are racing to replace their wires with **fibre-optic cables** to deliver more data and better picture quality. Fibre optics can carry signals that can make on-screen delivery as sharp as a computer screen.

DIRECT-TO-HOME SYSTEMS

DTH, short for direct-to-home, could be cable's own comeuppance. DTH allows companies to transmit an array of channels directly to subscribers who have special antenna dishes—bypassing local cable companies. Early DTH experiments

DTH: Both Star Choice and Bell ExpressVu were among the first to offer HDTV and digital technology to Canadians. The first wave of digital channels in 2001 proved to be a boom for DTH providers in Canada.

had mixed results, but new DTH companies, without the expense of wiring communities, seem to have the potential to undercut cable company rates and further fragment the television market. Canada's first two DTH satellite systems are Star Choice and Bell ExpressVu. The CRTC claims that by 2004, 2.4 million Canadians will subscribe to a DTH service.

Telephone companies, meanwhile, are upgrading their lines with fibre-optic cables in both Canada and the U.S. These cables can carry a great number of high-quality signals, including video, which means that telephone companies have the potential to compete with cable companies in delivering television services. Because far more homes are wired for telephone than for cable, especially in rural areas, today's cable companies may face stiff new competition from the telephone companies.

CBC: Links to CBC programs.

www.tv.cbc.ca

CTV: Details on all CTV's shows.

www.ctv.ca

CanWest Global: Official site of Canada's third network.

www.canwestglobal.com/ links.html#tv

Over-the-Air Networks

TRADITIONAL NETWORKS

For over 40 years, national networks dominated television in the U.S. and Canada. **NBC**, **CBS**, and **ABC** were the major players in the U.S., while **CBC** and **CTV** dominated the Canadian airwaves. New national networks, like **CanWest Global** in Canada and **WB** and **UPN** in the U.S. have begun to challenge the dominance of the traditional networks.

A network affiliation is an asset to local stations. Programs offered by the networks are of a quality that an individual station cannot afford to produce. With quality network programs, stations attract larger audiences than they could on their own. Larger audiences mean that stations can charge higher rates for local advertisements in the six to eight minutes per hour that the networks leave open for affiliates to fill. Stations also profit directly from affiliations, and the networks share their advertising revenue with affiliates.

Network–affiliate relations are not entirely money-making bliss. The networks, whose advertising rates are based on the number of viewers they have, would prefer that all affiliates carry all their programs. Affiliates, however, sometimes have sufficient financial incentives to pre-empt network programming. Broadcasting a local hockey tournament can generate lots of local advertising. The networks would also prefer that affiliates confine their quest for advertising to their home areas, leaving national ads to the networks. Local stations, however, accept national advertising on their own, which they schedule inside and between programs, just as they do local advertising.

The networks have learned to pay more heed to affiliate relations in recent years. Unhappy affiliates have been known to leave one network for another. This happened in 1994 when Fox lured 12 stations away from the big three U.S. networks, eight of them from CBS alone. Networks once required affiliates to carry most network programs, which guaranteed network advertisers a large audience. Most stations, however, were not bothered by the requirement, which dated to network radio's early days, because they received a slice of the network advertising revenue.

CANADIAN NETWORKS

At Present, there are three national networks in Canada. Two of them are privately owned, while one, the CBC, is Canada's national public broadcaster.

The CBC was created by an act of Parliament back in 1936 as a radio network. CBC television began in 1952. Today, despite cutbacks in funding, the CBC has developed a loyal following for its programming on several media platforms. CBC television programming outlets include CBC television in both English and French, CBC Newsworld, and Galaxie, a pay audio service available through digital cable and DTH. Some of CBC television's best known shows include *Hockey Night in Canada*, *This Hour Has 22 Minutes*, *Made in Canada*, *Twitch City*, and the documentary *Canada: A People's History*.

While the CBC is Canada's public network, CTV was Canada's first privately owned national network. It began broadcasting in 1961 with only eight affiliates. Today, Bell GlobeMedia, a subsidiary of BCE, owns CTV. CTV stations reach over 99 percent of English Canada with their programming. In addition to being a conventional, "over-the-air" broadcaster, CTV also boasts quite a collection of specialty

CTV was Canada's first privately owned network. It began broadcasting in 1961. Today, it's part of Bell GlobeMedia.

Fifth Estate. CBC Television's *Fifth Estate* has a long-standing reputation as one of CBC's elite news programs.

channels. These include CTV-NewsNet, Talk TV, the Comedy Network, Outdoor Life Network, and TSN. In addition to airing American programming, CTV stations also promote Canadian television with shows such as *Open Mike with Mike Bullard*, *Mason Lee: On the Edge*, *The Associates*, and *Cold Squad*. The CTV network has also aired some of the most watched Canadian movies, such as *Murder Most Likely*, *Milgaard*, *Lucky Girl*, and *The Sheldon Kennedy Story*.

From humble beginnings at CKND (Winnipeg) in 1974, lawyer and journalist Izzy Asper has built a media empire in Canada. Through a series of buyouts and takeovers spanning almost 30 years, CanWest Global became Canada's third national network and second private national network in 2000. Its 11 stations in eight provinces reach over 88 percent of Canadian viewers. CanWest has interests in both conventional television and in specialty channels. Channels under the CanWest banner include Prime and ROB-TV. Some of the more notable Canadian productions aired by CanWest are *Bob and Margaret*, *Blackfly*, and *Blue Murder*.

In *Canada's Cultural Industries*, Paul Audley sums up the history of television in Canada well. He writes, "the general pattern from the beginning of television in 1952 until the present has been one of a rapidly expanding private television broadcasting system and an underfinanced public system." Given the changes of the late 20th and early 21st centuries, this still appears to be true. Writing in *Maclean's*, Peter C. Newman argues that Canadians need the CBC to become important again. Says Newman, "with our kids watching 900 hours or more of TV a year—and at least 80 percent of it spreading the gospel of the American way of life—we must maintain a vibrant indigenous alternative." Private broadcasters would disagree with Newman, claiming that the Canadian identity can be preserved by the private sector.

NBC: Access to the peacock network.

www.nbc.com

CBS: Eye on the net.

www.cbs.com

ABC: Television links.

www.abc.com

Fox: 20th Century Fox Television.

www.fox.com

WB-TV: Links to the WB.

www.thewb.com

UPN-TV: Shows, schedules, and news for UPN.

www.upn.com

PBS Online: Public TV links and previews.

www.pbs.org

Mike Bullard. America has Leno and Letterman; Canada has Mike Bullard. While other Canadian late-night talk shows have come and gone, *Open Mike with Mike Bullard* has been a ratings success. He is seen on both the Comedy Network and CTV. Both are owned by Bell Globe Media.

THE AMERICAN NETWORKS

U.S. television had four networks to begin with, but few cities had more than two stations. Because NBC and CBS both had been household words since the early days of radio, they were the first choices of local stations in lining up an affiliation. Upstart ABC, in the radio business only since 1943, survived in television through a cash infusion that accompanied a 1953 merger with **United-Paramount Theaters**. The DuMont Network, namesake of picture-tube developer Allen DuMont, folded in 1955. Meanwhile, as more cities acquired a third station, ABC grew and eventually rivalled the other networks for viewers.

With federal funding provided in 1967, the Public Broadcasting Service began providing programs to non-commercial stations. While PBS has offered some popular programs, such as *Sesame Street*, commercial stations did not see it as much of a threat. In fact, with its emphasis on informational programming such as the *MacNeil-Lehrer News Hour*, *Nova*, and quality drama and arts, PBS relieved public pressure on commercial stations for less profitable highbrow programming.

Media baron **Rupert Murdoch** launched a fourth network in 1987 after buying seven non-network stations in major cities and the Twentieth Century-Fox Film Corporation, which gave him production facilities and a huge movie library. Murdoch's new Fox network recruited affiliates among other independent stations nationwide with a late-night talk show, then Sunday night programming, and then Saturday night shows. By 1994, with a full prime-time line-up and having outbid CBS for NFL football, Fox raided eight stations from CBS.

Today, the older networks—ABC, CBS, and NBC—each have about 200 affiliates. Fox, with about 190, is catching up, but many Fox stations don't have evening newscasts to draw viewers into a whole evening of programming, which means Fox has far fewer viewers than the other networks. Also, most Fox affiliates are UHF stations, which, in general, have fewer viewers than stations in the VHF lower-end of the television spectrum. Newcomers UPN and WB are further dividing the viewership for the traditional networks.

Pat Mitchell. People came to know Pat Mitchell in the 1980s as the first producer and host of a nationally syndicated talk show, the Emmy-winning *Woman to Woman.* Later she was the CNN and Turner executive in charge of producing original nonfiction programming. In 2000 she became president of PBS. Her job: To develop programming to increase the noncommercial network's visibility. Prime-time ratings typically had been at 2.0 on a scale that had commercial network shows at 10.0 and higher.

Cable Television

ROOTS OF CABLE

Cable companies, which provide signals by coaxial or fibre-optic cable, have siphoned viewers away from the traditional over-the-air networks. Cable and over-the-air broadcasters are now rivals, but it always wasn't so.

In the early 1950s, the networks and local affiliates reached only major cities. TV signals, like FM radio, do not follow the curvature of the earth, so communities 70 or 80 kilometres away were pretty much out of range. One by one, small-town entrepreneurs, following the lead started in London, Ontario, in 1951, hoisted antennas on nearby hilltops to catch television signals from the nearest cities with over-the-air stations. These systems, called **CATV** for community antenna television, ran a cable down into town to deliver pictures to houses from the hilltop antenna. Everybody was happy; small towns got big-city television, local businesspeople made money, and the networks were able to reach audiences they would not otherwise have reached. As a result, networks were able to increase their advertising rates.

THE CABLE CHALLENGE

Today the major commercial networks, which deliver programming via over-the-air local affiliates, face a significant challenge from cable television. In 1972 the networks watched helplessly as a new company, Home Box Office (HBO), began providing movies and special sports events by **microwave relay** to local cable companies, which set up a separate channel and charged subscribers an extra fee to tune in to the programs. HBO made hardly a dent in network viewership, but in 1975 the company switched to an orbiting satellite to relay its programs, which made the service available to every cable system in the United States and 265 000 homes. HBO itself still was hardly a threat to the big three networks, but within months the owner of an independent station in Atlanta, **Ted Turner**, began beaming his signal to an orbiting satellite that retransmitted the signal to subscribing cable systems—the start of Superstation WTBS. This increasing variety of cable-delivered programming, plus the wiring of more and more communities for cable in the 1970s, began draining viewers from the traditional networks.

Canadian Cable Television Association: Information on the cable industry's suppliers and products, as well as statistics and a history of the industry.

www.ccta.ca

PAY SERVICES AND SPECIALTY CHANNELS

Meanwhile, other pay services joined HBO. These included Showtime, Cinemax, Disney, and Playboy, which further divided the television audience. In Canada, the CRTC licensed the first pay networks, SuperChannel, the Movie Network, C Channel, and Super Ecran, in 1982. In 1984, the first five Canadian specialty networks—TSN, MuchMusic, ChinaVision, Cathay, and Telelatino—began broadcasting and luring viewers away from the traditional Canadian networks with niche programming, movies, and events. Today, the television landscape in Canada is fast approaching the mythical "500 channel" universe with a wide variety of specialty channels available on both traditional and digital cable. In addition, **pay-per-view** services, offered by cable companies to subscribers, who are charged for each program they watch, are coming into their own. Viewer's Choice Canada is available in 90 percent of Canadian homes with cable and DTH. French Canada has Canal Indigo for first-run movies and sporting events.

Television Programming

PRODUCING ENTERTAINMENT PROGRAMS

The networks produce some entertainment programs themselves, but over many years, the networks relied mostly on independent companies for their shows. This is also becoming the norm in Canadian television. The independent companies create prototype episodes called **pilots** to entice the networks and channels to buy the whole series, usually a season in advance. When a network buys a series, the show's producers work closely with network programming people on details. Because networks are responsible for the programs they feed their affiliates, the networks have **standards and practices** people who review every program for content acceptability, and they may order changes to be made. Although this is gatekeeping, not true censorship, these people who control the standards and practices are sometimes called "censors."

At all three major U.S. networks, the "censorship" units have been downsized in recent years—in part because of greater audience and government acceptance of risqué language and forthright dramatizations. This does not mean there are no limits. In 1993 ABC pushed some people's tolerance with the new *NYPD Blue* program. Many advertisers were cautious at first about signing up for the program. The criticism, mostly from the religious right, led by the Reverend David Wildmon, was offset by the critical acclaim the program received. The program also drew large audiences. Many advertisers, despite the criticism, couldn't pass up *NYPD Blue* as an effective vehicle to air their messages. Undeterred, in 1994 Wildmon and his followers launched a US$3 million campaign against the program, the network, and the sponsors, but decision makers, including regulators, weren't listening. This kind of opposition is seen less often in Canada, but it may be on the rise.

Besides buying programs from independent producers, networks buy motion pictures, some that have already been on the movie-house circuit and on pay television, and others made expressly for the networks. Hollywood studios are among the largest producers of network entertainment programs.

Like the networks, single stations also buy independently produced entertainment programs. To do this, the stations go to distributors, called **syndicators**, who package programs specifically for sale to individual stations, usually for one-time use. Syndicators also sell programs that previously appeared on the networks. These off-network programs, as they are called, sometimes include old episodes of programs still playing on the networks. *Murder, She Wrote*, a successful CBS program, went off-net in 1987 to the USA cable network while new episodes were still being produced for CBS. Local stations, like the networks, also buy old movies from motion picture companies for one-time showing.

PRODUCING ADVERTISEMENTS

Many television stations have elaborate facilities that produce commercials for local advertisers. In some cities, stations provide production services free, but the general practice is to charge production fees. These fees, usually based on studio time, vary widely but can run hundreds of dollars an hour. They can be a significant revenue source for stations. Except in the smallest markets, stations do not have a monopoly on producing commercials. Independent video production houses are also available to advertisers to put together commercials, which are then provided ready-to-play to stations.

Television Regulation in Canada

THE FOWLER COMMISSION

The evolution of television in Canada paralleled the growth of radio, a system with both public and private broadcasting. Initially, private television broadcasters had to apply to the CBC for broadcast licences. Private broadcasters were not happy; they felt a conflict of interest existed. During this time, even private broadcasters had to carry 10 hours of CBC programming each week. How could the CBC, a broadcaster itself, also be responsible for overseeing private broadcasting?

In 1955 a Royal Commission into broadcasting was formed. The **Fowler Commission**, headed by Robert Fowler, analyzed Canadian broadcasting from the points of view of culture and regulations. Its report, tabled in 1957, formed the basis of the **Broadcasting Act** of 1958. Diefenbaker's Conservatives passed the act in July 1958. Among the changes to Canadian broadcasting policy were:

- The forming of the **Board of Broadcast Governors (BBG)**, which would oversee the granting of broadcasting licences.
- Official government recognition of private broadcasters in Canada. This allowed stations to affiliate themselves with a body other than the CBC. This would lead to the formation of Canada's first private television network, CTV.
- Programming that was as Canadian in "content and character" as possible. In 1959 government policy decreed that 45 percent of programming had to be Canadian in nature and that the percentage was to rise to 55 percent by 1962.

THE 1968 BROADCASTING ACT

In March of 1968, another Broadcasting Act further defined the broadcast system and the function it should serve in Canada. This act resulted in the formation of the Canadian Radio-Television Commission (CRTC). The changes to television were as follows:

- The CRTC replaced the BBG and had the power to regulate broadcasting in Canada.

- The CBC was given its mandate to provide a national broadcasting service in both official languages and to provide Canadian programming that helped develop national unity and allowed for Canadian cultural expression.
- Television broadcasters should provide 60 percent Canadian content.
- Canadian broadcasting should be owned and operated by Canadians.

THE 1991 BROADCASTING ACT

In 1975 the CRTC became the Canadian Radio-television and Telecommunications Commission when it assumed responsibility for regulating the telephone industry. In 1991 a new Broadcasting Act was issued to help further define broadcasting and cultural issues in Canada. The new act:

- Stressed the importance of programming that was Canadian in content and character. The act also admitted that it was easier to fill Canadian content quotas than to produce programs that audiences would watch.
- Redefined the CBC's role as the national broadcaster, which was to help create a "Canadian consciousness." However, no attempt to define the term "Canadian consciousness" was made; nor was the issue of funding addressed.
- Explained that cable companies should efficiently deliver Canadian services and stations at a reasonable cost.

1998 TELEVISION POLICY CHANGES

While the Broadcasting Act itself wasn't changed, the CRTC's policies on television were changed in 1998. The changes offered broadcasters some flexibility in acquiring and scheduling Canadian programs, notably:

- Canadian stations still needed to schedule 60 percent Canadian content overall, with at least 50 percent during the "peak viewing period" of 7 p.m. until 11 p.m., seven days a week.
- Included in this 50 percent of Canadian content during this time are "priority programs," such as Canadian-produced entertainment magazines, documentaries, regionally produced programs, dramas, and comedies.

These changes shift the emphasis for Canadian television stations from producing Canadian programs to scheduling them. This is closer to the American model of producing television shows. This has meant an increase in work for the Canadian independent TV production sector. Canada has many successful independent television producers, including Alliance-Atlantis, Cinar, Nelvana, S and S, and Salter Street. These companies also have an eye not only for producing television that is (as the CRTC requires) "Canadian in content and character," but is also exportable to the United States. Canadian production houses have been quite successful in producing children's programming such as *Caliou*, *Arthur*, and *The Magic School Bus*, while S and S has had success in the U.S. with *The Red Green Show*. Alliance-Atlantis produces and distributes shows such as *The Associates*, *Drop the Beat*, and *Total Recall 2070* for both the Canadian and U.S. markets.

Canadian television, although often maligned, has come into its own. Regulatory changes by the CRTC have made producing Canadian programming more reliant on the viewing habits of Canadians rather than just producing a Canadian show to fill airtime in order to fulfill **CanCon** requirements. The goal for Canadian networks, according to Michael McCabe, former president of the Canadian Association of Broadcasters, is viewing. Says McCabe, "viewing is what really counts. Not just how many hours we have or how many dollars we spend. These are just proxies for what should be the real goal—more Canadians watching, being informed by and, most importantly, enjoying Canadian television."

Evaluating Television

POPULIST MEASURES

Television and advertising executives get the ratings, called Nielsens, in the U.S. In Canada, broadcasters get ratings from ACNielsen Canada or the Bureau of Measurement Canada (BBM). These are tabulations on how many people watched network shows the night before. Although networks grumble at the ratings and attack survey methods when ratings dip, all parties have agreed to use the numbers to adjust advertising rates. Millions of dollars ride on the ratings. A network that had promised 3 million viewers to an advertiser will have to reduce its bill for the commercials if fewer people tune in. Ratings are used the same way for cable and lots of local programming. They are a reasonably reliable indicator of the popularity of programs.

QUALITY MEASURES

Some awards are measures of quality. Peabody Awards for news carry a lot of weight, as do DuPonts. The Academy of Television Arts and Sciences, sponsor of the **Emmy Awards,** offers peer review. Academy members, all television people, choose the annual winners. In Canada, the Academy of Canadian Film and Television hosts the **Gemini Awards** to shine the spotlight on the best television produced in Canada,

The West Wing. The idealistic NBC/CTV series *The West Wing,* about a hypothetical but believable White House staff in continual turmoil, won a record-setting nine Emmy awards in 2000.

MEDIA DATABANK 5.2

The Best in Canadian Television

TV Guide polls its readers every year to vote on their favourite Canadian TV shows and stars. Some recent favourites include:

- Best Dramatic TV Show: *DaVinci's Inquest* (CBC), *Cold Squad* (CTV)
- Best Comedy Series: *This Hour Has 22 Minutes* (CBC), *Royal Canadian Air Farce* (CBC), *Red Green Show* (CBC)
- Best Newsmagazine: *W-5* (CTV), *The Fifth Estate* (CBC)
- Best Kids' Show: *Sesame Park* (CBC), *Arthur* (Syndication)
- Best Animated Show: *Bob and Margaret* (Global), *It's the Mr. Hell Show* (Comedy Network)
- Best Talk Show Host: Mike Bullard, Michael Landsberg, Vicki Gabareau

Source: TV Guide, August 11, 2001.

while the Genies honour the best Canadian movies. Industry politics can be a factor, but nobody challenges the quality of works, performances, and contributions that win these awards. In one sense, these awards represent both populist and elitist values. The television and film industries, by nature, are audience-responsive. As such, the Genies, Geminis, and Emmys are a measure of commercial success. At the same time, excellence is a value in Gemini or Emmy considerations.

Television and Canadian Movies

Bohdan Szuchewycz and Jeannette Sloniowski, in *Canadian Communications: Issues in Contemporary Media and Culture*, sum up the plight of Canadian movies like this: "Canadian Movies: Not Coming to a Cinema Near You." Due to economic and distribution issues, Canadian movies make up less than 5 percent of all screen time at movie houses in Canada. Because of this, television is often the only outlet for Canadian films. Canadian channels, both conventional and specialty, are the primary outlet for Canadian movies to be seen by Canadians. As a result of exposure on television, the Canadian Film and Television Production Association announced that over 40 percent of revenue earned by Canadian movies came from pay television. This may increase in the future with the launching of digital specialty channels such as the Independent Film Channel in late 2001.

A 1998 government committee on the status of the Canadian film industry came to the conclusion that television was the best way to bring Canadian movies to Canadians. The Feature Film Advisory Committee (1999) came up with several recommendations to help produce Canadian movies:

- The CBC should budget up to $25 million to produce Canadian movies.
- The CRTC should insist that private broadcasts commit a portion of their budgets to acquiring and scheduling Canadian movies and to make sure that Canadian movies are broadcast during peak viewing periods.

- Ottawa should budget $150 million to help in the production and distribution of Canadian movies.

Canadian movies have always lived in the shadow of American fare. As a result, they have had to struggle to mature and gain acceptance in this country. In his article "American Domination of the Motion Picture Industry," **Garth Jowett** points out that Canada has always been dependent on Hollywood for movies. Jowett writes, "from the outset, Canada because of its geographic situation was considered to be merely one of the many marketing areas designated by the American film industry." Jowett also claims that most Canadians have always preferred Hollywood movies to British or Canadian films. However, this does not mean filmmaking traditions do not exist in this country.

From the earliest days of the medium, movies were shot and produced in Canada. Douglas Fetherling says that the first film shot in Canada was in Manitoba in 1897. Many other short films followed; however, the first Canadian feature film wasn't made until 1913. *Evangeline* was a five-reel film produced by the Canadian Biograph Company of Halifax. Based on a poem by Longfellow about the flight of the Acadians, it was shot on location in the Annapolis Valley. It featured an American cast and turned a profit. The Canadian Biograph Company was never able to match the success of *Evangeline*. The same was true of other early Canadian filmmakers; it's estimated that only about 70 Canadian feature films were produced before 1939, the year the National Film Board of Canada was established.

American movie mogul D.W. Griffith, whose narrative style was influential in the development of Hollywood movies, visited Toronto in 1925. During that visit, he told Canadian officials that Canada should make Hollywood-type movies to trade with the United States. Twenty years later, a British filmmaker disagreed with him and the Canadian film industry went in another direction. That man was John Grierson, and the National Film Board was born.

NATIONAL FILM BOARD

One of the most high-profile Canadian film organizations is the **National Film Board (NFB)**. Formed by an act of Parliament in 1939 to "interpret Canada to Canadians," the board's first commissioner was John Grierson, a British documentary filmmaker. Grierson advocated a strong national film industry. He wanted to make movies that celebrated Canada's geographic and social diversity. In a statement about government film policy, Grierson said that while Canada could never compete with the glamour of Hollywood, it should not abandon the idea of a national film industry. Grierson felt that making short, inexpensive films about Canadians and their experiences could complement more expensive Hollywood fare, while still giving Canadians a cinematic voice. Grierson also believed that films should tackle social issues and that filmmakers should try to produce films that make a difference.

During World War II, the NFB produced several propaganda films in support of the war effort. *The World in Action* and *Canada Carries On*, both narrated by Lorne Greene, were two popular NFB war films. A 1941 feature, *Churchill's Island*, won the first of nine Oscars for Canada's National Film Board. During the war period, the NFB didn't just make propaganda films. *Alexis Tremblay: Habitant* (1943) examined the mythical lifestyle of rural French Canadians, while *Eskimos of the Eastern Arctic* (1944) portrayed Inuit life.

Telefilm Canada: Sheila Copps's agency dedicated to developing and promoting the Canadian film, television, video, and multimedia industries.
www.telefilm.gc.ca

NFB: The National Film Board of Canada.
www.nfb.ca

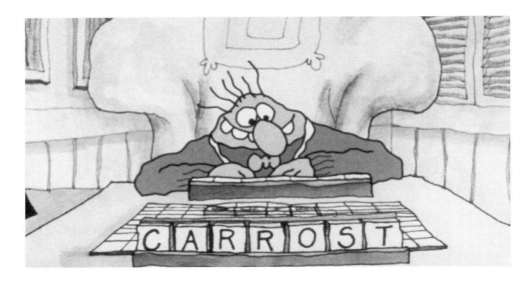

NFB Classic. Richard Condie's Genie Award-winning *The Big Snit* (1985) is just one of many NFB animated shorts to receive plaudits world-wide. The NFB continues to trailblaze in the spirit of Norman McLaren.

After the war, Grierson returned to England, but the NFB continued to make successful documentary films. During this time, it became known for a style called cinéma vérité, which roughly translated means "truth in cinema." For the NFB, cinéma vérité has meant documentaries by Canadians about Canadians.

The NFB is also known for its animation. The board's animation roots can be traced back to the arrival of Norman McLaren in 1941. Although he made 59 films for the NFB, including the propaganda movies *V for Victory* (1941) and *Keep Your Mouth Shut* (1944), animation was McLaren's first love. While his films have won more than 200 international awards, his best-known work is the 1953 Oscar-winning short *Neighbours*. The eight-minute antiwar film is about two neighbours fighting over a flower. The dispute escalates into tribal warfare. The film used live actors, but they were animated with the same techniques used to animate puppets and drawings.

In 1950 Parliament passed the National Film Act, which changed the NFB's mandate to include producing, promoting, and distributing films in the national interest. In the NFB's early days, it would send projectionists from city to city and town to town to show its latest offerings in arenas, community centres, and even fields. These films were also shown in movie houses and eventually on television. NFB films were (and still are) distributed by public libraries, schools, universities, and colleges.

The 1980 NFB classic *The Sweater*, based on a story by Roch Carrier about a French Canadian boy who orders a Montreal Canadiens jersey but receives a Toronto Maple Leafs jersey by mistake from "Monsieur Eaton," was re-released in 1998. It was shown in Famous Players theatres as the short prior to the Hollywood science-fiction movie *Deep Impact*.

Some classic NFB films include *A Place Called Chiapas* (1998), *The Champagne Safari* (1996), *Bob's Birthday* (1995), *Manufacturing Consent* (1992), and the controversial *The Boys of St. Vincent* (1992).

The future of the NFB is cloudy. Some argue that its funding should be increased, while others say that government money would be better spent on producing more feature films. Today, the NFB enjoys regular showings on television on several specialty channels, both digital and analogue.

FEATURE FILMS IN CANADA

Despite its success in the documentary and animated areas, Canada, with the exception of Quebec, has left the bulk of dramas and literary adaptations to the Americans. The feature film industry in Canada remained largely dormant until the 1960s. In 1964 two films marked the unofficial start of the feature film industry in Canada. They were Don Owen's *Nobody Waved Goodbye* and Gilles Groulx's *Le Chat dans le sac*. Both of these films were NFB productions, but they were feature films shot in the documentary tradition and featured regional themes without the glamour of Hollywood movies. The better-known Canadian films from this era include *Goin' Down the Road* (1970), *Mon Oncle Antoine* (1971), *Paperback Hero* (1973), *Between Friends* (1973), and the classic *The Apprenticeship of Duddy Kravitz* (1974).

By the late 1970s, government incentives and tax breaks for producers investing in Canadian feature films created a glut of product—some good, some bad. Films like *Why Shoot the Teacher?* (1978), *Outrageous* (1979), *Atlantic City* (1980), *Scanners* (1981), and the largest-grossing Canadian movie of all time, *Porky's* (1982), were all produced during this time.

Today, both federal and provincial governments in Canada help fund the production of Canadian movies. This funding covers the NFB and feature films. However, in the last 10 years, the federal government has made it clear that filmmakers in this country can't rely on federal funding through Telefilm Canada alone to make movies. Movies in Canada today are not only financed with federal money, but with provincial and private money. Most Canadian media powerhouses offer funding for the production of Canadian movies. For example, the Rogers Telefund and TMN both offer filmmakers financing for their projects.

MEDIA DATABANK 5.3

The Best of Canadian Films

The United States has the Oscars; Canada has the Genie Awards, which are awarded annually to the best in Canadian movies by the Academy of Canadian Cinema and Television. Here's a list of recent Genie award winners for best picture in Canada:

1990:	*Jesus of Montreal*
1991:	*Black Robe*
1992:	*Naked Lunch*
1993:	*Thirty-Two Short Films About Glenn Gould*
1994:	*Exotica*
1995:	*Le Confessional*
1996:	*Lilies*
1997:	*The Sweet Hereafter*
1998:	*The Red Violin*
1999:	*Sunshine*
2000:	*Maelström*
2001:	*Atanarjuat*

The Sweet Hereafter.
Canadian directors, such as Atom Egoyan, have achieved critical success both here and abroad.

Canadian Films—What are we to make of them?
An interesting critique of current Canadian film-making.

www.arts.uwaterloo.ca/ FINE/juhde/gp-ca981.htm

AMERICAN VS. CANADIAN MOVIES: WHAT'S THE DIFFERENCE?

Why are Canadian movies different from American movies? Notice that the question doesn't imply that Canadian movies are "worse" than American movies, although that seems to be the mythology. For students of communication and decoders of texts, the questions really should be: "What makes Canadian movies different from American films?" and "What do our films say about our culture?"

While certainly funding, marketplace economics, and distribution have all played a role in the development of the Canadian film industry and the "look" of Canadian films, there may be other differences as well. **Peter Harcourt**, in his essay "Introduction" (1976), argues that Canadian movie scripts symbolically reflect "our own social uncertainties—both our uncertainty of action as a nation and our own present lack of security in dealing with ethnic and cultural problems which, throughout our vast nation, we are trying to define ourselves."

This uncertainty is clearly evident in the films of one of Canada's best-known filmmakers, Atom Egoyan. Harcourt, in the film journal *Film Quarterly*, described Egoyan's work as "expressing the classic Canadian dilemma as formulated by Northrop Frye... Egoyan devises films that register the personal uncertainties of people who are striving to find a place of rest within a culture not their own." David Cronenberg's films also feature these themes, which don't always feature the happy endings of Hollywood cinema. According to Cronenberg, both he and Egoyan "have a horror of the cheap emotional affect of Hollywood movies." Canadian-born director James Cameron, who not only directed *Titanic*, but *True Lies*, *The Abyss*, and *Terminator*, doesn't share this allergy to making American-style movies. He's one Canadian who happens to do it rather well. However, it might be argued that even in Cameron's Hollywood blockbusters, there is a certain element of uncertainty.

Uncertainty is part of the Canadian way of life; the uncertainties of the French–English debate and the uneasiness of living next door to the United States have all helped shape Canadian culture. Do you see this theme as part of the content of Canadian films? Do an analysis of any Canadian film you have seen. Is this theme present? How is it signified? Here's a list of Canadian films (French and English) that will help get you started:

James Cameron. Canadian James Cameron won an Academy Award for directing the 1997 blockbuster *Titanic*. An Oscar is recognized as a mark of accomplishment because it is the film industry itself, the Academy of Motion Picture Arts and Sciences, that selects the winners.

- *Nobody Waved Goodbye* (1964)
- *Goin' Down the Road* (1970)
- *Mon Oncle Antoine* (1971)
- *Paperback Hero* (1973)
- *The Apprenticeship of Duddy Kravitz* (1974)
- *Decline of the American Empire* (1987)
- *Exotica* (1994)
- *Whale Music* (1994)
- *The Sweet Hereafter* (1997)
- *The Hanging Garden* (1997)
- *Crash* (1997)
- *August 32nd on Earth* (1998)
- *The Red Violin* (1998)
- *Sunshine* (1999)
- *The Art of War* (2000)
- *Maelström* (2000)
- *Atanarjuat* (2001)

media future

television

The pell-mell impact of the web on older mass media portends special importance for television. These two media share many qualities. Both television and web messages are visual, in motion, auditory, and live. Not to be overlooked, however, is that both are received by appliances that are widely available. Television sets are in 98 percent of homes, and web-linked computers are in a majority and the number is growing. Television and the web are well into the process of melding into a single medium.

Common delivery appliances, like WebTV and TiVo, have a foothold already. Cross-platform content is also here with streaming. Major media companies have simultaneous delivery. Will the web subsume television? Or will television subsume the web? It won't be a question of one disappearing into the other as much as an integration that wipes out the distinctions we see today between these media. Will Canadian broadcasters become cablecasters or webcasters?

CHAPTER WRAP-UP

Television initially patterned itself after radio. Companies that were heavily involved in radio were also the television heavyweights. Even television's programming mimicked radio's. The networks were the most powerful shapers of television, leading in entertainment programming and news. Gerald Levin and then Ted Turner led a restructuring when they realized that they could deliver programs to local cable companies via orbiting satellites. Convergence is also a key factor, as once large broadcast companies, including CTV and CanWest Global, are becoming multi-platform media corporations.

QUESTIONS FOR REVIEW

1. How does television influence people and society in the short term and the long term?
2. Describe the development of television technology.
3. How much of an impact does American television have on Canadian culture?
4. How has television expanded beyond over-the-air delivery?
5. Describe the development of Canadian television.
6. What are Steve Smith's views on Canadian television content?
7. What are some of the changes convergence is bringing to television?
8. What role does the CRTC play in Canadian television?
9. What is the role of the NFB?

QUESTIONS FOR CRITICAL THINKING

1. How did Philo Farnsworth's image dissector employ electronics to pick up moving images and relay them to faraway screens?
2. How has digital technology changed television?
3. Outline the development of television networks in both the U.S. and Canada.
4. Should there be Canadian content regulations for Canadian television? For Canadian movie houses?
5. What is meant by the NFB's mandate to "explain Canada to Canadians"?
6. What makes Canadian television different from American television? What about Canadian movies versus American movies?
7. What have the most significant changes been in Canadian television over the last five years?

FOR KEEPING UP TO DATE

Playback, Broadcaster, and *Broadcast Dialogue* are broadcasting trade journals. *Television/Radio Age* is another trade journal.

Journal of Broadcasting and Electronic Media and the *Canadian Journal of Communication* are quarterly scholarly journals published by the Broadcast Education Association.

Consumer magazines that deal extensively with television programming include *Entertainment* and *TV Guide.*

Newsmagazines that report on television issues more or less regularly include *Newsweek, Maclean's,* and *Time.*

Business Week, Forbes, and *Fortune* track television as a business.

Major newspapers with strong television coverage include the *Los Angeles Times,* the *New York Times,* the *National Post,* the *Toronto Star,* the *Globe and Mail,* and the *Wall Street Journal.*

FOR FURTHER LEARNING

2001 Annual Report, CanWest Global Communications.

2001 Annual Report, CBC.

2001 Annual Report, CTV.

Erik Barnouw. *Tube of Plenty: The Evolution of American Television* (Oxford, 1975).

John Bugailiskis. "TV Finally Gets Interactive." *Broadcaster* April 2000).

Warren Bennis and Ian Mitroff. *The Unreality Industry* (Carol Publishing, 1989).

Roger Bird. *Documents in Canadian Broadcasting* (Carleton University Press, 1988).

Bray, Jim. "New Television a Bright Clear Idea" (www.technofile.com/articles/canadian_hdtv.html).

Robert Brehl. "Specialty Channels Change TV Patterns," *Globe and Mail* (March 21, 1998).

David Clandfield. *Canadian Film* (Oxford University Press, 1987).

Mark Christensen and Cameron Stauth. *The Sweeps* (Morrow, 1984).

CRTC. Broadcasting Policy Monitoring Report, 2001.

CRTC. "The New Policy on Canadian Television: More Flexibility, Diversity and Programming Choice."

Harvey Enchin. "Film Industry Has Its Critics." *Globe and Mail* (September 8, 1997).

Douglas Fetherling. *Documents in Canadian Film* (Broadview Press, 1988).

Seth Feldman and Joyce Nelson. *Canadian Film Reader* (Peter Martin and Associates, 1977).

Graham Fraser and Doug Saunders. "New Policy Aims to Raise Profile of Film Industry." *Globe and Mail* (February 4, 1998).

Louis Giannetti and Jim Leach. *Understanding Movies: Canadian Edition* (Prentice-Hall/Allyn and Bacon, 1998).

Hyatt, Laurel. "Canadian Content Key to New Television Policy." *Broadcaster* (July 1999).

Garth Jowett and James M. Linton. *Movies as Mass Communication* (Sage, 1980).

Ed Joyce. *Prime Times, Bad Times* (Doubleday, 1988).

Danylo Hawaleshka, "Converging on Your Living Room." *Maclean's* (August 6, 2001).

Helen Holmes and David Tara. *Seeing Ourselves: Media Power and Policy in Canada*.

Daphne Lavers. "PTV: The Next Greatest Thing." *Broadcast Dialogue* (August 2001).

Mary Lu Carnevale. "Untangling the Debate over Cable Television." *Wall Street Journal* (March 19, 1990): 107, B1, B5, B6.

Gayle Macdonald. "The Vast Picture Show." *Globe and Mail* (January 17, 1998).

McGrath, John. "The Smart Road to HDTV in Canada" *Broadcaster Magazine* (July 2000).

Joshua Meyrowitz. *No Sense of Place: The Impact of the Electronic Media on Social Behavior* (Oxford, 1985).

Minister of Public Works and Government Services Canada. *A Review of Canadian Feature Film Policy—Discussion Paper* (February 1998).

Peter C. Newman. "Save the Country by Salvaging the CBC." *Maclean's* (February 19, 1996).

Patricia Pearson. "The Sweet Here and Now." *Saturday Night* (April 1998).

Lucas A. Powe, Jr. *American Broadcasting and the First Amendment* (University of California Press, 1987).

John P. Robinson and Mark R. Levy. *The Main Source* (Sage, 1986).

Ted Rogers. "Interactive TV Means the Best Is Yet to Come." *Broadcast Dialogue* (November 1999).

Doug Saunders. "We Want Flubber?" *Globe and Mail* (February 14, 1998).

Bohdan Szuchewycz and Jeannette Sloniowski. *Canadian Communications: Issues In Contemporary Media and Culture* (Prentice Hall, 2001).

Mary Vipond. *The Mass Media in Canada* (James Lorimer and Company, 1992).

Peter Waal. "The Making of James Cameron." *Saturday Night*, (March 1998).

Jennifer Wells. "Izzy's Dream." *Maclean's* (February 19, 1996).

Hank Whittemore. *CNN: The Inside Story* (Little, Brown, 1990).

Chapter 6

Pull or Push? The impact of the Internet cannot be overstated, but is it a mass medium? Most theorists and the CRTC claim it is not broadcasting, but it is a mass medium that has had an incredible impact on the traditional mass media.

The Web

MEDIA TIMELINE

Internet and Web

1945	Vannevar Bush proposes a memex machine for associative links among all human knowledge.
1947	AT&T develops the transistor.
1962	Ted Nelson introduces the term *hypertext*.
1969	U.S. Defense Department creates the ARPAnet network linking military contractors and researchers.
1973	Mead Data Central opens Lexis, the first online full-text database.
1978	Mead Data Central goes online with Nexis, the first online database with national news publications.
1979	CompuServe begins service to consumers.
1989	Tim Berners-Lee devises coding that makes the World Wide Web possible.
1993	Marc Andreessen creates the Mosaic browser, followed by Netscape.
1999	CRTC decides "not to regulate the Internet at this time."
2000	U.S. federal judge finds Microsoft monopolistic, and orders its break-up.

MEDIA IN THEORY

Pull–Push Model

The communication revolution requires a new model to understand new ways that the media are working. One new model classifies some media as passive. These are pull media, which you steer. Examples are the traditional media, like radio and television, over which you have control to pull in a message. You can turn them on or off. You can pick up a book and put it down. You can go to a movie or not.

Push media, on the other hand, propel messages at you whether invited to or not. A simple, low-tech example is a recorded voice in a grocery store aisle that encourages you to buy a certain brand of corn flakes as you pass by the cereal display. Push media are taking sophisticated forms with the World Wide Web and new technologies that are making the media more pervasive than ever. They're always on.

Some push media you can program include:

- A belt-loop beeper that updates the score on a hockey game you can't watch while you're doing something else.
- News and travel updates from Egypt you ask for after booking airline tickets for a vacation to the Pyramids.

Other push media intrude gently or in-your-face without you doing any programming:

- A heads-up automobile windshield display that flashes directions to nearby repair shops when sensors detect your engine is overheating.

- Banners across your computer screen that advertise products that your past online purchases indicate you're likely to want.
- Wall screens that push items at you based on assumptions about your interests—like music video samplers for a performing star who is popular on a radio station you listen to.

The editors of *Wired* magazine, describing push media, give this example:

> You are in your study, answering e-mail from the office when you notice something happening on the walls. Ordinarily, the large expanse in front of you features a montage generated by Sci-Viz—a global news feed of scientific discoveries, plus classic movie scenes and 30-second comedy routines. You picked this service because it doesn't show you the usual disaster crap, yet the content is very lively, a sort of huge screen saver. Which you usually ignore. But just now you notice a scene from your hometown, something about an archeological find. You ask for the full video. This is always-on, mildly in-you-face networked media.

No model is perfect, which means push media and pull media are extremes that rarely exist in reality. Most media messages are push-pull hybrids. The "media wall" in the *Wired* magazine example intrudes without a specific invitation, but it also leaves it to you to choose what to pull in when you want more detail. Most emerging new media have such hybrid capabilities.

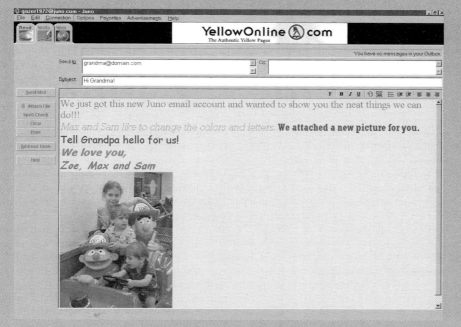

By Invitation, Sort of. Juno offers free Internet connections to anyone who is willing to have advertisements superimposed on their screen. "The price is right," said one wag. These commercial messages, which can be tailored to your buying habits and interests, are an example of push media. They're in your face. Although you've accepted Juno's terms, they aren't really invited. They're being pushed at you.

CERN: Tim Berners-Lee quietly created the World Wide Web while working at this European particle physics lab.

www.cern.ch

24 Hours in Cyberspace: Chronicling a day in the life of the web.

www.cyber24.com

The World Wide Web Consortium: Based out of MIT, this organization develops and promotes common protocols to ensure the interoperability of the World Wide Web.

www.w3.org

The World Wide Web

A NEW MASS MEDIUM

Single-handedly, **Tim Berners-Lee** invented the **World Wide Web.** Then, unlike many entrepreneurs who have used the web to amass quick fortunes, Berners-Lee devoted his life to refining the web as a medium of communication open to everyone for free.

Berners-Lee, an Oxford engineer, came up with the web concept because he couldn't keep track of all his notes on various computers in various places. It was 1989. Working at **CERN,** a physics lab in the Swiss Alps, he proposed a system to facilitate scientific research by letting scientists' computers tap into each other. In a way, the software worked like the brain. In fact, Berners-Lee said that the idea was to keep "track of all the random associations one comes across in real life and brains are supposed to be so good at remembering, but sometimes mine wouldn't."

Working with three software engineers, Berners-Lee had a demonstration up and running within three months. As Berners-Lee travelled the globe to introduce the web at scientific conferences, the potential of what he had devised became clear. The web was a system that could connect all information with all other information.

The key was a relatively simple computer language known as **HTML,** short for **hypertext markup language,** which, although it has evolved over the years, remains the core of the web. Berners-Lee also developed the addressing system that allows computers to find each other. Every web-connected computer has a unique address, a **universal resource locator** (URL). For it all to work, Berners-Lee also created a protocol that actually links computers: **HTTP,** short for **hypertext transfer protocol.**

As you would expect, Berners-Lee had offers galore from investors and computer companies to build new ways to derive profits from the web. He said no. Instead, he has chosen the academic life. At the Massachusetts Institute of Technology he works out of spartan facilities as head of the **W3 consortium,** which sets the protocol and coding standards that are helping the World Wide Web realize its potential.

It's hard to overrate Berners-Lee's accomplishment. The web is the information infrastructure that likely will, given time, eclipse other media. Some liken Berners-Lee to Johannes Gutenberg, who centuries earlier had launched the age of mass communication with the movable type that made mass production of the written word possible.

Original Webmaster. Tim Berners-Lee and his associates at a Swiss research facility created new Internet coding in 1989, dubbing it the World Wide Web. Today the coding is the heart of global computer communication.

IMPACT OF THE WORLD WIDE WEB

From a dizzying array of new technologies, the World Wide Web emerged in the mid-1990s as a powerful new mass medium. But what is the web? It is where ordinary people can go on their computer screens and, with a few clicks of a mouse button, can find a vast array of information and entertainment that originates all over the world. Make no mistake, though: The web is not just singular on-screen pages. The genius of the web is that on-screen pages are linked to others. It is the people browsing the web, not editors and programmers, who choose which on-screen pages to go to, and which to pass by, and in what sequence. It's an almost seamless journey from an ad for a new movie, to a biography on the movie's leading lady in the canoe.ca/jam archives, to books about the actress at chapters.indigo.ca. In short, the web is an interface for computers that allows people anywhere to connect to any information anywhere else on the system.

How significant is the web as a mass medium? Here are some more facts and figures from Statistics Canada's *Household Internet Use Survey*, released in 2001:

- 51 percent of Canadians consider themselves regular Internet users, with using e-mail the most cited reason for going online.
- Alberta had the highest percentage of Internet penetration; Quebec the lowest.
- 6.9 million Canadian households have Internet access; 61 percent of those homes had users who spent over 20 hours online per week
- Canadians with higher incomes and education were more likely to be frequent Internet users.
- 91 percent of Canadians use e-mail on a regular basis.

Source: Adapted from Statistics Canada's Internet Site, www.statcan.ca/Daily/English/ 010726/d010726a.htm, July 26, 2001.

THE WEB IN CONTEXT

The terms *web* and *Internet* are often tossed around loosely, leading to lots of confusion. The fundamental network that carries messages is the Internet. It dates to a military communication system created in 1969. The early Internet carried mostly text.

The web is a structure of codes that permits the exchange not only of text but also of graphics, video, and audio. Web codes are elegantly simple for users who don't even need to know them to tap into the web's content. The underlying web codes are accepted universally, which makes it possible for anyone with a computer, a modem, and a web connection to tap into anything introduced from anywhere on the globe. The term *web* comes from the spidery links among millions of computers that tap into the system—a maze that not even a spider could visualize and that becomes more complex all the time.

For most practical purposes, it is the web that's a mass medium, with messages posted for mass audiences. Other messages on the web, mostly e-mail, are more point-to-point communication than mass communication.

The prefix **cyber-** is affixed almost casually to anything involving communication via computer. *Cyberspace* is the intangible place where the communication occurs. *Cyberporn* is sexual naughtiness delivered on-screen. A *cyberpunk* is a kid obsessed with computer protocols and coding. The term *cyberspace* was introduced by science-fiction novelist and Vancouverite **William Gibson** in his book *Neuromancer*. At that point, in 1984, he saw a kind of integration of computers and

William Gibson aleph: The essential information collection about the author William Gibson.

www.8op.com/gibson

human beings. Paraphrasing a bit, here is Gibson's definition of *cyberspace*: "A consensual hallucination experienced daily by billions of people in every nation. A graphic representation of data abstracted from the banks of every computer in the human system. Unthinkable complexity. Lines of light ranged in the nonspace of the mind. Clusters and constellations of data."

BANDWIDTH LIMITATIONS

The first newspaper and magazine forays onto the web were mostly text. Gradually, simple graphics and small photos joined the mix. Why not full-blown graphics, intense in colour and detail? In a word: **bandwidth.** Bandwidth is the capacity available on a cable for transmission. There's only so much room. It's the same issue that prevents an unlimited number of television stations from being on the air—not enough channel room. On the Internet, text and simple graphics take up relatively little bandwidth. Fancy graphics take more, which means that they require more time to transmit. Super-detailed photos can take as long as several minutes.

Music and video require lots of bandwidth, which raises the question: Will there ever be enough Internet space for real-time radio and television? How about full-length movies? With improvements in transmission technology, they're coming.

FIBRE-OPTIC CABLE.   In the 1990s telephone and cable companies began replacing their cables with high-capacity lines made of **fibre-optic cable.** With fibre-optic cable, messages now are sent as pulses of light—theoretically at 300 000 kilometres an hour—rather than as much slower electrical pulses. The increases in capacity have been dramatic.

MULTIPLEXING.   With **multiplexing** technology a message is broken into bits for transmission through whatever cable pipelines have room at the moment. Then the bits are reassembled at the delivery point. So instead of a message getting clogged in a pipeline that's already crammed, the messages move in small bits called packets, each packet going through whatever pipeline has room. The message ends up at its destination faster.

CNET's Bandwidth Meter: A quick online test that measures the speed of your Internet connection.

webservices.cnet.com/ bandwith

Improving Download Time. The more complex a graphical web message, the longer the downloading takes. Video takes forever, it seems, as you wait. Download times will improve as people acquire faster modems for their computers and as more capacity is built into the Internet, but real-time live video is a long way off. An interim solution is streaming, which downloads into your computer while you're doing other things. You can begin watching while the download is still in progress.

	Today's Modem 56 kilobits per second	Future Modem, Upgraded Bandwith 4 megabits per second
Simple image 2 megabits	35.7 seconds	0.5 seconds
Short animation 72 megabits	21.5 minutes	18 seconds
Long animation 4.3 gigabits	21.4 hours	18 minutes

COMPRESSION. **Compression** technology has been devised that screens out nonessential parts of messages so that they need less bandwidth. This is especially important for graphics, video, and audio, which are incredibly code-heavy. Coding for a blue sky in a photo, for example, need not be repeated for every dot of colour. Even without redundant coding, the sky still appears blue. Audio too is loaded with redundant coding.

STREAMING. When a message is massive with coding, such as audio and video, the message can be segmented with the segments stored in a receiving computer's hard drive for replay even before all segments of the message have been received. This is called **streaming.** Most audio and video today is transmitted this way, which means some downloading delay—often only seconds. The more complex the coding is, the longer it takes.

The Internet

THE INFORMATION HIGHWAY

The Internet had its origins in a 1969 U.S. Defense Department computer network called **ARPAnet,** for Advanced Research Project Agency. The Pentagon built the network for military contractors and universities doing military research to exchange information. In 1983, the **National Science Foundation,** whose mandate is to promote science, took over part of the network to give researchers access to four costly supercomputers at Cornell, Illinois, Pittsburgh, and San Diego. The new civilian network was an expensive undertaking, but the ARPAnet infrastructure was already in place. Also, the expense of the new component was far less than installing dozens of additional $10 million supercomputers that would have duplicated those at the original four core computer sites.

This new National Science Foundation network attracted more and more institutional users, many of which had their own internal networks. For example, most schools and organizations contribute to CA*Net, which is the backbone for educational Internet use in Canada. As a backbone system that interconnects networks, **internet** was the name that fit. The expense of operating the Internet is borne by the institutions and organizations that tie their computers into it.

Commerce and the Web

WEB COMMERCE

Today, the Internet has become a household word in Canada; hardly any major retailer is without a web presence. Web commerce, or "e-commerce," accounted for roughly $417 million worth of online business by Canadians in 1999, according to Statistics Canada. Global Internet commerce for Canadian businesses is expected to reach over $90 billion by 2003.

POINT OF PURCHASE. Web retailers display their wares on-screen, take orders, and ship the products. The old **point-of-purchase** concept, catching consumers at the store with displays and posters, has taken on a whole new meaning. In the cyberworld the point of purchase is not the merchant's shop alone but the consumer's computer screen.

Industry Canada's Office of Consumer Affairs: Provides information and education for the consumer engaging in e-commerce.

strategis.ic.gc.ca/ sc_consu/consuaffairs/ engdoc/oca.html

BUSINESS TO BUSINESS. Another form of web commerce goes by the buzzword B2B, short for business-to-business commerce. Businesses that service other businesses have taken to the web to supplement their traditional means of reaching their customers.

ADVERTISING FORMS. The web also carries advertising. At many websites the advertising is like a traditional ad that promotes a product or service and steers potential customers either to more information or to a place to make a purchase. These ads are akin to those in magazines, newspapers, radio, and television. At these dot-coms, the noncommercial content is the attraction. You won't find Torstar's waymoresports.com touting that it has great ads. Rather, the dominant consumer product is sports news. Just as in the print editions of the *Toronto Star,* the site sells advertisers on the access it provides them to an audience attracted by the content.

Channel 4000: WCCO TV's commercially successfully Internet site.

www.channel4000.com

WEB ADVERTISING

Many retailing dot-coms were profitable early on, but the going was slow for media companies that looked to advertising to pay the freight for expensive content such as news. Not until 1997 was any profit reported from a website that was intending to be advertising supported. The first was the Channel 4000 site, operated by the Minneapolis television station WCCO.

The lure of advertising revenue was at the heart of many business plans for news sites in the late 1990s. Venture capitalists poured billions of dollars into these sites. Building these sites into revenue producers took longer than expected. At some sites, investors pulled the plug. Others quietly went out of business. The 2000 shakeout may hasten the day when websites become proven advertising-supported media units. No one doubts the potential of this medium, especially in Canada. In fact, on a per-capita basis, Canada has a highest penetration of Internet use out of any country in the world—including the U.S.—according to the Internet Advertising Bureau of Canada.

With such encouraging numbers, why weren't websites rolling in advertising dough? Despite the 2000 shakeout, there remained too many sites chasing too few advertising dollars. In time, demand was sure to catch up with supply, but the problem was here and now. A more serious problem was that web advertisers were never quite sure what they were buying. Measuring and categorizing the web audience were not easy.

THE WEB'S ADVERTISING REACH

Despite upbeat data from Statistics Canada and the Internet Advertising Bureau about Canadians who use the web, there remains a hitch in developing the web as a major advertising medium. Nobody has devised tools to measure traffic at a web site in meaningful ways. Such data are needed to establish advertising rates that will give advertisers confidence that they're spending their money wisely. For traditional media, advertisers look to standard measures like **cost per thousand** (CPM) to calculate the cost effectiveness of ads in competing media. Across-the-board comparisons aren't possible with the web, however—at least not yet.

The most-cited measure of web audiences is the **hit.** Every time someone browsing the web clicks an on-screen icon or on-screen highlighted section, the computer server that offers the web page records a hit. Some companies that operate web sites tout hits as a measure of audience, but savvy advertisers know hits are a misleading indicator of audience size. The online edition of *Wired* magazine, *HotWired*, for example, records an average 100 hits from everybody who taps in. *HotWired*'s 600 000 hits on a heavy day come from a mere 6000 people.

Another measure of web usage is the **visit,** a count of the people who visit a site. But visits are also misleading. At *Playboy* magazine's website, 200 000 visits are scored on a typical day, but that doesn't mean that *Playboy* cyber-ads are seen by 200 000 different people. Many of the same people visit again and again on a given day.

Some electronic publications charge advertisers by the day, others by the month, others by the hit. But because of the vagaries of audience measurements, there is no standard pricing. Knowing that the web cannot mature as an advertising medium until advertisers can be given better audience data, electronic publications have asked several companies, including Nielsen Canada and BBM, to devise tracking mechanisms. But no one expects data as accurate as press runs and broadcast ratings any time soon.

Evaluating the Web

ACCURACY ON THE WEB

The web has been called a democratized mass medium because so many people create web content. Almost anybody can put up a site. A downside of so much input from so many people is that the traditional media gatekeepers aren't necessarily present to ensure accuracy. To be sure, there are many reliable sites with traditional gatekeeping, but the web is also littered with junk.

Of course, unreliable information isn't exclusive to the web. But among older media, economic survival depends on finding and keeping an audience. Unreliable newspapers, for example, eventually lose the confidence of readers. People stop buying them, and they go out of business. The web has no such intrinsic economic imperative. A site can be put up and maintained with hardly any capital—in contrast to a newspaper, which requires tons of newsprint and barrels of ink, not to mention expensive presses, to keep coming out. Bad websites can last forever.

To guard against bad information, web users should pay special heed to the old admonition: Consider the source. Is the organization or person behind a site reliable? If you have confidence in the *National Post* as a newspaper, you can have the same confidence in its website. Another news site, no matter how glitzy and slick, may be nothing more than a lunatic working alone in a dank basement somewhere recasting the news with a perverse twist and whole-cloth fiction.

In research reports, footnotes or endnotes need to be specific on web sources, including URL addresses. This allows people who read a report to go to the web source to make their own assessment—just as traditional footnotes allow a reader to go to the library and check a source.

Even with notations, a report that cites web sources can be problematic. Unlike a book, which is permanent once it's in print, web content can be in continuing flux. What's there today can be changed in a minute—or disappear entirely. To address this problem at least in part, notation systems specify that the date and time of the researcher's web visit be included.

In serious research, you can check whether an online journal is refereed. A mission statement will be on the site with a list of editors and their credentials and a statement on the journal's editorial process. Look to see whether articles are screened through a **peer review** process.

Lycos: Web scanning and links to topic areas.

www.lycos.ca

World Wide News Sources on the Internet: An alphabetical listing by country of major news services.

www.discover.co.uk/NET/ NEWS/news.html

AltaVista: This fast, powerful search engine scans every word in thousands of sites to match the key words you gave it to get started. AltaVista is good if you need to search for very specific information.

www.altavista.ca

Excite: The web and Usenet plus links to reference freeware, dictionaries, and encyclopedias.

www.excite.ca

The Webby Awards:
Recognizing excellence
on the web.

www.webbyawards.com

Yahoo: How do you find
good stuff on the Inter-
net? Search engines like
Yahoo, one of the first
search engines, ask you
to type in key words about
what you're looking for,
then give you a directory
of likely sites.

www.yahoo.ca

STRENGTHS OF SITES

Several organizations issue awards to excellent websites. The most prestigious are the **Webby** awards, a term contrived from the nickname for the somewhat parallel Emmy awards of television. Many web awards, though, are for design and graphics, not content, although there are many measures of a site's excellence.

CONTENT. The heart of all mass media messages is the value of the content. For this, traditional measures of excellence in communication apply—such as accuracy, clarity, and cohesion.

NAVIGABILITY. Does the site have internal links so you can move easily from page to page and among various points on the site? Among the mass media, navigability is a quality unique to the web.

EXTERNAL LINKS. Does the site connect to related sites on the web? The most distinctive feature of the web as a mass medium is interconnectivity with other sites on the global network. Good sites exploit this advantage.

INTUITIVE TO USE. The best sites have navigational aids for moving around a site seamlessly and efficiently. These include road signs of many sorts, including clearly labelled links.

Media People

Microsoft Chief

Bill Gates

Bill Gates was well into his courses at Harvard when his high school buddy Paul Allen drove across the country from Seattle to convince him to drop out. Gates did. The pair went to Albuquerque and set up shop to do computer stuff. Their company, Microsoft, today is the world's largest software producer, and it is moving rapidly into creating a dominant web presence. It also is becoming a major creator of media content. With the company's success, Gates became the world's richest person. By 2001, he was worth US$80 billion. At one point, his assets were growing at US$30 million a day.

In Albuquerque in 1976, Gates acquired the code that became the Microsoft Disk Operating System, usually abbreviated as MS-DOS and pronounced *m-s-doss*. Allen and Gates persuaded computer hardware manufacturers to bundle MS-DOS with their units, which

pre-empted competitors. The bundling also gave Microsoft a growing and gigantic market for software application programs that operated only on MS-DOS. The company's word-processing program, Microsoft Word, for example, dominates globally. So do various Microsoft Windows operating systems that have updated MS-DOS.

With their initial success, Gates and Allen moved the company to their hometown, Seattle, where it remains. Allen bowed out after a debilitating disease was diagnosed (falsely, it turned out). Allen's departure left Gates in charge. Today, the company operates out of a 35-building campus in suburban Redmond.

Critics say that Microsoft products are neither the best nor the most innovative. These critics attribute the company's success to cutthroat competitive practices and marketing muscle, rather than product excellence. Detractors have built websites that revile Gates as an unconscionable monopolist. Gates, who subscribes to Darwin's "survival of the fittest" theory, tried to explain away the criticism as envy.

But in 2000 a federal judge sided with the U.S. antitrust prosecutors and ordered that Microsoft be broken up. Gates vowed to challenge the decision.

LOADING TIMES. Well-designed sites take advantage of the web as a visual medium with images. At the same time, pages should load quickly so users don't have to wait and wait and wait for a page to write itself onto their screens. This means the site needs a balance. Overdoing images, which require lots of bandwidth, works against rapid downloads. Absence of images makes for dull pages.

Web Technology

TRANSISTORS

Three researchers at AT&T's **Bell Labs** developed the **semiconductor** switch in 1947. **Walter Brattain, John Bardeen,** and **William Shockley,** who would receive the 1956 Nobel Prize, took pieces of glasslike silicon (just sand, really) and devised a way to make them respond to a negative or positive electrical charge. These tiny units, first called **transistors,** now more commonly called semiconductors or chips, functioned very rapidly as on-off switches. The on-off technology, in which data are converted to on-off codes, is called **digitization** because data are reduced to a series of digits, 1 for on, 0 for off.

DIGITIZATION. As might be expected, Bell researchers tried applying digitization to telephone communication. Soon they found ways to convert the human voice to a series of coded pulses for transmission on telephone lines to a receiver that would change them into a simulation of the voice. These pulses were digital on-off signals that were recorded so fast at one end of the line and reconstructed so fast at the other that they sounded like the real thing.

COMPRESSION. Bell Labs also devised techniques to squeeze different calls onto the same line simultaneously, which increased the capacity of the telephone network. With traditional telephone technology, only one message could be carried at a time

Google: One of the Internet's most versatile and comprehensive search engines.

www.google.ca

Transistor Inventors. The transistor, also called a semiconductor switch, can be likened to a tiny triple-decker sandwich. The sandwich, made of silicon, responds to slight variations in electrical current that allow incredibly fast processing of data that has been converted into on-off signals. In addition to speed, the transistor ushered in miniaturization of data-processing equipment and storage devices. Since 1947, when Bell Labs engineers devised the transistor, it has become possible to store thousands of pages of text on a device as small as a pinhead and to transmit them almost instantly to other devices, like your home computer. The 1956 Nobel Prize went to Bell Labs' Walter Brattain, John Bardeen, and William Shockley for inventing the transistor.

on a telephone line. With digitization, however, a new process called multiplexing became possible. Tiny bits of one message could be interpreted with tiny bits of other messages for transmission and then sorted out at the other end. Few people foresaw that digitization and compression would revolutionize human existence, let alone do it so quickly.

MINIATURIZATION. Radio and television were the first mass media beneficiaries of the transistor. In the 1940s, broadcast equipment was built around electrical tubes, which looked somewhat like light bulbs. These tubes heated up and eventually burned out and consumed massive amounts of electricity. Transistors, on the other hand, could perform the same functions with hardly any electricity and no heat. Important too, transistors were much, much smaller than tubes and much more reliable.

Not only did the use of transistors dramatically reduce the size and weight of broadcast equipment, the size of computers shrank as well. In the 1940s, early computers, based on tube technology, were so big it took entire buildings to house them and large staffs of technicians to operate them. Today, the Marquardt Corporation estimates that all the information recorded in the past 10 000 years can be stored in a cube two metres by two metres by two metres.

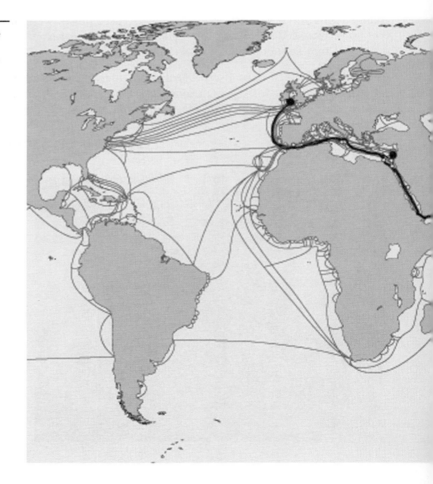

Global Fibre Optics. The Fiberoptic Link Around the Globe, "FLAG" for short, is the longest engineering project in human history—a 28 000-kilometre communication link of England and Japan. The lighter lines are other undersea fibre-optic routes that are planned or in place. The world is being wired for faster World Wide Web communication.

There seems no end to **miniaturization.** IBM has developed a computer drive that, using **giant magneto-resistance (GMR)** technology, crams an incredible 100 million digital characters on a thumbtack-size disk. IBM now expects to be producing GMR disks that can accommodate 2 billion characters on a thumbtack. That's equivalent to about 2000 novels.

EFFICIENCIES.   Transistor-based equipment costs less to manufacture and operates with incredible efficiency. The National Academy of Science estimates it cost US$130 000 to make 125 multiplications when the forerunners of today's computers were introduced in the 1940s. By 1970 the cost was a mere $4. Today, it can be done for pennies.

FIBRE OPTICS

While AT& T was building on its off-on digital technology to improve telephone service in the 1960s, **Corning Glass** developed a cable that was capable of carrying light at incredible speeds—theoretically 300 000 kilometres per second. It was apparent immediately that this new fibre-optic cable, made out of silicon, could carry far more digitized multiplex messages than could copper. The messages were encoded as light pulses rather than as the traditional electrical pulses for transmission.

The International Telecommunication Union: Governments and companies coordinate global telecom networks and services through this Geneva-based organization.

www.itu.int

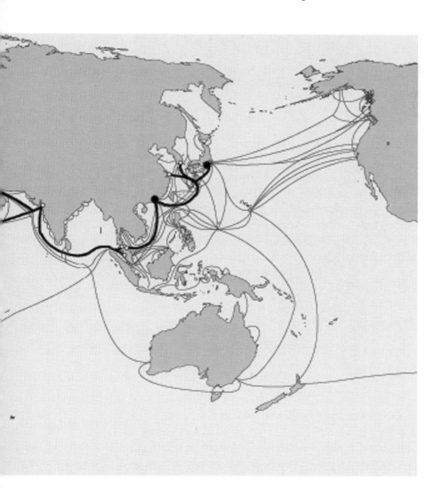

By the 1980s, new equipment to convert data to light pulses for transmission was in place, and long-distance telephone companies were replacing copper lines with fibre-optics, as were local cable television systems. Today, with semiconductor switching combined with optical fibre cable, a single line can carry 60 000 telephone calls simultaneously. In addition to voice, the lines can carry all kinds of other messages that have been broken into digitized pulses. With fibre-optic cable, the entire *Oxford English Dictionary* can be sent in just seconds. Such speed is what has made the web a mass medium that can deliver unprecedented quantities of information so quickly.

Nonlinear Communication

HYPERTEXT AND THE WEB

Until recently, we were all accustomed to mass messages flowing from start to finish in the sequence that mass communicators figured would be most effective for most people. Many mass messages still flow linearly. Newscasts, as an example, start with the most important item first. A novel builds climatically to the final chapter. A television commercial catches your attention at the start and names the advertiser in the sign-off. This is **linear communication**.

Vannevar Bush, a leading thinker of his time, noted to *Atlantic* magazine readers in 1945 that knowledge had expanded exponentially in the 20th century, but the means for "threading through" the maze was "the same as used in the days of square-rigged ships." Bush proposed a machine he called **memex** to mimic human thinking in organizing material. With his memex, people could retrieve information through automated association with related information.

Alas, Bush's memex was never built, but a generation later, technologist **Ted Nelson**, who may have heard his grandfather read Bush's article aloud, picked up on the idea. In his 1962 book *Literary Machines*, Nelson coined the term **hypertext** for an alternate way for people to send and receive information. Nelson also used the term *nonsequential writing*, but it was *hypertext* that stuck.

To better understand how hypertext works, pretend you're a few years into the future and you're studying a new edition of this book. You're at your computer screen because the book is in on-screen, nonlinear hypertext. Your professor has assigned you to study the journalism chapter, which you open up on-screen. You can read the chapter linearly from start to finish, or you also can move your on-screen cursor to highlighted words, called hot spots, hot keys, or links, and click on them to switch elsewhere in the book or to other documents for detail that interests you. Consider the following paragraph:

> Years later, reflecting on the instant success of his *New York Sun*, Benjamin Day shook his head in wonderment. He hadn't realized at the time that the *Sun* was such a milestone. Whether he was being falsely modest is something historians can quibble over. The fact is that the *Sun*, which Day founded in 1833, discovered mass audiences on a scale never before envisioned and ushered in the era of modern mass media

You can click on *New York Sun* and go to a screen with a thumbnail history of the newspaper with its own hot spots. You decide to click the penny newspapers hot

Vannevar Bush: Bush's 1945 *Atlantic* magazine article, proposing a new relationship between human beings and knowledge, is available online.

www.isg.sfu.ca/~duchier/ misc/vbush

Vannevar Bush. After World War II a leading intellectual, Vannevar Bush, proposed a machine that would hold all the information accumulated in human history. People using the machine could retrieve whatever they wanted in whatever sequence they wanted. The machine, which Bush called memex, was never built, but the concept is the heart of today's hypertext.

spot. Up comes a list of 14 leading one-cent newspapers. You could click on any of the 14 to go to screens with information about them. Instead, you choose a hot spot on a list of options at the bottom of the screen: Scholarship 1960–69. There you find a list of nine books and 61 articles in academic journals on the Penny Press Period from the 1960s, and you can go to summaries, tables of contents, or full texts of any of them. The hyperlinks are limitless, and at any time you can reverse your course to a previous screen to choose a hot term to go on yet another pathway.

In primitive ways, people have done a kind of hypertext learning for centuries. In the library, a researcher may have two dozen books open and piled on a desk, with dozens more reference books handy on a shelf. Moving back and forth among the books, checking indexes and footnotes, and fetching additional volumes from the library stacks, the researcher is creating new meanings by combining information in new sequences. The computer has accelerated that process and opened up thousands of resources, all on-screen, for today's scholars.

PRE-HYPERTEXT INNOVATIONS

Although hypertext itself is not new, the shift from linear presentation in traditional media has been gradual. A preliminary stage was merely casting text in digital form for storage and transmission. This is what other early online services like **Nexis** did, providing linear full-text news stories from cooperating newspapers. While a major step forward at the time, full-text is derisively called **shovelware** by hypertext enthusiasts because it is simply moved from a traditional medium to another without much adaptation to the unique characteristics of the new medium. Shovelware falls short of the potential of the web.

How Hypertext Works. At a glance, on-screen hypertext looks like any other text, but there is a difference. Hypertext contains links within the text to other documents. By clicking your cursor on shaded, underlined, or coloured text, or graphics, you can go instantly to your choice of other documents. This illustration, adapted from one by Kevin Hughes, a student systems programmer at Honolulu Community College, shows how you can move from the term hypertext in one document to a history of hypertext, or to a dictionary definition of hypertext. These new documents themselves have links to other documents. As Hughes puts it: "Continually selecting text would take you on a free-associative tour of information. In this way, hypertext links, called hyperlinks, can create a complex virtual web of connections." Those connections can include hypermedia—sounds, images, and movies.

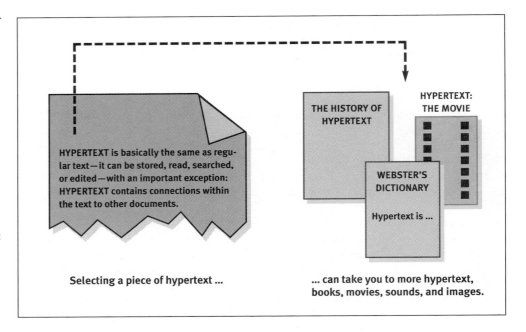

HYPERTEXT is basically the same as regular text—it can be stored, read, searched, or edited—with an important exception: HYPERTEXT contains connections within the text to other documents.

Selecting a piece of hypertext ...

THE HISTORY OF HYPERTEXT

HYPERTEXT: THE MOVIE

WEBSTER'S DICTIONARY

Hypertext is ...

... can take you to more hypertext, books, movies, sounds, and images.

The **Media Lab** at the Massachusetts Institute of Technology came up with the next refinement: the *Daily Me,* an experimental digital newspaper that provided subscribers information only on subjects they specified in advance. Take, for example, a car buff who follows hockey and who earns a living running a grocery store in Brandon, Manitoba. For this person, a customized *Daily Me* would include news on the automobile industry, the NHL, the AHL's Manitoba Moose, the local hockey team the Brandon Wheat Kings, livestock and produce market reports, news summaries from Manitoba, and a brief summary of major national and world news.

MIT's *Daily Me* innovation took commercial form at the *Wall Street Journal,* which in 1995 launched the first customizable electronic newspaper. It was called **Personal Journal,** with the subtitle: "Published for a Circulation of One." *Personal Journal,* which cost US$18 a month plus 50 cents per update, offered whatever combination a subscriber wanted of business and general coverage by category, market tables and selected quotes, sports, and weather. Such customization, matching content to a user's interest, is now common.

HYPERTEXT NEWS

The potential of digital news was realized with the web. When *USA Today* established a website, it offered a hypertext product—not shovelware. *USA Today* webmasters broke the newspaper's content into web page-size components, updated them 24 hours a day as events warranted, and linked every page with others. Every day, readers can choose among thousands of connections, in effect creating their own news package by moving around among the entire content of the newspaper. Hot spots include links to archived material from previous coverage that *USA Today*'s webmasters thought some readers would want to draw on for background.

All the major news products coming online today are state-of-the-art hypertext ventures. Some websites offer users an opportunity to communicate immediately back to the creators of the products.

HYPERFICTION

While digital technology is revolutionizing many aspects of human communication, it is unclear whether all literary forms will be fundamentally affected, but there have been experiments with hypertext fiction. For example, the computer games *Myst*, *Riven*, and *Myst III: Exile* put players in dreamlike landscapes where they wander through adventures in which they choose the course of events. Options, of course, are limited to those the authors put into the game, but the player has a feeling of creating the story rather than following an author's plot. These games represent a new dimension in exploration as an experiential literary form.

Some futurists see interactivity overtaking traditional forms of human story-telling, and the term **hyperfiction** has been applied to a few dozen pioneer hypertext novels. One hyperfiction enthusiast, Trip Hawkins, who creates video games, laid out both sides in a *New York Times* interview: "Given the choice, do viewers really want to interact with their entertainment? Watching, say, *Jurassic Park*, wouldn't they prefer to have Steven Spielberg spin the tale of dinosaurs munching on their keepers in an island theme park?" For himself, however, Hawkins says, "I want to be on the island. I want to show that I could have done better than those idiots did. I could have gotten out of that situation."

Editor & Publisher: The online edition of the trade journal covers both the online and traditional print news industries.
www.mediainfo.com

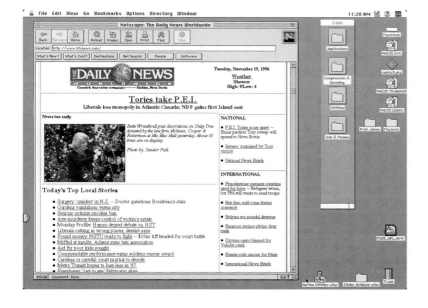

First Online. *The Halifax Daily News* was Canada's first online newspaper. Internet surfers can read local, national, and international stories at the click of a button. Many other newspapers have also gone online in Canada.

Convergence Issues

TECHNOLOGICAL CONVERGENCE

Johannes Gutenberg brought mass production to books, and the other primary print media, magazines and newspapers, followed. People never had a problem recognizing differences among books, magazines, and newspapers. When sound recording and movies came along, they too were distinctive, and later so were radio and television. Today, the traditional primary media are in various stages of transition to digital form.

As the magazine *The Economist* noted, once-discrete media industries "are being whirled into an extraordinary whole." Writing in *Quill* magazine, Kevin Manay put it this way:

> All the devices people use for communicating and all the kinds of communication have started crashing together into one massive megamedia industry. The result is that telephone lines will soon carry TV shows. Cable TV will carry telephone calls. Desktop computers will be used to watch and edit movies. Cellular phone-computers the size of a notepad will dial into interactive magazines that combine text, sound and video to tell stories.

This **technological convergence** is no better illustrated at a corporate level than the mergers of BCE, CTV, and the *Globe and Mail* or CanWest and Hollinger in 2000.

UNIVERSAL ACCESS

Although web use is growing dramatically, the fact is that not everybody has access or, probably, ever will. StatsCan says that people are more likely to be Internet users and computer owners if they have higher than average income. What about everybody else? This is a profound public policy question, especially in Canada, which prides itself on assuring equality for every citizen on basic matters like access to information.

MEDIA DATABANK 6.1

Canadians on the Internet

According to the CRTC and the Convergence Consulting Group, these are the most popular household ISPs (Internet Service Providers) in Canada:

Company	Market Share
Sympatico	8%
Telus	7%
Rogers	7%
Shaw	7%
AOL Canada	5%

(Source: CRTC Broadcast Policy Monitoring Report, 2000)

One line of reasoning is that the government should not guarantee **universal access**. This rationale draws on the interstate highway system as an analogy. The government builds the roads, but individuals provide the vehicles to drive around on the system. The counter-argument is that access to information will become so essential to everyone's well-being that we could end up with a stratified society of info-rich and info-poor people. Such a knowledge gap hardly is the ideal.

In Canada, the government feels that accessing the Internet is an important social issue. As part of its "Connecting Canadians" strategy, Industry Canada provides public Internet access to Canadians, usually through libraries and community centres. It hopes to make Canada the most connected country in the world.

CYBERPORNOGRAPHY

The debate over what to do about censorship on the Internet is ongoing. The sheer volume of information uploaded to the Internet on a daily basis, the equivalent of about 300 pages per second, makes censoring and policing the Internet difficult, if not impossible. Pornographic images, stories, and games are widely available on the Internet. This material can be accessed through the World Wide Web, in newsgroups, or via e-mail.

In 2001, Justice Minister Anne McLellan introduced a bill that would make simple possession of child pornography a criminal offence. This means that even simply surfing to a site with child pornography would be illegal in Canada. The person would not need to download or distribute the images. It would also make communicating over the Internet in order to entice young children to engage in sexual acts illegal. This includes e-mail or chat room conversations. The law was clearly aimed at pedophiles using the

Cyberporn: One of the more significant issues arising out of new computer technology is that of pornography. Parents are concerned about what images their children may accidentally stumble across, while businesses are also worried about time lost on the job due to surfing for pornography.

Internet for their gratification. While the RCMP may be able to charge people with possessing these images, it's impossible to track down some of the international sites that are distributing the images. Laws recognize borders; the Internet doesn't.

The Web and the CRTC

The **CRTC** was the first broadcast regulator in the world to address the issue of controlling the Internet. In its 1999 decision, Canada's broadcast regulator announced it would not regulate the Internet at this time, as it doesn't fall under the authority of Canada's Broadcasting Act. Among the reasons they cited for their conclusion:

- The Internet is not, by definition, broadcasting. Its messages are largely communicated using alphanumeric text.
- The Internet does not replace broadcasting; it simply complements it.
- Since web material can be customized by the user, its messages are broadcast for a mass audience in the same way a radio or television broadcast is. The web is "push" media.
- There is already a large Canadian presence on the Internet
- The CRTC felt that the Criminal Code and the use of content-filtering software by the users would be the best way to deal with offensive content on the Internet.

The Web

Futurists are scrambling—fruitlessly, it seems—to sort through technological breakthroughs to figure out where it's all going. Their vision extends only a few months ahead at best. Amid all the haze, two realities are clear. First, bandwidth improvements will expand capacity exponentially for the transmission and exchange of messages. Second, the web will untether itself from the landlines on which most messages move today. A wireless future will make the web a medium of ultimate portability. The possibilities that will come with further miniaturization of equipment and compression of messages are mind-boggling.

As the technological breakthroughs leapfrog over each other, we will see the traditional media shift increasingly to the web. Don't expect to wake up one morning, though, and find that the world is paperless and local television stations have vanished. Just as the horse and buggy and the automobile coexisted for 40 years, so too will e-books and paper books. Web TV will still be television as we know it today, and many people will be satisfied with a living room set pretty much as now—although with bigger screens, sharper pictures, and movie-house sound quality.

In short, media companies will need to use two redundant modes to maximize the audience. Already we see this with over-air radio stations that stream online, magazines and newspapers on paper and on the web, and recordings that are at the record store and also downloadable.

CHAPTER WRAP-UP

The web utilizes the global Internet, so computers anywhere can exchange digitized data—including text, visuals, and audio. Many media companies are investing heavily in cyberspace, and the expansion of high-capacity fibre-optic cable networks will increase capacity tremendously so that audio and moving visuals are on tap live on any computer screen connected to the Internet. Two-way communication via the web already is standard fare. With every passing day, more mass communication is occurring on the web.

QUESTIONS FOR REVIEW

1. How can the web be defined as a new and distinctive mass medium?
2. How is the web related to the Internet?
3. What is the difficulty with the web as an advertising medium?
4. What is the effect of digitization and fibre-optic cable on mass communication?
5. What is the connection between the web and hypertext?
6. Will hypertext change the way that human beings create stories and receive them?
7. Why was digitizing a necessary prelude to the web?
8. Should public policy guarantee everyone, including children, total access to the web?

QUESTIONS FOR CRITICAL THINKING

1. Will it ever be possible to condense all human knowledge into an area smaller than the four-square-metre cube described by the Marquardt Corporation?
2. What makes books, magazines, newspapers, sound recordings, movies, radio, and television different from one another? What will become of these distinctions in coming years?
3. Trace the development of the technology that has made the web possible.
4. What were the innovations that Tim Berners-Lee introduced that are revolutionizing mass communication?
5. How does hypertext depart from traditional human communication? And does hypertext have a future as a literary form?
6. What obstacles would you have in designing public policy to assure access for every citizen to the web?
7. Some people say there is no point in trying to regulate cyberporn. Do you agree? Disagree? Why?
8. Some mass media may be subsumed by the web. Pretend you are a futurist and create a timeline for this to happen.
9. What should the role for the CRTC be, if any, regarding regulating the Internet?

FOR KEEPING UP TO DATE

Industry Standard is the main trade journal of e-commerce.

The magazine *Wired* offers hep coverage of cyber-developments, issues, and people.

Trade journals *Editor & Publisher, Advertising Age, Broadcast Dialogue*, and *Broadcaster* have excellent ongoing coverage of their fields.

InfoWorld covers the gamut of cybernews. Widely available news media that explore cyberissues include *Time, Newsweek*, and *Maclean's*.

Don't overlook surfing the web for sites that track web developments, including Canada's Internet Advertising Bureau.

FOR FURTHER LEARNING

ACNeilsen. *ACNeilsen Measures the Net*.

Vannevar Bush. "As We May Think." *Atlantic Monthly* (July 1945).

Robert Brehl. "Brave New World." *Toronto Star* (March 30, 1996).

Canada, The Information Highway Advisory Council. The Challenge of the Information Highway (1995). Available at **www.info.ic.gc.ca/info-highway/ih.html.**

CRTC. *Broadcast Policy Monitoring Report* (CRTC, 2000).

CRTC. "CRTC Won't Regulate the Internet." (CRTC, May 19, 1999).

"Crime in Cyberspace." *Maclean's* (May 22, 1995), pp. 50–58.

Martha FitzSimons, editor. *Media, Democracy and the Information Highway* (Freedom Forum Media Studies Center, 1993).

Robert Lucky. *Silicon Dreams* (St. Martin's, 1989).

Kevin Maney. "Will the Techno Tsunami Wash Us Out?" *Quill* (March 1994), pp. 16–18.

JoAnn Napier. "Online Advertising Rise 96% in a Year." *Ottawa Citizen* (March 20, 2000).

John V. Pavlik. *New Media Technology: Cultural and Commercial Perspectives* (Allyn & Bacon, 1995).

Mark Slouka. *War of the Worlds* (Basic Books, 1996).

Statistics Canada. "Household Internet Use Survey." *The Daily* (July 26, 2001).

Chapter 7

Terrible News. In the days following September 11, 2001, the world's attention was focused on the aftermath of the terrorist attacks on the United States. News coverage was completely preoccupied with the events unfolding in New York City and Washington, DC. As horrific images of the collapse of the World Trade Center's twin towers were played over and over again on every news broadcast, many lesser stories went unreported.

News

MEDIA IN THEORY

Personal Values in News: The Role of the Journalist

This just in . . . Canadians love news. A 1998 Angus Reid survey found that over 75 percent of Canadians are interested in following the news, with local and national news stories topping the list of the kinds of news that interest us the most. Although Canadians have a hunger for news, few ask the question: "what is news?" It's not an easy question to answer in practice or in theory. Unfortunately, there is no one single definition of news. In *Canadian Broadcast News: The Basics*, journalism professor **Brian Green** says that news is "the significant, the unusual, that which affects us." However, the definition of what is "significant" is open to personal interpretation. Veteran U.S. journalist Chet Huntley once quipped, "news is what I decide is news." This contributes to the independence and autonomy that characterize news work. Journalists know they have a high level of responsibility in deciding what to report as news. While most reporters will agree on the newsworthiness of some events and issues, such as a catastrophic storm or a tax proposal, their judgments will result in stories that take different slants and angles. On events and issues whose newsworthiness is less obvious, reporters will differ even on whether to do a story.

Journalists' Personal Values and Bias

The journalistic ideal, an unbiased seeking of truth and an unvarnished telling of it, dictates that the work be done without partisanship. Yet as human beings, journalists have personal values that influence all that they do, including their work. Because the news judgment decisions that journalists make are so important to an informed citizenry, we need to know what makes these people tick. Are they left-wingers? Are they ideological zealots? Are they quirky and unpredictable? Are they conscientious?

A sociologist who studied stories in the American news media for 20 years, **Herbert Gans** concluded that journalists have a typical North American value system. Gans identified primary values, all in the North American mainstream, that journalists use in making their news judgments:

- *Ethnocentrism.* Journalists see things through their culture's eyes, which affects news coverage.
- *Commitment to democracy and capitalism.* Coverage of other governmental forms dwells on corruption, conflict, protest, and bureaucratic malfunction. Gans also found that when they report corruption and misbehaviour in business, journalists treat them as aberrations.
- *Small-town pastoralism.* Like most of their fellow citizens, journalists romanticize rural life. Given similar stories from metropolitan Vancouver and tiny Estevan, Saskatchewan, editors usually opt for the small town. This helps explain the success of Wayne Rostad's long-running *On the Road Again* series on CBC.
- *Individualism tempered by moderation.* Gans found that journalists love stories about rugged individuals who overcome adversity and defeat powerful forces. This is a value that contributes to a negative coverage of technology as something to be feared because it can stifle individuality.

- *Social order.* Journalists cover disorder—earthquakes, catastrophes, protest marches, the disintegrating nuclear family, and transgressions of laws and mores. This coverage, noted Gans, is concerned not with glamorizing disorder but with finding ways to restore order.

When asked if biases exist in journalism, **David Rooney**, author of *Reporting and Writing for Canadian Journalists*, says, "of course they do. No one gets through life without acquiring political attitudes and prejudices and journalists are no different in that regard. But, for the most part, conscientious reporters keep their biases out of their copy. They leave it to fellow journalists—the columnists and editorial writers—to openly advocate particular policies or ideologies."

Critics of the news media come in many colours. Conservatives are the most vocal, charging that the media slant news to favour liberal causes. Liberal critics see it in the opposite light. The most recurrent charge, however, is that the media are leftist, favouring liberal over conservative views, and change over the status quo. In the final analysis, news is the result of journalists scanning their environment and making decisions, first on whether to cover certain events and then on how to cover them. The decisions are made against a backdrop of countless variables, many of them changing during the reporting, writing, and editing processes.

News Media Traditions: U.S. and Canada

COLONIAL PERIOD

In the colonial period, **Benjamin Harris** published the first colonial newspaper, *Publick Occurrences,* in Boston in 1690. He was in hot water right away, alleging that the king of France was having an affair with his son's wife. In the colonies just as in England, a newspaper needed royal consent. The governor had not consented, and Harris was put out of business after one issue.

Even so, Harris's daring was a precursor for emerging press defiance against authority. In 1733 **John Peter Zenger** started a paper in New York in competition with the existing Crown-supported newspaper. Zenger's *New York Journal* was backed by merchants and lawyers who disliked the royal governor. From the beginning the newspaper antagonized the governor with items challenging his competence, and finally the governor arrested Zenger. The trial made history. Zenger's attorney, **Andrew Hamilton**, argued that there should be no punishment for printing articles that are true. Hamilton's argument prevailed, and Zenger, who had become a hero for standing up to the Crown, was freed.

Zenger Trial. Printer John Peter Zenger, in the dock, won his 1735 trial for criticizing New York's royal governor. The victory fed a colonial exuberance that culminated 46 years later in winning the U.S. revolution against British rule.

PARTISAN PERIOD

After the American Revolution, newspapers divided along partisan lines. What is called the Federalist period in American history is also referred to as the **partisan period** among newspaper historians. Intense partisanship characterized newspapers of the period, which spanned roughly 50 years to the 1830s.

Initially the issue was over a constitution. Should the nation have a strong central government or remain a loose coalition of states? James Madison, Alexander Hamilton, **Thomas Jefferson**, and other leading thinkers exchanged ideas with articles and essays in newspapers. The *Federalist Papers*, a series of essays printed and reprinted in newspapers throughout the nation, were part of the debate. After the U.S. Constitution was drafted, partisanship intensified, finally culminating lopsidedly when the Federalist party both controlled the Congress and had their leader, **John Adams**, in the presidency.

In firm control and bent on silencing their detractors, the Federalists ramrodded a series of laws through Congress in 1798. One of the things these laws, the **Alien and Sedition Acts**, prohibited was "false, scandalous, malicious" statements about government. Using these laws, **Matthew Lyon**, a member of Congress, was jailed for a letter to a newspaper editor that accused President Adams of "ridiculous pomp, foolish adulation, selfish avarice." Lyon, an anti-Federalist, was sentenced to four months in jail and fined $1000. Although he was tried in Rutland, Vermont, he was sent to a filthy jail more than 60 kilometres away. When editor Anthony Haswell printed an advertisement to raise money for Lyon's fine, he was jailed for abetting a criminal. The public was outraged at Federalist heavy-handedness. This outrage showed itself in the election of 1800. Jefferson was elected president, and the Federalists were thumped out of office.

PENNY PRESS PERIOD

In 1833, when he was 22, the enterprising **Benjamin Day** started a newspaper that changed American journalism: the *New York Sun*. At a penny a copy, the *Sun* was within reach of just about everybody. Other papers were expensive, an annual subscription costing as much as a full week's wages. Unlike other papers, distributed mostly by mail, the *Sun* was hawked every day on the streets. The *Sun*'s content was different too. It avoided the political and economic thrust of the traditional papers, concentrating instead on items of interest to common folk. The writing was simple,

Newseum: The interactive museum of news.

www.newseum.org

Media History Project: Promoting the study of media history from petroglyphs to pixels.

mediahistory.umn.edu

Penny Press Period. When Benjamin Day launched the *New York Sun* in 1833 and sold it for one cent a copy, he ushered in an era of cheap newspapers that common people could afford. The penny press period also was marked by newspapers with stories of broad appeal, as opposed to the political and financial papers of the preceding partisan period.

straightforward, and easy to follow. For a motto for the *Sun*, Day came up with "It Shines for All," his pun fully intended.

Day's *Sun* was an immediate success. Naturally, it was quickly imitated, and the **penny press period** began. Partisan papers that characterized the partisan period continued, but the mainstream of American newspapers came to be in the mould of the *Sun*.

Merchants saw the unprecedented circulation of the **penny papers** as a way to reach great numbers of potential customers. Advertising revenue meant bigger papers, which attracted more readers, which attracted more advertisers. Day, as a matter of fact, did not meet expenses by selling the *Sun* for a penny a copy. He counted on advertisers to pick up a good part of his production cost. In effect, advertisers subsidized readers, just as they do today.

Several social and economic factors made the penny press possible. The first variable was the Industrial Revolution. With new steam-powered presses, hundreds of copies an hour could be printed. Urbanization was a key factor. Workers flocked to the cities to work in new factories, creating a great pool of potential newspaper readers for advertisers. Immigration from impoverished parts of Europe also boosted sales. Most were eager to learn English and found that penny papers, with their simple style, were good tutors. The last factor was an overall rise in literacy in the United States.

Several New York newspaper publishers, concerned about the escalating expense of sending reporters to gather far-away news, got together in 1848 to share stories. They called their cooperative venture the **Associated Press (AP)**, a predecessor of today's giant global news service. So that AP stories could be used by member news-papers of different political persuasions, reporters were told to write from a nonpar-tisan point of view. The result was a fact-oriented kind of news writing often called **objective reporting.** It was widely imitated and still is the dominant reporting style for event-based news stories in all the news media.

YELLOW PRESS PERIOD

The quest to sell more copies led to excesses that are illustrated by the Pulitzer-Hearst circulation war in New York in the 1890s, in what came to be known as the **yellow press period.**

Joseph Pulitzer, a poor immigrant, made the *St. Louis Post-Dispatch* into a finan-cial success. In 1883, Pulitzer decided to try a bigger city. He bought the *New York World* and applied his formula. He emphasized human interest, crusaded for worthy causes, and ran lots of promotional hoopla. Pulitzer's *World* also featured solid jour-nalism. His star reporter, **Nellie Bly,** epitomized the two faces of the Pulitzer formula for journalistic success. For one story, Bly feigned mental illness, entered an insane asylum, and emerged with scandalous tales about how patients were treated. It was enterprising journalism of great significance, and reforms resulted.

Joseph Pulitzer

William Randolph Hearst

Journalistic Sensationalism. Rival New York newspaper publishers Joseph Pulitzer and William Randolph Hearst tried to outdo each other daily with anti-Spanish atrocity stories from Cuba, many of them trumped up. Some historians say the public hysteria fuelled by Pulitzer and Hearst helped precipitate the Spanish-American War, especially after the U.S. battleship *Maine* exploded in Havana's harbour. Both Pulitzer and Hearst claimed it was a Spanish attack on an American vessel, although a case can be made that the explosion was accidental.

In San Francisco, Pulitzer had a young admirer, **William Randolph Hearst.** With his father's Nevada mining fortune and mimicking Pulitzer's New York formula, Hearst made the *San Francisco Examiner* a great success. In 1895 Hearst decided to go to New York and take on the master. He bought the *New York Journal* and vowed to "out-Pulitzer" Pulitzer. The inevitable resulted. To outdo each other, Pulitzer and Hearst launched crazier and crazier stunts. Not even the comic pages escaped the competitive frenzy. Pulitzer ran the *Yellow Kid*, and then Hearst hired the cartoonist away. Pulitzer hired a new one, and both papers ran the yellow character and plastered the city with yellow promotional posters. The circulation war was nicknamed "yellow journalism," and the term came to be a derisive reference to sensational excesses in news coverage.

The yellow excesses reached a feverish peak as Hearst and Pulitzer covered the growing tensions between Spain and the United States. Fuelled by hyped atrocity stories, the tension eventually exploded in war. One story in particular epitomizes the no-holds-barred competition between Pulitzer and Hearst. Although Spain had consented to all demands by the United States, Hearst sent the artist Frederic Remington to Cuba to cover the situation. Remington cabled back: "Everything is quiet. There is no trouble here. There will be no war. Wish to return." Hearst replied: "Please remain. You furnish pictures. I'll furnish war."

The yellow tradition still lives. The *New York Daily News*, founded in 1919 and almost an immediate hit, ushered in a period that some historians characterize as **jazz journalism.** It was just Hearst and Pulitzer updated in tabloid form with an emphasis on photography. Today, newspapers like the commercially successful *National Enquirer* are in the yellow tradition.

HISTORY OF JOURNALISM IN CANADA

Wilfred Kesteron's research on the history and growth of journalism in Canada is regarded as the definitive work in this area. Kesterton observes that Canadian journalists work under a libertarian press system, and that they are fuelled by ideals similar to those that characterized the partisan and colonial periods in U.S. history. In his *Guide to the Canadian News Media*, Peter Desbarats comments that journalism in Canada "has been closer to Main Street USA than to Fleet Street." By this he means that Canadian news traditions followed the U.S. model and not the British model. A comparison of the press periods in Canada and the U.S. seems to indicate that similar ideals developed, albeit at a different times. Kesterton breaks down the journalism in Canada into four periods.

THE TRANSPLANT PERIOD IN CANADIAN JOURNALISM (1752–1807). Kesterton refers to this press period as the **transplant period** due to the fact that Canada's first newspapers were literally American newspapers or publishers that transplanted, or resettled, in Canada. The *Halifax Gazette*, Canada's first newspaper, was published by John Bushnell, who moved from Boston in 1752. The oldest newspaper in existence, the *Quebec Gazette* was started by two printers from Philadelphia in 1764. The *Halifax Gazette* appeared every two weeks and had about 70 subscribers, while the *Quebec Gazette* had about 150 subscribers when it first began publishing. As conditions improved and immigrants began moving down the St. Lawrence and into Upper Canada, other newspapers began publishing.

Early to Print. A snapshot of the Monday March 23rd, 1752 edition of *The Halifax Gazette*—Canada's first newspaper.

As with their early American counterparts, most of the first papers in Canada were organs for the fledgling governments of British North America. Most of the content of these three- or four-page newsletter-type sheets contained government information with a sprinkling of news from "back home." It was felt that for the settlements in the New World to be successful, the government needed this voice to inform and educate settlers. These newspapers were also a primitive advertising tool for early Canadian merchants. The first ads in Canadian newspapers appeared in 1752 when the *Halifax Gazette* printed three ads for a lawyer, a clerical service, and for butter. While some ads appeared in these publications, the main source of income for most early newspapers was printing government information. Therefore, the success of newspapers during this time was contingent on government support, both financial and ideological. As a result, most of these papers didn't "rock the boat." In 1766, The *Halifax Gazette* dared to question the government on the new Stamp Tax. As a result, the government suspended publication of the *Gazette*.

SECOND CANADIAN PRESS PERIOD: GROWTH (1807–1858).   Following the War of 1812, immigration in Canada flourished, particularly in Upper Canada, where the population doubled by the mid-1820s. Combine this population surge with the effects of the Industrial Revolution and you will begin to understand the changing social climate in Canada. People stopped working at home or in the fields and began to work in factories. These factors contributed to the growth of newspapers, and thus to what Kesterton refers to as the **growth period** of Canadian journalism. At the end of the War of 1812, Canada had only a handful of newspapers; by the mid-1820s, that number had risen to almost 300. Canada's first daily newspaper arrived in 1833 with Montreal's *Daily Advisor*.

As in the time of the penny press period in the U.S., this growth in immigration and urbanization created markets for Canadian newspapers. As a result, newspapers were less dependent on government revenue for their economic success. This, in turn, created a kind of "partisan" press period in Canada, as newspapers began to take sides along political lines. Often, newspaper editors were also politicians and their papers were labelled as "Tory" or "Reform" papers. Newspapers would take sides on political issues.

The most significant example of this period in Canadian journalism history involved Joseph Howe. On New Year's Day, 1835, Howe published "the letter" signed by "the people" in his *Novascotian*. In the letter, he accused the local police and the lieutenant-governor of corruption: "it is known that from the pockets of the poor and distressed, at least 1,000 pounds are drawn yearly and pocketed by men whose services the country might very well spare." Despite the fact that Howe was charged with seditious libel under the criminal codes of the day, and the presiding judge instructed the jurors to bring back a verdict of guilty, a jury acquitted him of libel in only ten minutes. The jury felt that publishing something that is true shouldn't be illegal. As with the earlier American example of Zenger's *New York Journal*, the message for Canadian journalists was clear; freedom of the press and intellectual freedom were important principles.

THIRD CANADIAN PRESS PERIOD: WESTWARD GROWTH (1858–1900).

During the latter half of the 1800s, immigration and migration became two important factors in the growth of Canadian newspapers. As the Canadian population increased, it moved west and north and newspapers soon followed. Kesterton calls this the **westward growth** period of Canadian journalism. The gold rushes in the West made Victoria, British Columbia, a centre for commerce and transportation. In 1858, the *Victoria Gazette* and *Anglo American* began publishing. New papers also began publishing in central and eastern Canada: the *Montreal Star* in 1869, the *Toronto Telegram* in 1876, and the *Ottawa Journal* in 1885. By the turn of the century, over 1200 newspapers were serving Canada's population, which at that time stood at close to 5.5 million people.

This period was also a sort of "partisan period" for Canadian journalism. The debate over Confederation, the Riel Rebellion, or the completion of the Canadian National Railway were the subject of many an article. D'Arcy McGee, George Brown, and Joseph Howe were among the country's most opinionated journalists.

Changes in technology were important aspects of this period. Steam-powered presses were commonplace by the 1850s. In the last half of the 19th century, the world was becoming "wired." **Samuel Morse**'s invention of the telegraph in 1844 would change journalism forever. Reporters for Western newspapers could be sent to the East Coast to cover the Confederation debates in Charlottetown. However, the technology wasn't perfect and would often break down. Editors instructed their reporters to tell the most important information first in case telegraph lines failed as a story was being transmitted. That way, when a story was interrupted, editors would have at least a few usable sentences.

The structure that developed during this period was known as the **inverted pyramid** and, it turned out, was popular with readers because it allowed them to learn what was most important at a glance. Also, the inverted pyramid helped editors fit stories into the limited confines of a page—a story could be cut off at any paragraph and the most important parts remained intact.

FOURTH CANADIAN PRESS PERIOD: THE TWENTIETH CENTURY ONWARDS.

In the 1900s, journalism came of age in Canada. Although immigration levels and migration patterns were inconsistent due to the World Wars and the Depression during the first half of the 20th century, improvements in technology helped the newspaper grow to new heights. This technology included better printing presses and better-quality newsprint, which helped improve the form of the newspaper. Improvements in communication and transportation helped distribution. Due to these changes and the continuing growth of cities, the large metropolitan daily as a business enterprise became the norm for many newspapers.

News agencies arrived in Canada during this period. The **Canadian Press (CP)** was founded in 1917. Prior to the arrival of CP, newspapers received their information from the Associated Press via the Canadian Pacific Railway. To complement the AP service, the CPR would pay freelancers along their routes to gather information to be distributed across Canada. In 1907 the CPR told the three Winnipeg newspapers that their AP reports would be telegraphed to them from Minnesota. Not only would their service be cut, but the cost was to be doubled. Looking for a cheaper way to fill the void of Canadian news, the three newspapers formed their own news agency, the Western Associated Press (WAP). The new service provided news stories for several Western papers. It grew to the point where it became a strong competitor for AP and the CPR in Canada. A series of legal battles ensued, and then ended with the CPR getting out of the news distribution business, and CP was officially launched in 1910. A statute of Parliament officially made the Canadian Press a corporation in 1923. Over 300 journalists write stories for CP.

Television also added an element to Canadian journalism. In *A Guide to Canadian News Media*, Peter Desbarats reports that by the late 1950s, Canadian news programs were becoming in depth and analytical. René Lévesque's *Point de mire* and Pierre Berton's *Close-Up* were popular newsmagazine-style shows. CTV aired its first nightly newscast in 1961 with Harvey Kirck as the anchor. Today, people tune in to the trustworthy images of Lloyd Robertson and the *CTV National News* or Peter Mansbridge on CBC's *The National*.

Probably the best-known newsmagazine in the 1960s was *This Hour Has Seven Days*, hosted by Laurier LaPierre and Patrick Watson. It debuted in the fall of 1964. The program become known for its controversial style and was taken off the air in 1966 after only 50 episodes. *W-5* began broadcasting in 1966 on CTV and is now the longest-running newsmagazine in North America. CBC's *Fifth Estate* is also known for hard-hitting, take-no-prisoners journalism.

Broadcast News (BN) is a news agency for Canadian broadcasters. It's a collective between CP and Canada's broadcasters, which was created in 1954. Before then, broadcasters bought news stories from newspapers and CP and rewrote them for broadcast. BN operates 24 hours a day, seven days a week, and provides news in both official languages to over 500 subscribers.

The Canadian Press: Homepage for the cooperatively owned national news agency.

www.cp.org

Canadian Newsmagazine. Wei Chen is one of the hosts of CTV's *W-5*, the longest running newsmagazine program in North America.

NewsWatch Canada:
NewsWatch monitors the diversity and thoroughness of news coverage in Canada's media, with a focus on identifying blind spots and double standards. The site includes a Top Ten list of underreported stories.

newswatch.cprost.sfu.ca

NEWS MEDIA TRADITIONS FROM THE VARIOUS PRESS PERIODS

History has helped journalism develop various practices that are evident in both Canada and the U.S. today. While not all traditions are found in every piece of journalism, some of these include:

- The news media actively try to mould government policy and mobilize public sentiment. Today this is done primarily on the editorial page.
- Journalists are committed to seeking truth, which was articulated in Zenger's and Howe's "truth defence."
- Inverted pyramid story structures and writing that appeals to general audiences to make reading the news easier.
- A strong orientation to covering events, including the ferreting out of news.

Media People

Sue Prestedge

WTSN

Sue Prestedge

Sports journalism made history in Canada on September 7, 2001. For the first time anywhere, a digital channel devoted to covering women's sports went on the air. WTSN, the Women's Sports Network, owned by Bell Globe Media, is devoted to the covering women's sports in Canada. It is not "a female version of TSN," says **Sue Prestedge,** a senior vice president with the network. Prestedge spent about 20 years in news and sports broadcasting at CBC. She is the only female winner of celebrated Foster Hewitt Award for Outstanding Sports Broadcasting for her coverage of the 1984 Olympics. She also spent six years as a journalism professor at Mohawk College in Hamilton before accepting her role with WTSN.

Two factors that need to be present in any successful broadcast venture—the channel must have a clearly defined audience and support from advertisers. Prestedge says that WTSN has both. Prestedge has an interesting perception about the WTSN's viewers: "Primarily, our audience is women between 18 and 49, but eventually it's not going to be all women. Fathers are also involved with the daughter's sports, as supporters and coaches. As the network grows, so will the audience."

She would also like younger viewers, like her three daughters, to come home from school or soccer practice and turn on WTSN. As well, advertisers, particularly those that have sports-related products for women, were also keen on the idea of an all-women's sports channel, says Prestedge. It offered them a chance to reach an audience they might not have otherwise reached.

The role of the journalist in deciding what is newsworthy is always an issue and the reporters for WTSN are no exception. Says Prestedge, "WTSN keeps in touch with grass roots reporters at their CTV affiliates to alert us to sports stories about women that are out there." She also feels that WTSN may be paving the way for more jobs for women in sports journalism. Says Prestedge, "many women work in local sports departments, but few have national exposure or prominence. I would hope that in the next few years we should be able to see more women on national sports broadcasts covering Major League Baseball, the NHL, and the CFL."

At first, some females thought that WTSN would "ghettoize" women's sports coverage. Prestedge says that WTSN doesn't ghettoize women's sports, but simply offers more coverage of women's sports. Her goal for WTSN is simple: to cover and promote women's sports by giving Canadian female sports journalists a chance to tell these stories. One of these shows, *Benchmarks*, focuses on Canadian athletes and the power brokers of women's sports in Canada. WTSN was also able to gain the broadcast rights for highlights of women's events at the 2002 Winter Olympics in Salt Lake City.

- A commitment by some journalists to social improvement and a willingness to crusade against corruption.
- Being on top of unfolding events and providing information to readers quickly.
- A detached, neutral perspective in reporting events, a tradition fostered by CP, BN, and AP.
- A strong ideology that government should keep its hands off the press.

Variables Affecting News

NEWS HOLE

A variable affecting what ends up being reported as news is called the **news hole**. In newspapers the news hole is the space left after the advertising department has placed all the ads it has sold in the paper. The volume of advertising determines the number of total pages, and generally, the bigger the issue, the more room for news. Newspaper editors can squeeze fewer stories into a thin Monday issue than a fat Wednesday issue.

In broadcasting, the news hole tends to be more consistent. A 30-minute television newscast may have room for only 24 minutes of news, but the format doesn't vary. When the advertising department doesn't sell all six minutes available for advertising, it usually is public service announcements, promotional messages, and program notes—not news—that pick up the slack. Even so, the news hole can vary in broadcasting. A 10-minute newscast can accommodate more stories than a five-minute newscast, and, as with newspapers, it is the judgment of journalists that determines which events make it.

NEWS FLOW AND STAFFING

Besides the news hole, the **flow** of news varies from day to day. A story that might be played prominently on a slow news day can be passed over entirely in the competition for space on a heavy news day.

On one of the heaviest news days of all time, in 1989, death claimed Iran's Ayatollah Khomeini, a central figure in United States foreign policy; Chinese young people and the government were locked in a showdown in Tiananmen Square; the Polish people were voting to reject their one-party Communist political system; and a revolt was underway in the Soviet republic of Uzbekistan. That was a heavy news day, and the flow of major nation-rattling events pre-empted stories that otherwise would have been news.

Whether reporters are in the right place at the right time can affect coverage. A radio station's city government coverage will slip when the city hall reporter is on vacation or if the station can't afford a regular reporter at city hall. When Iraq invaded Kuwait by surprise in August 1990, it so happened that almost all the U.S. and European reporters assigned to the Persian Gulf were on vacation or elsewhere on assignment. An exception was Caryle Murphy of the *Washington Post*. Like everyone else, Murphy hadn't expected the invasion, but she had decided to make a routine trip from her Cairo bureau for a firsthand look at Kuwaiti affairs. Only by happenstance did Murphy have what she called "a front-row seat for witnessing a small nation being crushed." Competing news organizations were devoid of eyewitness staff coverage until they scrambled to fly people into the region.

CAJ: The Canadian Association of Journalists is a national organization that serves Canadian journalists working in print, radio, and television.

www.eagle.ca/caj

PERCEPTIONS ABOUT AUDIENCE

How a news organization perceives its audience affects news coverage. The *National Enquirer* lavishes attention on unproven cancer cures that the *Saskatoon Leader-Post* treats briefly if at all. The *Wall Street Journal* sees its purpose as news for readers who have special interests in finance, the economy, and business. Canada's ROB-TV was established to serve an audience more interested in quick market updates and analysis than is provided by their local newscast. CTVNewsNet may lead newscasts with a coup d'état in another country, while Newsworld leads with a new government economic forecast.

AVAILABILITY OF MATERIAL

The availability of photographs and video is also a factor in what ends up being news. Television is often faulted for overplaying visually titillating stories, such as fires, and underplaying or ignoring more significant stories that are not photogenic. The media are partial to stories with strong accompanying visuals, as shown with images of the tornado in Alberta, school shootings in Orleans, Ontario, and Taber, Alberta, and the pomp and ceremony of the funeral of former prime minister Pierre Trudeau.

COMPETITION

One trigger of adrenalin for journalists is landing a scoop and, conversely, being scooped. Journalism is a competitive business, and the drive to outdo other news organizations keeps news publications and newscasts fresh with new material.

Competition also has an unglamorous side. Journalists constantly monitor each other to identify events that they missed and need to catch up on to be competitive. This catch-up aspect of the news business contributes to similarities in coverage, which scholar Leon Sigal calls the **consensible nature of news**. It also is called "pack" and "herd" journalism.

Non-Newsroom Influences on News

ADVERTISER INFLUENCE

Special interests sometimes try to squelch stories or insist on self-serving angles. Usually, these attempts are made quietly, even tacitly, among executives—what is known as "country-club decision-making." Sometimes the pressure is exerted on media advertising people, who quietly exert influence on the newsroom.

Pressure sometimes occurs after a story appears, sending clear signals never to do it again. In an egregious California case in 1994, the local car dealers' association yanked US$1 million in advertising out of the *San José Mercury News* after the paper ran an in-depth consumer article on how to buy a car. The dealers didn't like the negotiation tips and other insider information that reporter Mark Schwanhausser included in the story. The *Mercury News* hasn't done that kind of story since. In an interview with *Columbia Journalism Review,* Schwanhausser talked about a chilling effect: "When you start guessing what people will react to, you can find all kinds of reasons not to write a story."

To their credit, most news organizations place allegiance to their audiences ahead of pleasing advertisers, as Terry Berger, president of an advertising agency representing the Brazilian airline Varig, found out from *Condé Nast's Traveler*, a travel magazine. After an article on air pollution in Rio de Janeiro, Berger wrote to the magazine: "Is your editorial policy then to see how quickly you can alienate present and potential advertisers and at the same time convince your readers to stick closer to home? I really think that if you continue with this kind of editorial information, you are doing both your readers and your advertisers a disservice." Unintimidated, the magazine's editor, Harold Evans, did not recant. Not only did Evans print the letter, but he followed with this comment: "Mrs. Berger is, of course, entitled to use her judgment about where she advertises Brazil's national airline. I write not about that narrow commercial issue, but about her assertion that it is a disservice to readers and advertisers for us to print true but unattractive facts when they are relevant. This goes to the heart of the editorial policy of this magazine. We rejoice in the enrichments of travel, but our aim is to give readers the fullest information, frankly and fairly, so they can make their own judgments."

CORPORATE POLICY

No matter how committed journalists may be to truth-seeking and truth-telling, the people in charge have the final word on matters big and small. It is owners, publishers, general managers, and their immediate lieutenants who are in charge. Their corporate responsibilities dictate that they are business executives before all else, even if once they were journalists. Executives sometimes make self-serving decisions on coverage that gall the journalists who work for them, but such is how chains of command work.

Lowell Bergman, former executive producer at *60 Minutes*, recalls his days at CBS: "You could not do a story about a supplier or major advertiser. You could try to do it, but you were taking a lot of risks getting close to the limit." At both ABC and CBS, Bergman said, he was told that the networks would not initiate a critical story about the business practices and histories of National Football League team owners. The networks, of course, stood to derive handsome revenue from airing NFL games if they were awarded contracts for play-by-play coverage.

Admonitions not to go near certain stories are not in written policy, although they are real. ABC news people got an unusually overt reminder when Michael Eisner, chair of Disney, which owns ABC, said in an interview, "I would prefer ABC not to cover Disney. I think it's inappropriate." Eisner went on to say that *ABC News* knew of his preference.

In fairness, it must be said that media owners generally are sensitive to their truth-seeking and truth-telling journalistic responsibilities and assiduously avoid calling the shots on news coverage. Journalists who are bothered by wrong-headed news decisions have three choices: persuade wayward owners of the error of their ways, comply with directives, or quit and go work for a respectable journalistic organization.

SOURCE PRESSURE

Journalists sometimes feel external pressure directly. At the courthouse, valuable sources turn cold after a story appears that they don't like. A tearful husband begs an editor not to use his wife's name in a story that points to her as a bank embezzler. A bottle of Chivas Regal arrives at Christmas from a sports publicist who says she appreciates the excellent coverage over the past year. Most journalists will tell you that their commitment to truth overrides external assaults on their autonomy. Even so, external pressures exist.

The relationship between journalists and publicists can be troublesome. In general, the relationship works well. Publicists want news coverage for their clients and provide information and help reporters to line up interviews. Some publicists, however, are more committed to advancing their clients' interests than to advancing truth, and they work to manipulate journalists into providing coverage that unduly glorifies their clients.

Staging events is a publicity tactic to gain news coverage that a cause would not otherwise attract. Some staged events are obvious hucksterism, such as Evel Knievel's ballyhooed motorcycle leaps across vast canyons in the 1970s and local flagpole-sitting stunts by celebrity disc jockeys. Covering such events is usually part of the softer side of news and, in the spirit of fun and games and diversion, is relatively harmless.

Of more serious concern are staged events about which publicists create a mirage of significance to suck journalists and the public into giving more attention than they deserve. For example, consider:

- The false impression created when hundreds of federal workers are released from work for an hour to see an incumbent's campaign speech outside a government office building.
- The contrived photo opportunity at which people, props, and lighting are carefully, even meticulously, arranged to create an image on television.
- Stunts that bring attention to a new product and give it an undeserved boost in the marketplace.

Staged events distort a balanced journalistic portrayal of the world. Worse, they divert attention from truly significant events.

Gatekeeping in News

GATEKEEPERS' RESPONSIBILITIES

Just as a reporter exercises judgment in deciding what to report and how to report it, judgment also is at the heart of the gatekeeping process. Hardly any message, except live reporting, reaches its audience in its original form. Along the path from its originator to the eventual audience, a message is subject to all kinds of deletions, additions, and changes of emphasis. With large news organizations, this process may involve dozens of editors and other persons.

Most **gatekeepers** are invisible to the news audience, working behind the scenes and making crucial decisions in near-anonymity on how the world will be portrayed in the evening newscast and the next morning's newspaper. Herbert G. Kariel and Lynn A. Rosenvall, both associated with the University of Calgary, refer to gatekeepers as "filters," in their book *Places in the News: A Study of News Flows*. Kariel and Rosenvall say, "on any given day, only a small fraction of all the happenings that occur in the world are published in any newspaper at all, and many of those published in one newspaper do not appear in others." They list several hypothetical filters that impact news coverage. The first are "source filters":

- A journalist must be present at the event in order to report on it.
- The journalist must decide to write a story on the event, if he or she believes it to be newsworthy.

■ An editor at a news agency determines if the story will be distributed on a regional, national, or international basis.

The second type of filter is a "destination filter." These occur at the local news level where local editors make judgments on what stories are appropriate for their local markets. The size of the newsroom also acts as a filter. Larger newsrooms will have more stories to choose from and more time and space to include stories.

This work is based on the ideas of gatekeeping outlined by Wilbur Schramm in 1960:

> Suppose we follow a news item, let us say, from India to Indiana. The first gatekeeper is the person who sees an event happen. This person sees the event selectively, noticing some things, not others. The second gatekeeper is the reporter who talks to this "news source." Now, of course, we could complicate this picture by giving the reporter a number of news sources to talk to about the same event, but in any case the reporter has to decide which facts to pass along the chain, what to write, what shape and colour and importance to give to the event. The reporter gives his message to an editor, who must decide how to edit the story, whether to cut or add or change. Then the message goes to a news service where someone must decide which of many hundreds of items will be picked up and telegraphed to other towns, and how important the story is, and therefore how much space it deserves.
>
> At a further link in the chain, this story will come to a . . . news service and here again an editor must decide what is worth passing on to the . . . newspapers and broadcasting stations. The chain leads us on to a regional and perhaps a state news service bureau, where the same decisions must be made; always there is more news than can be sent on—which items, and how much of the items, shall be retained and retransmitted? And finally when the item comes to a local newspaper, an editor must go through the same process, deciding which items to print in the paper.
>
> Out of news stories gathered by tens of thousands of reporters around the world, only a few hundred will pass the gatekeepers along the chains and reach a local newspaper editor, who will be able to pass only a few dozen of those on to the newspaper reader.

GATEKEEPING: THE HOMOLKA AND BERNARDO TRIALS

The trials of Paul Bernardo and Karla Homolka provide an interesting case study of gatekeeping. The St. Catharines, Ontario, couple were convicted in the abduction and deaths of Kristen French of St. Catharines and Leslie Mahaffey of nearby Burlington. During the course of a regular shift, most reporters go about their duties as gatekeeper without much thought; it becomes second nature. However, reporters on this beat were made keenly aware of their role as gatekeepers and the power they held.

NICAR: National Institute of Computer Assisted Reporting.

www.nicar.org

Pulitzer Prize: The top prize for top work.

www.pulitzer.org

FACSNET: Improving journalism through education.

www.facsnet.org

Jim Romenesko's Media News: A daily clearinghouse of news-related links and information.

www.poynter.org

Mike and his Pals. While only a small percentage of daily happenings around the world "make" the news on any given day, political stories are often seen as "newsworthy" by gatekeepers. Daily scrums are one way that gatekeepers can get to the newsmakers.

In 1993, at Karla Homolka's trial, Judge Francis Kovacs issued a publication ban. The reason Kovacs gave for the ban was simple; it was to help ensure that Paul Bernardo received a fair trial. The ban proved to be problematic because much of the banned information was broadcast on American television and posted on the Internet in various newsgroups. But the role of Canadian journalists as gatekeepers was clearly defined; the gate had been locked. Journalists were only to report news that had been officially released by the court. Most journalists felt the ban was wrong as it interfered with the autonomy of their work and went against all the ideals Canadian journalism was based on, but most reporters complied with the ruling.

While the ban became the topic of discussion surrounding Homolka's trial, it's interesting to note that for many journalists, having to deal with the lifting of the ban at Paul Bernardo's trial in 1995 proved to be a much more difficult task. Kirk Makin of the *Globe and Mail* described the Bernardo beat as, "a hyperactive little community, consumed by deadlines and a sense that we were involved in something big. Those of us who were together for the entire trial shared the camaraderie of veterans, if only because the things we heard and saw were often too searing to convey to friends and family. Particularly in the beginning, the mind was unwilling, the tongue unable."

While reporting the details of Homolka's trial might have been liberating, other factors made reporting difficult for the gatekeeper during the Bernardo trial. This included not only the volume of evidence released about both Bernardo and Homolka, but the nature of the evidence itself, which was graphically violent and sexual. How did one report such horrible acts?

The *National Post*'s **Anne Marie Owens** held a unique position as gatekeeper. A journalist for the *St. Catharines Standard* at the time, she was the reporter assigned to the story when Kristen French was abducted in 1992 until the conviction of Paul Bernardo in 1995. Her experience on the Bernardo beat sheds some interesting light on the role of the gatekeeper. Most studies of the news-gathering process tend to state that news beats are highly routine. But these two trials were anything but routine. Homolka's trial lasted less than two days. Owens describes it as orchestrated and neatly packaged. You were given the information and told what to report.

Bernardo's trial was different. In contrast to Homolka's trial, there was an abundance of information. Like Makin, Owens found the facts difficult to write about. Not only did she find the story repulsive, but she was also a reporter in a community that was trying to understand how something so horrible could happen in their hometown. The rapes and murders had shattered what Gans might refer to as the "small town pastoralism" of St. Catharines. Owens was also writing stories that might be read by the victims' families and friends. Owens remembers, "listening to stuff that is sometimes unfathomable. The information that came out was so unlike anything else that the *Standard* normally covers. I had anticipated that there would be explicit information and details that would become, as gruesome as they were, relevant. There was so much awful information. Our job wasn't to give people all of it, it was to allow people to understand what had happened and give them enough details so they knew what happened. That was tough."

Journalism Trends

CONVERGENCE AND CANADIAN JOURNALISM

In 2001, the **CRTC** had to deal with the issue of convergence and editorial control. TVA, CTV, and CanWest Global were asked how they were planning to handle issues of newsroom policy and editorial decision making. Leonard Asper, president and CEO of CanWest Global Communications, had this vision of journalists in a converged media world, "in the future, journalists will wake up, write a story for the web, write a column, take their cameras, cover an event and do a report for TV and file a video clip for the web. What we have really acquired is a quantum leap in the product we offer advertisers and a massive, creative content-generation machine."

Quebec media giant, TVA, on the other hand, wanted to keep the broadcast and print newsrooms separate, saying "information professionals working in the newsrooms of TVA, LCN and LCN affiliates shall at no time transmit, receive, exchange or discuss information by phone, fax, Internet or other technology with information professionals working in the newsroom of Quebecor newspapers."

According to the Broadcasting Act, radio and television stations in Canada must provide varied and comprehensive coverage of significant issues. While the CRTC has no control over what happens in print newsrooms, they do have a say in what goes on in broadcast newsrooms. In their 2001 decisions concerning TVA, Global, and CTV, the CRTC's viewpoint is clear—keep editorial decisions between multimedia platforms within conglomerates separate. They have made it clear that they do not agree with Leonard Asper's view of journalism in the future. To the CRTC, this adds to the diversity of voices within the Canadian broadcasting system.

EXPLORATORY REPORTING

Norman Cousins acquired his reputation as a thinker when he edited the magazine *Saturday Review*. A premier journal under Cousins, the magazine tackled issues in depth and with intelligence. A few years later, Cousins said he couldn't find much of that kind of journalism in magazines anymore: "The best magazine articles in the U.S. today are appearing not in magazines but in newspapers." Cousins was taking note of a profound late-20th-century change in the concept of news: **exploratory reporting**. Newspapers and to a lesser extent television were tackling difficult issues that earlier were almost the exclusive provinces of magazines. Cousins especially admired the *Los Angeles Times*, which runs thoroughly researched, thoughtful pieces. It is not unusual for the *Los Angeles Times* to commit weeks, even months, of reporters' time to develop major stories, nor is that unusual at other major newspapers and some smaller ones.

Although newspapers have never been devoid of in-depth coverage, the thrust through most of their history has been to chronicle events: meetings, speeches, deaths, catastrophes. The emphasis began changing noticeably in the 1960s as it dawned on journalists that chronicling easily identifiable events was insufficient to capture larger, more significant issues and trends.

The failure of event-based reporting became clear when northern American cities were burning in race riots in the late 1960s. Journalists had missed one of the 20th century's most significant changes in the U.S.: the northward migration of southern blacks. The superficiality of mere chronicling was underscored in early coverage of the Vietnam War. By focusing on events, journalists missed asking significant questions about the flawed policies until it was too late. Newspapers expanded significantly beyond a myopic focus on events in the 1970s for three reasons:

- Recognition that old ways of reporting news were not enough.
- Larger reporting staffs that permitted time-consuming enterprise reporting.
- Better-educated reporters and editors, many with graduate degrees.

MEDIA DATABANK 7.1

How Canadians Get Their News

Here is a summary of findings of Canadians and their news habits, according to a 1998 telephone survey by the Angus Reid Group.

Media used "a great deal" for news information:

TV	60%
Newspapers	46%
Radio	37%
Weeklies	29%
Internet	9%

In regards to news reporting in general, the survey said:

- 56 percent of Canadians felt that reporters focus too much on the personal lives of those in the public eye.
- 45 percent think that business newspapers print what big companies tell them to print.
- 32 percent feel the level of in-depth coverage is just right.
- 22 percent say that journalists should be able to print anything they want.

Source: Canadians and the News Media, Angus Reid Group, 1998.

Newspapers, profitable as never before, were able to hire larger staffs that permitted them to try more labour-intensive, exploratory kinds of journalism. Instead of merely responding to events, newspapers, particularly big ones, began digging for stories. Much of this **investigative journalism** was modelled on the *Washington Post's* doggedness in covering **Watergate,** the White House-authorized break-in at the Democratic national headquarters during the 1972 U.S. presidential campaign. Twenty years earlier, the Watergate break-in scandal probably would not have gone beyond three paragraphs from the police beat. In 1972, however, the persistence of *Post* reporters **Carl Bernstein** and **Bob Woodward** posed so many questions about morality in the White House that eventually Nixon resigned and 25 aides went to jail.

SOFT NEWS

The success of the *National Enquirer*, whose circulation began to skyrocket in the 1960s, was not unnoticed, and when Time, Inc., launched *People* magazine and the *New York Times* launched *Us* magazine, gossipy celebrity news gained a kind of respectability. In this period, the newspaper industry began sophisticated research to identify what readers wanted, and then fine-tuned the content mix that would improve market penetration. As a result, many dailies added "People" columns. The news services began receiving requests for more offbeat, gee-whiz items of the sensational sort. Newspapers have always run such material, but more is being printed today to appeal to a broader audience. Many newspapers today also carry more consumer-oriented stories, lifestyle tips, and entertainment news. This is called **soft news.** In her 1997 content analysis of Toronto's supper-hour newscast, *Toronto Star* journalist Antonia Zerbisias said, "hard news is often hard to find." Her article states that on average, only about 43 percent of any newscast is "hard news."

Identifying Good Journalism

AUDIENCE DIMENSIONS

For decades the sensationalizing *National Enquirer* has been the largest-circulation newspaper in the United States. On ABC radio Paul Harvey's entertaining presentation and oddball items drew the medium's largest news audiences. Audience size, of course, is one measure of success, but it's a measure that misses a qualitative question: Is a news product popular because it's good?

For 4 million U.S. readers, the *National Enquirer* is good. They keep buying it, every week. Among Canadian daily newspapers, the *Toronto Star* and the *Globe and Mail* are the national circulation leaders—but with less circulation in Canada than the *Enquirer*. Are they not as good? The quantitative measures of circulation, reach, penetration, visits, and hits, while useful to advertisers, aren't much help for individuals in choosing news sources that meet their needs.

EVALUATIVE CRITERIA

Rather than following the pack, discerning people develop their own criteria for evaluating news sources. There are no cookie-cutter formulas. One size doesn't fit all. Among criteria to consider are the following:

ACCURACY, BALANCE, AND FAIRNESS. Deadline pressures, at the heart of news reporting, can work against accuracy—and balance and fairness take time. Some errors are forgivable, like those that occur in reporting an airliner hijacking, with all the attendant confusion. Unforgivable are doctored quotes, out-of-context data, and slanted editing. The triad of accuracy, balance, and fairness comprise a reasonable expectation for news media performance.

INTERPRETATION. Are journalists trying to help the audience make sense of what's happening? This interpretive aspect of journalism is tricky because a journalist's individual values are an underlying factor that, by their nature, aren't shared by everyone. The challenge for news consumers is to identify journalists whose judgment they trust to sort through information and present it in a meaningful context.

ORIGINAL CONTENT. News organizations package information from many sources. So much information is available from so many places that some newsrooms, especially in network radio, do nothing more than packaging. They hardly ever send a reporter out on the street, let alone to a war zone. A news organization deserves points for generating its own on-scene reporting. For example, when the Milosevic dictatorship ended in Yugoslavia in 2000, CNN kept two reporters in the country to track details.

NEWS

Today a great issue is whether journalism can insulate itself from the agendas of the giant corporations that own most journalistic enterprises when interests conflict. Classic cases: How does ABC cover Disney? How does the *National Post* cover Global? A 2000 Pew Research Center survey found that almost one-third of journalists believe that their newsrooms ignore stories that might conflict with the financial interests of their owners or advertisers.

The issue of *editorial independence* is essential to truth-seeking, truth-telling, and inspiring audience trust. That's the main concern of the CRTC when it comes to convergence in Canada.

AOL Time Warner has devised a policy that might serve as an industry model. Norman Pearlstine, editor-in-chief of the company's magazines, has a mandate to "provide unbiased coverage of the myriad interests of advertisers and of Time Warner itself." The mandate has been signed by the parent company's board of directors and chief executive. Says Pearlstine, "If readers think there are stories that we're keeping from them or that there are stories that we're pulling our punches on, we're out of business. If you're going to have a magazine, it's clear to me that you have to have the highest level of editorial independence."

Is this a road that other media conglomerates will take with their news operations? Time will tell.

CHAPTER WRAP-UP

Journalism is an art, not a science. Judgments, rather than formulas, determine which events and issues are reported and how—and no two journalists approach any story exactly the same way. This leaves the whole process of gathering and telling news subject to second-guessing and criticism. Journalists ask themselves all the time whether there are ways to do a better job. All journalists can do is try to find truth and to relate it accurately. Even then, the complexity of modern news-gathering—which involves many people, each with an opportunity to change or even kill a story—includes dozens of points at which inaccuracy and imprecision can creep into a story that started out well.

QUESTIONS FOR REVIEW

1. What contemporary news practices are rooted in the various press periods in Canada and the U.S.?

2. What personal values do journalists bring to their work? Does this affect what is reported and how?

3. What variables beyond journalists' control affect news?

4. What pressures from outside the media affect news reporting?

5. What responsibilities do journalists have as gatekeepers?

6. Is there a contradiction between the two contemporary journalistic trends of exploratory reporting and soft news?

QUESTIONS FOR CRITICAL THINKING

1. The 19-year-old son of the premier of a troubled Central American country in which the CIA has deep involvement died, perhaps of a drug overdose, aboard a Northwest Airlines plane en route from Tokyo to Singapore. On the plane was a young female country-western singer, his frequent companion in recent weeks. The plane was a Boeing 747 manufactured in Washington state. Northwest's corporate headquarters is in Minnesota. The death occurred at 4 a.m. Eastern time. Consider the six elements of news—proximity, prominence, timeliness, consequence, currency, and drama—and discuss how this event might be reported on morning television newscasts in Miami, Minneapolis, Nashville, Seattle and the District of Columbia. How about in Managua? Singapore? Tokyo? Rome? Istanbul? Johannesburg? What if the victim were an ordinary college student? What if the death occurred a week ago?

2. Explain news judgment.

3. How do the news hole and news flow affect what is reported in the news media?

4. *Time* and *Maclean's* carry cover stories on the same subject one week. Does this indicate that executives of the magazine have conspired, or is it more likely to be caused by what Leon Sigal calls the consensible nature of news?

5. How does the nature of news provide ammunition to conservatives to criticize the news media as leftist promoters of change?

6. Discuss whether the news media reflect mainstream values. Do you see evidence in your news media of an underlying belief that democracy, capitalism, rural small-town life, individualism, and moderation are virtues?

7. Do you feel that the mass media revel in disorder? Consider Herbert Gans's view that the media cover disorder from the perspective of identifying ways to restore order.

8. If a college president calls a news conference and makes a major announcement, who are the gatekeepers who determine how the announcement is covered in the campus newspaper?

FOR KEEPING UP TO DATE

Among publications that keep current on journalistic issues are *Columbia Journalism Review, Quill, American Journalism Review,* and *Editor & Publisher.*

Bridging the gap between scholarly and professional work is *Newspaper Research Journal.*

FOR FURTHER LEARNING

Angus Reid Group. "Canadians and the News Media." (*Canadian Corporate News*, 1998).

Jim Bawden. "Taking Care of Business," *Starweek Magazine* (May 17, 1997).

L. Brent Bozell III and Brent H. Baker, eds. *And That's the Way It Isn't: A Reference Guide to Media Bias* (Media Research Center, 1990).

Canada. Volume 6 of the Kent Commission on Newspapers, *Canadian News Services* (Ottawa: Supply and Services, 1981).

Canada. Volume 2 of the Kent Commission on Newspapers, *The Journalists* (Ottawa: Supply and Services, 1981).

Peter Desbarats. *Guide to the Canadian News Media* (Harcourt Brace, 1990).

Daniel J. Czitrom. *Media and the American Mind: From Morse to McLuhan* (University of North Carolina Press, 1982).

Hazel Dicken-Garcia. *Journalistic Standards in the Nineteenth Century* (University of Wisconsin Press, 1989).

Edwin and Michael Emery. *The Press and America,* 4th ed. (Prentice Hall, 1984).

Mark Fishman. *Manufacturing the News* (University of Texas Press, 1980).

Thomas L. Friedman. *From Beirut to Jerusalem* (Farrar, Straus & Giroux, 1989).

Herbert J. Gans. *Deciding What's News: A Study of CBS Evening News, NBC Nightly News, Newsweek and Time* (Pantheon, 1979).

Brian Green. *Canadian Broadcast News* (Harcourt Canada, 2001).

Jane T. Harrigan. *Read All About It! A Day in the Life of a Metropolitan Newspaper* (Globe Pequot Press, 1987).

Norman E. Isaacs. *Untended Gates: The Mismanaged Press* (Columbia University Press, 1986).

Ryszard Kapuscinski. *The Soccer War* (Alfred A. Knopf, 1991).

H.G. Kariel and L.A. Rosenvall. *Places in the News: A Study of News Flows* (Carleton University Press, 1995).

Wilfred Kesterton. *A History of Journalism in Canada* (McClelland and Stewart, 1967).

Anne Kingston. "Pamela Wallin's Wild Kingdom." *Saturday Night* (June, 1997).

Brooke Kroeger. *Nellie Bly: Daredevil, Reporter, Feminist* (Random House, 1994).

Molly Moore. *A Woman at War: Storming Kuwait With the U.S. Marines* (Scribner's, 1993).

Michael Parenti. *Inventing Reality: The Politics of the Mass Media* (St. Martin's, 1988).

David F. Rooney. *Reporting and Writing for Canadian Journalists* (Prentice Hall, 2001).

Michael Schudson. *Discovering the News: A Social History of American Newspapers* (Basic Books, 1978).

Pamela J. Shoemaker with Elizabeth Kay Mayfield. *Building a Theory of News Content: A Sythesis of Current Approaches* (Journalism Monographs, No. 103, June 1987).

David H. Weaver and G. Cleveland Wilhoit. *The American Journalist: A Portrait of U.S. News People and Their Work,* 2nd ed. (Indiana University Press, 1991).

Anthony Wilson-Smith. "Wall to Wall News." *Maclean's* (March 2, 1998).

Antonia Zerbisias. "The News About TV News." *Toronto Star* (July 20, 1997).

Chapter 8

Firestone Crisis. In early 2000, tire manufacturer Firestone was faced by an usual increase in warranty claims citing their tires as a factor in numerous highway accidents. Could good public relations have pre-empted the crisis at Firestone?

MEDIA TIMELINE

Evolution of Public Relations

1859	Charles Darwin advances survival-of-the-fittest theory, which leads to social Darwinism.
1880s	Public becomes dissatisfied with unconscionable business practices justified with social Darwinism.
1906	Ivy Lee begins the first public relations agency.
1917	George Creel heads a federal agency that generates support for World War I.
1927	Arthur Page becomes the first corporate public relations vice president.
1930s	Paul Garrett creates the term *enlightened self-interest* at General Motors.
1953	The Canadian Public Relations Society is formed.
1965	Public Relations Society of America creates the accreditation system.
1970s	Herb Schmertz pioneers adversarial public relations at Mobil Oil.
1987	Public Relations Society of America adopts an ethics code.

Public Relations

Media in Theory

Public Relations as "Sleaze?"

Public relations operates in the realm of what Canadian **Joyce Nelson** calls the "legitimacy gap" in her book *The Sultans of Sleaze: Public Relations and the Media*. The term *legitimacy gap* was coined by business professor Prakesh Sethi to describe the difference between a corporate image and the corporate reality. Nelson applies Jungian psychology to the term in her analysis of public relations. She argues that a corporation has two sides: a persona and a shadow. The persona is its corporate image, the positive image that is promoted via advertising; the shadow is its dark side, which is not usually seen in the news media and certainly not in advertising. According to Nelson, the shadow may include "the ways in which their [the corporation's] activities infringe upon our health and

safety, our environment, to our oppression or that of others, despite what all their persona-related activity would like us to believe." When something happens that threatens the persona and reveals the shadow of a corporation, public relations professionals are called to fix the problem.

Nelson provides an interesting example. Within two weeks during the summer of 1981, Ontario Hydro was involved in two environmental accidents. First it dumped heavy water containing 3500 curies of radiation into the Ottawa River. The event received front-page coverage in the *Globe and Mail* and was reported on television news. A week later, almost 4000 gallons (18 000 litres) of radioactive water was accidentally spilled at Ontario Hydro's Bruce Nuclear

Power Plant. More than twice as much tritium—about 8000 curies—was released in the accident. These incidents created a problem for Ontario Hydro. The nuclear power industry's persona is centred around concern for public safety and the environment. But Nelson argues that these spills raised questions about the safety of nuclear power, thus revealing Hydro's shadow.

The second incident received less coverage in both the *Globe and Mail* and the *Toronto Star*. One of the reasons for this may have been "information overload"; perhaps the news media were simply tired of writing about problems at nuclear power plants. According to Nelson, another reason the second accident received less negative coverage had to do with the well-crafted press release that ended up as a news story in the *Toronto Star*. Consider the lead of the news story: "Armed with mops, pails and pumps, an Ontario Hydro crew has recovered 3400 gallons of radioactive heavy water at the Bruce Nuclear Power plant." This passage succeeds in diverting attention from the accident by focusing instead on the clean-up. Any suspicions the reader may have about the corporation's shadow are discarded. The story goes on to outline the cost, of the clean-up in detail, which underlines Hydro's commitment to protecting the environment, whatever the cost, and thus reinforces its corporate image, or persona. The story makes no mention of damage to the surrounding area.

Bruce Livesey, a Toronto journalist, concurs with Nelson's ideas. In his article "PR Wars: How the PR Industry Flacks for Big Business," Livesey says the "corporations that befoul the environment, sell shoddy and dangerous products . . . are increasingly turning to the PR industry for assistance." Understanding how the media works is an important element in public relations. It's no surprise then that many public relations practitioners were journalists earlier in their careers. Livesey claims that economics is one reason: the starting salary for a journalist at the *Globe and Mail* is $672 a week, while a job as a PR person for the Ontario government, just down the road (literally and metaphorically) from the *Globe* pays $819 a week.

Nelson sees public relations as the art of controlling information. In theoretical terms, this can be viewed as agenda setting. Nelson argues that there is a serious problem when public relations professionals can shape, either entirely or in part, the content of a newspaper or newscast. A well-written and well-publicized press release, like the one written about the spill of heavy water, not only starts the process of communication but effectively ends it as well by determining the discourse surrounding it.

The Canadian Public Relations Society would agree—and disagree—with the ideas of Livesey and Nelson. In the article "Truth Pays Dividends with the Public," Jean Valin argues that up to 50 percent of the public will not believe most media messages due to a perceived lack of trust of the media. However, Valin discounts Nelson's idea that public relations is "smoke and mirrors." She says that in the end, "organizations will always be well served by telling the truth. It takes a long time to build your credibility and an even longer time to rebuild it . . . this provides all the more reason to practice good public relations and avoid the pitfalls of manipulation and disinformation—honesty pays."

Importance of Public Relations

A YOUNG GIRL'S STORY

In tearful and dramatic testimony, a 14-year-old Kuwaiti girl told a U.S. congressional committee that she had witnessed horrible atrocities when Iraqi troops invaded her homeland. She described soldiers pulling babies out of hospital incubators and leaving them on the floor to die. This was October 1990, while U.S. President George Bush was engaged both in massive military build-up in preparation to retake Kuwait from the Iraqis and in a massive campaign at home to convince Congress and the American people that military intervention was justified.

Within a few days, Congress voted narrowly to let President Bush proceed with the war preparations. Of course, much more than the girl's testimony shaped public feelings, but for many people her account was riveted indelibly in their minds. Also, the testimony, as well as the U.S. military intervention, marked a huge success for the giant Hill & Knowlton public relations company.

After the Iraqi blitzkrieg into Kuwait in August 1990, well-heeled Kuwaiti leaders who had fled their country founded a group called Citizens for a Free Kuwait to generate U.S. support for their cause. As the CBC's *Fifth Estate* revealed in its 1992 documentary *To Sell a War*, the group hired Hill & Knowlton, which has 290 employees in Washington alone, to send lobbyists to Congress to make their client's case. The company arranged for Kuwaiti sympathizers to give television, radio, newspaper, and magazine interviews.

Hill & Knowlton was engaged in classic public relations activities: advising a client on how to present the best possible case to groups it wants to win over to its view and then helping the client accomplish its purposes. For Hill & Knowlton's services, the exiled Kuwaiti government paid US$11.9 million. It was a bargain, to whatever extent the expenditure contributed to the multination military and diplomatic mobilization against Iraq and the eventual expulsion of Iraqis from Kuwaiti soil. The Kuwaitis got the most bang for their buck, however, from the testimony of 14-year-old Nayirah al-Sabah.

Hill & Knowlton: At this website, Hill & Knowlton details its international services. These include crisis and issue management, business-to-business communication, media relations, research, design, event management, and sponsorship.

www.hillandknowlton.com

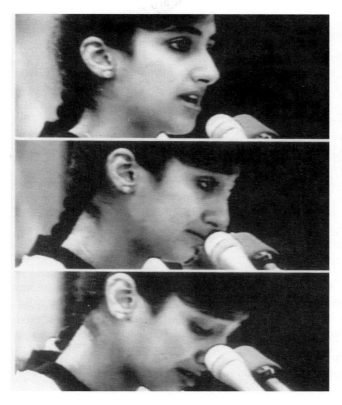

Tearful and Compelling. Fourteen-year-old Nayirah al-Sabah told Congress that she had witnessed Iraqi troops committing atrocities in her Kuwaiti homeland. Her testimony, it was learned later, was arranged by the Hill & Knowlton public relations agency, and her claims were wildly exaggerated in an attempt to arouse U.S. public sentiment against the Iraqi invaders so they would intervene militarily. Critics have raised serious questions about the appropriateness of Hill & Knowlton's role in trying to influence U.S. public policy on behalf of Kuwaiti clients.

Canadian Public Relations Society: Canada's only professional public relations society, representing more than 1500 PR practitioners across the country.

www.cprs.ca

Institute for Public Relations: Research and education to improve the practice of public relations.

www.instituteforpr.com

Council of Public Relations Firms: This site is a new window on a public relations industry that has been too long shrouded in mystery and myth.

www.prfirms.org

PR Watch: The Center for Media & Democracy is a nonprofit, public-interest organization funded by individuals and nonprofit foundations and dedicated to investigative reporting on the public relations industry. The Center serves citizens, journalists, and researchers seeking to recognize and combat manipulative and misleading PR practices.

www.prwatch.org

Early in October, two months after the Iraqi invasion, officials from the Kuwaiti embassy in Washington escorted Nayirah to the Hill & Knowlton office to tell her story. The potential for the girl's story was clear right away to Lauri Fitz-Pegado, a senior H&K vice president. The agency contacted U.S. House of Representatives member Tom Lantos, co-chair of the congressional Human Rights Caucus, and set up a hearing for Nayirah to testify. The news media were advised to be there for dynamite revelations.

The hearing lived up to Hill & Knowlton's advance billing. Nayirah choked back tears as she explained that she had been working as a volunteer at the hospital under an assumed name, and then she told about the dreadful infanticides. Among other atrocities she described was how teen-age friends had been tortured with electricity. CNN carried the testimony live, evening newscasts led with it, newspapers bannered it, and magazines featured it. Amnesty International, which tracks political terrorism worldwide, reported the baby massacre based on Nayirah's testimony, and the Red Crescent cited it before the United Nations.

Later, it turned out that Hill & Knowlton may have been duped. Although many Iraqi atrocities occurred in Kuwait, investigators were never able, even after the war, to corroborate Nayirah's story of the baby massacre. Furthermore, journalists raised questions about a cozy connection between H & K and Congressman Tom Lantos, who arranged the hearing at which Nayirah testified. Questions were raised whether Citizens for a Free Kuwait was a legitimate grassroots organization or a front manufactured for Kuwaiti interests by Hill & Knowlton. Additional doubts surfaced when it was learned that Nayirah was actually the daughter of the Kuwaiti ambassador, which had not been announced at the hearings. To that issue, Hill & Knowlton said it had needed to protect her and her family members from Iraqi death squads.

DEFINING PUBLIC RELATIONS

Edward Bernays, the public relations pioneer, lamented how loosely the term **public relations** is used. To illustrate his concern, Bernays told about a young woman who approached him for career advice. He asked her what she did for a living. "I'm in public relations," she said. He pressed her for details, and she explained that she handed out flyers. It's unfortunate, but the term public relations sometimes is used loosely. Some people think it means backslapping, glad-handing, and smiling prettily to make people feel good. The fact, however, is that public relations goes far beyond good interpersonal skills. The Canadian Public Relations Society says that public relations is "the management function which evaluates public attitudes, identifies the policies of an individual or organization with the public interest, and plans and executes a program of action to earn public understanding and acceptance." An IPSO Reid poll, released in 2000, claimed that 96 percent of Canadian CEOs felt that good public relations was essential for businesses today.

Four steps are necessary for public relations to accomplish its goals:

IDENTIFY EXISTING RELATIONSHIPS. In modern society, institutions have many relationships. A college, for example, has relationships with its students, its faculty, its staff, its alumni, its benefactors, the neighbourhood, the community, the legislature, other colleges, accreditors of its programs, and perhaps unions. The list could go on and on. Each of these constituencies is called a public—hence the term public relations.

EVALUATE THE RELATIONSHIPS. Through research, the public relations practitioner studies these relationships to determine how well they are working. This evaluation is an ongoing process. A college may have excellent relations with the legislature one year and win major appropriations, but after a scandal related to the president's budget the next year, legislators may be downright unfriendly.

DESIGN POLICIES TO IMPROVE THE RELATIONSHIPS. The job of public relations people is to recommend policies to top management to make these relationships work better, not only for the organization but also for the partners in each relationship. **Paul Garrett,** a pioneer in corporate relations, found that General Motors was not seen in friendly terms during the Great Depression, which put the giant automaker at risk with many publics, including its own employees. GM, he advised, needed new policies to seem neighbourly—rather than as a far-removed, impersonal, monolithic industrial giant.

IMPLEMENT THE POLICIES. Garrett used the term **enlightened self-interest** for his series of policies intended to downsize GM in the eyes of many of the company's publics. Garrett set up municipal programs in towns with GM plants, and grants for schools and scholarships for employees' children. General Motors benefited from a revised image and, in the spirit of enlightened self-interest, so did GM employees, their children, and their communities.

Public relations is not a mass medium itself, but PR uses the media as tools to accomplish its goals. The number of people in most of the publics with which public relations practitioners need to communicate is so large that it can be reached only through the mass media. The influence of public relations on the news media is extensive. Half of the news in many newspapers originates with formal statements or news releases from organizations that want something in the paper. It is the same with radio and television.

Misconceptions about public relations include the idea that it is a one-way street for institutions and individuals to communicate to the public. Actually, the good practice of public relations seeks two-way communication between and among all the people and institutions concerned with an issue.

Origins of Public Relations

MOGULS IN TROUBLE

Nobody would be tempted to think of **William Henry Vanderbilt** as very good at public relations. In 1882, it was Vanderbilt, president of the New York Central Railroad, who said, "The public be damned," when asked about the effect of changing train schedules. Vanderbilt's utterance so infuriated people that it became a banner in the populist crusade against robber barons and tycoons in the late 1800s. Under populist pressure, state governments set up agencies to regulate railroads. Then the U.S. government established the Interstate Commerce Commission to control freight and passenger rates. Government began insisting on safety standards. Labour unions formed in the industries with the worst working conditions, safety records, and pay. Journalists added pressure with muckraking exposés on excesses in the railroad, coal, and oil trusts; on meat-packing industry frauds; and on patent medicines.

The leaders of industry were slow to recognize the effect of populist objections on their practices. They were comfortable with **social Darwinism,** an adaptation of **Charles Darwin**'s survival-of-the-fittest theory. In fact, they thought themselves forward-thinking in applying Darwin's theory to business and social issues. It was only

Crisis Management. Something went wrong at a Union Carbide chemical factory at Bhopal, India, and more than 2000 people died. It was the worst industrial accident in history. Union Carbide fumbled at first in dealing with media inquiries. Company guards denied access to a reporter who wanted to visit a Union Carbide plant in West Virginia that manufactured the same chemical as the Bhopal plant. A few days later, however, the company invited reporters inside the gates en masse. The turnaround represented a realization that shutting out the news media was engendering public suspicions about Union Carbide's culpability in the Bhopal disaster. In contrast, openness can inspire public confidence.

Museum of Public Relations: Established in 1997 by Spector & Associates, the museum showcases successful public relations programs since the birth of the PR industry.

www.prmuseum.com

a few years earlier, in 1859, that Darwin had laid out his biological theory in *On the Origin of Species by Means of Natural Selection*. To cushion the harshness of social Darwinism, many tycoons espoused a paternalism toward those whose "fitness" had not brought them fortune and power. No matter how carefully put, the paternalism seemed arrogant to the "less fit."

George Baer, a railroad president, epitomized both social Darwinism and paternalism in commenting on a labour strike: "The rights and interests of the laboring man will be protected and cared for not by labor agitators but by the Christian men to whom God in His infinite wisdom has given the control of the property interests of the country." Baer was quoted widely, further fuelling sentiment against big business. Baer may have been sincere, but his position was read as a cover for excessive business practices by barons who assumed superiority to everyone else.

Meanwhile, social Darwinism came under attack as circuitous reasoning: economic success accomplished by abusive practices could be used to justify further abusive practices, which would lead to further success. Social Darwinism was a dog-eat-dog outlook that hardly jibed with democratic ideals, especially not as described in the preamble to the U.S. Constitution, which sought to "promote the general welfare, and secure the blessings of liberty" for everyone—not for only the chosen "fittest." Into these tensions at the turn of the last century came public relations pioneer Ivy Lee.

THE IDEAS OF IVY LEE

Coal mine operators, like the railroad magnates, were held in the public's contempt at the turn of the last century. Obsessed with profits, caring little about public sentiment or even the well-being of their employees, the mine operators were vulnerable in the new populist wave. Mine workers organized, and 150 000 in Pennsylvania went out on strike in 1902, shutting down the anthracite industry and disrupting coal-dependent industries, including the railroads. The mine operators snubbed reporters, which probably contributed to a pro-union slant in many news stories and worsened the operators' public image. Not until six months into the strike, when President Theodore Roosevelt threatened to take over the mines with Army troops, did the operators settle.

Shaken finally by Roosevelt's threat and recognizing Roosevelt's responsiveness to public opinion, the mine operators began reconsidering how they went about their business. In 1906, with another strike looming, one operator heard about **Ivy Lee,** a young publicist in New York who had new ideas about winning public support. He was hired. In a turnabout in press relations, Lee issued a news release that announced, "The anthracite coal operators, realizing the general public interest in conditions in the mining regions, have arranged to supply the press with all possible information." Then followed a series of releases with information attributed to the mine operators by name—the same people who earlier had preferred anonymity and refused all interview requests. There were no more secret strike strategy meetings. When operators planned a meeting, reporters covering the impending strike were informed. Although reporters were not admitted to the meetings, summaries of the proceedings were given to them immediately afterward. This relative openness eased longstanding hostility toward the operators, and a strike was averted.

Lee's success with the mine operators began a career that rewrote the rules on how corporations deal with their various publics. Among his accomplishments were the following:

CONVERTING INDUSTRY TOWARD OPENNESS. Railroads had notoriously secretive policies not only about their business practices but even about accidents. When the **Pennsylvania Railroad** sought Ivy Lee's counsel, he advised against suppressing news—especially on things that inevitably would leak out anyway. When a train jumped the rails near Gap, Pennsylvania, Lee arranged for a special car to take reporters to the scene and even take pictures. The Pennsylvania line was applauded in the press for the openness, and coverage of the railroad, which had been negative for years, began changing. A "bad press" continued plaguing other railroads that persisted in their secretive tradition.

TURNING NEGATIVE NEWS INTO POSITIVE NEWS. When the U.S. Senate proposed investigating International Harvester for monopolistic practices, Lee advised the giant farm implement manufacturer against reflexive obstructionism and silence. A statement went out announcing that the company, confident in its business practices, not only welcomed but also would facilitate an investigation. Then began a campaign that pointed out International Harvester's beneficence toward its employees. The campaign also emphasized other upbeat information about the company.

PUTTING CORPORATE EXECUTIVES ON DISPLAY. When workers at a Colorado mine went on strike, company guards fired machine guns and killed several men. More battling followed, during which two women and 11 children were killed. It was called the **Ludlow Massacre,** and **John D. Rockefeller, Jr.,** the chief mine owner, was pilloried for what had happened. Rockefeller was an easy target. Like his father, widely despised for the earlier standard oil monopolistic practices, John Jr. tried to keep himself out of the spotlight, but suddenly mobs were protesting at his mansion in New York and calling out, "shoot him down like a dog." Rockefeller asked Ivy Lee what he should do. Lee

Ludlow Massacre. Colorado militiamen opened fire during a 1914 mine labour dispute and killed women and children. Overnight, John D. Rockefeller became the object of public hatred. It was a Rockefeller company that owned the mine, and even in New York, where Rockefeller lived, there were rallies asking for his head. Public relations pioneer Ivy Lee advised Rockefeller to tour the Ludlow area as soon as tempers cooled to show his sincere concern and to begin work on a labour contract to meet the concerns of miners. Rockefeller ended up a popular character in the Colorado mining camps.

Ivy Lee

began whipping up articles about Rockefeller's human side, his family, and his generosity. Then, on Lee's advice, Rockefeller announced he would visit Colorado to see conditions himself. He spent two weeks talking with miners at work and in their homes and meeting their families. It was a news story that reporters could not resist, and it unveiled Rockefeller as a human being, not a far-removed, callous captain of industry. One myth-shattering episode occurred one evening when Rockefeller, after a brief address to miners and their wives, suggested that the floor be cleared for a dance. Before it was all over, John D. Rockefeller, Jr., had danced with almost every miner's wife, and the news stories about the evening did a great deal to mitigate antagonism and distrust toward Rockefeller. Back in New York, with Lee's help Rockefeller put together a proposal for a grievance procedure, which he asked the Colorado miners to approve. It was ratified overwhelmingly.

AVOIDING PUFFERY AND FLUFF. Ivy Lee came on the scene at a time when many organizations were making extravagant claims about themselves and their products. Circus promoter **P.T. Barnum** made this kind of **puffery** a fine art in the late 1800s, and he had many imitators. It was an age of puffed-up advertising claims and fluffy rhetoric. Lee noted, however, that people soon saw through hyperbolic claims and lost faith in those who made them. In launching his public relations agency in 1906, he vowed to be accurate in everything he said and to provide whatever verification anyone requested. This became part of the creed of good practice in public relations, and it remains so today.

Structure of Public Relations

POLICY ROLE OF PUBLIC RELATIONS

When U.S. giant AT&T needed somebody to take over public relations in 1927, the president of the company went to magazine editor **Arthur Page** and offered him a vice presidency. Before accepting, Page laid out several conditions. One was that he

Media People

Edward Bernays

Edward Bernays

After graduation from college in 1912, Edward Bernays tried press agentry. He was good at it, landing free publicity for whoever would hire him. Soon his bosses included famous tenor Enrico Caruso and actor Otis Skinner. Bernays felt, however, that his success was tainted by the disdain in which press agents were held in general. He also saw far greater potential for affecting public opinion than his fellow press agents did. From Bernays's discomfort and vision was born the concept of modern public relations. His 1923 book *Crystallizing Public Opinion* outlined a new craft he called public relations.

Bernays saw good public relations as counsel to clients. He called the public relations practitioner a "special pleader." The concept was modelled partly on the long-established lawyer-client relationship in which the lawyer, or counsellor, suggests courses of action. Because of his seminal role in defining what public relations is, Bernays sometimes is called the "Father of PR," although some people say the honour should be shared with Ivy Lee.

No matter, there is no question of Bernays's ongoing contributions. He taught the first course in public relations in 1923 at New York University. Bernays encouraged firm methodology in public relations, a notion that was captured in the title of a book he edited in 1955: *The Engineering of Consent*. He long advocated the professionalization of the field, which laid the groundwork for the accreditation of the sort the Public Relations Society of America has developed.

Throughout his career Bernays stressed that public relations people need a strong sense of responsibility. In one reflective essay, he wrote, "Public relations practiced as a profession is an art applied to a science in which the public interest and not pecuniary motivation is the primary consideration. The engineering of consent in this sense assumes a constructive social role. Regrettably, public relations, like other professions, can be abused and used for anti-social purposes. I have tried to make the profession socially responsible as well as economically viable." When asked by agents of fascist dictators Francisco Franco and Adolf Hitler to improve their images in the United States, Bernays declined, saying, "I wouldn't do for money what I wouldn't do without money."

Bernays became the Grand Old Man of public relations, still attending PRSA and other professional meetings past his 100th birthday. He died in 1993 at age 102.

---

have a voice in AT&T policy. Page was hardly on an ego trip. He had seen too many corporations that regarded their public relations arm merely as an executor of policy. Page considered PR itself as amanagement function. To be effective as vice president for public relations, Page knew that he must contribute to the making of high-level corporate decisions as well as executing them.

Barbara L. Pollock, of the Canadian Public Relations Society, agrees that public relations is an important management tool. Says Pollock: "Communications and information are the primary tools of tomorrow's manager. In fact, today's organizations already spend the majority of time in public relations and if their managers are not trained to handle it, they will get others that are."

HOW PUBLIC RELATIONS IS ORGANIZED

No two institutions are organized in precisely the same way. At some large Canadian corporations, over 100 people may work in public relations. In smaller organizations, PR may be one of several hats worn by a single person. Except in the smallest operations, the public relations department usually has three functional areas of responsibility:

DynaComm Public Relations: With links to wit and wisdom.

www.infopoint.com/sc/ business/dynacomm/ index.html

Edelman Worldwide: Worldwide PR firm with dozens of high-end corporate clients.

www.edelman.com

Fleishman-Hillard: Complete treatment of an international company in four languages.

www.fleishman.com

Ketchum: This giant public relations agency waxes eloquently at this elegant thematic website. Ketchum welcomes you with this message: "Enter with an open mind. Or pick one up while you're here."

www.ketchum.com

EXTERNAL RELATIONS. **External public relations** involves communication with groups and people outside the organization, including customers, dealers, suppliers, and community leaders. The external-relations unit usually is responsible for encouraging employees to participate in civic activities. Other responsibilities include arranging promotional activities like exhibits, trade shows, conferences, and tours.

Public relations people also lobby government agencies and legislators on behalf of their organization, keep the organization abreast of government regulations and legislation, and coordinate relations with political candidates. This may include fund-raising for candidates and coordinating political action committees.

In hospitals and nonprofit organizations, a public relations function may include recruiting and scheduling volunteer workers.

INTERNAL RELATIONS. **Internal public relations** involves developing optimal relations with employees, managers, unions, shareholders, and other internal groups. In-house newsletters, magazines, and brochures are important media for communicating with organizations' internal audiences.

MEDIA RELATIONS. Communication with large groups of people outside an organization is practicable only through the mass media. An organization's coordinator of **media relations** responds to news media queries, arranges news conferences, and issues news releases. These coordinators coach executives for news interviews and sometimes serve as their organization's spokesperson.

PUBLIC RELATIONS AGENCIES

Even though many organizations have their own public relations staff, they may go to **public relations agencies** for help on specific projects or problems. Hundreds of companies specialize in public relations counsel and related services. It is a big business. Gross revenue at Fleishman-Hillard, Canada's largest PR firm, is close to $40 million.

The biggest agencies offer a full range of services on a global scale. Hill & Knowlton has offices in Cleveland, its original home; Dallas; Frankfurt; Geneva; London; Los Angeles; New York, now its headquarters; Paris; Rome; Seattle; and Washington, DC. The agency will take on projects anywhere in the world, either on its own or by working with local agencies.

Besides full-service agencies, there are specialized public relations companies, which focus on a narrow range of services. For example, clipping services cut out

MEDIA DATABANK 8.1

Top Public Relations Firms in Canada

These are the largest public relations firms in Canada, according to a survey conducted by *Marketing Magazine*. The list was compiled based on companies that provided financial information.

Company	*Gross Revenues, 2000 (in Canadian Dollars)*
1. Fleishman-Hillard	$39 346 743
2. Bench Mark Porter Novelli	$5 941 045
3. Environics Communications	$4 759 766
4. High Road Communications	$2 170 000
5. LaFleur Communication Marketing	$1 291 595

Source: Marketing Magazine, *June 25, 2001. Reprinted with permission.*

and provide newspaper and magazine articles and radio and television items of interest to clients. Among specialized agencies are those that focus exclusively on political campaigns. Others coach corporate executives for news interviews, and others coordinate trade shows.

Public Relations Services

ACTIVITIES BEYOND PUBLICITY

Full-service public relations agencies provide a wide range of services built on two of the cornerstones of the business: **publicity** and **promotion**. These agencies are ready to conduct media campaigns to rally support for a cause, create an image, or turn a problem into an asset. Publicity and promotion, however, are only the most visible services offered by public relations agencies. There are several others:

LOBBYING. Every province has public relations practitioners whose specialty is representing their clients to legislative bodies and government agencies, or **lobbying**. In one sense, lobbyists are expediters. They know local traditions and customs, and they know who is in a position to affect policy. Lobbyists advise their clients, which include trade associations, corporations, public interest groups, and regulated utilities and industries, on how to achieve their goals by working with legislators and government regulators. Many lobbyists call themselves "government relations specialists."

POLITICAL COMMUNICATION. Every provincial capital has political consultants whose work mostly is advising candidates for public office in **political communication**. Services include campaign management, survey research, publicity, media relations, and image consulting. Political consultants also work on elections, referendums, recalls, and other public policy issues.

Infomart: An online repository of clippings offering information on Canadian news and business. A valuable tool for the PR practitioner.

www.informart.ca

Weber Shandwick Worldwide: An international PR firm that brands itself as "the world's most powerful communications consultancy."

www.webershandwick.com

IMAGE CONSULTING. **Image consulting** has been a growing specialized branch of public relations since the 1970s. Jacqueline Thompson, author of the *Directory of Personal Image Consultants*, listed 53 entries in 1981 and has been adding up to 157 new entries a year since then. About these consultants, said Thompson: "They will lower the pitch of your voice, remove your accent, correct your 'body language,' modify your unacceptable behavior, eliminate your negative self-perception, select your wardrobe, restyle your hair, and teach you how to speak off the cuff or read a speech without putting your audience to sleep."

FINANCIAL PUBLIC RELATIONS. Financial public relations dates back to the 1920s and 1930s. It is the job of people in financial PR to know not only the principles of public relations but also the complex regulations governing the promotion of securities in corporate mergers, acquisitions, new issues, and stock splits.

FUND-RAISING. Some public relations people specialize in fund-raising and membership drives. Many university and community colleges, for example, have their own staffs to perform these functions. Others look to fund-raising firms to manage capital drives. Such an agency employs a variety of techniques, from mass mailings to telephone soliciting, and charges a percentage of the amount raised. This is a growing field, given the current economic climate, which has led both the federal and provincial governments to cut back on grants and funding.

CONTINGENCY PLANNING. Many organizations rely on public relations people to design programs to address problems that can be expected to occur. This is known as **contingency planning.** Airlines, for example, need detailed plans for handling inevitable plane crashes—situations requiring quick, appropriate responses under tremendous pressure. When a crisis occurs, an organization can turn to public relations people for advice on dealing with it. Some agencies specialize in **crisis management,** which involves picking up the pieces either when a contingency plan fails or when there was no plan to deal with a crisis.

POLLING. Public-opinion sampling is essential in many public relations projects. Full-service agencies can either conduct surveys themselves or contract with companies that specialize in surveying.

EVENTS COORDINATION. Many public relations people are involved in coordinating a broad range of events, including product announcements, news conferences, and convention planning. Some in-house public relations departments and agencies have their own artistic and audio-visual production talent to produce brochures, tapes, and other promotional materials. Other agencies contract out for those services.

PUBLIC RELATIONS AND ADVERTISING

Both public relations and **advertising** involve persuasion, but most of the similarities end there. Public relations has responsibility in shaping an organization's policy. It is a management activity. Advertising is not. The work of advertising is much narrower. It focuses on selling a service or product after all the management decisions have been made. Public relations "sells" points of view and images, which are intangibles and therefore hard to measure. In advertising, success is measurable with tangibles, like sales, that can be calculated from the bottom line.

Taking on the Media. After ABC television reported that tobacco companies spiked cigarettes to make them more addictive, R.J. Reynolds responded with a multi-prong campaign to tell its side. The tobacco company sued ABC. The company also ran advertorials in the *Wall Street Journal* and elsewhere featuring the chairman of the company. Adversarial responses to the media are not mainstream public relations, but they are becoming more frequent. General Motors used adversarial public relations against NBC after the network rigged a GM truck to explode in order to support a claim that they were prone to fires in collisions. GM filed a suit and went public with evidence that NBC's video was staged. After extracting an apology from a humiliated NBC, GM dropped its suit.

When an organization decides it needs a persuasive campaign, there is a choice between public relations and advertising. One advantage of advertising is that the organization controls the message. By buying space or time in the mass media, an organization has the final say on what it says in its advertising messages.

In public relations, in contrast, an organization tries to influence the media to tell its story its way, but the message that goes out is actually up to the media. A news reporter, for example, may lean heavily on a public relations person for information about an organization, but the reporter may also gather information from other sources, and, in the end, it is the reporter who writes the story. The result, usually, is that a news story carries more credibility than advertisements with mass audiences. The disadvantage to an organization is the risk that comes with surrendering control over the message that goes to the public.

JOINT PROJECTS

For many persuasive campaigns, organizations use both public relations and advertising. Increasingly, public relations and advertising people find themselves working together—an overlap resulting from the decisions of many major ad agencies to acquire public relations agencies.

INSTITUTIONAL ADVERTISING. Public relations and advertising crossovers are hardly new. One area of traditional overlap is **institutional advertising**, which involves producing ads to promote an image rather than a product. The fuzzy, feel-good ads of the CIBC that feature images of Canadian mythology are typical.

INTEGRATED MARKETING. A new hybrid, with elements of public relations, advertising, and marketing, emerged in the 1990s. Called **integrated marketing communication,** the idea is to use any and all means to make a product part of a targeted consumer's mindset. It is not enough to advertise in the traditional media to mass audiences or even subgroups. Rather, the goal is to immerse a product in the mindset of individual consumers by focusing a diverse array of messages in their experience.

To describe integrated marketing communication, called IMC, media critic James Ledbetter suggests thinking of the old Charlie the Tuna ads, in which a cartoon fish made you chuckle and identify with the product—and established a brand name. That's not good enough for IMC. "By contrast," Ledbetter says, "IMC encourages tuna buyers to think about all aspects of the product. If polls find that consumers are worried about dolphins caught in tuna nets, then you might stick a big 'Dolphin Safe' label on the tins and set up a Web site featuring interviews with tuna fishermen." The new wave of IMC, according to one of its primary texts, is "respectful not patronizing; dialogue-seeking, not monologic; responsive—not formula-driven. It speaks to the highest point of common interest—not the lowest common denominator."

Media Relations

OPEN MEDIA RELATIONS

The common wisdom among public relations people today is to be open and candid with the mass media. It is a principle that dates to Ivy Lee, and case studies abound to confirm its effectiveness. A classic case study on this point is the Tylenol crisis. Johnson & Johnson had spent many years and millions of dollars to inspire public confidence in its product Tylenol, and by 1982 the product was the leader in a crowded field of headache remedies, with 36 percent of the market. Then disaster struck. Seven people in Chicago died after taking Tylenol capsules laced with cyanide. James Burke, president of Johnson & Johnson, and Lawrence Foster, vice president for public relations, moved quickly. Within hours, Johnson & Johnson:

- Halted the manufacture and distribution of Tylenol.
- Removed Tylenol products from retailers' shelves.
- Launched a massive advertising campaign requesting people to exchange Tylenol capsules for a safe replacement.
- Summoned 50 public relations employees from Johnson & Johnson and its subsidiary companies to staff a press centre to answer media and consumer questions forthrightly.
- Ordered an internal company investigation of the Tylenol manufacturing and distribution process.
- Promised full cooperation with government investigators.
- Ordered the development of tamper-proof packaging for the reintroduction of Tylenol products after the contamination problem was resolved.

Investigators determined within days that an urban terrorist had poisoned the capsules. Although the news media exonerated Johnson & Johnson of negligence, the company nonetheless had a tremendous problem: how to restore public confidence in Tylenol. Many former Tylenol users were reluctant to take a chance, and the Tylenol share of the analgesic market dropped to 6 percent.

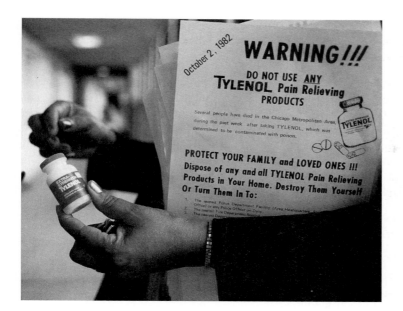

Product-Tampering Crisis. When cyanide-laced Tylenol capsules killed seven people in Chicago, the manufacturer, Johnson & Johnson, responded quickly. Company president James Burke immediately pulled the product off retailers' shelves and ordered company publicists to set up a press centre to answer news media inquiries as fully as possible. Burke's action and candour helped restore the public's shaken confidence in Tylenol, and the product resumed its significant market share after the crisis ended. It turned out that it had been a disturbed person outside Johnson & Johnson's production and distribution system who had contaminated the capsules rather than a manufacturing lapse.

James Burke

To address the problem, Johnson & Johnson called in the Burson-Marsteller public relations agency. Burson-Marsteller recommended a media campaign to capitalize on the high marks the news media had given the company for openness during the crisis. Mailgrams went out inviting journalists to a 30-city video teleconference to hear James Burke announce the reintroduction. Six hundred reporters turned out, and Johnson & Johnson officials took their questions live.

To stir even wider attention, 7500 **media kits** had been sent to newsrooms the day before the teleconference. The kits included a news release and a bevy of supporting materials: photographs, charts, and background information. The resulting news coverage was extensive. On average, newspapers carried 32 column inches of copy on the announcement. Network television and radio as well as local stations also afforded heavy coverage. The massive media-based public relations campaign worked. Within a year, Tylenol had regained 80 percent of its former market share, and today, in an increasingly crowded analgesic field, Tylenol is again the market leader with annual sales of US$670 million, compared with US$520 million before the cyanide crisis.

Sarah Evans, of the Canadian Public Relations Society, says that "this is the classic example in public relations annals of how to deal with a situation. You take immediate action, you worry about people first, you provide as much information as you can as fast as you've got it. Did Johnson and Johnson stock suffer? No. Did Tylenol suffer? No."

PROACTIVE MEDIA RELATIONS

Although public relations campaigns cannot control what the media say, public relations people can help shape how news media report issues by taking the initiative. In the Tylenol crisis, for example, Johnson & Johnson reacted quickly and decisively

Burson-Marsteller: Profiles of how they manage public perception.

www.bm.com

Medialink: PR with a decidedly broadcast slant.

www.medialink worldwide.com

PRNewswire: News about companies searchable by industry.

www.prnewswire.com

and took control of disseminating information, which, coupled with full disclosure, headed off false rumours that could have caused further damage. This is an example of **proactive media relations.**

PROACTIVE CRISIS RESPONSES. A principle in crisis management is to seize leadership on the story. This involves anticipating what journalists will want to know and providing it to them before they even have time to formulate their questions. Ivy Lee did this time and again, and Johnson & Johnson did it in 1982.

For successful crisis management, public relations people need strong ongoing relationships with an organization's top officials. Otherwise, when a crisis strikes, they likely will have difficulty rounding up the kind of breaking information they need to deal effectively with the news media.

ONGOING MEDIA RELATIONSHIPS. Good media relations cannot be forged in the fire of a crisis. Organizations that survive a crisis generally have a history of solid media relations. Their public relations staff people know reporters, editors, and news directors on a first-name basis. Many public relations people, in fact, are seasoned journalists themselves, and they understand how journalists go about their work. It is their journalistic background that made them attractive candidates for their PR jobs.

SOUND OPERATING PRINCIPLES. An underlying strength that helped see Johnson & Johnson through the Tylenol crisis was the company's credo. The credo was a written vow that Johnson & Johnson's first responsibility was to "those who use our products and services." The credo, which had been promoted in-house for years, said: "every time a business hires, builds, sells or buys, it is acting for the people as well as for itself, and it must be prepared to accept full responsibility." With such a sound operating principle, Johnson & Johnson's crisis response was, in some respects, almost reflexive.

AMBIVALENCE IN MEDIA RELATIONS

Despite the advantages of open media relations, there are companies that choose not to embrace that approach. Some corporations take a middle ground, currying media coverage selectively. This is an example of **ambivalent media relations.** IBM, which receives 30 000 media queries a year, frets that news coverage would underscore its sheer size. IBM turns away questions on many issues, including the company's long-term planning. The corporation's PR chief, Seth McCormick, spurns Ivy Lee's maxim that corporate executives should be "on display." In an interview, McCormick told *Fortune*: "We control what is said about the company through the sparsity of heads for the outside world to talk to. We like it that way."

Although IBM ignores the common wisdom about media relations, the corporation shows up frequently in rankings of the most respected companies in the world. An interesting question is whether IBM's reputation is due to its posture on media relations or in spite of it.

Procter & Gamble is another major company that generally is tight-lipped about how it conducts its business, with the notable exception of product promotions. Another notable exception was Procter & Gamble's full-scale public relations campaign in the 1980s to squelch persistent rumours that its corporate symbol—the moon and stars—had roots in Satanism.

Messing Up. The Exxon public-relations operations bungled badly when a tanker went aground off Alaska in 1989, causing a gigantic environmental disaster. Exxon Chairman Lawrence Rawl remained silent for a week. Exxon was slow to mobilize its cleanup crews and then blamed Coast Guard and state authorities for delays. Also, Exxon tried to handle media inquiries with a one-person press centre, which was hardly sufficient. Things worsened. Amid media finger-pointing at the captain of the ship, Joseph Hazelwood, Exxon publicly abandoned him. Public sympathy shifted to the captain when it turned out that the media had given him a worse rap than he was due.

Lawrence Rawl

ADVERSARIAL PUBLIC RELATIONS

Public relations took on aggressive, even feisty tactics when Mobil Oil decided in the 1970s not to take media criticism lightly any more. **Herb Schmertz**, vice president for Mobil's public affairs, charted a new course by:

- Filing formal complaints with news organizations when coverage was unfair in the company's view.
- Taking Mobil's case directly to the general public with paid advertising, **advertorials** as they are called, a splicing of the words "advertising" and "editorial," that explained the company's views.
- Sending corporate representatives on media tours to spread Mobil's side to as many constituencies as possible. Schmertz's energetic counterattacks, an example of **adversarial public relations**, were a departure from conventional wisdom in pubic relations, which was to let criticism go unanswered or, at most, to complain privately to executives of news organizations about negative coverage as unwarranted. The conventional wisdom was that a public response would only bring more attention to the negative coverage.

In abandoning passivity, Mobil was adapting what sports fans call the Red Auerbach technique. Auerbach, the legendary coach of the Boston Celtics, was known for criticizing referees. He realized they would never change a call, but he believed that refs would be less inclined to make questionable calls against the Celtics if they knew that Auerbach would jump all over them. Mobil President Rawleigh Warner, Jr., explained the new Mobil policy this way: "People know that if they take a swipe at us, we will fight back."

Schmertz employed the full range of PR tools in 1974 when ABC aired a television documentary that raised critical questions about the U.S. oil industry. Mobil objected first to ABC and then fired off a formal complaint to the National News Council, a volunteer media watchdog group. Mobil claimed 32 inaccuracies and instances of unfairness and requested that the council investigate. Mobil also issued an unusually lengthy news release, quoting from the documentary and offering point-by-point rebuttals.

Six Mobil executives were given a crash course on giving good interviews and sent out to meet the news media. In two years, the executives and other Mobil representatives appeared on 365 television and 211 radio shows and talked with 80 newspaper reporters. Schmertz encouraged them to take the offensive. To counter the ABC impression that the oil industry still engaged in the bad practices of its past, Schmertz told executives to stress that such information was outdated. "Put the shoe on the other foot," he said, advising the Mobil executives to say the impression left by the ABC documentary was "comparable to Mobil's producing a documentary about today's television industry and pointing to a 1941 FCC decree requiring RCA to rid itself of one of its networks as evidence of a current conspiracy."

Advertorials were part of Mobil's initiatives. Under Schmertz, as much as US$6 million a year went into newspaper and magazine ads, explaining the company's position. Mobil also began producing its own television programs on energy issues and providing them free to stations. The programs had a journalistic tone, and many stations ran them as if they were actual documentaries rather than part of Mobil's media campaign.

Herb Schmertz

Mobil Advertorial. Many public relations practitioners seek to avoid confrontation, but Herb Schmertz of Mobil bought space in newspapers and magazines beginning in the 1970s to lay out his company's positions on controversial issues and even to be confrontational. Schmertz tackled the news media when he felt Mobil had not received a fair shake in coverage. These position statements are called "advertorials" because they are in space purchased as advertising and their content is like an editorial.

The jury is still out on whether Schmertz's aggressive sparring is good policy. Most organizations continue to follow the traditional thinking that taking on the media only generates more attention about the original bad news. On the other hand, Schmertz's approach has been tried by some major corporations. Bechtel, Illinois Power, and Kaiser Aluminum all have called for independent investigations of stories that reflected badly on them.

Another adversarial approach, although not recommended by most public relations people, is for an offended organization to sever relations with the source of unfavourable news—an **information boycott**. In 1954, in a spectacular pout, General Motors cut off contact with *Wall Street Journal* reporters and withdrew advertising from the newspaper. This approach carries great risks:

■ By going silent, an organization loses avenues for conveying its message to mass audiences.

■ An organization that yanks advertising to punish detractors is perceived negatively for coercively wielding its economic might.

■ An organization that quits advertising in an effective advertising medium will lose sales.

A boycott differs from Schmertz's adversarial approach in an important respect. Schmertz responds to negative news by contributing to the exchange of information and ideas, which is positive in a democratic society. An information boycott, on the other hand, restricts the flow of information. Today, GM's policy has returned to the conventional wisdom of not arguing with anyone who buys paper by the ton and ink by the barrel.

Professionalization

A Tarnished Heritage

Unsavoury elements in the heritage of public relations remain a heavy burden. P.T. Barnum, whose name became synonymous with hype, attracted crowds to his stunts and shows in the latter 1800s with extravagant promises. Sad to say, some promoters still use Barnum's tactics. The claims for snake oils and elixirs from Barnum's era live on in commercials for pain relievers and cold remedies. The early response of tycoons to muckraking attacks, before Ivy Lee came along, was **whitewashing**—covering up the abuses but not correcting them. It is no wonder that the term "PR" sometimes is used derisively. To say something is "all PR" means it lacks substance. Of people whose apparent positive qualities are a mere façade, it may be said that they have "good PR."

Although journalists rely heavily on public relations people for information, many journalists look with suspicion on PR practitioners. Not uncommon among seasoned journalists are utterances like: "I've never met a PR person I couldn't distrust." Such cynicism flows partly from the journalists' self-image as unfettered truth seekers whose only obligation is serving their audiences' needs. PR people, on the other hand, are seen as obligated to their employers, whose interests do not always dovetail with the public good. Behind their backs, PR people are called "flaks," a takeoff on the World War II slang for antiaircraft bursts intended to stop enemy bombers. PR **flakkers,** as journalists use the term, interfere with journalistic truth seeking by putting forth slanted, self-serving information, which is not necessarily the whole story.

The journalism–PR tension is exacerbated by a common newsroom view that PR people try to get free news hole space for their messages rather than buy airtime and column inches. This view may seem strange considering that Hill & Knowlton, one of Canada's largest PR firms, estimates that 50 to 90 percent of all news stories either originate with or contain information supplied by PR people. It is also strange considering that many PR people are former news reporters and editors. No matter how uncomfortable PR people and journalists are as bedfellows, they are bedfellows nonetheless.

Some public relations people have tried to leapfrog the negative baggage attached to the term "PR" by abandoning it. **Public information**, as well as *public affairs, corporate communication,* and plain old *communication,* have been used by public relations firms as synonyms for PR.

Standards and Certification

In 1948, two public relations groups, one in Montreal, the other in Toronto, merged. By 1953, they became the **Canadian Public Relations Society (CPRS)**; in 1957 they become recognized as a national society. Today, CPRS has over 1500 members across Canada. The association adopted the following code of professional standards. Although CPRS is a Canadian association, its codes clearly reflect lessons learned in both the U.S. and Canada. Here is their code of ethics:

Canadian Public Relations Society Code of Professional Standards

Members of the Canadian Public Relations Society feel strongly about standards within the profession and abide by the following codes of ethics:

- A member shall practice public relations according to the highest professional standards.
- A member shall deal fairly and honestly with the communications media and the public.
- A member shall practice the highest standards of honesty, accuracy, integrity and truth, and shall not knowingly disseminate false or misleading information.
- A member shall deal fairly with past or present employers/clients, with fellow practitioners, and with members of other professions.
- A member shall be prepared to disclose the name of their employer or client for whom public communications are made and refrain from associating themselves with anyone that would not respect such policy.
- A member shall protect the confidences of present, former and prospective employers/clients.
- A member shall not represent conflicting or competing interests without the express consent of those concerned, given after a full disclosure of the facts.
- A member shall not guarantee specified results beyond the member's capacity to achieve.
- Members shall personally accept no fees, commissions, gifts or any other considerations for professional services from anyone except employers or clients for whom the services were specifically performed. *(Reprinted by permission of the CPRS.)*

In a further professionalization step, the CPRS established a certification process. Those who meet the criteria and pass exams are allowed to place **APR**, which stands for accredited public relations professional, after their names. The criteria are:

- Being recommended by an already accredited CPRS member.
- Five years of full-time professional experience.
- Passing an eight-hour written examination on public relations principles, techniques, history, and ethics.
- Passing an oral exam conducted by three professionals.

The process is rigorous. Typically, a third of those who attempt the examination fail it the first time. Once earned, certification needs to be renewed through continuing education, and the right to use "APR" can be taken away if a member violates the CPRS code. About 1500 CPRS members hold APR certification.

CHAPTER WRAP-UP

When Ivy Lee hung up a shingle in New York for a new publicity agency in 1906, he wanted to distance himself from the huckstering that marked most publicity at the time. To do that, Lee promised to deal only in legitimate news about the agency's clients, and no fluff. He invited journalists to pursue more information about the agency's clients. He also vowed to be honest and accurate. Those principles remain the defence of good public relations practice today.

QUESTIONS FOR REVIEW

1. What is public relations? How is public relations connected to the mass media?

2. Why did big business become interested in the techniques and principles of public relations beginning in the late 1800s?

3. How is public relations a management tool?

4. What is the range of activities in which public relations people are involved?

5. What kind of relationship do most people strive to have with the mass media?

6. Why does public relations have a bad image? What are public relations professionals doing about it?

QUESTIONS FOR CRITICAL THINKING

1. When Ivy Lee accepted the Pennsylvania Railroad as a client in 1906, he saw the job as "interpreting the Pennsylvania Railroad to the public and interpreting the public to the Pennsylvania Railroad." Compare Lee's point with Arthur Page's view of public relations as a management function.

2. How are public relations practitioners trying to overcome the complaints from journalists that they are flakkers interfering with an unfettered pursuit of truth?

3. What are Edward Bernays' views on public relations?

4. How do public relations agencies turn profits?

5. When does an institution with its own in-house public relations operation need to hire a PR agency?

6. Explain the concept of enlightened self-interest.

7. How did the confluence of the following three phenomena at the turn of the last century contribute to the emergence of modern public relations?

   - The related concepts of social Darwinism, a social theory; laissez-faire, a government philosophy; and paternalism, a practice of business.

   - Muckraking, which attacked prevalent abuses of the public interest.

   - Advertising, which had grown since the 1830s as a way to reach great numbers of people.

8. Showman P.T. Barnum epitomized 19th-century press agentry with extravagant claims, such as promoting the midget Tom Thumb as a Civil War general. To attract crowds to a tour by an unknown European soprano, Jenny Lind, Barnum labelled her "the Swedish Nightingale." Would such promotional methods work today? Keep in mind that Barnum, explaining his methods, once said, "There's a sucker born every minute."

FOR KEEPING UP TO DATE

The trade journal *O'Dwyer's PR Services* tracks the industry on a monthly basis.

Other sources of ongoing information are *Public Relations Journal, Public Relations Quarterly*, and *Public Relations Review*

FOR FURTHER LEARNING

Scott M. Cutlip, Allen H. Center, and Glen M. Broom. *Effective Public Relations, 6th ed.* (Prentice Hall, 1985).

Ray Eldon Hiebert. *Courtier to the Crowd: The Story of Ivy Lee and the Development of Public Relations* (Iowa State University Press, 1966).

Bruce Livesey. "PR Wars: How the PR Industry Flacks for Big Business." *Canadian Dimension* (November-December, 1996).

Marketing Magazine. "The Rankings." June 25, 2001.

George S. McGovern and Leonard F. Guttridge. *The Great Coalfield War* (Houghton Mifflin, 1972).

Kevin McManus. "Video Coaches." *Forbes* 129 (June 7, 1982).

Lael M. Moynihan. "Horrendous PR Crises: What They Did When the Unthinkable Happened." *Media History Digest* 8 (Spring–Summer 1988): 1, 19–25.

Joyce Nelson. *The Sultans of Sleaze* (Between the Lines, 1989).

Barbara Pollock. "A Profession for Tomorrow." Canadian Public Relations Society **website:www.cprs.ca/cprsprof_tom.html**, July 9, 1998.

Herbert Schmertz and William Novak. *Good-bye to the Low Profile: The Art of Creative Confrontation* (Little, Brown, 1986).

Ray Truchansky. "In Today's Business World, Good PR is Priceless." *Edmonton Journal* (April 7, 2001).

Jean Valin. "Truth Pays Dividends with Public." Canadian Public Relations Society website: **www.cprs.ca/cprstruth.htm**, July 9, 1998.

Perry Dean Young. *God's Bullies: Power Politics and Religious Tyranny* (Henry Holt, 1982).

Chapter 9

Advertising

MEDIA TIMELINE

Development of Advertising

	1468	William Caxton promotes a book with the first printed advertisement.
	1704	Joseph Campbell includes advertisements in the Boston News-Letter.
	1833	Benjamin Day creates the *New York Sun* as a combination news and advertising vehicle.
	1869	Wayland Ayer opens the first advertising agency, in Philadelphia.
	1890s	Brand names emerge as an advertising technique.
	1899	Anson McKim opens the first Canadian advertising agency.
	1950s	Ernest Dichter pioneers motivational research.
	1950s	David Ogilvy devises brand imaging technique.
	1950s	Jack Trout devises positioning technique.
	1957	James Vicary claims success for subliminal advertising.
	1960s	Rosser Reeves devises unique selling proposition technique.
	1963	Canadian Code of Advertising Standards is established.

Media in Theory

Analyzing Ads

If research means to "look again," the question becomes how can we look at ads? As artifacts of communication, advertisements can be considered texts to be read and analyzed. Two ways in which communication scholars do this is through content analysis and semiotic analysis.

As a research tool, content analysis has its roots in the social sciences. It's an empirical method that measures denotation (or first-order signifieds) in an ad. In other words, it counts what is physically present in an advertisement and nothing more. It is an objective, structured, and scientific way of looking at ads. A simple content analysis might involve counting the number of women in ads for household products and comparing them to the number of men in the same type of ad. If the research indicated that more women than men were being used to sell these products, the researcher might claim that this is an example of sexism in advertising, as women are represented in terms of traditional stereotypes. Content analysis is often used by **MediaWatch**, which is a national volunteer organization that keeps an eye on the Canadian media. Through content analysis, MediaWatch claims that even in the 21st century, the majority of women appearing in advertisements tend to be cast in the role of consumer—they are rarely seen as an "expert" or "celebrity."

Unlike content analysis, semiotic analysis has its roots in the humanities. As we've seen before, it's a method used to look at connotation (or second-order signifieds) in ads. Instead of following the structured, scientific format of content analysis, semiotics analyzes an ad in terms of the interplay of signs, signifiers, and signifieds. In this way, the researcher can uncover the ideology or mythology in an ad or a series of ads.

Griselda Pollock, in "What's Wrong with Images of Women?" offers a unique and simple semiotic method for reading sexism in an ad. The myths behind the signs for both men and women need to be addressed because it's hard to talk about good or bad images of women (or men, for that matter) without comparing how the opposite gender is represented in advertising images. Pollock, therefore, argues that a semiotic analysis of gender images needs to treat men and women as separate signs, each with specific

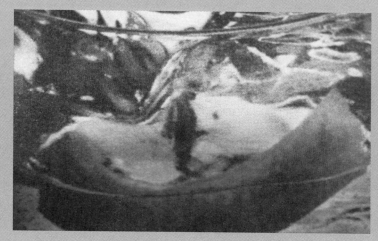

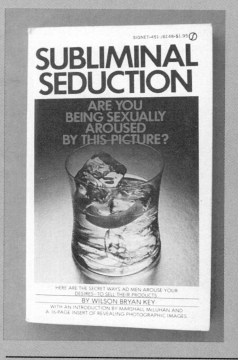

Sex in the Clams? Author Wilson Bryan Key is convinced that Madison Avenue hides sex in advertisements to attract attention and sell products. To demonstrate his point, he outlines the human figures that he saw in an orgy in a photograph of clam strips on a restaurant menu. Can you see the hidden sex that Key claims was designed into the liquor ad photos? Most advertising people, who dismiss his claims, cannot see it either. It's a good example of what communication theorists call connotation.

signifiers and signifieds. She argues that the idea of images of women "needs to be challenged and replaced by the notion of woman as a signifier in an ideological discourse in which one can identify the meanings that are constructed in relation to other signifiers . . . A useful device for initiating this kind of work is the use of male/female reversals."

Her classic example of female/male reversals is the juxtaposition of a 19th-century French nude photo of a woman holding a tray of apples up to her breasts, bearing the caption "Achetez les pommes," with a nude man, holding a tray of bananas near his crotch. While the example is a humorous one, it does uncover certain mythologies about how images of men and women are constructed. The first image is a redundant one; women are often compared to fruit in Western culture. The second image is entropic because it is unexpected. Pollock's point is this: if the ad creates a strange connotation when a man is put in place of a woman, you have uncovered what communication theorists call the dominant ideology and what Barthes would call myth. The role reversal may also be done by substituting "he" for "she" in advertising copy.

Both semiotic analysis and content analysis have strengths and weaknesses. In *Social Communication in Advertising*, Leiss, Klein, and Jhally explain that while content analysis is an objective method of looking at ads and works best on a large scale using many ads, it doesn't really explain how audiences interpret and decode the images within the text itself. They say that semiotic analysis works well if you are reading a single ad.

Motivational Research

Whatever naïveté North Americans had about opinion-shaping was dispelled by the mid-20th century. Sinister possibilities were realized in the work of Joseph Goebbels, the Nazi minister of propaganda and public enlightenment. In the Pacific, the Japanese aimed the infamous Tokyo Rose radio broadcasts at GIs to lower their morale. Then, during the Korean War, a macabre fascination developed with the so-called brainwashing techniques used on American prisoners of war. In this same period, the work of Austrian psychiatrist Sigmund Freud, which emphasized hidden motivations and repressed sexual impulses, was being popularized in countless books and articles.

No wonder, considering this intellectual context, advertising people in the 1950s looked to the social sciences to find new ways to woo customers. Among the advertising pioneers of this period was **Ernest Dichter**, who accepted Freud's claim that people act on motivations that they are not even aware of. Depth interviewing, Dichter felt, could reveal these motivations, which could then be exploited in advertising messages.

Dichter used his interviewing, called **motivational research**, for automotive clients. Rightly or wrongly, Dichter determined that the American male was loyal to his wife but fantasized about a mistress. Men, he noted, usually were the decision makers in purchasing a car. Then, in what seemed a quantum leap, Dichter equated sedans, which were what most people drove, with wives. Sedans were familiar, reliable. Convertibles, impractical for many people and also beyond their reach financially, were equated with mistresses—romantic, daring, glamorous. With these conclusions in hand, Dichter devised advertisements for a new kind of sedan without a centre door pillar. The hardtop, as it was called, gave a convertible effect when the windows were down. The advertising clearly reflected Dichter's thinking: "You'll find something new to love every time you drive it." Although they were not as solid as sedans and tended to leak air and water, hardtops were popular among automobile buyers for the next 25 years.

Dichter's motivational research led to numerous campaigns that exploited sexual images. For Ronson lighters, the flame, in phallic form, was reproduced in extraordinary proportions. A campaign for Ajax cleanser, hardly a glamour product, had a white knight charging through the street, ignoring law and regulation with a great phallic lance. Whether consumers were motivated by sexual imagery is hard to establish. Even so, many campaigns flowing from motivational research worked.

Subliminal Advertising

The idea that advertising can be persuasive at subconscious levels was taken a step further by market researcher **Jim Vicary**, who coined the term **subliminal advertising**. Vicary claimed in 1957 that he had studied the effect of inserting messages like "Drink Coca-Cola" and "Eat popcorn" into movies. The messages, although flashed too fast to be recognized by the human eye, still registered in the brain and, said Vicary, prompted moviegoers to rush to the snack bar. In experiments at a New Jersey movie house, he said, Coke sales increased 18 percent and popcorn almost 60 percent. Vicary's report stirred great interest, and also alarm, but researchers who tried to replicate his study found no evidence to support his claim.

Despite Vicary's dubious claims, psychologists have identified a phenomenon they call **subception**, in which certain behaviour sometimes seems to be triggered by messages perceived subliminally. Whether the effect works outside laboratory experiments and whether the effect is strong enough to prod a consumer to go to buy something is uncertain. Nevertheless, there remains a widespread belief among the general population that subliminal advertising works, and fortunes are being made by people who peddle various devices and systems with extravagant claims that they can control human behaviour. Among these are the "hidden" messages in stores' sound systems that say shoplifting is not nice.

This idea that advertising is loaded with hidden messages has been taken to extremes by **Wilson Bryan Key**, who spins out books alleging that plugs are hidden in all kinds of places for devil worship, homosexuality, and a variety of libertine activities. He has accused the Nabisco people of baking the word "sex" into Ritz crackers. At Howard Johnson restaurants, he has charged, placemat pictures of plates heaped with clams portray orgies and bestiality. Though widely read, Key offers no evidence beyond his own observations and interpretations. In advertising circles, his views are dismissed as amusing but wacky. The view of Nabisco and Howard Johnson is less charitable.

In 1990 Wilson Bryan Key's views suffered a serious setback. He was a primary witness in a highly publicized Nevada trial on whether the Judas Priest heavy metal album *Stained Glass* had triggered the suicide of an 18-year-old youth and the attempted suicide of his 20-year-old friend. The families said that the pair had obsessed about a Judas Priest album that dealt with suicide and that one song was subliminally embedded with the words "Do it" over and over. The families' attorneys hired Key as an expert witness to help make their point. From Key's perspective, the case did not go well. Millions of television viewers who followed the trial strained to make out the supposed words "Do it," but even when isolated from the rest of the music, they were almost impossible to make out. It turned out the sounds were neither lyrics nor even vocal but rather instrumental effects. Members of Judas Priest testified that they had not equated the sound to any words at all and had inserted it for artistic effect, hardly to encourage suicide. The jury sided with Judas Priest, and Key left town with his wobbly ideas on subliminal messages having taken a serious blow under a jury's scrutiny.

David Ogilvy, founder of the Ogilvy & Mather agency, once made fun of claims like Key's, pointing out the absurdity of "millions of suggestible consumers getting up from their armchairs and rushing like zombies through the traffic on their way to buy the product at the nearest store." The danger of "Vote Bolshevik" being flashed during the *NBC Nightly News* is remote, and whether it would have any effect is dubious.

Importance of Advertising

ADVERTISING AND CONSUMER ECONOMIES

Advertising is a major component of modern economies. In *Canadian Advertising in Action*, Keith Tuckwell estimates that Canadian companies spend over $8 billion a year on advertising. General Motors of Canada alone spends about $130 million on advertising each year. When production of goods and services is up, so is advertising spending. When production falters, as it did in the early 1990s, many manufacturers, distributors, and retailers pull back their advertising expenditures.

The essential role of advertising in a modern consumer economy is obvious if you think about how people decide what to buy. If a shoe manufacturer were unable to tout the virtues of its footwear by advertising in the mass media, people would have a hard time learning about the product, let alone knowing whether it is what they want.

ADVERTISING AND PROSPERITY

Advertising's phenomenal continuing growth has been a product of a plentiful society. In a poor society with a shortage of goods, people line up for necessities like food and clothing. Advertising has no role and serves no purpose when survival is the question. With prosperity, however, people have not only discretionary income but also a choice of ways to spend it. Advertising is the vehicle that provides information and rationales to help them decide how to enjoy their prosperity.

Besides being a product of economic prosperity, advertising contributes to prosperity. By dangling desirable commodities and services before mass audiences, advertising can inspire people to greater productivity, so that they can have more income to buy the things that are advertised.

Advertising Age: The online magazine for the advertising industry.

adage.com

Institute of Canadian Advertising: This site has essays about advertising, a showcase of successful ad campaigns, a reading list, and a list of Canadian ad agencies.

www.ica-ad.com

Place-Based Media. Advertisers are dabbling with alternatives to the traditional media for delivering their messages. Newspapers stand to lose grocery advertising to in-store coupon dispensers like this Actmedia device, located right on the shelf near the advertised product. Advertisers using Actmedia pay to have the devices stocked with up to 1500 coupons a month.

Canadian Marketing Association: This is the largest marketing association in Canada and the primary advocate on legislative matters for marketers. The site includes a history of the organization and its code of ethics.

www.the-cma.org

IAA: The International Advertising Association is a global partnership of advertisers, agencies, and related services.

www.iaaglobal.org

Advertising also can introduce efficiency into the economy by allowing comparison shopping without in-person inspections of all the alternatives. Efficiencies also can result when advertising alerts consumers to superior and less costly products and services, which displace outdated, outmoded, and inefficient offerings.

Said Howard Morgens when he was president of Procter & Gamble: "Advertising is the most effective and efficient way to sell to the consumer. If we should ever find better methods of selling our type of products to the consumer, we'll leave advertising and turn to these other methods." Veteran advertising executive David Ogilvy made the point this way: "Advertising is still the cheapest form of selling. It would cost you $25,000 to have salesmen call on a thousand homes. A television commercial can do it for $4.69." McGraw-Hill, which publishes trade magazines, has offered research that a salesperson's typical call costs $178, a letter $6.63, and a phone call $6.35. For 17 cents, says McGraw-Hill, an advertiser can reach a prospect through advertising. Although an advertisement does not close a sale, it introduces the product and makes the salesperson's job easier and quicker.

ADVERTISING AND DEMOCRACY

Advertising took off as a modern phenomenon in the United States and Canada more than elsewhere, which has given rise to a theory that advertising and democracy are connected. This theory notes that North Americans, early in their history as a democracy, were required by their political system to hold individual opinions. They looked for information so that they could evaluate their leaders and vote on public policy. This emphasis on individuality and reason paved the way for advertising: Just as people looked to the mass media for information on political matters, they also came to look to the media for information on buying decisions.

In authoritarian countries, on the other hand, people tend to look to strong personal leaders, not reason, for ideas to embrace. This, according to the theory, diminishes the demand for information in these nondemocracies, including the kind of information provided by advertising.

Advertising has another important role in democratic societies in generating most of the operating revenue for newspapers, magazines, television, and radio. Without advertising, many of the media on which people rely for information and for the exchange of ideas on public issues would not exist as we know them.

Origins of Advertising

STEPCHILD OF TECHNOLOGY

Advertising is not a mass medium, but it relies on media to carry its messages. Johannes Gutenberg's movable type, which permitted mass production of the printed word, made mass-produced advertising possible. First came flyers, then advertisements in newspapers and magazines. In the 1800s, when technology created high-speed presses that could produce enough copies for larger audiences, advertising used them to expand markets. With the introduction of radio, advertisers learned how to use electronic communication. Then came television. Today, Canadian advertisers are looking to the Internet for possibilities.

Flyers were the first form of printed advertising. The British printer **William Caxton** issued the first printed advertisement in 1468 to promote one of his books. Early newspapers listed cargo arriving from Europe and invited readers to come, look, and buy.

INDUSTRIAL REVOLUTION SPIN-OFFS

Steam-powered presses made large press runs possible. Factories drew great numbers of people to jobs within geographically small areas to which newspapers could be distributed quickly. The jobs also drew immigrants who were eager to learn—from newspapers as well as other sources—about their adopted country. Industrialization also created unprecedented wealth, giving even labourers a share of the new prosperity. A consumer economy was emerging, although it was primitive by today's standards.

A key to the success of the early penny press was that, at a penny a copy, its newspapers were affordable for almost everyone. Of course, production expenses exceeded a penny a copy. Just as the commercial media do today, the penny express looked to advertisers to pick up the slack. As Ben Day wrote in his first issue of the *New York Sun*: "The object of this paper is to lay before the public, at a price within the means of everyone, all the news of the day, and at the same time afford an advantageous medium for advertising." Day and imitator penny press publishers sought larger and larger circulations, knowing that merchants would see the value in buying space to reach so much buying power.

National advertising took root in the 1840s as railroads, another creation of the Industrial Revolution, spawned new networks for mass distribution of manufactured goods. National brands developed, and their producers looked to magazines, also delivered by rail, to promote sales. By 1869 the rail network linked the Atlantic and Pacific coasts.

PIONEER AGENCIES

By 1869, most merchants recognized the value of advertising, but they grumbled about the time it took away from their other work. In that grumbling, a young Philadelphia man sensed opportunity. **Wayland Ayer**, aged 20, speculated that merchants, and even national manufacturers, would welcome a service company to help them create advertisements and place them in publications. Ayer feared, however, that his idea might not be taken seriously by potential clients because of his youth and inexperience. So when Wayland Ayer opened a shop, he borrowed his father's name for the shingle.

In 1872, Toronto newspapers began selling advertising space to clients outside their area. The *Toronto Mail* sent a young man to Montreal to sell advertising space. **Anson McKim** saw this as a great opportunity and he began to act as a broker for other publications in south-central Ontario. By 1889, McKim opened Canada's first ad agency in Montreal, A. McKim and Company. McKim also published the first directory of media in Canada, *The Canadian Newspaper Directory*, in 1892.

The Ayer and McKim agencies had forerunners in space brokers who, beginning in 1842 with Volney Palmer, bought large blocks of newspaper space at a discount, broke up the space, and resold it to advertisers at a mark-up, usually 25 percent. Space brokers, however, did not create advertisements. The Ayer agency not only created ads but also offered the array of services that agencies still offer clients today:

- Counsel on selling products and services.
- Design services, actually creating advertisements and campaigns.
- Expertise on placing advertisements in media.

Advertising Agencies

AGENCY STRUCTURE

Full-service advertising agencies conduct market research for their clients, design and produce advertisements, and choose the media in which the advertisement will run. The 500 leading agencies employ 120 000 people worldwide. The responsibilities of people who work at advertising agencies fall into the following broad categories:

CREATIVE POSITIONS. This category includes copywriters, graphics experts, and layout people. These creative people generally report to **creative directors**, art directors, and copy supervisors.

CLIENT LIAISON. Most of these people are **account executives**, who work with clients. Account executives are responsible for understanding clients' needs, communicating those needs to the creative staff, and going back to clients with the creative staff's ideas.

MEDIA BUYING. Agency employees called **media buyers** determine the most effective media in which to place ads and then place them there. Publications such as *Canadian Rates and Data (CARD)* are used by media buyers to determine costs and placement.

MARKET RESEARCH. Agency research staffs generate information on target consumer groups, data that can guide the creative and media staffs.

Many agencies also employ technicians and producers who turn ideas into camera-ready proofs, colourplates, videotape, and film and audio cartridges, although a lot of production work is contracted to specialty companies. Besides full-service agencies, there are creative boutiques, which specialize in preparing messages; media buying houses, which recommend strategy on placing ads; and other narrowly focused agencies.

AGENCY–MEDIA RELATIONS

Because agencies are so influential in deciding where advertisements are placed, the mass media give them a 15 percent discount. A newspaper that lists $100 per column inch as its standard rate charges agencies only $85. The agencies, however, bill their clients the full $100 and keep the 15 percent difference. This discount, actually a **commission system,** is available only to agencies. Besides the 15 percent commission, agencies receive an additional 2 percent discount from media units by paying cash for space and time. Because these media discounts are offered only to ad agencies, advertisers themselves would not receive them if they did their advertising work in-house.

The commission system causes a problem for agencies because their income is dependent on the frequency with which advertisements are placed. The fluctuations can be great, which makes it difficult for the agencies to meet their regular payroll. To even out their income, some agencies have shifted to a **fee system**. Arrangements

Recount Pizza. Knowing that people order lots of pizza during television football games, Pizza Hut's ad agency, BBDO, scrambled to capitalize on the huge audience following the recounts after the 2000 U.S. presidential election. To promote the new Insider pizza, the narrator suggested being part of history: "Someday you can tell your grandkids you were there when Florida decided the next President by voting for Bush—no Gore . . . no, no, Bush . . . no, Gore . . . Well, at least you can tell them you tried the Insider pizza."

vary, but it is common for the client to be billed for the agency's professional time and research plus an agreed-on percentage. The fee system reduces gigantic fluctuations in agency income when clients change their media spending because revenue is derived from fees for services, not a percentage of space and time purchases. Another advantage of the fee system is that clients who pay fees for services are not suspicious that their agencies are being self-serving when they recommend bigger and bigger campaigns.

MEDIA ROLE IN CREATING ADVERTISING

Agencies are the most visible part of the advertising industry, but more advertising people work outside agencies than for agencies. The media themselves have advertising staffs that work with agency media buyers on placing advertisements. These staffs, comprised of ad reps, also design and produce material for smaller advertisers. Broadcast networks, magazines, and radio and television stations also have their own sales staffs.

ADVERTISER ROLE IN ADVERTISING

Although they hire agencies for advertising services, most companies have their own advertising expertise among the in-house people who develop marketing strategies. These companies look to ad agencies to develop the advertising campaigns that will help them meet their marketing goals. For some companies, the **advertising director** or advertising manager is the liaison between the company's marketing strategists and the ad agency's tacticians. Large companies with many products have in-house **brand managers** for this liaison. Although it is not the usual pattern, some companies have in-house advertising departments and rely hardly at all on agencies.

Placing Ads

MEDIA ADVERTISING PLANS

Agencies create **media plans** to insure that advertisements reach the right target audience. Developing a media plan is no small task. Consider the number of media outlets available: daily newspapers, weeklies, general-interest magazines, radio stations, and television stations. Other possibilities include banners on websites, direct mail, billboards, blimps, skywriting, and even printing the company's name on coffee mugs.

Media buyers have formulas for deciding which media are best for reaching potential customers. The most common formula is called **CPM,** short for cost per thousand. If airtime for a radio advertisement costs 7.2 cents per thousand listeners, and if space for a magazine advertisement costs 7.3 cents per thousand readers, and if both can be expected to reach equally appropriate target audiences, and if all other things are equal, radio—with the lower CPM—will be the medium of choice.

Media buyers have numerous sources of data to help them decide where advertisements can be placed for the best results. The **Audit Bureau of Circulations,** created by the newspaper industry in 1914, provides reliable information based on independent audits of the circulation of most newspapers. Survey organizations like Nielsen and the Bureau of Measurement conduct surveys on television and radio audiences. Standard Rate and Data Service publishes volumes of information on media audiences, circulations, and advertising rates.

MEDIA FOR ADVERTISING

Here are the advantages and disadvantages of major media as advertising vehicles:

NEWSPAPERS. The hot relationship that Marshall McLuhan described between newspapers and their readers attracts advertisers. Newspaper readers are predisposed to consider information in advertisements seriously. Studies show that people, when ready to buy, look more to newspapers than to other media. Because newspapers are tangible, readers can refer back to advertisements just by picking up the paper a second time, which is not possible with ephemeral media like television and radio. Coupons are possible in newspapers. Newspaper readers tend to be older, better educated, and have higher incomes than television and radio audiences. Space for newspaper ads usually can be reserved as late as 48 hours ahead, and 11th-hour changes are possible. Twenty-five percent of advertising revenue is spent on newspaper ads in Canada.

However, newspapers are becoming less valuable for reaching young adults with advertising messages. To the consternation of newspaper publishers, there has been an alarming drop in readership by this group in recent years, and it appears that, unlike their parents, young adults are not picking up the newspaper habit as they mature.

Another drawback to newspapers as an advertising medium is that, being printed on cheap paper, the ads do not look as good as in slick magazines. Also, most people recycle their newspapers within a day or so, which means that, unlike magazines, there is not much opportunity for readers to happen upon an ad a second or third time.

MAGAZINES. Accounting for about 11 percent of advertising revenue in Canada, magazines have many of the advantages of newspapers, plus a longer **shelf life**, an advertising term for the amount of time that an advertisement remains available to readers. Magazines remain in the home for weeks, sometimes months, which offers greater exposure to advertisements. People share magazines, which give them high **pass-along circulation**. Magazines are more prestigious, with slick paper and splashier graphics. With precise colour separations and enamelled papers, magazine advertisements can be beautiful in ways that newspaper advertisements cannot. Magazines, specializing as they do, offer more narrowly defined audiences than newspapers.

On the downside, magazines require reservations for advertising space up to three months in advance. Opportunities for last-minute changes are limited, often impossible.

RADIO. Radio stations with narrow formats offer easily identified target audiences. Time can be bought on short notice, with changes possible almost until airtime. Comparatively inexpensive, radio lends itself to repeated play of advertisements to drive home a message introduced in more expensive media like television. Radio also lends itself to jingles that can contribute to a lasting image. The CRTC claims that about 14 percent of all advertising money spent in Canada is spent on radio.

However, radio offers no opportunity for a visual display, although the images listeners create in their minds from audio suggestions can be more potent than those set out visually on television. Radio is a mobile medium that people carry with them. The extensive availability of radio is offset, however, by the fact that people tune in and out. Another negative is that many listeners are inattentive. Also, there is no shelf life.

TELEVISION. As a moving and visual medium, television can offer unmatched impact, and the rapid growth of both network and local television advertising, far outpacing other media, indicates its effectiveness in reaching a diverse mass audience. It is also the number one choice among Canadian advertisers, accounting for 34 percent of advertising revenue. Some of the benefits of TV are intangible. The Television Bureau of Canada says that TV "has an aura of importance. It is a prestigious medium, enhancing the advertisers' image by its use."

Drawbacks include the fact that production costs can be high. So are rates. The expense of television time has forced advertisers to go to shorter and shorter advertisements. A result is **ad clutter**, a phenomenon in which advertisements compete against each other and reduce the impact of all of them. Placing advertisements on television is a problem because demand outstrips the supply of slots, especially during prime hours. Slots for some hours are locked up months, even whole seasons, in advance.

ONLINE SERVICES. One advantage of **online advertising** is that readers can click to deeper and deeper levels of information about advertised products. A lot more information can be packed into a layered online message than within the space and time confines of a print or broadcast ad. High-resolution colour is standard, and the technology is available for moving pictures and audio. The Internet Advertising Bureau of Canada estimates that Internet advertising grew from $24.5 million in 1998 to over $100 million in 2000. Banners account for about 70 percent of all Internet ad revenue in Canada.

Advertisers are not abandoning traditional media, but they are experimenting with online possibilities. For mail-order products, orders can be placed over the Internet right from the ad. For some groups of potential customers, online advertising has major advantages. To reach college students, almost all of whom have computer access, online advertising makes sense.

The downside of website advertising is that the Internet is accessible only to people with computers, modems, and Internet accounts. Of course, the percentage of the computer-knowledgeable population is mushrooming and will continue to do so.

Pitching Messages

IMPORTANCE OF BRANDS

A challenge for advertising people is the modern-day reality that mass-produced products aimed at large markets are essentially alike: Toothpaste is toothpaste is toothpaste. When the product is virtually identical to the competition, how can one toothpaste-maker move more tubes?

BRAND NAMES. By trial and error, tactics were devised in the late 1800s to set similar products apart. One tactic, promoting a product as a **brand** name, aims to make a product a household word. When it is successful, a brand name becomes almost the generic identifier, like Coke for cola and Kleenex for facial tissue.

Techniques of successful brand name advertising came together in the 1890s for an English product, Pears' soap. A key element in the campaign was multimedia saturation. Advertisements for Pears' were everywhere—in newspapers and magazines and on posters, vacant walls, fences, buses, and street posts. Redundancy hammered home the brand name. "Good morning. Have you used Pears' today?" became a good-natured greeting among Britons that was still being repeated 50 years later. Each repetition reinforced the brand name.

IABC: The Internet Advertising Bureau of Canada represents Internet publishers and advertisers who hope to bring structure and standards to the industry.

www.iabcanada.com

Internet Profiles Corp.: How much to charge for Internet advertising? They show the way.

www.ipro.com

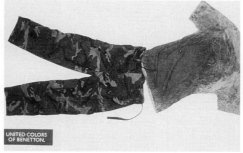

Oliviero Toscani

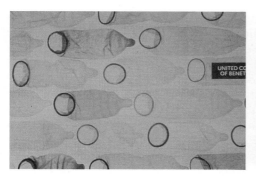

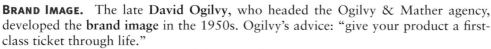

Benetton with Message. For years Benetton, the global casual clothing retailer, has run controversial ads drawing attention to social issues more than the company's products. A 1994 campaign in 25 countries featured a bloody military uniform from Bosnia, recovered from the family of a young man who died in combat. It was a haunting photo. Oliviero Toscani, Benetton's creative director who shoots the company's ads, says the goal is to position Benetton as a socially conscious marketer. The attention-getting 1991 "flying condoms" ad, said Toscani, was aimed to combat the disease AIDS. Even so, in the United States, *Self*, *Mademoiselle*, and *Cosmopolitan* rejected it for fear of offending readers. There were objections also with a follow-up campaign that Benetton claimed celebrated love, but which some cautious publications thought trod too closely on taboos. Some Benetton ads are quite entropic and are excellent texts to decode using semiotic techniques.

BRAND IMAGE.   The late **David Ogilvy**, who headed the Ogilvy & Mather agency, developed the **brand image** in the 1950s. Ogilvy's advice: "give your product a first-class ticket through life."

Explaining the importance of image, Ogilvy once said:

> Take whisky. Why do some people choose Jack Daniel's, while others choose Grand Dad or Taylor? Have they tried all three and compared the taste? Don't make me laugh. The reality is that these three brands have different images which appeal to different kinds of people. It isn't the whisky they choose, it's the image. The brand image is 90 percent of what the distiller has to sell. Give people a taste of Old Crow, and tell them it's Old Crow. Then give them another taste of Old Crow, but tell them it's Jack Daniel's. Ask them which they prefer. They'll think the two drinks are quite different. They are tasting images.

Image has also been important in Canadian advertising. **Jerry Goodis**, a veteran of Canadian advertising, claims that to get consumers to be loyal to your product,

Ogilvy & Mather: The Ogilvy & Mather agency maintains this website, with a brief biography of brand guru David Ogilvy. You can link to his landmark 1955 speech, "The Image and the Brand." The agency prides itself on responding to all inquiries, including those from students seeking help on research projects.

www.ogilvy.com

you need to keep the brand name front and centre. Goodis used this philosophy in creating some of the best-known Canadian commercials, including "at Speedy, you're a somebody" and "Harvey's makes your hamburger a beautiful thing."

LOWEST COMMON DENOMINATOR

Early brand-name campaigns were geared to the largest possible audience, sometimes called an LCD, or **lowest common denominator**, approach. The term "LCD" is adapted from mathematics. To reach an audience that includes members with IQs of 100, the pitch cannot exceed their level of understanding, even if some people in the audience have IQs of 150. The opportunity for deft touches and even cleverness is limited by the fact they might be lost on some potential customers.

Lowest common denominator advertising is best epitomized in contemporary advertising by USP, short for **unique selling proposition**, a term coined by **Rosser Reeves** of the giant Ted Bates agency in the 1960s. Reeves's prescription was simple: Create a benefit of the product, even if from thin air, and then tout the benefit authoritatively and repeatedly as if the competition doesn't have it. One early USP campaign flaunted that Schlitz beer bottles were "washed with live steam." The claim sounded good—who would want to drink from dirty bottles? However, the fact was that every brewery used steam to clean reusable bottles before filling them again. Furthermore, what is "live steam"? Although the implication of a competitive edge was hollow, it was done dramatically and pounded home with emphasis, and it sold beer. Just as hollow a competitive advantage was the USP claim for Colgate toothpaste: "Cleans Your Breath While It Cleans Your Teeth."

Perhaps to compensate for a lack of substance, many USP ads are heavy-handed. Most people have heard about fast-fast-fast relief from headache remedies or that heartburn relief is spelled R-O-L-A-I-D-S. USP can be unappealing, as acknowledged even by the chairman of Warner-Lambert, which makes Rolaids, who once laughed that his company owed the American people an apology for insulting their intelligence over and over with Bates's USP slogans. Warner-Lambert was also laughing all the way to the bank over the USP-spurred success of Rolaids, Efferdent, Listermint, and Bubblicious.

A unique selling proposition, however, need be neither hollow nor insulting. Leo Burnett, founder of the agency bearing his name, refined the USP concept by insisting that the unique point be real. For Maytag, Burnett took the company's slight advantage in reliability and dramatized it with the lonely Maytag repairman.

MARKET SEGMENTS

Rather than pitching to the lowest common denominator, advertising executive **Jack Trout** developed the idea of **positioning**. Trout worked to establish product identities that appealed not to the whole audience but to a specific audience. The cowboy image for Marlboro cigarettes, for example, established a macho attraction beginning in 1958. Later, something similar was done with Virginia Slims, aimed at women.

Positioning helps distinguish products from all the LCD clamour and noise. Advocates of positioning note that there are more and more advertisements and that they are becoming noisier and noisier. Ad clutter, as it is called, drowns out individual advertisements. With positioning, the appeal is focused and caters to audience segments, and it need not be done in such broad strokes.

Campaigns based on positioning have included:

- Johnson & Johnson's baby oil and baby shampoo, which were positioned as an adult product by advertisements featuring athletes.
- Alka-Seltzer, once a hangover and headache remedy, which was positioned as an upmarket product for stress relief among health-conscious, success-driven people.

REDUNDANCY TECHNIQUES

You'll remember from Chapter 1 that a redundant message is one that's easy to decode. Advertising people learned the importance of redundancy early on. To be effective, an advertising message must be repeated, perhaps thousands of times. Redundancy, however, is expensive. To increase effectiveness at less cost, advertisers use several techniques:

- **Barrages.** Scheduling advertisements in intensive bursts called **flights** or **waves**.
- **Bunching.** Promoting a product in a limited period, like running advertisements for school supplies in late August and September.
- **Trailing.** Running condensed versions of advertisements after the original has been introduced, as AT&T did with its hostility advertisements on workplace tensions beginning in 1987. Powerful 60-second advertisements introduced the campaign, followed in a few weeks by 15-second versions. Automakers introduce new models with multi-page magazine spreads, following with single-page placements.
- **Multimedia trailing.** Using less expensive media to reinforce expensive advertisements. Relatively cheap drive-time radio in major markets is a favourite follow-through to expensive television advertisements created for major events like the Super Bowl.

NEW ADVERTISING TECHNIQUES

Ad people are concerned that traditional modes are losing effectiveness. People are overwhelmed. Consider, for example, that a major grocery store carries 30 000 items, each with packaging that screams "buy me." More commercial messages are put there than a human being can handle. The problem is ad clutter. Advertisers are trying to address the clutter in numerous ways, including stealth ads, new-site ads, and alternative media. Although not hidden or subliminal, stealth ads are subtle—even covert. You might not know you're being pitched unless you're attentive, really attentive.

STEALTH ADS. **Stealth ads** fit so neatly into the landscape that the commercial pitch seems part of the story line. In 1996 the writers for four CBS television programs, including *The Nanny*, wrote Elizabeth Taylor into their scripts. And there she was, in over two hours of programming one winter night, wandering in and out of sets looking for a missing string of black pearls. Hardly coincidentally, her new line of perfume, Black Pearls, was being introduced at the time.

The gradual convergence of information and entertainment, called infotainment, has a new element: advertising. *Seinfeld* characters on NBC munched junior mints. The M&M/Mars candy company bought a role for Snickers in the Nintendo game *Biker Mice from Mars*. In 1997, Unilever's British brand Van den Bergh Foods introduced a video game that stars its Peperami snack sausage. In movies promotional plugs have become a big-budget item. The idea is to seamlessly work the presence of commercial products into a script without a cue—nothing like the hopelessly dated "and now a word from our sponsors."

Harvey's. Branding is an effective way to promote not only a product, but an image.

Less subtle is the **infomercial**, a program-length television commercial dolled up to look like a newscast, a live-audience participation show, or a chatty talk show. With the proliferation of 24-hour television service and of cable channels, airtime is so cheap at certain hours that advertisers of even offbeat products can afford it. Hardly anybody is fooled into thinking that infomercials are anything but advertisements, but some full-length media advertisements, like Liz Taylor wandering through CBS sitcoms, are cleverly disguised.

A print media variation is the **'zine**—a magazine published by a manufacturer to plug a single line of products with varying degrees of subtlety. 'Zine publishers, including such stalwarts as IBM and Sony, have even been so brazen as to sell these wall-to-wall advertising vehicles at newsstands. In 1996, if you bought a splashy new magazine called *Colors,* you paid $4.50 for it. Once inside, you probably would realize it was a thinly veiled ad for Benetton casual clothes. *Guess Journal* may look like a magazine, but guess who puts it out as a 'zine: the makers of the Guess fashion brand.

Stealth advertisements try "to morph into the very entertainment it sponsors," wrote Mary Kuntz, Joseph Weber, and Heidi Dawley in *Business Week.* The goal, they said, is "to create messages so entertaining, so compelling—and maybe so disguised—that rapt audiences will swallow them whole, oblivious to the sales component."

MEDIA DATABANK 9.1

Top Advertising Agencies in Canada

Here are the largest creative advertising agencies in Canada, according to a survey done by *Marketing Magazine.* Some of these companies are part of international advertising agencies:

Firm	Gross Revenues*	Major Canadian Clients
Cossette Communication Group	$ 109 910 000	Air Canada, Bell Canada
MacLaren McCann	$ 91 500 000	Royal Bank, Labatt's
Young and Rubicam	$ 77 788 222	Kraft, Molson's
Maxxcom	$ 70 161 000	Honda Canada
BBDO Canada	$ 65 181 851	Building Box, *Globe and Mail*

*All figures in Canadian dollars and represent domestic business.
Source: Marketing Magazine, *June 25, 2001.*

NEW-SITE ADS. Ironically, solving the problem of ad clutter by going underground with stealth ads contributes to the clutter. Sooner or later, it would seem, people would also tire of advertising omnipresence. Snapple stickers adorn kiwis and mangoes at the grocery. Sports stadiums named for department stores or other companies, like the Air Canada Centre in Toronto and the Montreal Canadiens' Molson Centre, try to weave product names into everyday conversation and the news. Sports events galore bear the names of high-bidding sponsors. How omnipresent can advertising become? Consider the Bamboo lingerie company that stencilled messages on sidewalks: "From here, it looks like you could use some new underwear."

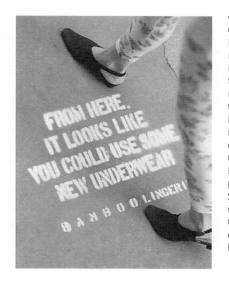

Omnipresent Ads. Bamboo Lingerie's stencilled sidewalk messages may have been unsettling to some folks, but they sold underwear. Like many advertisers worried that their messages are lost in ad-crammed traditional media, Bamboo has struck out for nontraditional territory to be noticed. Regina Kelley, director of strategic planning for the Saatchi & Saatchi agency in New York said, "Any space you can take in visually, anything you can hear, in the future will be branded."

Advertising Regulation

GATEKEEPING REGULATION BY MEDIA

A dramatic reversal in thinking about advertising occurred in the 20th century. The earlier **caveat emptor** mindset, "buyer beware," tolerated extravagant claims. Anybody who believed that the same elixir could cure dandruff, halitosis, and cancer deserved to be conned, or so went the thinking. Over the years, due partly to the growing consumer movement, the thinking changed to **caveat venditor**, "seller beware," placing the onus on the advertiser to avoid misleading claims and to demonstrate the truth of claims.

The advertising industry in Canada must adhere to a variety of laws and regulations, most notably the **Competition Act**. This is a federal statute that covers many different aspects of advertising in Canada. According to the act, any representation (flyer, brochure, in-store display, newspaper ad, material on the Internet or on radio or television) that offers a product or service for sale must adhere to specific guidelines. Some specific aspects covered by the act include false and misleading advertising, bait-and-switch advertising, selling at a higher than advertised price, and testimonials. Fines levied under the Competition Act can be steep. For example, in 1998, the Hudson's Bay Company was fined $600 000 for misleading advertising. The ads in question were for bicycles. Flyers and in-store displays suggested that the sale prices were for a limited time only, when in fact the prices were in effect for a much longer time. This created a false sense of urgency in the ads. In 1997, Click Modelling and Talent Agency of Canada was fined $200 000 for a series of ads claiming that acting and modelling jobs were available through their company when, in fact, the company was selling modelling courses and photographs.

INDUSTRY SELF-REGULATION

In advertising's early days, newspapers and magazines skirted the ethics question posed by false advertisements by saying their pages were open to all advertisers. Under growing pressure, publications sometimes criticized dubious advertisements editorially, but most did not ban them. **Edward Bok,** who made *Ladies' Home Journal* a runaway success in the 1890s, crusaded against dishonest advertising. In one exposé on Lydia E. Pinkham's remedies for "female maladies," Bok reported that Lydia, to whom women readers were invited in advertisements to write for advice, had been dead for 22 years. Yet the advertisements continued.

Codes for broadcast advertising have come and gone over the years; all were voluntary with stations that chose to subscribe. The print media also have seen a variety of industry-wide codes, all voluntary. Most publications spurn misleading advertisements. Many university and community college newspapers refuse advertisements from term-paper services. Some metropolitan papers turn away advertisements for pornographic movies.

A case can be made that the media do not go far enough in exercising their prerogative to ban dubious advertisements. Critics argue that on nettling questions, such as the morality of printing ads for carcinogenic tobacco products, with major revenue at stake, many newspapers and magazines sidestep a moral judgment, run the advertisements, and reap the revenue. The critics note, for example, that most commercial broadcasters ran cigarette advertisements until the federal government intervened. The media, so goes the argument, are too devoted to profits to do all the regulating they should.

The advertising industry itself has numerous organizations that try, through ethics codes and moral suasion, to eradicate falsity and deception. Besides the explicit purposes of these self-policing mechanisms, their existence can be cited by advertising people to argue that their industry is able to deal with misdeeds itself with a minimum of government regulation.

ADVERTISING STANDARDS CANADA

Advertising Standards Canada (ASC) is the self-regulatory body that oversees advertising in Canada. The ASC administers many industry codes. The Canadian Code of Advertising Standards, which has been in place since 1963, includes 15 clauses with an emphasis on the following themes:

- Clear and accurate information on the price, availability, and performance of goods or services.
- No deceptive price claims.
- Warranties and guarantees must be fully explained.
- Products cannot be shown encouraging use that may be dangerous.
- Children's advertising shouldn't exploit their naïveté; nor should it harm them physically, morally, or emotionally.
- If the good or service is prohibited to minors, for instance tobacco or alcohol, its advertising cannot appeal to underage people.
- Advertising cannot exploit violence, gender, or sexuality. It should always be in good taste.

Problems and Issues

ADVERTISING CLUTTER

Leo Bogart of the Newspaper Advertising Bureau noted that the number of advertising messages doubled through the 1960s and 1970s, and except for the recession at the start of the 1990s, the trend continues. This proliferation of advertising creates a

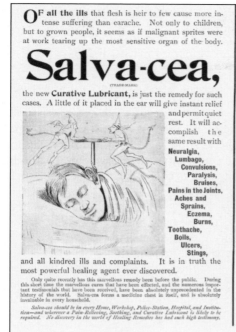

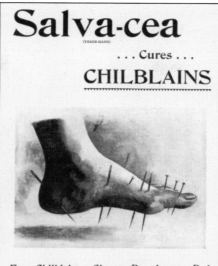

Miracle Cures. Potions and gizmos for curing just about whatever ails you led to government regulation of advertising.

problem—too many ads. CBS squeezed so many ads into its coverage of the 1992 Winter Olympics that some viewers felt the network regarded the games as a sideshow. Even in regular programming, the frequency of ads has led advertisers to fret that their individual ads are being lost in the clutter. The problem has been exacerbated by the shortening of ads from 60 seconds in the early days of television to today's widely used 15-second format.

Ad clutter is less of an issue in the print media. Many people buy magazines and newspapers to look at ads as part of the comparative shopping process. Even so, some advertisers, concerned that their ads are overlooked in massive editions, such as a three-kilogram metro Sunday newspaper or a 700-page bridal magazine, are looking for alternative means to reach potential customers in a less cluttered environment.

The clutter that marks much of commercial television and radio today may be alleviated as the media fragment further. Not only will demassification create more specialized outlets, such as narrowly focused cable television services, but there will be new media. The result will be advertising aimed at narrower audiences. On the downside, people are increasingly frustrated by "pop up" or "pop under" ads that automatically open up new windows in their web browsers while they surf the Internet. This also creates clutter.

EXCESSES IN CREATIVITY

Advertisers are reviewing whether creativity is as effective an approach as hard sell. Harry McMahan studied Clio Awards for creativity in advertising and discovered that 36 agencies that produced 81 winners of the prestigious awards for advertisements had either lost the winning account or gone out of business.

Predicts advertising commentator E.B. Weiss: "Extravagant license for creative people will be curtailed." The future may hold more heavy-handed pitches, perhaps with over-the-counter regimens not only promising fast-fast-fast relief but also spelling it out in all caps and boldface with exclamation marks: **F-A-S-T! F-A-S-T! F-A-S-T!!!**

ADVERTISING EFFECTIVENESS

Long-held assumptions about the effectiveness of advertising itself are being questioned. **Gerald Tellis**, a researcher, put together a sophisticated statistical model that found that people are relatively unmoved by television advertisements in making brand choices, especially on mundane everyday products like toilet paper and laundry detergents.

Tellis's conclusions began with consumer purchasing studies. Not surprisingly, considering its self-interest, the advertising industry has challenged Tellis's studies. Meanwhile, Tellis and other scholars have continued the studies.

The jury is still out on whether Tellis is correct in his doubts about television advertising, on whether the style of advertising makes a difference, or on whether it is just ads for generic products, such as toilet paper and detergent, that are virtually identical and that fail to influence consumers when they are in the store picking products off the shelves.

MEDIA DATABANK 9.2

Advertising in Canadian Schools?

A hotly debated subject in the last few years in Canada is the emergence of advertising in the classroom. Both public and post-secondary institutions in Canada have had to struggle with the economic and ethical dimensions of this matter. A 1999 survey of Canadians by the Angus Reid Group shows how divided we are on this issue. They were asked if they agreed or disagreed with corporations donating equipment to schools (such as computers) in exchange for being able to advertise in the classroom:

- Fifty-three percent of Canadians were in favour; 46 percent were not.
- The strongest support came from Quebec (62 percent agreed), while only 49 percent agreed in Alberta and Ontario.
- Education was a variable: 45 percent of those with a post-secondary education agreed, compared with 58 percent of high school graduates.
- Age was also a factor: 64 percent of those aged 18 to 34 agreed, while only 44 percent of those over 55 agreed.

Source: Angus Reid Group and the Globe and Mail, *June 22, 1999.*

advertising

As an advertising medium, the web seems so exciting and new, but soon the web will be old hat. The future is interactivity with a hodgepodge of wireless devices through which messages can be highly individualized. Because these don't constitute a clearly defined medium, at least not yet, the vague term *new media* is applied to them. Despite the vagueness, nobody disputes the potential of these media as advertising platforms.

The wireless media encompass mobile phones, beepers, wireless laptop computers, and pocket and palm devices—and who knows what else is coming along? Each device has an identifying code, which can be read by the sender. Because the devices are used by individuals whose demographic characteristics—and buying patterns— can be identified, messages can be narrowly focused. Most important, however, is that individuals can talk back. If an advertising message strikes a chord, the user can immediately tap into more information and even make a purchase. Hence, the term *interactivity*.

The new Wireless Application Protocol, WAP for short, means the new devices all speak the same language. With this universal protocol, pitches can be directed at you no matter which device you're using at the moment.

How near is the future? Ovum, a British research company, projects that wireless advertising, only worth US$4 million in 2000, will reach US$4.2 billion by 2005—a thousand-fold increase over five years. Worldwide, says Ovum, the total will exceed US$16 billion.

Nobody's crystal ball predicts the disappearance of existing advertising platforms, but the new media are further dispersing the ways for advertisers to reach their customers.

CHAPTER WRAP-UP

The role of advertising in mass media cannot be overstated. Without advertising, most media would go out of business. In fact, in the 1960s, when advertisers switched to television from the giant general-interest magazines, those magazines went under. Today, the rapid expansion of cable networks is possible only because advertisers are buying time on the new networks to reach potential customers. In one sense, advertisers subsidize readers, viewers, and listeners who pay only a fraction of the cost of producing publications and broadcasts. The bulk of the cost is paid by advertisers, who are willing to do so to make their pitches to potential customers who, coincidentally, are media consumers.

Besides underwriting the mass media, advertising is vital for a prosperous, growing consumer economy. It triggers demand for goods and services, and it enables people to make wise choices by providing information on competing products. The result is efficiency in the marketplace, which frees more capital for expansion. This all speaks to an intimate interrelationship involving advertising in a democratic and capitalistic society.

Today, as democracy and capitalism are reintroduced in Central and Eastern Europe, advertising can be expected to have an essential role in fostering new consumer economies. American, Canadian, European, and Japanese advertising agencies will be called on for their expertise to develop campaigns for goods and services that will make for better lives and stronger economies. This process will provide a greater revenue base for the mass media in these countries, which will result in better journalistic and entertainment content.

QUESTIONS FOR REVIEW

1. Why is advertising essential in a capitalistic society?
2. Trace the development of advertising since the time of Johannes Gutenberg.
3. What is the role of advertising agencies?
4. Why do some advertisements appear in some media and not other media?
5. What are the major tactics used in advertising? Who devised each one?
6. How do advertising people use psychology and research to shape their messages?
7. Explain the differences between semiotic and content analysis.
8. Does advertising still follow the dictum "let the buyer beware"?
9. What are some problems and unanswered issues in advertising?

QUESTIONS FOR CRITICAL THINKING

1. How does the development of modern advertising relate to Johannes Gutenberg's technological innovation? To the Industrial Revolution? To long-distance mass transportation? To mass marketing?
2. Why does advertising flourish more in democratic than in autocratic societies? In a capitalistic more than in a controlled economy? In a prosperous society?
3. What were the contributions to advertising of Wayland Ayer, Rosser Reeves, Jack Trout, Ernest Dichter, Wilson Bryan Key, and David Ogilvy?
4. What are the responsibilities of advertising account executives, copywriters, media buyers, researchers, brand managers, ad reps, and brokers?
5. What are the advantages of the commission system for advertising agency revenue? Of the fee system? What are the disadvantages of both?
6. Describe these advertising tactics: brand name promotion, unique selling proposition, lowest common denominator approach, positioning, and redundancy.
7. How is ad clutter a problem? What can be done about it?
8. How has Advertising Standards Canada improved the image of companies that advertise, agencies that create advertisements, and media that carry advertisements? Give examples.

FOR KEEPING UP TO DATE

Weekly trade journals are *Advertising Age* and *AdWeek*. Scholarly publications include *Journal of Marketing Research* and *Journal of Advertising*. The *New York Times* regularly reports on the industry.

Marketing Magazine is an excellent trade journal that looks at marketing, advertising, and public relations from a Canadian perspective.

The Journal of Consumer Psychology includes analysis, reviews, reports, and other scholarship on the role of advertising in consumer psychology.

FOR FURTHER LEARNING

Mary Billard. "Heavy Metal Goes on Trial." *Rolling Stone* (July 12–26, 1990): 582–583 double issue, 83–88, 132.

Russell Elman. *Media Law Study Book* (Media Studies Department, Mohawk College, Hamilton, Ontario).

Stephen Fox. *The Mirror Makers: A History of American Advertising and Its Creators* (Morrow, 1984).

Jerry Goodis. *Good!s.* (Fitzhenry and Whiteside, 1991).

Industry Canada. *Annual Report of the Director of Investigation and Research, The Competition Act*, for the year ending March 31, 1998.

Wilson Bryan Key. *Subliminal Seduction: Ad Media's Manipulation of a Not So Innocent America* (New American Library, 1972).

Otto Kleppner, Thomas Russell, and Glenn Verrill. *Advertising Procedure*, 8th ed. (Prentice Hall, 1990).

William Liess, Stephen Klein, and Sut Jhally. *Social Communication in Advertising* (Nelson Canada, 1990).

Bob Levenson. *Bill Bernbach's Book: A History of the Advertising That Changed the History of Advertising* (Random House, 1987).

Nancy Millman. *Emperors of Adland: Inside the Advertising Revolution* (Warner Books, 1988).

David Ogilvy. *Confessions of an Advertising Man* (Atheneum, 1963).

David Ogilvy. *Ogilvy on Advertising* (Vintage, 1985).

Griselda Pollock. "What's Wrong with Images of Women?" in *Screen Education* 24 (Autumn, 1977).

Anthony Pratkanis and Elliot Aronson. *Age of Propaganda: The Everyday Use and Abuse of Persuasion* (W. H. Freeman, 1992).

Ronald H. Rotenberg. *Advertising: A Canadian Perspective* (Allyn and Bacon, 1986)

Paul Rutherford. *The New Icons? The Art of Television Advertising* (University of Toronto Press, 1994).

Michael Schudson. *Advertising: The Uneasy Persuasion: Its Dubious Impact on American Society* (Basic Books, 1984).

Alan Shanoff. *Advertising and Law* (Hallion Press, 1995).

Keith J. Tuckwell. *Canadian Advertising in Action* (Prentice Hall, 2000).

ickle Audience. Television executives look to survey research to find ways to reach more viewers. In 1994, CNN's ratings were down 25 percent from a year earlier. That prompted the network to scrap some soft-news programs, including *Living in the '90s*, and to create new call-in sports and news programs, one with a live audience. CNN's problem is that it cannot sustain the huge audience it draws when everybody is intently interested in major news, like the O.J. Simpson case, Operation Desert Storm, the 1999 NATO attacks on Serbia, or the September 11, 2001, terrorist attacks on the U.S. The network typically draws only about 100 000 viewers. Although CNN's audience is educated, affluent, and attractive to advertisers, more viewers would mean more revenue. CNN accounted for 70 percent of Turner Broadcasting System's operating earnings before Turner was absorbed by Time Warner.

MEDIA TIMELINE

Media Research

1914	Advertisers' publications are created by the Audit Bureau of Circulations to verify circulation claims.
1929	Archibald Crossley conducts the first listenership survey.
1932	George Gallup uses quota sampling in an Iowa election.
1936	Gallup uses quota sampling in a U.S. presidential election.
1940S	A.C. Nielsen conducts a demographic listenership survey.
1944	BBM is established in Canada.
1948	Gallup uses probability sampling in a U.S. presidential election.
1970S	SRI introduces VALS psychographics.
1974	Jonathan Robbin introduces PRIZM geodemographics.
1990S	BBM and Nielsen Media Canada begin offering web ratings.
2000	Portable People Meters are introduced to track listenership for radio and television, including cable.

Media Research

Media in Theory

Applied and Theoretical Research

Media-sponsored research looks for ways to build audiences, to enhance profits, and to program responsibly. In contrast, mass communication scholarship asks theoretical questions that can yield new understandings, regardless of whether there is a practical application.

Media-Sponsored Research

Studies sponsored by mass media companies seek knowledge that can be put to use, or applied. This is called **applied research.** When broadcasters underwrite research on media violence, they want answers to help make programming decisions. Audience measures and analysis are applied research, which can be put to work to enhance profits.

Mass media research ranges from developing new technology to seeking historical lessons from previous practices. Some fields of applied media research are discussed below.

Technological Research. Mass media companies and their suppliers finance research into technology to take economic advantage of new opportunities. Early radio in Canada, for example, was spearheaded by businesspeople at the CNR, who saw it as a business opportunity. Ink manufacturers introduced nonsmudge soybean inks in the late 1980s for newspapers. Besides cutting-edge **technological research,** media companies also sponsor finding out ways to adapt innovations developed in other fields, such as computers and satellites, to reduce costs, improve profits, and remain competitive.

Public Policy Analysis.   The media have intense interests in how changes in public policy will affect their business. Analysts anticipated correctly that the television networks would go to satellites to send programs to their affiliates, but they failed to anticipate that network affiliates would use their new downlink dishes to pick up programming from non-network sources and accelerate the fragmentation of the television industry. The CRTC and CAB (Canadian Association of Broadcasters) often engage in policy analysis.

Financial Studies.   Whether the *Financial Post* recommends that investors be bullish on CTV stock depends on how analysts interpret CTV's periodic financial reports. Even privately held media companies are subject to analysis. Competitors make decisions based on their assessment of the marketplace and all the players.

Opinion Surveys.   When anchor Dan Rather began wearing a sweater on the *CBS Evening News*, ratings improved. The network learned about the "sweater factor" from audience **opinion surveys.** Survey research helps media executives make content decisions—whether to expand sports coverage, to hire a disc jockey away from the competition, or to axe a dubious sitcom.

Mass Communication Scholarship

In contrast to applied research, **theoretical research** looks for truths regardless of practical application. Scholars consider most theoretical research on a higher level than applied research, partly because the force that drives it is the seeking of truths for their own sake rather than for any economic goal. The *Canadian Journal of Communication* is one such academic journal. Below are some of the kinds of studies and analyses that are the subject of theoretical research.

Effects Studies.   The greatest ferment in mass communication scholarship has involved questions about effects. In the 1920s, as mass communication theory took form, scholars began exploring the effects of

mass communication and of the mass media themselves on society and individuals. Conversely, scholars are also interested in how ongoing changes and adjustments in society influence the mass media and their content. The research is known as **effects studies.**

Process Studies.   A continuing interest among scholars is the mystery of how the process of mass communication works. Just as human beings have developed theories to explain other great mysteries, such as thunder being caused by unhappy gods thrashing about in the heavens, mass communication scholars have developed, in **process studies**, a great many explanations to help us understand mass communication.

Examples of these theories include the diverse models that scholars have created of the mass communication process. You might recall the general, concentric circle, and narrative models from Chapter 1. None of these models is as way out as the thrashing-gods explanation for thunder, but their diversity indicates that many questions still need to be asked and explored before we can ever develop the kind of understanding about mass communication that scientists now have about thunder.

Gratifications Studies.   Beginning in the 1940s, studies about how and why individuals use the mass media attracted scholarly interest. These today are called **uses and gratifications studies.**

Content Analysis.   George Gerbner, a scholar of media violence, studied the 8 p.m. hour of network television for 19 years and found an average of 168 violent acts a week. Gerbner arrived at his disturbing statistic through **content analysis**, a research method involving the systematic counting of media content. Gerbner's tallying became a basic reference point for important further studies that correlated media-depicted violence with changes in incidents of violence in society at large.

MediaWatch is a national volunteer network that monitors various issues in the media. Content analysis is one of their techniques. Through content analysis, MediaWatch surveyed 16 Canadian newspapers in 1998 and found that women were grossly underrepresented. Only 25 percent of reporters and

20 percent of newsmakers were female. When compared to studies in the early 1990s, this represented no significant change to the representation of women in the Canadian media.

Historical Studies.   Some scholars specialize in deriving truths about the mass media and mass communication by examining evidence from the past.

Harold Innis's *Empire and Communication* is a classic example of a historical study.

Critical Studies.   Scholars who are engaged in critical studies question underlying institutions and their economic, philosophical, and political assumptions that shape the mass media. The semiotic school falls under the umbrella term critical studies.

Public-Opinion Surveying

THE SURVEYING INDUSTRY

Angus Reid Group: The official polling company for the *Globe and Mail* and CTV. Recent news items include "Canadians more like Swedes when it comes to Internet use" and "63% of Canadians say they're less likely to buy GM foods."

www.Angusreid.com

Environics Research Group: They originally focused on public opinion polling for political parties, and then in the early 1980s, with Quebec polling firm CROP Inc., began conducting a yearly evaluation of social change in Canada known as the Social Values Monitor.

erg.environics.net

Polls: The Gallup Poll people explain how they conduct polls.

www.gallup.com/poll/ faq/faq000101.asp

Public-opinion surveying is a business whose clients include major corporations, political candidates, and the mass media. Hundreds of companies are in the survey business, most performing advertising and product-related opinion research for private clients. During election campaigns, political candidates become major clients. There are dozens of other survey companies that do confidential research for and about the media. Their findings are important because they determine what kind of advertising will run and where, what programs will be developed and broadcast, and which ones will be cancelled. Some television stations even use such research to choose anchors for major newscasts.

PROBABILITY SAMPLING

Although polling has become a high-profile business, many people do not understand how questions to a few hundred individuals can tell the mood of millions. In the **probability sampling** method pioneered by **George Gallup** in the 1940s, four factors figure into accurate surveying:

SAMPLE SIZE. To learn how students from a certain college or university feel about abortion on demand, you start by asking one student. Because you can hardly generalize from one student to the whole student body of 2000, you ask a second student. If both agree, you start developing a tentative sense of how students at this college feel, but because you cannot have much confidence in such a tiny sample, you ask a third student, and a fourth, and a fifth. At some point between interviewing just one and all 2000 students, you can draw a reasonable conclusion.

How do you choose **sample size**? Statisticians have found that **384** is a magic number for many surveys. Put simply, no matter how large the **population** being sampled, if every member has an equal opportunity to be polled, you need ask only 384 people to be 95 percent confident that you are within 5 percentage points of a precise reading. For a lot of surveys, that is close enough. Here is a breakdown, from Philip Meyer's *Precision Journalism*, a book for journalists on surveying, on necessary sample sizes for 95 percent confidence and being within 5 percentage points:

Population Size	Sample Size
Infinity	384
500 000	384
100 000	383
50 000	381
10 000	370
5 000	357
3 000	341
2 000	322
1 000	278

At a community college with a total enrolment of 2000, the sample size would need to be 322 students.

SAMPLE SELECTION. The process of choosing whom to interview is known as **sample selection**. Essential in probability sampling is giving every member of the population being sampled an equal chance to be interviewed. If, for example, you want to know how Albertans intend to vote, you cannot merely go to an Edmonton street corner and survey the first 384 people who pass by. You would need to check a list of the province's registered voters and then divide by the magic number, 384:

$$\frac{675\ 000}{384} = 1758$$

You would need to talk with every 1758th person on the list. At your school, 2000 divided by 322 would mean an interval of 6.2. Every sixth person in the student body would need to be polled.

MARGIN OF ERROR. For absolute precision, every person in the population must be interviewed, but such precision is hardly ever needed, and the process would be prohibitively expensive and impracticable. Pollsters, therefore, must decide what is an acceptable **margin of error** for every survey they conduct. This is a complex matter, but, in simple terms, you can have a fairly high level of confidence that a properly designed survey with 384 respondents can yield results within 5 percentage points, either way, of being correct. If the survey finds that two candidates for provincial office are running 51 to 49 percent, for example, the race is too close to call with a sample of 384. If, however, the survey says that the candidates are running 56 to 44 percent, you can be reasonably confident who is ahead in the race because, even if the survey is 5 points off on the high side for the leader, the candidate at the very least has 51 percent support (56 percent minus a maximum 5 percentage points for possible error). At best, the trailing candidate has 49 percent (44 percent plus a maximum 5 percentage points for possible error).

Increasing the sample size will reduce the margin of error. Meyer gives this breakdown:

Population Size	Sample Size	Margin of Error
Infinity	384	5 percentage points
Infinity	600	4 percentage points
Infinity	1067	3 percentage points
Infinity	2401	2 percentage points
Infinity	9605	1 percentage point

Professional polling organizations that sample voters typically use sample sizes between 1500 and 3000 to increase accuracy. Also, measuring subgroups within the population being sampled requires that each subgroup, such as men and women, or Catholics and non-Catholics, be represented by 384 properly selected people.

CONFIDENCE LEVEL. With a sample of 384, pollsters can claim a relatively high 95 percent **confidence level**; that is, they are within 5 percentage points of being on the mark. For many surveys, this is sufficient statistical validity. If the confidence level needs to be higher, or if the margin of error needs to be decreased, the number of people surveyed will need to be increased. In short, the level of confidence and margin of error are inversely related. A larger sample can improve confidence, just as it can also reduce the margin of error.

QUOTA SAMPLING

Besides probability sampling, pollsters survey cross-sections of the whole population. With **quota sampling**, a pollster checking an election campaign interviews a sample of people that includes a quota of men and women that corresponds to the number of male and female registered voters. The sample might also include an appropriate quota of Liberals, New Democrats, Conservatives, and Reformers; of poor, middle-income, and wealthy people; of Catholics, Jews, and Protestants; of the employed and unemployed; and other breakdowns significant to the pollster.

Both quota and probability sampling are valid if done correctly, but Gallup abandoned quota sampling because he could not pinpoint public opinion closer than 4 percentage points on average. With probability sampling, he regularly came within 2 percentage points.

EVALUATING SURVEYS

Sidewalk interviews cannot be expected to reflect the views of the population. The people who respond to such polls are self-selected by virtue of being at a given place at a given time. Just as unreliable are call-in polls with 800 or 900 telephone numbers. These polls test the views only of people who are aware of the poll and who have sufficiently strong opinions to want to be heard.

Journalists run the risk of being duped when special-interest groups suggest that news stories be written based on their privately conducted surveys. Some organizations selectively release self-serving conclusions.

Incompetence in designing a survey can mar results. Surveys by college research methodology classes are notorious. Results can be seriously skewed if even one student, perhaps under deadline pressure at the end of a semester, fakes data and is not caught.

Media People

George Gallup

George Gallup was excited. His mother-in-law, Ola Babcock Miller, had decided to run for secretary of state. If elected, she would become not only Iowa's first Democrat but also the first woman to hold the state-wide office. Gallup's excitement, however, went beyond the novelty of his mother-in-law's candidacy. The campaign gave him an opportunity to pull together his three primary intellectual interests: survey research, public opinion, and politics. In that 1932 campaign George Gallup conducted the first serious poll in history for a political candidate. Gallup's surveying provided important barometers of public sentiment that helped Miller to gear her campaign to the issues that were most on voters' minds. She won and was re-elected twice by large margins.

Gallup devoted himself to accuracy. Even though he predicted Roosevelt's victory in the 1936 U.S. presidential election, Gallup was bothered that his reliability was not better. His method, quota sampling, could not call a two-way race within 4 percentage points. With quota sampling, a representative percentage of women and men was surveyed, as was a representative percentage of Democrats and Republicans, Westerners and Easterners, Christians and Jews, and other constituencies.

In 1948 Gallup correctly concluded that Thomas Dewey was not a shoo-in for U.S. president. Nonetheless, his pre-election poll was 5.3 percentage points off. So he decided to switch to a tighter method, probability sampling, which theoretically gave everyone in the population being sampled an equal chance to be surveyed. With probability sampling, there was no need for quotas because, as Gallup explained in his folksy Midwestern way, it was like a cook making soup: "When a housewife

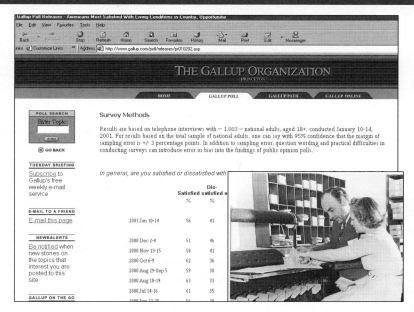

George Gallup Jr.   Sorting data has become more sophisticated since George Gallup Jr. took over the polling organization from his father.

wants to test the quality of the soup she is making, she tastes only a teaspoonful or two. She knows that if the soup is thoroughly stirred, one teaspoonful is enough to tell her whether she has the right mixture of ingredients." With the new method, Gallup's **statistical extrapolation** narrowed his error rate to less than 2 percentage points.

Even with improvements pioneered by Gallup, public opinion surveying has detractors. Some critics say that polls influence undecided voters toward the front-runner—a bandwagon effect. Other critics say that polls make elected officials too responsive to the momentary whims of the electorate, discouraging courageous leadership. George Gallup, who died in 1984, tirelessly defended polling, arguing that good surveys give voice to the "inarticulate minority" that legislators otherwise might not hear. Gallup was convinced that public-opinion surveys help to make democracy work.

In response to sloppy and dishonest surveying, the Associated Press insists on knowing methodology details before running poll stories. The AP tells reporters to ask:

- *How many?* Any survey of fewer than 384 persons selected randomly from the population group has a greater margin for error than is usually tolerated.
- *When was the poll taken?* Opinions shift over time. During election campaigns, shifts can be quick, even overnight.
- *Who paid?* With privately commissioned polls, reporters should be sceptical, asking whether the results being released constitute everything learned in the survey. The timing of the release of political polls to be politically advantageous is not uncommon.
- *What's the margin of error?* Margins of error exist in all surveys unless everyone in the population is surveyed. If the margin of error exceeds the margin between candidates, the results are indicative only that the race is tight.
- *How were questions asked?* Whether a survey was conducted over the telephone or face to face in homes is important. Polls conducted on street corners or in shopping malls are not worth much statistically unless the question is what the people at a particular street corner or mall think. Mail surveys are also flawed unless surveyors follow up on people who do not answer the original questionnaires.
- *What was asked?* Drafting questions is an art. Sloppily worded questions yield sloppy conclusions. Leading questions and loaded questions can skew results. So can question sequencing.

It is at great risk that a polling company's client misrepresents survey results. Most polling companies, concerned about protecting their reputations, include a clause in their contracts with clients that gives the pollster the right to approve the release of findings. The clause usually reads: "When misinterpretation appears, we shall publicly disclose what is required to correct it, notwithstanding our obligation for client confidentiality in all other respects."

LATTER-DAY STRAW POLLS

Many media outlets dabble, some say irresponsibly, with phone-in polling on public issues. The initial vehicle was the **900 telephone number**, which listeners could phone to register yea or nay on a question. This type of survey is called a **straw poll**. MuchMusic and TSN often invite their viewers to log onto their websites to answer their "question of the day." Also dubious are the candid camera features, popular in weekly newspapers, in which a question is put to citizens on the street. The photos of half a dozen individuals and their comments are then published, often on the editorial page.

Measuring Audience Size

BROADCAST RATINGS

Radio and television audiences are difficult to measure, but advertisers still need counts to help them decide where to place ads and what is a fair price. To keep track of broadcast audiences, a whole **ratings** industry, now with about 200 companies worldwide, has developed. **Nielsen Media Research** tracks network television viewership. Since 1944, Canadian broadcast audiences have also been measured by the **Bureau of Measurement (BBM)**.

A.C. Nielsen: Nielsen Media Research, the famous TV ratings company, is the leading provider of television information services in the United States and Canada.

www.nielsenmedia.com

BBM: The Bureau of Measurement is a not-for-profit company that produces ratings information about TV, radio, and interactive media audiences.

www.bbm.ca

MEDIA DATABANK 10.1

Nielsen Canada Ratings

Each week, Nielsen Canada releases the Top 10 shows for the previous week. Here are the Canadian ratings for the week of February 18 to 24, 2002.

Rank	Program	Network	Total (000s)
1	OLYMPIC - CLOSING. CER. (A)/ Salt Lake 2002	CBC Full	4601
2	OLYMPIC PRIME (A) / Various	CBC Full	2614
3	OLYMPIC DAY (A) / Various	CBC Full	1607
4	SATURDAY REPORT (A)	CBC Full	1287
5	NATIONAL NEWS/OLYMPIC (A)	CBC Full	1274
6	CTV EVENING NEWS (A)	CTV	1240
7	ALLY MCBEAL (A)	CTV	1174
8	LAW AND ORDER: SVU (A)	CTV	1122
9	LAW & ORDER (A)	CTV	1113
10	C.S.I. (A)	CTV	1091

Source: Reprinted by permission of Nielsen Media Research.

Radio ratings began in 1929 when advertisers asked American pollster Archibald Crossley to determine how many people were listening to network programs. Crossley checked a small sample of households and then extrapolated the data into national ratings, the same process that radio and television audience-tracking companies still use, although there have been refinements.

In the 1940s, Nielsen began telling advertisers which radio programs were especially popular among men, women, and children. Nielsen also divided listenership into age brackets: 18–34, 35–49, and 50 plus. These were called **demographic** breakdowns. When Nielsen moved into television monitoring in 1950, it expanded audience data into more breakdowns, including income, education, religion, occupation, neighbourhood, and even which products the viewers of certain programs use frequently.

While Archibald Crossley's early ratings were sponsored by advertisers, today networks and individual stations also commission ratings to be done. The television networks pass ratings data on to advertisers immediately. Local stations usually recast the raw data for brochures that display the data in ways that put the station in the most favourable light. These brochures are distributed by station sales representatives to advertisers. While advertisers receive ratings data from the stations and networks, major advertising agencies have contracts with research companies to gather audience data to meet their specifications.

BBM and Nielsen Media Research both provide useful data for Canadian advertisers. BBM measures radio, television, and web audiences, while Nielsen Media Canada focuses on the Internet and television.

AUDIENCE MEASUREMENT TECHNIQUES

The primary techniques, sometimes used in combination, for measuring broadcast audiences are the following:

INTERVIEWS. In his pioneer 1929 listenership polling, Archibald Crossley placed telephone calls to randomly selected households. Today, many polling companies use telephone **interviews** exclusively. Some companies conduct face-to-face interviews, which can elicit fuller information, although it is more expensive and time-consuming.

DIARIES. Many ratings companies give forms to selected households to record what stations were on at particular times. Some companies distribute **diaries** to every member of a household. BBM's diaries go to everybody over age 12 in selected households, which provide data on age and gender preferences for certain stations and programs. Participants mail these diaries back to BBM, which then tabulates the results.

BBM began using diaries to tabulate data about Canadians' viewing and listening habits in 1956. Initially, BBM issued a household diary to participants in its survey. Participants would record information about the entire household and their

Measuring Broadcast Audiences. Many audience measurement companies ask selected households to keep diaries on their listening and viewing habits. Through statistical extrapolations, these companies claim they can discover the size of the total audience for particular programs and stations. This Nielsen Media Research diary asks participants to list who is watching, which allows broadcast executives and advertisers to learn demographic details about this audience. Under pressure for more accurate television ratings, audience measurement companies are shifting from written diaries to electronic meters. With a meter, members of participating households punch in when they start watching. With more advanced meters, punching in is not even required. The meters sense who is watching by body mass, which is programmed into the meter for every member of the household when it is installed.

viewing and listening habits in this diary. In 1967, BBM started to issue personal diaries, which helped tabulate data about a specific person within that house. In 1975, the bureau began to provide separate diaries for radio and television.

Using a probability sample in each market in Canada, BBM measures television viewing on a weekly basis; while radio stations are rated for about four months each year, with an eight-week ratings period in both the spring and the fall. In larger markets, like Toronto, Montreal, and Vancouver, BBM also has a summer ratings period.

BBM now asks radio listeners to answer additional questions about their favourite products and restaurants, and about how much money they spend per week on food. This gives the bureau additional data that may be useful to radio stations when selling their airtime. Asking questions like these may uncover opportunities for niche advertising.

METERS. For television ratings both BBM and Nielsen Media Canada have installed meters to record when television sets are on and to which channels they are tuned. Nielsen has 3100 households wired with meters in Canada, with another 4000 in the United States. BBM began using people meters in 1998 in Vancouver. Today, it measures audiences from coast to coast. BBM uses this data to augment its diary-based research into the television viewing habits of Canadians.

In the United States in 2000, Nielsen and Arbitron jointly tested portable meters for people to carry around. The pager-size **Portable People Meters,** weighing approximately 70 grams, were set to pick up inaudible signals transmitted with programs. The goal was to track away-from-home audiences at sports bars, offices, and airports. Tracking those "lost listeners" could affect ratings. The "walking meters," as they are called, also track commuter radio habits for the first time. The **passive meters** don't require people to remember to turn them on, press buttons, or make entries.

WEB AUDIENCE MEASURES

There are a number of ways to measure the traffic at a website, some more accurate than others. On the one hand, ISPs (Internet service providers) offer a regular traffic report on the number of "hits" on a website. Software is also available to help monitor web traffic. However, the most reliable data come from the companies who know media research best.

Both BBM and Nielsen Media Canada offer their clients a web "ratings" service. BBM's New Media Division's web auditing not only offers information about the number of hits to the website, but also the top referring links, most accessed pages, the amount of time spent at the site, and visits by time and day. Nielsen Media's NetRatings measures Internet use not only in Canada, but in 26 other countries. NetRatings information is dependent on interest. For example, it can offer information to advertisers about traffic to a website and it can also provide specific information to people interested in e-commerce, media, and finance.

How accurate are web ratings? Some major content providers claim the ratings undercount their users. Such claims go beyond self-serving comments because, in fact, different rating companies come up with widely divergent ratings. The question

Walking Meter. The latest broadcast audience-measuring device is a 70-gram gizmo for people to carry wherever they go. The portable meters track listening that is missed by household meters. The meters pick up an inaudible code embedded in the audio of television, radio, and streamed programs. When people get home, they put the meters in a dock that transmits accumulated data to Nielsen and Arbitron computers for aggregation.

Arbitron: The radio research people.

www.arbitron.com

DoubleClick: DoubleClick claims to be the industry leader at using technology, media, and data expertise to create solutions that help advertisers and publishers unleash the power of the web for branding, selling products, and building relationships with customers. The site lets you create your own customized DoubleClick media kit.

www.doubleclick.net

is: Why can't the ratings companies get it right? The answer, in part, is that divergent data flow from divergent methodologies. Data need to be viewed in terms of the methodology that was used. Also, the infant web ratings business undoubtedly is hobbled by methodology flaws that have yet to be identified and corrected.

NEWSPAPER AND MAGAZINE AUDITS

The number of copies a newspaper or magazine puts out, called **circulation**, is fairly easy to calculate. It is simple arithmetic involving data like press runs, subscription sales, and unsold copies returned from newsracks. Many publishers follow strict procedures, which are checked by independent audit organizations, such as the **Audit Bureau of Circulations (ABC)**, to assure advertisers that the system is honest and circulation claims comparable.

The Audit Bureau of Circulations was formed in 1914 to remove the temptation for publishers to inflate their claims to attract advertisers and hike ad rates. Inflated claims, contagious in some cities, were working to the disadvantage of honest publishers. Today, most newspapers belong to ABC, which means that they follow the bureau's standards for reporting circulation and are subject to the bureau's audits.

The **Print Measurement Bureau (PMB)** tracks magazine sales in Canada. In 2001, they introduced a new method to measure readership in Canada. The "recent reading" method doesn't measure how many magazines have been sold, but rather how many have been read. A survey asks respondents when they last read an issue of *Maclean's* or *Reader's Digest*. PMB feels that this helps paint a truer picture of how successful Canadian magazines are. This method is also used worldwide to measure magazine readership.

CRITICISM OF RATINGS

However sophisticated the ratings services have become, they have critics. Many fans question the accuracy of ratings when their favourite television program is cancelled because the network finds the ratings inadequate. Something is wrong, they say, when the viewing preferences of a few thousand households determine network programming for an entire nation. Though it seems incredible to someone unknowledgeable about statistical probability, the sample base of major ratings services is considered sufficient to extrapolate reliably on viewership and listenership.

Ratings have problems, some of them inherent in differing methodologies. For example, in 2001, Statistics Canada reported that TV viewing among Canadians was down in 1999. They attributed the drop in ratings to people watching more movies and logging on to the Internet more. However, Nielsen Media Research disputed the claims, saying that TV viewing trends had actually increased. Nielsen says that the Statistics Canada survey only used data from a short four-week period in the fall of 1999, which is too small a sample to draw any meaningful conclusions from. Nielsen's data was culled from 2500 people meters across Canada.

The reality is that, while as close to "scientific" as possible, ratings can be problematic for many reasons:

DISCREPANCIES. When different ratings services come up with widely divergent findings in the same market, advertisers become suspicious. Minor discrepancies can be

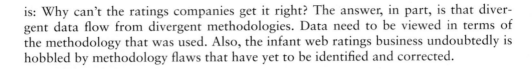

ABC: The Audit Bureau of Circulations was created in 1914 to establish and enforce ground rules for circulation accounting, and to provide published reports of verified circulation data to buyers and sellers of print advertising space.

www.accessabc.com

explained by different sampling methods, but significant discrepancies point to flawed methodology or execution.

SLANTED RESULTS.   Sales reps of some local stations, eager to demonstrate to advertisers that their stations have large audiences, extract only the favourable data from survey results. It takes a sophisticated local advertiser to reconcile slanted and fudged claims. Unfortunately, this seems to be a common occurrence.

SAMPLE SELECTION.   Some ratings services select their samples meticulously, giving every household in a market a statistically equal opportunity to be sampled. Some sample selections are seriously flawed: How reliable, for example, are the listenership claims of a rock 'n' roll station that puts a disc jockey's face on billboards all over town and then sends the disc jockey to a teenage dance palace to ask about listening preferences?

HYPING.   Ratings-hungry stations have learned how to build audiences during **sweeps** weeks in February, May, and November, when major local television ratings are done.

RESPONDENT ACCURACY.   Respondents don't always answer truthfully. People have an opportunity to tell interviewers or diaries that they watched an artsy film on Showcase instead of less classy fare. Shock radio and trash television may have more audience than the ratings show.

ZIPPING, ZAPPING, AND FLUSHING.   Ratings services measure audiences for programs and for different times of day, but they do not measure whether commercials are watched. Advertisers are interested, of course, in whether the programs in which their ads are sandwiched are popular, but more important to them is whether people are actually watching the ads.

This vacuum in audience measurements was documented in the 1960s when somebody with a sense of humour correlated a major drop in Chicago water pressure with the Super Bowl halftime. Football fans were getting off the couch by the thousands at halftime to go to the bathroom. Advertisers were missing many people because viewers were watching the program but not the ads. This **flush factor** was also at work with all other programs. Television viewers find all kinds of things to do when the commercials come on—go to the refrigerator, let the dog in, chat with someone else watching the program. The same thing happens in radio. With a push-button car radio, drivers easily change stations whenever an ad comes up to find a station that is playing music or delivering news.

This problem has been exacerbated with the advent of hand-held television remote controls. Viewers can **zip** from station to station to avoid commercials, and when they record programs for later viewing they can **zap** out the commercials. The Association of Canadian Advertisers calls this practice "commercial avoidance."

Measuring Audience Reaction

FOCUS GROUPS

Television consulting companies measure audience reaction with **focus groups**. Typically an interview crew goes to a shopping centre, chooses a dozen individuals by gender and age, and offers them cookies, soft drinks, and $25 each to sit down and watch a taped local newscast. A moderator then asks their reactions, sometimes with loaded and leading questions to open them up. It is a tricky research method that depends highly on the skill of the moderator. In one court case, an anchor who lost her job as a result of responses to a focus group complained that the moderator contaminated the process with prejudicial assertions and questions:

■ "This is your chance to get rid of the things you don't like to see on the news."
■ "Come on, unload on those sons of bitches who make $100 000 a year."
■ "Let's spend 30 seconds destroying this anchor. Is she a mutt? Be honest about this."

Even when conducted skilfully, focus groups have the disadvantage of reflecting the opinion of the loudest respondent.

GALVANIC SKIN CHECKS

Consulting companies hired by television stations run a great variety of studies to determine audience reaction. Local stations, which originate news programs and not much else, look to these consultants for advice on news sets, story selection, and even which anchors and reporters are most popular. Besides surveys, these consultants sometimes use **galvanic skin checks**. Wires are attached to individuals in a sample group of viewers to measure pulse and skin reactions, such as perspiration. Advocates of these tests claim that they reveal how much interest a newscast evokes and whether it is positive or negative.

These tests were first used to check audience reaction to advertisements, but today some stations look to them in deciding whether to remodel a studio. A dubious use, from a journalistic perspective, is using galvanic skin checks to determine what kinds of stories to cover and whether to find new anchors and reporters. The skin checks reward short, photogenic stories like fires and accidents rather than significant stories, which tend to be longer and don't lend themselves to flashy video. The checks also favour good-looking, smooth anchors and reporters regardless of their journalistic competence. One wag was literally correct when he called this "a heart-throb approach to journalism."

If It Bleeds, It Leads. Audience researchers have found newscast ratings go up for stations that consistently deliver graphic video. This has prompted many stations to favour fire stories, for example, even if the fire wasn't consequential, if graphic video is available. The ratings quest also prompts these stations to favour crimes and accidents over more substantive stories, like government budgets, that don't lend themselves to gripping graphics.

PROTOTYPE RESEARCH

Before making major investments, media executives need as much information as they can obtain to determine how to enhance a project's chances for success or whether it has a chance at all. This is known as **prototype research**. The American Research Institute of Los Angeles specializes in showing previews of television programs and even promotional ads to sample audiences. It is a method originated by movie studios, which invite people to advance showings and watch their reaction to decide how to advertise a new film most effectively, how to time the film's release, and even whether to re-edit the film.

In network television, a prototype may even make it on the air in the form of a pilot. One or a few episodes are tested, usually in prime time with a lot of promotion, to see if the audience goes for the program concept. Some made-for-television movies actually are test runs to determine whether a series might be spun off from the movie.

Audience Analysis

DEMOGRAPHICS

Early in the development of public-opinion surveying, pollsters learned that broad breakdowns had limited usefulness. Archibald Crossley's pioneering radio surveys, for example, told the number of people who were listening to network programs, which was valuable to the networks and their advertisers, but Crossley's figures did not tell how many listeners were men or women, urban or rural, old or young. Such breakdowns of overall survey data, called **demographics**, were developed in the 1930s as Crossley, George Gallup, and other early pollsters refined their work.

Today, if demographic data indicate a political candidate is weak in the prairies, campaign strategists can gear the candidate's message to western concerns. Through demographics, advertisers keen on reaching young women can identify magazines that will carry their ads to that audience. If advertisers seek an elderly audience, they can use demographic data to determine where to place their television ads.

While demographics remains valuable today, newer methods can break the population into categories that have even greater usefulness. These newer methods, which include geodemography, psychographics, and cohort analysis, provide lifestyle breakdowns.

GEODEMOGRAPHICS

Computer whiz **Jonathan Robbin** provided the basis for more sophisticated breakdowns in 1974 when he began developing his **PRIZM** system for **geodemography**. From U.S. census data, Robbin grouped every zip code by ethnicity, family life cycle,

Adrenalin Video. Television producers know from research what kinds of videos excite viewers. During the Persian Gulf war, combat footage was repeated again and again under voice-overs that told about war developments. This led some observers to say that war coverage had become video entertainment.

Geodemographics. Many magazines can customize their advertising and editorial content to match the interests of readers through sophisticated geodemographic audience analysis. *Time* demonstrated the potential of its TargetSelect geodemographic program by printing the name of each subscriber as part of the cover art for the November 26, 1990, issue. The cover underscored the point of the lead article about the sort of TargetSelect sophistication also used by "junk mail" companies to match fliers sent through the mail with the likeliest customers for their products.

housing style, mobility, and social rank. Then he identified 34 factors that statistically distinguished neighbourhoods from each other. All this information was cranked through a computer programmed by Robbin to plug every zip code into 1 of 40 clusters. Here are the most frequent clusters created through PRIZM, which stands for Potential Rating Index for Zip Markets, with the labels Robbin put on them.

- *Blue-Chip Blues.* These are the wealthiest blue-collar. About 13 percent of these people are university graduates.
- *Young Suburbia.* Child-rearing outlying suburbs. Roughly 5.3 percent of the population.
- *Golden Ponds.* Rustic mountain, seashore, or lakeside cottage communities; 5.2 percent of the population.
- *New Beginnings.* Fringe-city areas of singles' apartment complexes, garden apartments, and trim bungalows. About 4.3 percent of the general population.
- *New Homesteaders.* Exurban boom towns of young mid-scale families; 4.2 percent of population.

   The potential of Robbin's PRIZM system was clear at *Time*, *Newsweek*, and *McCall's*, which re-sorted subscriber lists and created new zoned editions to allow advertisers to mix and match their messages with a great variety of subaudiences of potential customers. Cadillac could choose editions aimed at these PRIZM neighbourhoods:

- *Blue-Blood Estates.* Wealthiest neighbourhoods; university grads, 51 percent.
- *Money and Brains.* Posh big-city enclaves of townhouses, condos, and apartments; university grads, 46 percent.

For its household products, Colgate-Palmolive might focus on:

- *Blue-Collar Nursery.* Middle-class, child-rearing towns; university grads, 10 percent.

Geodemographic breakdowns are used not only for magazine advertising but also for editorial content. At Time Warner magazines, geodemographic analysis permits issues to be edited for special audiences. *Time*, for example, has a 600 000 circulation edition for company owners, directors, board chairs, presidents, and other titled officers and department heads. Among others are editions for physicians and students.

Theoretically, using PRIZM geodemographic breakdowns and other data, newsmagazines customize their agribusiness coverage for chicken farmers, offer expanded golf coverage for golf fans, and beef up articles on problems of the aged in the Gray Power and Golden Ponds PRIZM clusters. More book reviews might be added for Town and Gowns, the PRIZM cluster for university towns. In a 1990 stunt that demonstrated the potential for customizing magazines, *Time* printed the name of each subscriber in big print as part of the cover art, using the same computerized ink-jet printing that it uses for localizing advertisements.

PSYCHOGRAPHICS

A refined lifestyle breakdown introduced in the late 1970s, **psychographics**, divides the population into lifestyle segments. One leading psychographics approach, the Values and Life-Styles program, known as **VALS** for short, uses an 85-page survey that was used to identify broad categories of people:

NEED-DRIVEN PEOPLE.

- *Survivors.* This is a small downscale category that includes pensioners who worry about making ends meet.
- *Sustainers.* These people live from paycheque to paycheque. Although they indulge in an occasional extravagance, they have slight hope for improving their lot in life. Sustainers are a downscale category and aren't frequent advertising targets.

OUTER-DIRECTED PEOPLE.

- *Belongers.* Comprising about 38 percent of the population, these people are conformists who are satisfied with mainstream values and are reluctant to change brands once they're satisfied. Belongers are not very venturesome. They tend to be churchgoers and television watchers.

- *Emulators.* Comprising 10 percent of the population, these people aspire to a better life but, not quite understanding how to do it, go for the trappings of prosperity. Emulators are status seekers, prone to suggestions on what makes the good life.

- *Achievers.* Comprising about 20 percent of the population, these are prosperous people who pride themselves on making their own decisions. They're an upscale audience to which a lot of advertising is directed. As a group, achievers aren't heavy television watchers.

INNER-DIRECTED PEOPLE.

- *I-Am-Me's.* Comprising 3 percent of the population, these people work hard to set themselves apart and are susceptible to advertising pitches that offer ways to differentiate themselves, which gives them a kind of subculture conformity. SRI International, which developed the VALS technique, characterized the I-am-me as "a guitar-playing punk rocker who goes around in shades and sports an earring." Rebellious youth, angry and maladjusted, fit this category.

VALS: Now that you've read all about VALS in the textbook, see where you fit in on the value and lifestyle hierarchy. You might be surprised after responding to this site's questionnaire.

future.sri.com/vals

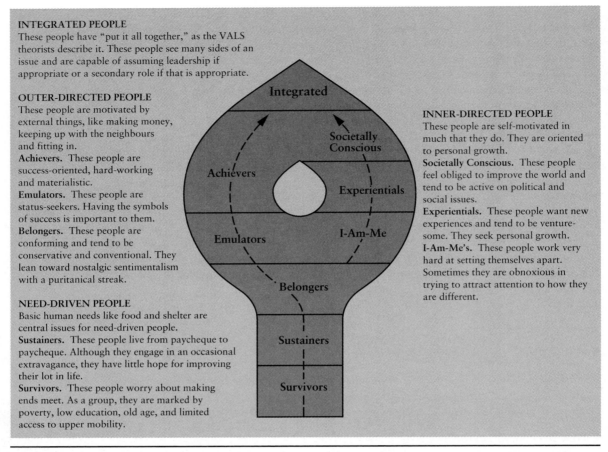

INTEGRATED PEOPLE
These people have "put it all together," as the VALS theorists describe it. These people see many sides of an issue and are capable of assuming leadership if appropriate or a secondary role if that is appropriate.

OUTER-DIRECTED PEOPLE
These people are motivated by external things, like making money, keeping up with the neighbours and fitting in.
Achievers. These people are success-oriented, hard-working and materialistic.
Emulators. These people are status-seekers. Having the symbols of success is important to them.
Belongers. These people are conforming and tend to be conservative and conventional. They lean toward nostalgic sentimentalism with a puritanical streak.

NEED-DRIVEN PEOPLE
Basic human needs like food and shelter are central issues for need-driven people.
Sustainers. These people live from paycheque to paycheque. Although they engage in an occasional extravagance, they have little hope for improving their lot in life.
Survivors. These people worry about making ends meet. As a group, they are marked by poverty, low education, old age, and limited access to upper mobility.

INNER-DIRECTED PEOPLE
These people are self-motivated in much that they do. They are oriented to personal growth.
Societally Conscious. These people feel obliged to improve the world and tend to be active on political and social issues.
Experientials. These people want new experiences and tend to be venture-some. They seek personal growth.
I-Am-Me's. These people work very hard at setting themselves apart. Sometimes they are obnoxious in trying to attract attention to how they are different.

VALS Hierarchy. Developmental psychologists have long told us that people change their values as they mature. Today, many advertisers rely on the Values and Life-Styles Model, VALS for short, which was derived from developmental psychology, to identify potential consumers and to design effective messages. Relatively few messages are aimed at survivors or sustainers, who have little discretionary income. However, belongers and people on the divergent outer-directed or inner-directed paths are lucrative advertising targets for many products and services.

- *Experientials.* Comprising 5 percent of the population, these people are venture-some, willing to try new things in an attempt to experience life fully. They are a promising upscale audience for many advertisers.
- *Societally Conscious.* Comprising 11 percent of the population, these people are aware of social issues and tend to be politically active. The societally conscious also are upscale and inner-directed, and they tend to prefer reading to watching television.

INTEGRATED PEOPLE.

- *Integrateds.* Comprising only 2 percent of the population, integrateds are both creative and prosperous—willing to try different products and ways of doing things, and they have the wherewithal to do it.

Applying psychographics is not without hazard. The categories are in flux as society and lifestyles change. SRI researchers charted growth in the percentage of

I-am-me's, experientials, and the societally conscious in the 1980s and projected that they would be one-third of the population within a few years. Belongers were declining.

Another complication is that no person fits absolutely the mould of any one category. Even for individuals who fit one category better than another, there is no single mass medium to reach them. VALS research may show that achievers constitute the biggest market for antihistamines, but belongers also head to the medicine cabinet when they're congested.

COHORT ANALYSIS

Marketing people have developed **cohort analysis**, a specialized form of demographics, to identify generations and then design and produce products with generational appeal. Advertising people then gear media messages with the images, music, humour, and other generational variables that appeal to the target cohort. The major cohorts are dubbed:

- **Generation X.** Those who came of age in the 1980s.
- **Baby Boomers.** Those who came of age in the late 1960s and 1970s.
- **Post-War Generation.** Those who came of age in the 1950s.
- **World War II Veterans.** People who came of age in the 1940s.
- **Depression Survivors.** Those who came of age during the economic depression of the 1930s.

Cohort Analysis. When Oldsmobile realized in the 1980s that young buyers weren't maturing into clones of their parents, the company flaunted its cars with the advertising slogan "It's not your father's Oldsmobile." Unfortunately for Olds, the cars were not much different and sales continued to skid. Today, marketing and advertising people are using cohort analysis to develop products, not just slogans, to appeal to different generations. Chrysler did this in the late 1990s, dropping plans for the LHX luxury car which might have appealed to people in their 50s a generation ago but not to today's aging Baby Boomers. For the new 50-something generation, Chrysler created the Plymouth Prowler hotrod, which stirred wonderful memories in affluent car-buyers who grew up in the 1960s and 1970s.

Cohort analysis has jarred traditional thinking that people, as they get older, simply adopt their parents' values. The new 50-plus generation, for example, grew up on Coke and Pepsi drinks and some of them, to the dismay of coffee growers, prefer to start the day with cola—not the coffee their parents drank.

The Chrysler automobile company was early to recognize that Baby Boomers aren't interested in buying Cadillac-type luxury cars even when they have amassed the money to afford them. In 1996, Chrysler scrapped plans for a new luxury car to compete with Cadillac and instead introduced the $50 000 open-top 1997 Plymouth Prowler that gave Baby Boomers a nostalgic feel for the hotrods of their youth. Chrysler also determined that greying Baby Boomers preferred upscale Jeeps to the luxo-barge cars that appealed to the Post-War Generation.

Advertising people who use cohort analysis know that Baby Boomers, although now in their 50s, are still turned on to pizzas and the Rolling Stones. In short, the habits of their youth stick with a generation as it gets older. What appealed to the 30-something a decade ago won't necessarily sail with today's 30-something set. David Bostwick, Chrysler's marketing research director, puts it this way: "Nobody wants to become their parents."

CHAPTER WRAP-UP

Both theoretical research, which mostly is campus-based, and applied research, which the media eagerly fund, use many of the same tools. A unifying tool of these disparate research approaches is public-opinion sampling. It is used to track public opinion, which is essential in public relations work; to learn which television programs are the most watched, which is essential in programming and advertising decisions; and to determine the effects of media and how people use the media, which are scholarly endeavours.

QUESTIONS FOR REVIEW

1. What do surveys tell the mass media about their audiences?

2. How is the size of mass media audiences measured?

3. How is the reaction of people to the mass media measured?

4. What are techniques of audience analysis?

5. Why are mass media organizations more interested in applied than theoretical research?

6. Explain what BBM and Nielsen Media Research do.

QUESTIONS FOR CRITICAL THINKING

1. Street-corner polls are called "straw polls" because they are based on such weak methodology. Explain how quota sampling and probability sampling are improvements.

2. What is the basis for arguments that public-opinion surveys subvert democracy? What is the counterargument?

3. The Audit Bureau of Circulations and television rating services like Nielsen Media Research and BBM are essential media services to advertisers. How are these services similar? How are they different?

4. How can local television and radio stations manipulate their ratings?

5. Explain how applied research and theoretical research differ.

FOR KEEPING UP TO DATE

Public Opinion Quarterly is a scholarly publication. *American Demographics* and *Public Opinion* have a lot of general-interest content for media observers.

FOR FURTHER LEARNING

James Atlas. "Beyond Demographics: How Madison Avenue Knows Who You Are and What You Want." *Atlantic* 254 (October 1984): 4, 49–58.

Charles O. Bennett. *Facts Without Opinion: First Fifty Years of the Audit Bureau of Circulations* (Audit Bureau of Circulations, 1965).

Keith Damsell. "Magazine Numbers Unravelled." *Globe and Mail* (July 6, 2001).

George Gallup. *The Sophisticated Poll Watcher's Guide* (Princeton Opinion Press, 1972).

Shearson A. Lowery and Melvin L. DeFleur. *Milestones in Mass Communication Research: Media Effects* (Longman, 1983).

Philip Meyer. *Precision Journalism,* 2nd ed. (Indiana University Press, 1979).

Alan Prendergast. "Wendy Bergin's Exclusive Hoax." *Washington Journalism Review* 13 (October 1991): 8, 30–34.

Philip Preville. "Do We Have A Sweeps Week?" *Saturday Night* (March 10, 2001).

William S. Rubens. "A Personal History of TV Ratings, 1929 to 1989 and Beyond." *Feedback* 30 (Fall 1989): 4, 3–15.

Michael J. Weiss. *The Clustering of America* (Harper & Row, 1988).

Richard Saul Wurman. *Information Anxiety* (Doubleday, 1989).

n Perry Barlow. He doubts the ditional notion that creativity is pendent on the financial incentive ated by copyright law. New technology, Barlow says, is rendering pyright concepts archaic—a cinating but contentious view.

Chapter 11

Media Timeline

Landmarks in Canadian Media Law and Ethics

1926	Canadian Association of Broadcasters is formed.
1928	First Royal Commission into broadcasting in Canada, the Aird Commission.
1932	Canadian Radio Broadcasting Act is passed.
1936	CBC is formed; it is Canada's public broadcaster and its first broadcast regulator.
1957	Fowler Report is released and the Board of Broadcast Governors (BBG) is formed to regulate broadcasters in Canada. It also introduces the idea of Canadian content for television.
1970	Canadian content for radio is introduced.
1982	Canadian Charter of Rights and Freedoms is passed into law, guaranteeing media freedom.
1990	SOCAN is formed in Canada.
1990	CBSC is formed by the Canadian Association of Broadcasters.
1992	Butler ruling on pornography.
1990S	CRTC begins a slow deregulation process of radio and television.
1997	Howard Stern arrives in Canada, raising questions about media ethics.
2001	CRTC says management teams for print and broadcast must be kept separate in multimedia conglomerates.
2001	Howard Stern is no longer on the air in Canada. His show is cancelled due to poor ratings.
2001	A review of the CRTC and Broadcasting Act is undertaken by the federal government.

Media Law and Ethics

Media in Theory

Media Convergence and Copyright Law

As John Perry Barlow envisions the future, giant media companies will shrivel. Convergence of the Mass Media makes it possible for people to acquire mass messages, like pop music, directly from artists. Such direct transactions between artists and consumers undermine the profitable role that media companies have been playing in the dissemination of messages.

To make his point, Barlow, cofounder of the Electronic Frontier Foundation, points to Napster's file-sharing technology that burst onto the scene in 1999. Until the courts stopped the practice in 2001, music fans used Napster to bypass media companies and traditional record-sales channels to acquire music directly from artists. Record companies were cut out.

What's happened with records, Barlow says, inevitably will happen with other kinds of mass messages.

No wonder media executives were watching closely when the record industry went to court to shut Napster down. The issue was **copyright** law, which guarantees that people who create intellectual property, like music, hold the right to benefit financially from their work. According to conventional wisdom, the financial incentive inspires creative people to keep producing and thus enrich society.

Until the web, creative people almost always turned over the ownership of their work to media companies because those companies owned the only means to disseminate messages to mass audiences. In exchange, media companies give a percentage of their revenue to the creative people.

In court against Napster, the record companies argued that composers, lyricists, and performers were in danger of losing their share of the revenue generated by the record companies. Without that financial incentive, according to these anti-Napster forces, creativity would suffer, perhaps dry up.

To that, Barlow said balderdash. He argues that creative people hardly need copyright protection to do their thing. Rhetorically, he asks, how about Shake-speare? Da Vinci? Homer? His point is that creativity is inherent in human nature and occurs independently of financial incentives. Further, Barlow says, technology makes it possible for the first time in modern history for creative people to reach mass audiences on their own. In short, as he sees it, the underlying premise for copyright is an archaic relic from earlier times. Equally archaic, he says, is the need for creative people to rely on media companies to disseminate their creative work and, in return, take a lion's share of the revenue. In short, Napster and similar technologies undermine the entire financial foundation on which media companies have been built.

In this chapter you will explore copyright to help you assess the merits of Barlow's argument, as well as that of the media companies. You also will learn about other aspects of mass media law, including the limits to media freedom in Canada. It's about the fences, both ethical and legal, that surround the media in Canada.

Electronic Frontier Foundation: Website for the organization co-founded by John Perry Barlow.

www.eff.org

Media Law in Canada

FREEDOM OF THE MEDIA IN CANADA

The **Canadian Charter of Rights and Freedoms** is the basis for both media law and ethics codes. Interestingly, in the U.S. "freedom of the press" has been a First Amendment Right since 1791. While the phrase "freedom of the press" was included in Canada's Bill of Rights in 1961, it only covered federal statutes and still wasn't a protected Constitutional right. Officially, the media in Canada have only held these press freedoms since Queen Elizabeth II signed the Constitution Act on April 17, 1982. In his *Pocket Guide to Media Law*, Stuart Robertson states that three specific parts of the Charter affect the Canadian media:

- *Section 1.* The Charter "guarantees the rights and freedoms set out in it subject only to such reasonable limits prescribed by law as can be demonstrably justified in a free and democratic society."
- *Section 2.* All Canadians have "freedom of thought, belief, opinion and expression, including freedom of the press and other media of communication."
- *Section 52(1).* "The Constitution of Canada is the supreme law of Canada, and any law that is inconsistent with the provisions of the Constitution is, to the extent of the inconsistency, of no force or effect."

Robertson goes on to argue that the Charter has affected the media in at least two ways. First, it has granted all Canadians the same basic rights and freedoms. Second, it protects everyone, including those who work in the media, from unfair limitations on expression.

However, although freedom of the media is listed in the Charter, it isn't guaranteed. That is made explicit in Section 1 of the Charter. The rights in the Charter are only guaranteed "to such reasonable limits prescribed by law as can be demonstrably justified in a free and democratic society." In simpler terms, this means that while there is media freedom, the media must also take responsibility for their actions.

PUBLICATION BANS

Publication bans are a uniquely Canadian legal occurrence. Under the **Young Offenders Act**, it is illegal to print or broadcast the name(s) of anyone under 18 who has been charged with or convicted of a crime. It also prohibits the naming of parents or siblings of those who have been charged, underage witnesses, or victims.

In addition to the publication ban on naming young defendants under the Young Offenders Act, there have been two recent noteworthy publication bans in Canada: the banning of evidence during the Karla Homolka murder trial and the banning, at least in Ontario and Quebec, of the showing of the CBC docudrama *The Boys of St. Vincent's*. Both publication bans were based on the same basic principle—the avoidance of affecting the outcome of cases before the courts. In Homolka's case, it was argued that evidence at her trial might influence jurors at the trial of Paul Bernardo. Meanwhile, a judge issued a broadcast ban on *The Boys of St. Vincent's* to protect the legal rights of four members of the Catholic Church who were on trial for sexually and physically abusing orphans. In both of these cases, it is felt that justice was better served by not informing the general public, at least for a short time. Once the trial of Paul Bernardo began and the case of the Catholic orphanage was completed, the publication bans were lifted.

THE CRTC AND THE BROADCASTING ACT

The **CRTC** (Canadian Radio-Television Telecommunications Commission) is the federal regulator in charge of regulating and supervising the broadcast media in Canada. It's an independent authority, whose mandate is "to maintain a delicate balance, in the public interest, between the cultural, social and economic goals of the legislation on broadcasting and telecommunications." Its roots and traditions go back as far as the 1929 Aird Commission. The CRTC has power over 5900 broadcasters in this country. It is the lawmaking authority for all television, radio, and DTH systems in Canada. The CRTC reports to the Prime Minister through the Minister of Canadian Heritage.

The CRTC is the political apparatus through which the spirit of the **Broadcasting Act** is made manifest. According to the CRTC, the main objective of the Broadcasting Act is "to ensure that all Canadians have access to a wide variety of high-quality Canadian programming." While specifics regarding the Broadcasting Act and its effect on radio and television content were discussed earlier in the text, the main thrust of the act is as follows:

- Canadian radio and television stations should be "effectively owned and operated by Canadians."
- The Canadian system has two parts: a public system and a private system.
- Canadian broadcasters should "safeguard, enrich and strengthen" life in Canada.
- Anyone who is involved in broadcasting in Canada is responsible for what he or she broadcasts.
- Adding another limitation to "freedom of the press" here in Canada, the Broadcasting Act specifically states that broadcasts should not include anything "in contravention of the law," nor should they contain obscenities, profanities, or false news.

With the convergence of various media in Canada, many are questioning the relevance of the CRTC and the Broadcasting Act. David Colville, interim chair of the CRTC, says that time will tell what effect convergence and the Internet will have on broadcasting. Colville says, "the feeling was that radio was going to kill the record industry and then television was going to kill radio and the cinema, then cable was going to kill over-the-air television, satellites were going to kill cable and so on. Yet here we are in 2001 and radio still exists and has found its particular niche and television still exists." As for the importance of the Broadcasting Act, Colville replies that the act itself is "technologically neutral," and that the most vital elements from the act are still Canadian content and programming.

Convergence has also created some interesting scenarios for the CRTC. While the CRTC does still have authority over broadcasters in Canada, it does not have any authority over print. This has produced a fascinating regulatory dilemma for the CRTC. Martha Wilson, CRTC commissioner, says that the CRTC still concerns itself with the question of diversity of voices in Canadian broadcast media. As a result of this worry, the CRTC has asked all conglomerations to keep their news management decisions separate from each other. As a condition of licence, the CRTC has required that CanWest, BCE, and TVA keep their newsroom management teams discrete and autonomous. TVA even volunteered to draft a special code of ethics and conduct regarding their separate newsroom policies.

Defamation and the Mass Media

CONCEPT OF DEFAMATION

If someone punches you in the face for no good reason, knocking out several teeth, breaking your nose, and causing permanent disfigurement, most courts would rule that your attacker should pay your medical bills. If your disfigurement or psychological upset causes you to lose your job, to be ridiculed or shunned by friends and family, or perhaps to retreat from social interaction, the court probably would order your attacker to pay additional amounts. Like fists, words can cause damage. If someone says or writes false, damaging things about you, you can sue for libel.

Defamation in Politics. Canadian Alliance Member of Parliament and former Alberta treasurer Stockwell Day was sued by lawyer Lorne Goddard. Day had been critical of Goddard's defending a pedophile. The pubic criticism of Goddard cost Day almost $800 000 in 2001.

Freedom of "thought, belief, opinion, and expression" and of the press is not a licence to say absolutely anything about anybody.

In Canada, libel is also referred to as **defamation**. Lawyer Michael G. Crawford, who has worked for both the CBC and CTV, defines defamation in *The Journalist's Legal Guide*, as the publication or broadcast of a statement that harms someone's reputation. If someone can prove the following three things, that person may be able to sue for defamation under Canadian law:

- The words or pictures were defamatory.
- The words and pictures were published or broadcast.
- The words or pictures refer to a specific, living person.

If a libelling statement is false, the utterer may be liable for millions of dollars in damages. When *Toronto Life* magazine published an article about the Reichmann family, the Reichmanns sued for $102 million. After four years in the courts, the case was settled out of court. *Toronto Life* issued a statement that it made "serious mistakes" in the research and writing of the story. In 1999, the *Red Deer Advocate* published a letter from Stockwell Day, then a member of the Alberta Legislature. In the letter, Day made defamatory remarks comparing a lawyer to a pedophile. Day tried to use the fair comment defence, but lost. The letter cost Day $792 000 in damages and legal costs.

These types of awards and cases are the foundation for what has become known as "libel chill." Many journalists, editors, and others in the media are deciding to play it safe and not publish controversial material that may result in a lawsuit. While this may make economic sense, one needs to question the role it plays in a democratic country that relies on information to educate its people.

DEFENCES FOR DEFAMATION

It is up to the media, in its defence, to prove any of the following to avoid conviction of defamation:

■ The person mentioned in the story or picture consented to its broadcast or publication.
■ The words or pictures are true.
■ The words or pictures were published under privilege. This means reporting and commenting fairly and accurately any comments made on public record. For example, quoting something that was said during a town council meeting, a courtroom, or contained in a media release would constitute privilege.
■ The words or pictures were fair comments.

What is fair comment? For the answer to this question, we look to the **Cherry Sisters**. People flocked to see the Cherry Sisters' act. Effie, Addie, Jessie, Lizzie, and Ella toured the United States with a song and dance act that drew big crowds. They were just awful. They could neither sing nor dance, but people turned out because the sisters were so funny. Sad to say, the Cherry Sisters took themselves seriously. In 1901, desperate for respect, they decided to sue the next newspaper reviewer who gave them a bad notice. That reviewer, it turned out, was Billy Hamilton, who included a lot of equine metaphors in his piece for the *Des Moines Leader*:

> Effie is an old jade of 50 summers, Jessie a frisky filly of 40, and Addie, the flower of the family, a capering monstrosity of 35. Their long skinny arms, equipped with talons at the extremities, swung mechanically, and anon waved frantically at the suffering audience. The mouths of their rancid features opened like caverns, and sounds like the wailings of damned souls issued therefrom. They pranced around the stage with a motion that suggested a cross between the *danse du ventre* and the fox trot—strange creatures with painted faces and hideous mien. Effie is spavined, Addie is stringhalt, and Jessie, the only one who showed her stockings, has legs with calves as classic in their outlines as the curves of a broom handle.

The outcome of the suit was another setback for the Cherrys. They lost in a case that established that actors or others who perform for the public must be willing to accept both positive and negative comments about their performance. This right of **fair comment and criticism**, however, does not make it open season on performers in aspects of their lives that do not relate to public performance. The *National Enquirer* could not defend itself when entertainer Carol Burnett sued for a story that described her as obnoxiously drunk at a restaurant. Not only was the description false (Carol Burnett abstains from alcohol), but Burnett was in no public or performing role at the restaurant. This distinction between an individual's public and private life has also been recognized in cases involving public officials. This is why Stockwell Day wasn't able to use this as a defence in his case.

The concept of malice is also important in defamation suits. The injured party must prove that information was published or broadcast with the specific intent of harming the person in the photograph or story. There is no legal defence if the plaintiff can prove malice on the part of the writer or broadcaster.

DEFAMATION AND THE INTERNET

Although this is new territory for the law, with no case law to look for precedents, it appears that defamation laws will extend to the Internet. On several occasions

Canadian police have forced ISPs (Internet service providers) to provide the names of anyone sending e-mail or posting messages anonymously. Still, the issue of defamation on the Internet isn't clear at this point. Lawyers David Potts and Sally Harris list several legal issues that will need to be defined before laws in this area are clear. One of the most difficult factors is jurisdiction. Where does the plaintiff live? Where does the defendant live? Where should litigation take place? How can decisions be enforced?

Copyright in Canada

Since, as social critic Walter Benjamin pointed out, we live in an age of mechanical reproduction where virtually anything can be copied mechanically or digitally, copyright has become a significant issue in Canadian communication. Think about it: Photocopiers, scanners, fax machines, VCRs, computers, CD burners, and dual cassette machines have made making copies easier than ever. Making copies of someone else's work, without their permission, is illegal in Canada.

The Canadian Copyright Act, governed by Heritage Canada and Industry Canada, covers all forms of communication: books, pamphlets, newspapers, magazines, maps, sheet music, movies, videos, and music. The act defines copyright as "the sole right to produce or reproduce the work of any substantial part thereof in any material form whatever or to perform the work or any substantial portion thereof in public." Basically, all original works are protected by copyright for the life of the creator, plus 50 years. The creator of the "act" of communication has the sole right to copy it or have it performed in public. That right may be granted to others. Generally speaking, you're not infringing on copyright when you're quoting a few lines from a magazine article in an essay.

Materials considered in the **public domain** are not covered by legislation. Facts, for example, cannot be copyrighted. Only the presentation of those facts falls upon copyright legislation. For example, if radio stations CXXX and CYYY cover the

Authors in a Dot-Com World. The National Writers Union, led by Jonathan Tasini, led a campaign for media companies to compensate freelance contributors when their works are recycled on websites. Among writers' targets was the *Boston Globe*. The newspaper insisted that once it bought a freelancer's piece for the newspaper, it owned the piece for whatever further use it wanted, including posting it on the web—without the author's permission and without sharing additional revenue generated from the website. The issue: who owns a writer's work under copyright law in the new age of the web.

Romance Plagiarism. Cynics think all romance novels are the same, but aficionados know the difference. It shook Janet Dailey fans in 1997 to learn that she had loosely paraphrased a passage from rival Nora Roberts. The publisher withdrew Dailey's book with the plagiarized passages, and the question was whether Dailey, whose 93 titles had sold more than 200 million copies, would ever recover from the tarnish. You decide how serious the transgression.

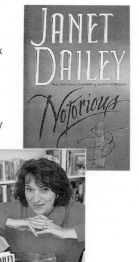

"Talk to me."

"It was just a dream as you said."

"You're hurting." He touched her cheek. This time she didn't jerk away, only closed her eyes. "You talk, I'll listen."

"I don't need anyone."

"I'm not going away until you talk to me."

—From *Sweet Revenge* (1989) by Nora Roberts

"Talk to me, Eden."

"It was only a dream, just as you said."

His fingers brushed her cheek. . . . She closed her eyes at the contact. "You need to talk about it. I'll listen."

"I don't need anyone," she insisted stiffly.

"I'm not leaving until you tell me about it."

— From *Notorious* (1996) by Janet Dailey

Nora Roberts   Janet Dailey

same fire, neither has violated copyright. The fire was a factual event. However, if radio station CYYY uses part of CXXX's broadcast on their newsmagazine, they have violated copyright. Ideas can't be copyrighted either unless they have manifested themselves in written or visual form. For instance, if you're working on a public relations campaign for a client and mention a few ideas to friends over a drink and they use the idea in public relations campaign for one of their clients, they have also not violated copyright. Unless they are protected trademarks, titles for songs and programs are not protected under current copyright legislation. If you're ever unsure about infringing on someone's copyright, contact your local MP for information regarding the Canadian Copyright Act.

The works of Canadians are also protected internationally under the copyright protection of the Berne Copyright Convention and the Universal Copyright Convention. These also protect the works of international artists in Canada. Several Canadian organizations exist to make sure that creators of communication content are compensated for their efforts and that copyright laws do not get broken.

COPYRIGHT AND PLAGIARISM

Perhaps the most fiercely loyal media fans are those who read romance novels and swear by a favourite author. On an Internet chatroom in 1997, romance writer Janet

Dailey found herself boxed into an admission that she had plagiarized from rival writer Nora Roberts. There is no scorn like that of creative people for those who steal their work, and Roberts was "very, very upset." HarperCollins recalled *Notorious*, Dailey's book that contained the **plagiarism**, and Roberts fans, many of them long-time Dailey detractors, began a hunt for other purloined passages.

What is plagiarism? Generally, it's considered passing off someone else's creative work as your own, without permission. It's still plagiarism if it's changed a bit, as was Dailey's loose paraphrasing.

The fact that Dailey's 93 books over 20 years had sold an average of more than 2 million each made the scandal all the juicier. In the end, Roberts proposed a financial settlement, and the proceeds went to promote literacy.

Everyone agrees that plagiarism, a form of thievery, is unethical, but the issue is not simple. The fact is that in many media people draw heavily on other people's ideas and works. Think about sitcom story lines that mimic each other, or the band-wagon of movies that follow an unexpected hit with an oddball theme. Journalists, most of whom consider themselves especially pristine compared to their media brethren, have standard practices that encourage a lot of "borrowing."

DIGITAL MEDIA AND COPYRIGHT ISSUES

The technological convergence of the traditional mass media is creating some new issues for copyright. The term digital media refers to any information that is stored in binary form (1s and 0s). This includes material stored in "fixed form" on the Internet, on CD, on CD-ROM, DVD, floppy disk, hard drives, and so on. The list is almost endless. The material can include text, music, and images.

Some of the legal issues remain the same for material stored in "traditional" or "digital" forms. For example, it must be original and in a fixed form. That being said, digital technology is stretching what was covered (or at the very least implied) under older copyright laws. In addition to the list of "rights" listed under the Copyright Act, some have introduced the following categories of "copyrights":

- Electronic rights
- Database rights
- Internet rights
- Multimedia rights

The courts in both Canada and the U.S. have decided that, under the law, the creator of an original work is entitled to compensation for each one of these types of rights and that each should be treated separately. Some of the landmark decisions regarding these types of rights include:

- Radio stations deciding *not* to stream audio over the Internet, as the issue of music licensing has not yet been addressed.
- Newspapers *not* reprinting articles written by "stringers," as they are only compensating for reprinting their articles in the traditional way.

MUSIC LICENSING IN CANADA

SOCAN, the Society of Composers, Authors and Music Publishers of Canada licenses the public performance of music. It was formed in 1990, when two other performing rights organizations, PROCAN (Performing Rights Organization of Canada) and CAPAC (Composers, Authors and Publishers Association of Canada) combined to form a new, not-for-profit organization. Its jurisdiction includes not only the playing of music on radio and television, but also in restaurants, by mobile disc jockeys, in parades, at sporting events, and at the movies. Almost anywhere you hear music, SOCAN is there to ensure that the writers of the song get paid. Copyright can be an issue if music is being used:

- on radio, television, in a movie or on the Internet;
- in a bar, restaurant, store, or shopping mall;
- in a concert setting; or
- in offices, including "on-hold" music on the telephone.

SOCAN: This site provides information on performing rights, copyright, licensing, and distribution.

www.socan.ca

SOCAN collects tariffs from anyone who uses music, and passes it along to the songwriters. No one, other than the songwriter, has the right in Canada to use a song's material in any way, shape, or form without permission. SOCAN recognizes several types of rights held by the songwriters when pertaining to music:

- *Performance rights.* These cover songwriters when their material is performed publicly. This can include a song on the radio, on television, or performed by a band at the local bar.
- *Reproduction rights.* There are two types of reproduction rights. Mechanical rights are the rights to copy the music onto a tape or CD, while synchronization rights refer to using the music in a film or video.
- *Moral rights.* A creator can claim violation of moral rights if, after selling performance and/or reproduction rights, they feel their original vision is altered. For example, members of the Canadian pop group The Parachute Club claimed their moral rights were violated first when their 1983 hit "Rise Up" was used in a commercial for frozen pizza, and then when the song was used promoting a political event in 1999. They felt their song, with its spiritual and self-empowering message, was morally diminished when it began to be associated with pizza and politicians.

SOCAN has several methods to assist in the collection of royalties for its members. These media outlets are surveyed several times each year for a listing of all music used. TV stations pay 1.8 percent of their gross revenue, while radio stations pay between 1.4 percent and 3.2 percent of their gross revenue, depending on the amount of music played. SOCAN also collects 3.0 percent of ticket sales at concerts in Canada.

Three other organizations license the use of music in Canada. AVLA, the Audio Visual Licensing Agency, overlooks the exhibition of music videos, while SODRAC (the Society for Reproduction Rights of Authors, Composers and Publishers in Canada Incorporated) and CMRRA (the Canadian Musical Reproduction Rights Agency Limited) authorize the reproduction of music (onto tapes and CDs) and the use of music in videos or film.

COPYRIGHT AND THE WEB

SOCAN is also currently negotiating licence fees for music transmitted along digital networks, including the music on the Internet. SOCAN is looking to set up a system whereby ISPs would pay a tariff, in much the same way radio and television stations do. Industry Canada has also looked into the affects of the Internet on copyright law in Canada. Some of the issues that emerged in their 1998 study include these:

■ Web browsers' "caching" material may comprise a form of reproduction.
■ Web links can't be copyrighted, but a collection of web links on a page may be eligible for copyright protection.
■ ISPs may be held liable for copyright infringements.

Other web legal issues were dealt with in the Digital Millennium Copyright Act in 1998. The law gives specific protection to companies and individuals who post original material on the web. Other people cannot legally take it for commercial purposes. This is the same fair-use exception that applies in traditional media. One such fair-use exception is quoting from a book in a review of the book.

Censorship in Canada

PORNOGRAPHY VS. OBSCENITY

If the Broadcasting Act states that Canadian broadcasters cannot broadcast anything "obscene," then why are sexually explicit movies available on Viewer's Choice Canada or on Showcase? The reason is simple; there is a difference between pornography and obscenity in Canada. This availability is due in large part to the 1992 **Butler ruling** by the Supreme Court of Canada. It has been the basis for the definition of obscenity in Canada. It ruled that any material that mixed sex with violence, included depictions of children having sex, or any sex that is degrading or dehumanizing, was obscene. Any other sexually explicit material would not seem to be considered obscene because, as the decision ruled, under Canada's Charter of Rights and Freedoms, laws can't "inhibit the celebration of human sexuality."

Legal definitions aside, censorship is nothing new in Canadian society. It exists at the provincial or the federal level. Consider the following:

■ In 1918, comedies were banned in Manitoba. They made the audience too giddy.
■ The importation of *Lady Chatterly's Lover* was banned by Canada Customs in 1930.
■ Norman Mailer's *The Naked and the Dead*, after being a bestseller in Canada for almost a year, was banned by the Minister of National Revenue in 1949.
■ An exhibit of work by artist Eli Langer was deemed pornographic in 1993.
■ The group Rockbitch was refused work permits by Immigration Canada in late 1997 because their act was "pornographic." The act includes real and simulated sex acts.
■ A 1997 concert by Marilyn Manson was cancelled in Calgary due to public pressure that the artist be banned.

Censorship is based on a culture's values, which, of course, change over time. Consider that at one time, the following films were banned or edited for release in Canada, yet they have all aired, uncut, on Showcase Television in Canada in the last few years: *Pretty Baby*, *The Tin Drum*, *Last Tango in Paris*, and *Devil in the Flesh*.

The Difficulty of Ethics

WHAT DID AVERY HAINES DO WRONG?

It began as just another Saturday morning shift at CTV NewsNet for **Avery Haines**. She was off the air, taping an introduction to a story on subsidies for farmers. She

Avery Haines. The Canadian journalist's comments sparked controversy one Saturday morning in January of 2000. Her comments were referred to as "racist" by some. Others felt that she was a victim of political correctness.

"tripped" up, flubbed her words, as announcers sometimes do. After her screw-up, she began talking off air with the technical staff. She said, "I kind of like this stuttering thing, it's like equal opportunity, right? We've got the stuttering newscaster, we've got the black, we've got the Asian, we've got the woman. I could be a lesbian, folk-dancing, black woman stutterer . . . in a wheel chair . . . with gimping rubber legs. Yeah, really, I'd have a successful career, let me tell you."

She paused to regain her composure and recorded a second take of the introduction to the news story on farm aid. This one was flawless. It was this second take that was supposed to air, not the first. A technical error resulted in the wrong introduction making it to air. Jim Slotek, writing in the *Toronto Sun*, said that Haines broke the cardinal rule for broadcasters, "never say anything in a studio you wouldn't say on air. There are just too many ways to get caught unawares." Haines did get "caught unawares." The negative response was immediate. Despite Haines's apologizing on air three times for the comments, calls and e-mails flooded CTV NewsNet.

CTV NewsNet promptly let Haines go. Henry Kowalski, CTV senior vice president of news, said that "the public must know that CTV takes this kind of behaviour as absolutely unacceptable." Moy Tam, of the Canadian Race Relations Foundation said, "we think they have dealt with the specific incident strongly." Writing in the *National Post*, Linda Mcquaig wrote, "does Ms. Haines think her career prospects would be better as a crippled black lesbian, rather than an attractive white heterosexual? In what galaxy would that be true?" Hamlin Grange, in the *Toronto Star* wrote, "I don't believe Avery Haines is a racist, sexist homophobe. I do believe she is naïve and ignorant of the harm comments such as this can have on some of her colleagues working in the news media."

The firing raised even more questions, not only about her comments, but the way CTV handled the situation. What was the real message behind her comments? Were they a shot at affirmative action programs? Were the comments racist?

Politically Correct? A very opinionated article from the Canadian Association of Free Expression about the Avery Haines controversy.

www.canadianfreespeech.com/press_releases/avery_haines.html

A Different View: A decidedly different take on what happened to Avery Haines.

www.newswire.ca/resource/pr-00-1-b.html

The Valour and the Horror: The film's producers maintain this site.

www.valourandhorror.com

Accuracy in Media: Official site of the media watchdog organization.

www.aim.org

Certainly stand-up comedians have said worse on the Comedy Network. Was the real ethical issue, as Jeff Gray argues in *Press Review*, that Haines stepped out of character during a newscast? It even made news in the U.S., where 81 percent of the viewers of *The View* with Barbara Walters thought that Haines should not have been fired. A Canadian poll found that 68 percent thought Haines's dismissal was wrong.

Christie Blatchford, writing in the *National Post,* said that Haines wasn't making fun of anyone but herself. According to Blatchford, "when she flubbed her lines on Saturday, her first instinct was to belittle herself, which is what women in general do and what Ms. Haines in particular does. The subtext of what she said was that Cheez Whiz, if she wasn't a pretty girl, she wouldn't have landed the gig in the first place. She had done nothing but make fun of herself and state the truth, which is that in the real world, companies, particularly those like television networks and newspapers, in the public eye, occasionally hire on the basis of gender, skin colour, disability or sexual preference."

Throughout it all, Haines was apologetic and contrite over the situation. After about a week of intense media scrutiny, Haines put things in perspective in the *National Post*: "It's only fucking television. It's not my son, it's not my husband, it's not my mum and dad." A few months after the incident, Haines was hired by CablePulse 24, Toronto's 24-hour news channel.

THE CASE OF *THE VALOUR AND THE HORROR*

When Canada's McKenna brothers, Brian and Terrance, made the documentary *The Valour and the Horror*, they had no idea of the controversy and ethical issues it would raise. The three-part series was broadcast on CBC in January of 1992. An estimated audience of six million Canadians saw it. Many viewers complained that the shows were historically inaccurate and that the McKennas had distorted the facts regarding Canada's role in World War II. Others saw the series as a documentary with a message—in war there is no valour, only horror. The series and the debate surrounding it provide a good example of the differences between media ethics and media law.

The programs that generated the most heat were the second and third in the series, *Desperate Battle* and *Death by Moonlight: Bomber Command*. These episodes featured archival footage of World War II, mixed with actors' renditions of those that were there. It was this mixture of "fact" and "fiction" that upset some and was the basis for much of the controversy. The battle over *The Valour and the Horror* was fought on ethical grounds. As we will discuss, all Canadian journalistic codes of conduct include passages that refer to the accuracy of content. This case painted an interested quandary. On the one hand, documentaries are supposed to present "true" information. However, documentaries are based on historical "facts" that are open to interpretation. According to William Morgan, the CBC ombudsman who wrote a report in response to a "substantial volume of cards and letters and other more detailed communications . . . many of them expressing anger" on *The Valour and the Horror*, the series violated several of the codes of CBC Policies and Standards. Among Morgan's charges:

- The documentary mixed real footage with the dramatization of events in a manner that could mislead the viewer.
- The series failed to present accurate material and did not present the information in a fair and balanced way in order to provide context for the viewer.

■ There were instances of "errors or confusion of fact." There were also "several significant unsubstantiated assertions or implications."

In the summer of 1992, the Senate held a hearing into the making of *The Valour and the Horror*. This resulted in CBC's then-president Gerard Veilleux apologizing to Canadian veterans. While the ombudsman for the CBC and its president may have had some ethical problems with the series, legally, according to a CRTC report on the broadcast, the McKennas did nothing wrong. They wrote, "while many—including veterans, historians and the (CBC's) Ombudsman—have cited material which seems to indicate that parts of the films may have been incorrect, the filmmakers too, appear to have reasonable grounds for the assertions made in series." A 1993 defamation lawsuit against the producers of *The Valour and the Horror* was dismissed.

Despite this backlash and a flurry of charges, many saw nothing wrong with the McKennas' representation of Canada's role during World War II. Among the positive responses to the series:

■ Pierre Berton wrote, "every schoolchild should be given the chance to see this documentary so that they may realize the horror, the misery, the cynicism, yes—the incompetence too—that accompanies war."
■ Max Hastings, an expert on Bomber Command, said, "I think the general tenor of your film reflects a fair picture of the bomber defensive and pays full tribute to the courage and sacrifice of the air crews who carried it out."

CANADIAN CODES OF ETHICS

The mass media abound with codes of ethics. Many newcomers to the mass media make an erroneous assumption that the answers to all the moral choices in their work exist in the prescriptions of these codes. While the codes can be helpful, ethics is not so easy. Attitudes toward codes of ethics vary, but most Canadian media organizations have a code, as do public relations and advertising associations. These codes go far beyond the question of "freebies," and at least try to address issues of social equality, controversy, offensive content, and fairness in handling complex stories. Many media critics feel that ethics are not taken as seriously as they might be. According to journalism professor Brian Green, one news director's perspective on ethics was as follows: "It's hard to remember you're here to drain the swamp when you're up to your ass in alligators." Peter Desbarats argues that many media critics feel that while the media may talk a good line when it comes to ethics, it's more talk than walk. Other critics feel that codes of ethics are merely public relations tools the media use to perpetuate the myth that they are holier than thou. This may or may not be true. But the fact remains that most Canadian media organizations have a **code of ethics** that, if nothing else, serves as a guideline to follow should an alligator creep up on them. The same applies to the public relations and advertising industries. These codes are based in Canadian law, but as codes, violation of them may not necessarily result in legal problems.

The study of ethics manifests itself in the world of media in the form of codes of conduct. Among the many media organizations that have codes of conduct for their members are the Canadian Association of Broadcasters, the Canadian Newspaper Association and the Radio and Television News Directors Association of Canada.

THE CANADIAN ASSOCIATION OF BROADCASTERS. Self-proclaimed as the voice of Canada's private broadcasters, the Canadian Association of Broadcasters, or **CAB,**

Online Ethics: A wealth of information on Canadian media ethics.

www.mediaethics.ca

Ethics Links: An online source of media ethics links from the University of British Columbia's Centre for Applied Ethics.

www.ethics.ubc.ca/ resources/media/inst.html

was founded by 13 broadcasters in 1926 as a voluntary organization that advocated self-rule for Canada's broadcasters with little, if any, government regulation. CAB was the lobby group for Canada's radio broadcasters prior to the findings of the Aird Commission in 1928. Currently, CAB represents 430 privately owned radio and television stations across Canada.

THE CANADIAN BROADCAST STANDARDS COUNCIL. In 1990 CAB formed the **CBSC** (Canadian Broadcast Standards Council). This is a self-regulating council funded for and by private broadcasters in Canada. Its mandate is to promote high standards in radio and television broadcasting through self-regulation.

Television viewers and radio listeners have filed a variety of complaints with the CBSC over the years. Many of those complaints had to deal with the arrival of Howard Stern on the radio in Canada. Stern made his Canadian radio debut on CHOM-FM in Montreal and Q-107 in Toronto in September of 1997. The show had been a popular choice for many years in the U.S. Stern's morning show has been broadcast from WXRK-RFM in New York since 1986. Both Canadian stations needed a ratings boost and turned to Stern's brand of humour for help. In terms of ratings, both stations, particularly Q-107, experienced huge increases in listenership.

But it wasn't the increase in listeners that had some people concerned. What concerned some, particularly the Canadian Broadcast Standards Council, was Stern's on-the-air sexist and racist comments. For example, during his first broadcast on CHOM-FM in Montreal, he referred to French-Canadians as "peckerheads" and "scumbags." During his first two weeks on the air, both the CRTC and the CBSC received as many complaints as they would normally receive in one year. The complaints related to several issues:

- The anti-French comments. Stern commented, "the biggest scumbags on the planet as I've said all along are not only the French in France, but the French in Canada."
- Sexist commentary particularly aimed at women. For example, Stern referred to women as "horny cows," "pieces of ass," and "dumb broads."
- Racist and homophobic commentary.

In their report responding to the complaints, the CBSC decided that Stern (and CHOM-FM and Q-107) had indeed "breached the provisions of the industry's Code of Ethics and Sex-Role Portrayal Code." The CBSC found that each episode of the *Howard Stern Show* during the weeks of September 1 and September 8, 1997, "contained abusive or discriminatory comments directed at French-Canadians and other identifiable groups, made sexist remarks or observations, or contained unsuitable language or descriptions of sexual activity during a broadcast period when children would be expected to listen to the radio."

However, since adherence to the codes is purely voluntary, neither station was obligated to do anything. For a time, there was a debate as to how both stations might respond to the decision. In the end, CHOM-FM dropped Stern in 1998, and Q-107 dropped his program in 2001 due to a decline in ratings.

In March of 2001, the CBSC developed the following five objectives for Canadian broadcasters:

- To continue to administer the codes of broadcast standards developed by the Canadian Association of Broadcasters, the Radio Television News Directors Association of Canada, and any other self-regulatory body that may be created.

Media People

Ron Cohen

Ron Cohen

Ron Cohen has been the National Chair of the Canadian Broadcast Standards Council since 1993. He's a writer, a lawyer, and was one of the founding members of the Academy of Canadian Cinema and Television back in 1979. He's also very passionate about the role of self-regulation in the Canadian media. The following is a reprint of his article that appeared in the November 1999 edition of Broadcast Dialogue magazine:

The Canadian Broadcast Standards Council is the cornerstone of a successful approach to a delicate subject—program content on the air. Does anything and everything go in the name of free speech? Possibly in the U.S., but not in Canada. It's not really our style. We're, well, reasonable and balanced in our approach to lots of things, including what goes on our airwaves. We have standards, broadcast standards. And the key is that they are administered on a self-regulatory basis. Funded by the industry, which remains hands off. An overall approach to the issue which sets us apart from most other western countries.

The CBSC administers four codes: the CAB Code of Ethics, the CAB Sex-Role Portrayal Code, the CAB Violence Code and the RTNDA of Canada Code of Journalistic Ethics. Both the Sex-Role and Violence Codes were created by private broadcasters and approved by the CRTC. The principles enunciated in these codes are Conditions of Licence for all broadcasters in Canada.

In some nearby nations, there are those who view any broadcast codes as the slippery slope on the way to fearsome government regulation, but, in Canada, our experience is diametrically opposed to that hypothetical prospect. If anything, the Canadian experience has been that official involvement in content issues has decreased since private broadcasters proposed the model of the CBSC in 1988.

It took a couple of years to move the concept from the drawing board into the public domain. Following the approval of the CAB's model by the CRTC, five Regional Councils were created to represent BC, the Prairies, Ontario, Quebec and the Maritimes.

It may be hard to believe but, in the 178 decisions released from our first decision until September 1999, 176 have been unanimous. CBSC Regional Council members never come to table with an ax to grind. No public representatives with the view that broadcasters are always wrong; no industry reps with the view that broadcasters are always right.

The resulting balance in the CBSC's decisions, even in the face of process-stressful Power Rangers and Howard Stern decisions, has provided credibility to the assertion by Canada's private broadcasters that they could regulate their own on-air conduct. And why should anyone have assumed the contrary? Doctors do it. So too accountants, lawyers, architects and most other professional groups. A good system is never better than when, even in the face of adverse decisions, the broadcasters continue to endorse and support the process.

I believe that the private broadcasters experiment has proven itself a nearly unqualified success. In comparative international terms, the CBSC's uniqueness is reflected in its blend of the public and industry, its entire reliance on private sector support, its decision making independence, and its adaptability to the needs of, and changes in, the public and the broadcasting system.

- To update and notify Canadians about the CBSC and their role within the self-regulatory process. This will include communicating CBSC code and decisions to the general public.
- To allow Canadians a channel for feedback for their complaints regarding Canadian programming on radio and television.
- To encourage resolution of complaints at the local level between the viewer/listener and the broadcaster. If this isn't possible, the CBSC will render its decision.
- To inform its members regarding sociological trends in broadcasting to help them make better programming choices.

RADIO AND TELEVISION NEWS DIRECTORS ASSOCIATION OF CANADA. The Radio and Television News Directors Association (RTNDA) was founded over 50 years ago. It's an international organization with affiliations in Canada. Recognizing the importance to a democracy of an informed public, the members of the RTNDA of Canada believe the broadcasting of factual, accurately reported and timely news and public affairs is vital. To this end, RTNDA members in Canada pledge to observe a code of ethics, which can be found at the RTNDA website.

CANADIAN NEWSPAPER ASSOCIATION CODE OF ETHICS. In 1919, the Canadian Daily Newspaper Association (CDNA) was formed. In 1996 it was renamed the Canadian Newspaper Association (CNA). The CNA represents 101 of Canada's English and French daily newspapers—99 percent of all newspapers sold in Canada on a daily basis. The CNA's statement of principles, which was originally adopted by the CDNA in 1977, was revised in 1995. This statement can be found at the CNA website. Some of the issues dealt with in the statement are freedom of the press, loyalty to the public good, accuracy, fairness, and community responsibility.

In general, the difficulty of ethics becomes clear when a news reporter is confronted with a conflict between moral responsibilities to different concepts. Consider the following issues.

RESPECT FOR PRIVACY

The code of the RTNDA prescribes that reporters will show respect for the dignity, privacy, and well-being of people "at all times." The prescription sounds excellent, but moral priorities such as dignity and privacy sometimes seem less important than other priorities.

COMMITMENT TO TIMELINESS

RTNDA: Check the RTDNA's code of ethics at their official site. They were updated in 2000.

www.rtndacanada.com

The code of the RTNDA also prescribes that reporters be "accurate, comprehensive, and fair." In practice, however, complete accuracy is jeopardized when reporters rush to the air with stories. It takes time to confirm details and be accurate—and that delays stories.

BEING FAIR

The code of the Canadian Public Relations Society prescribes dealing fairly with both clients and the general public. However, a persuasive message prepared on behalf of a client is not always the same message that would be prepared on behalf of the general public. Persuasive communication is not necessarily dishonest, but how information is marshalled to create the message depends on whom the PR person is serving.

CONFLICT IN DUTIES

Media ethics codes are well-intended, usually helpful guides, but they are simplistic when it comes to knotty moral questions. When media ethicians Clifford Christians, Mark Fackler, and Kim Rotzoll compiled a list of five duties of mass media practitioners, some of these inherent problems became obvious.

Sold-out Edition. Perhaps the most famous news photograph of all time was Tom Howard's shot of the electric chair execution of murderer Ruth Snyder. Knowing the Sing Sing warden wouldn't agree to a photo, Howard strapped a tiny camera to his ankle and, at the right moment, lifted his trouser leg and snapped the shutter with a trip wire. The exclusive photo goosed street sales of the *New York Daily News*, which had followed the lurid trial of Snyder and her lover for killing her husband. Such stories and a focus on photo coverage, typical of the *Daily News* under founder Joseph Patterson, boosted the newspaper's circulation to more than 2 million, the largest in the United States, in the 1940s.

DUTY TO SELF. Self-preservation is a basic human instinct, but is a photojournalist shirking a duty to subscribers by avoiding a dangerous combat zone?

Self-aggrandizement can be an issue too. Many college newspaper editors are invited, all expenses paid, to Hollywood movie premieres. The duty-to-self principle favours going: The trip would be fun. In addition, it is a good story opportunity, and, as a free favour, it would not cost the newspaper anything. However, what of an editor's responsibility to readers? Readers have a right to expect writers to provide honest accounts that are not coloured by favouritism. Can a reporter write straight after being wined and dined and flown across the continent by movie producers who want a gung ho story? Even if reporters rise above being affected and are true to conscience, there are the duty-to-employer and the duty-to-profession principles to consider. The newspaper and the profession itself can be tarnished by suspicions, no matter whether they are unfounded, that a reporter has been bought off.

DUTY TO AUDIENCE. Television programs that re-enact violence are popular with audiences, but are they a disservice because they frighten many viewers into inferring that the streets are more dangerous than they really are?

A journalist named Wicker tells a story about his early days on the police beat. He was covering a divorce case involving one spouse chasing the other with an axe. Nobody was hurt physically, and everyone who heard the story in the courtroom, except the divorcing couple, had a good laugh. "It was human comedy at its most ribald, and the courtroom rocked with laughter," he recalled years later. In writing his story, he captured the darkly comedic details so skilfully that his editor put the story on page one. Wicker was proud of the piece until the next day when the woman in the case called on him. Worn out, haggard, hurt, and angry, she asked, "Why did you think you had a right to make fun of me in your paper?"

The lesson stayed with him for the rest of his career. He had unthinkingly hurt a fellow human being for no better reason than evoking a chuckle, or perhaps a belly laugh, from his readers. To Wicker, the duty-to-audience principle would never again transcend his moral duty to the dignity of the subjects of his stories. Similar ethics questions are involved in whether to cite AIDS as a contributing factor to death in an obituary, whether to identify victims in rape stories, and whether to name juveniles charged with crimes.

DUTY TO EMPLOYER. Does loyalty to an employer transcend the ideal of pursuing and telling the truth when a news reporter discovers dubious business deals involving the parent corporation? This is a growing issue as the mass media become consolidated into fewer gigantic companies owned by conglomerates. In 1989, for example, investigative reporter Peter Karl of Chicago television station WMAQ broke a story that General Electric had manufactured jet engines with untested and sometimes defective bolts. Although WMAQ is owned by NBC, which in turn is owned by General Electric, Karl's exclusive, documented, and accurate story aired. However, when the story was passed on to the network itself, Marty Ryan, executive producer of the *Today* show, ordered that the references to General Electric be edited out.

DUTY TO THE PROFESSION. At what point does an ethically motivated advertising-agency person blow the whistle on misleading claims by other advertising people?

DUTY TO SOCIETY. Does duty to society ever transcend duty to self? To audience? To employer? To colleagues? Does ideology affect a media worker's sense of duty to society? Consider how Joseph Stalin, Adolf Hitler, and Franklin Roosevelt would be covered by highly motivated communist, fascist, and libertarian journalists.

Are there occasions when the duty-to-society and the duty-to-audience principles are incompatible? Nobody enjoys seeing the horrors of war, for example, but journalists may feel that their duty to society demands that they go after the most grisly photographs of combat to show how horrible war is and, thereby, in a small way, contribute to public pressure toward a cessation of hostilities and eventual peace.

Moral Principles

THE GOLDEN MEAN

The Greek philosopher **Aristotle**, writing almost 2400 years ago, devised the **golden mean** as a basis for moral decision making. The golden mean sounds simple and straightforward: Avoid extremes and seek moderation. Modern journalistic balance and fairness are founded on this principle.

The golden mean's dictate, however, is not as simple as it sounds. As with all moral principles, application of the golden mean can present difficulties. Consider the federal law that requires over-the-air broadcasters to give "equal opportunity" to candidates for public office. On the surface, this application of the golden mean, embodied in law, might seem to be reasonable, fair, and morally right, but the issue is far more complex. The equality requirement, for example, gives an advantage to candidates who hold simplistic positions that can be expressed compactly. Good and able candidates whose positions require more time to explain are disadvantaged, and the society is damaged when inferior candidates win public office.

While minute-for-minute equality in broadcasting can be a flawed application of the golden mean, Aristotle's principle is valuable to media people when making moral decisions, as long as they do not abdicate their power of reason to embrace formulaic tit-for-tat measurable equality. It

The Golden Mean. The Greek thinker Aristotle told his students almost 2400 years ago that right courses of action avoid extremes. His recommendation: moderation.

takes the human mind, not a formula, to determine fairness. And therein lies the complexity of the golden mean. No two human beings think exactly alike, which means that applying the golden mean involves individuals making judgment calls that are not necessarily the same. This element of judgment in moral decisions can make ethics intellectually exciting. It takes a sharp mind to sort through issues of balance and fairness.

"DO UNTO OTHERS"

The Judeo-Christian principle of "**Do unto others** as you would have them do unto you" appeals to most people. Not even the do-unto-others prescription, however, is without problems. Consider the photojournalist who sees virtue in serving a mass audience with a truthful account of the human condition. This might manifest itself in portrayals of great emotions, like grief. But would the photojournalist appreciate being photographed herself in a grieving moment after learning that her infant son had died in an accident? If not, her pursuit of truth through photography for a mass audience would be contrary to the "do-unto-others" dictum.

CATEGORICAL IMPERATIVES

About 200 years ago, German philosopher **Immanuel Kant** wrote that moral decisions should flow from thoroughly considered principles. As he put it, "Act on the maxim that you would want to become universal law." He called his maxim the **categorical imperative**. A categorical imperative, well thought out, is a principle that the individual who devised it would be willing to apply in all moral questions of a similar sort.

Kant's categorical imperative does not dictate specifically what actions are morally right or wrong. Moral choices, says Kant, go deeper than the context of the immediate issue. He encourages a philosophical approach to moral questions, with people using their intellect to identify principles that they, as individuals, would find acceptable if applied universally.

Universal Law. Immanuel Kant, an 18th-century German philosopher, urged people to find principles that they would be comfortable having applied in all situations. He called these principles *categorical imperatives*.

Utilitarianism. Journalists tend to like 19th-century British thinker John Stuart Mill's utilitarianism, which favours actions that result in the greatest good for the greatest number of people. This approach to ethics dovetails well with majority rule and modern democracy.

Kant does not encourage the kind of standardized approach to ethics represented by professional codes. His emphasis, rather, is on hard thinking. Says philosopher Patricia Smith, writing in the *Journal of Mass Media Ethics*: "A philosophical approach to ethics embodies a commitment to consistency, clarity, the principled evaluation of arguments, and unrelenting persistence to get to the bottom of things."

UTILITARIAN ETHICS

In the mid-1800s, British thinker **John Stuart Mill** declared that morally right decisions are those that result in "happiness for the greatest number." Mill called his idea the **principle of utility**. It sounds good to many of us because it parallels the democratic principle of majority rule, with its emphasis on the greatest good for the greatest number of people.

By and large, journalists embrace Mill's utilitarianism today, as evinced in notions like the *people's right to know*, a concept originally meant to support journalistic pursuit of information about government, putting the public's interests ahead of government's interests, but which has come to be almost reflexively invoked to defend pursuing very personal information about individuals, no matter what the human cost.

PRAGMATIC ETHICS

John Dewey, an American thinker who wrote in the late 1800s and early 1900s, argued that the virtue of moral decisions had to be judged by their results. A difficulty in Dewey's **pragmatic ethics** is that people do not have perfect crystal balls to tell them for sure whether their moral actions will have good consequences.

EGALITARIAN ETHICS

In the 20th century, philosopher **John Rawls** introduced the **veil of ignorance** as an element in ethics decisions. Choosing a right course of action, said Rawls, requires blindness to social position or other discriminating factors. This is known as **egalitarianism**. An ethical decision requires that all people be given an equal hearing and the same fair consideration.

To Rawls, a brutal slaying in an upscale suburb deserves the same journalistic attention as a slaying in a poor urban neighbourhood. All other things being equal, a $20 000 bank burglary is no more newsworthy than a $20 000 embezzlement.

SOCIAL RESPONSIBILITY ETHICS

The **Hutchins Commission**, a learned group that studied the mass media in the 1940s, recommended that journalists and other media people make decisions that serve the society responsibly. For all its virtues, the **social responsibility** system, like all ethics systems, has difficulties. For one thing, decision makers can only imperfectly foresee the effects of their decisions. It is not possible to predict with 100 percent confidence whether every decision will turn out to be socially responsible. Also, well-meaning people may differ honestly about how society is most responsibly served.

POTTER'S BOX

A Harvard Divinity School professor, **Ralph Potter**, has devised a four-quadrant model for sorting through ethics problems. Each quadrant of the square-like model called **Potter's Box** poses a category of questions. Working through these categories helps clarify the issues and lead to a morally justifiable position. These are the quadrants of Potter's Box:

SITUATION. In Quadrant 1, the facts of the issue are decided. Consider a newsroom in which a series of articles on rape is being developed, and the question arises whether to identify rape victims by name. Here is how the situation could be defined: the newspaper has access to a young mother who had been abducted and raped, and who is willing to describe the assault in graphic detail and to discuss her experience as a witness at the assailant's trial. Also, the woman is willing to be identified in the story.

VALUES. Moving to Quadrant 2 of Potter's Box, editors and reporters identify the values that underlie all the available choices. This process involves listing the positive and negative values that flow from conscience. One editor might argue: full, frank discussion on social issues is necessary to deal with them. Another might say: identifying the rape victim by name might discourage others from even reporting the crime. Other positions: publishing the name is in poor taste. The newspaper has an obligation to protect the victim from her own bad decision to allow her name to be

Clarifying Process. Potter's Box offers four categories of questions to help develop morally justifiable positions. Ralph Potter, the divinity professor who devised the categories, said to start by establishing the facts of the situation. Then identify values that underpin the options, recognizing that some values may be incompatible with others. Then consider the moral principles that support each of the values. Finally, sort through loyalties to all the affected interests. Potter's Box is not a panacea, but it gives people the assurance that they have worked through ethics issues in a thorough way.

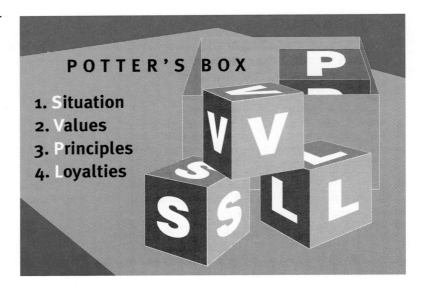

POTTER'S BOX

1. **S**ituation
2. **V**alues
3. **P**rinciples
4. **L**oyalties

used. The purpose of the rape series can be accomplished without using the name. Readers have a right to all the relevant information that the newspaper can gather. An editor who is torn between such anti-ethical thoughts is making progress toward a decision by at least identifying all the values that can be posited.

PRINCIPLES. In Potter's Quadrant 3, decision-makers search for moral principles that uphold the values they identified in Quadrant 2. John Stuart Mill's principle of utility, which favours the majority over individuals, would support using the victim's name because it could add poignancy to the story, enhancing the chances of improved public sensitivity and perhaps even lead to improved public policy, all of which, Mill would say, outweighs the harm that might come to an individual. On the other hand, people who have used Immanuel Kant's ideas to develop inviolable operating principles—categorical imperatives—look to their rule book: we never publish information that might offend readers. One value of Potter's Quadrant 3 is that it gives people confidence in the values that emerged in their debates over Quadrant 2.

LOYALTIES. In Quadrant 4, the decision-maker folds in an additional layer of complexity that must be sorted through: loyalties. The challenge is to establish a hierarchy of loyalties. Is the first loyalty to a code of ethics, and if so, to which code? To readers, and if so, to which ones? To society? To employer? To self? Out of duty to self, some reporters and editors might want to make the rape series as potent as possible, with as much detail as possible, to win awards and bring honour to themselves and perhaps a raise or promotion or bigger job with another newspaper. Others might be motivated by their duty to their employer: The more detail in the story, the more newspapers it will sell. For others, their duty to society may be paramount: The newspaper has a social obligation to present issues in as powerful a way as possible to spur reforms in general attitudes and perhaps public policy.

LIMITATIONS OF POTTER'S BOX

Potter's Box does not provide answers. Rather, it offers a process through which the key elements in ethics questions can be sorted out.

Also, Potter's Box focuses on moral aspects of a problem, leaving it to the decision-maker to examine practical considerations separately, such as whether prudence supports making the morally best decision. Moral decisions should not be made in a vacuum. For example, would it be wise to go ahead with the rape victim's name if 90 percent of the newspaper's subscribers would become so offended that they would quit buying the paper and, as a result, the paper would go out of business?

Other practical questions can involve the law. If the morally best decision is to publish the name but the law forbids it, should the newspaper proceed anyway? Does journalistic virtue transcend the law? Is it worth it to publish the name to create a public's-right-to-know issue or a freedom-of-speech issue? Are there legal implications, like going to jail or piling up legal defence costs?

Is it worth it to go against accepted practices and publish the victim's name? Deciding on a course of action that runs contrary to tradition, perhaps even contrary to some ethics codes, could mean being ostracized by other media people, whose decisions might have gone another way. Doing right can be lonely.

Unsettled, Unsettling Issues

PLAGIARISM

SWAPPING STORIES. Some creative work, like scholarship, requires that information and ideas be attributed to their sources. Journalists are not so strict, as shown by story swapping through the Canadian Press and Broadcast News. The Canadian Press picks up stories from its members and distributes them to other members, often without any reference to the source. Some CP publications and BN broadcasters do not even acknowledge CP as the intermediary.

Incredible as it may seem, journalistic tolerance for plagiarism allows radio stations to pirate the local newspaper for newscasts. Sometimes you can hear the announcer turning the pages. A sad joke that acknowledges this practice is that some stations buy their news, which is cheaper than hiring reporters to cover the community. So pervasive is the journalistic tolerance for "borrowing" that few newspapers even mildly protest when their stories are pirated.

NEWS RELEASES. In many newsrooms, the plagiarism question is clouded further by the practice of using news releases from public relations people word for word without citing the source. Even in newsrooms that rewrite releases to avoid the embarrassment of running a story that is exactly the same as the competition's, it is standard practice not to cite the source. Public relations people, who are paid for writing favourable stories on their clients, have no objections to being plagiarized, and news organizations find it an easy, inexpensive way to fill space. Despite the mutual convenience, the arrangement raises serious questions of ethics to which many in the media have not responded. The practice leaves the false impression that stories originating with news releases actually originated with the news organization. More serious is that the uncredited stories are a disservice to democracy. Marie Dunn White, in the *Journal of Mass Media Ethics*, wrote: "in order for the reader to evaluate the information he or she is receiving correctly and completely, he or she must know which information came from a press release and, therefore, may be biased."

MONITORING COMPETITION. Competitive pressure also contributes to fuzziness on the plagiarism issue. To avoid being skunked on stories, reporters monitor each other closely to pick up tips and ideas. Generally, reporters are not particular about where they pick up information as long as they are confident that it is accurate. For background, reporters tap newsroom libraries, databases, journals, books, and other sources, and, in the interest of not cluttering their stories, they do not use footnotes.

SUBLIMINAL MEMORY. Covering breaking events has its own pressure that puts journalists at special risk. Almost every journalist who writes under the pressure of a deadline has had the experience of writing a story and later discovering that phrases that came easily at the keyboard were actually somebody else's. In their voracious pursuit of information, reporters store phrases and perhaps whole passages subliminally in their memories. This happened to a drama critic who was horrified when a reader pointed out the similarity between his review of a play and an earlier review of the same play in another newspaper. Once aware of what he had done unwittingly, the critic offered his resignation. His editors instead moved him to the copy desk.

It's this concept of innocent recall that concerns Canadian columnist Don McGillivray, who argues that plagiarism is often a simple case of unintentionally borrowing from others. Journalists are like any other group of professionals: They like to "talk shop" when in the presence of other journalists. They discuss stories they've written and articles they've read. Later, while writing a story, a journalist may subconsciously remember a certain phrase from an earlier conversation with a colleague and use it in a story. Is this plagiarism? McGillivray doesn't think so. It's simply the outcome of a psychological process.

MISREPRESENTATION

Janet Cooke's meteoric rise at the *Washington Post* unravelled quickly the day after she received a Pulitzer Prize. Her editors had been so impressed with her story, "Jimmy's World," about a child who was addicted to heroin, that they nominated it for a Pulitzer Prize. The gripping tale began: "Jimmy is 8 years old and a third-generation heroin addict, a precocious little boy with sandy hair, velvety brown eyes and needle marks freckling the baby-smooth skin of his thin brown arms." Janet Cooke claimed that she had won the confidence of Jimmy's mother and her live-in man friend, a drug dealer, to do the story. Cooke said she had promised not to reveal their identities as a condition for her access to Jimmy.

The story, played on the front page, so shocked Washington that people demanded that Jimmy be taken away from his mother and placed in a foster home. The *Post* declined to help authorities, citing Cooke's promise of confidentiality to her sources. The mayor ordered the police to find Jimmy with or without the newspaper's help, and millions of dollars in police resources went into a door-to-door search. After 17 days, the police gave up knocking on doors for tips on Jimmy. Some doubts emerged at the *Post* about the story, but the newspaper stood behind its reporter.

Janet Cooke, 25 when she was hired by the *Post*, had extraordinary credentials. Her résumé showed a baccalaureate degree, magna cum laude, from Vassar; study at the Sorbonne in Paris; a master's degree from the University of Toledo; abilities in several languages; and two years of journalistic experience with the *Toledo Blade*. Said Ben Bradlee, editor of the *Post*, "She had it all. She was bright. She was well-spoken. She was pretty. She wrote well." She was black, which made her especially attractive to the *Post*, which was working to bring the percentage of black staff reporters nearer to the percentage of blacks in its circulation area.

"Jimmy's World" was published in September 1980. Six months later, the Pulitzer committee announced its decision and issued a biographical sheet on Janet Cooke. The Associated Press, trying to flesh out the biographical information, spotted discrepancies right away. Janet Cooke, it turned out, had attended Vassar one year but had not been graduated with the honours she claimed. The University of Toledo had no record of awarding her a master's. Suddenly, doubts that had surfaced in the days immediately after "Jimmy's World" was published took on a new intensity. The editors sat Cooke down and grilled her on the claims on which she was hired. No, she admitted, she was not multilingual. The Sorbonne claim was fuzzy. More importantly, they grilled her on whether there was really a Jimmy. The interrogation continued into the night, and finally Janet Cooke confessed all: There were no confidential sources, and there was no Jimmy. She had fabricated the story. She resigned, and the *Post*, terribly embarrassed, returned the Pulitzer.

In cases of outright fabrication, as in "Jimmy's World," it is easy to identify the lapses in ethics. When Janet Cooke emerged briefly from seclusion to explain herself, she said that she was responding to pressures in the *Post* newsroom to produce flashy, sensational copy. Most people found the explanation unsatisfying, considering the pattern of deception that went back to her falsified résumé.

Rigged Explosion. To illustrate a story on vehicle safety, NBC's *Dateline* showed a General Motors pickup truck exploding in a collision. Not told to viewers was that the explosion had been rigged for the cameras. The misrepresentation came to light when GM filed a suit, claiming it had been wrongly damaged. For most media people, the issue was one of ethics more than law. The misrepresentation in the re-creation violated the trust that the network had cultivated for its news. After an internal investigation, changes were ordered in the *Dateline* staff, and NBC News Vice President Michael Gartner soon found himself out of a job. Also, besides apologizing to GM, which then withdrew its suit, NBC apologized to its viewers.

There are **misrepresentations**, however, that are not as clearly unacceptable. Much debated are:

STAGING NEWS. To attract favourable attention to their clients, public relations people organize media events, a practice known as **staging events**. These are designed to be irresistible to journalists. Rallies and demonstrations on topical issues, for example, find their way onto front pages, magazine covers, and evening newscasts because their photogenic qualities give them an edge over less visual although sometimes more significant events. The ethics question is less important for publicists, who generally are up-front about what they are doing. The ethics question is more serious for journalists, who claim that their job is to present an accurate, balanced account of a day's events but who regularly overplay staged events that are designed by publicists to be photogenic and easy to cover.

RE-CREATIONS. A wave of **reality programs** on television that began in the late 1980s featured **re-enactments** that were not always labelled as such. Philip Weiss, writing in *Columbia Journalism Review*, offered this litany: shadows on the wall of a woman taking a hammer to her husband, a faceless actor grabbing a tin of kerosene to blow up his son, a corpse in a wheelbarrow with a hand dangling, a detective opening the trunk of a car and reeling from the smell of a decomposing body. While mixing re-creations with strictly news footage rankles many critics, others argue that it helps people understand the situation. The same question arises with docudramas, which mix actual events and dramatic re-creations.

SELECTIVE EDITING. The editing process, by its nature, requires journalists to make decisions about what is most worth emphasizing and what is least worth even including. In this sense, all editing is selective, but the term **selective editing** refers to making decisions with the goal of distorting. Selective editing can occur in drama too, when writers, editors, and other media people take literary licence too far and intentionally misrepresent.

FICTIONAL METHODS. In the late 1960s, many experiments in media portrayals of people and issues came to be called the **new journalism**. The term was hard to define because it included so many approaches. Among the most controversial were applications of fiction-writing methods on topical issues, an approach widely accepted in book publishing but suddenly controversial when it appeared in the news media. Character development became more important than before, including presumed insights into the thinking of people being covered. The view of the writer became an essential element in much of this reporting. The defence for these approaches was that traditional, facts-only reporting could not approach complex truths that merited journalistic explorations. The profound ethics questions that these approaches posed were usually mitigated by clear statements about what the writer was attempting. Nonetheless, it was a controversial approach to the issues of the day. There was no defence when the fictional approach was complete fabrication passing itself off as reality, as in "Jimmy's World."

GIFTS, JUNKETS, AND MEALS

In his 1919 book *The Brass Check,* a pioneer examination of newsroom ethics, **Upton Sinclair** told how news people took bribes to put stories in the paper. Today,

NewsWatch Canada: Independent research on the diversity and thoroughness of news coverage in Canada's media, with a focus on identifying blind spots and double standards. The site includes a Top Ten list of underreported stories.

newswatch.cprost.sfu.ca

media ethics codes universally condemn gifts and certainly bribes, but there still are many people who curry favour with the mass media through gifts, such as a college sports information director who gives a bottle of whisky at Christmas to a sports writer as a gesture of goodwill. Favours can take many forms: media-appreciation luncheons; free trips abroad, known as **junkets,** for the experience necessary to do a travel article; season passes to cover the opera; discounts at certain stores.

Despite the consistent exhortation of the ethics codes against gifts, favours, free travel, and special treatment and privileges, there is nothing inherently wrong in taking them if they do not influence coverage and if the journalist's benefactor understands that. The problem with favours is more a practical one than one of ethics. Taking a favour may or may not be bad, but it looks bad. Many ethics codes do not make this important distinction.

While ethics codes are uniform against **freebies,** as gifts and favours are called, many news organizations accept free movie, drama, concert, and other tickets, as well as recordings, books, and other materials for review. The justification usually is that their budgets allow them to review only materials that arrive free and that their audiences would be denied reviews if the materials had to be purchased. A counter-argument is that a news organization that cannot afford to do business properly should not be in business. Many news organizations, however, insist on buying tickets for their reporters to beauty pageants, sports events, and other things to which there is an admission fee. A frequent exception occurs when a press box or special media facility is available. With recordings, books, and free samples, some media organizations return them or pass them on to charity to avoid any appearance that they have been bought off.

When junkets are proposed, some organizations send reporters only if they can pay the fare and other expenses. An exception is made by some news organizations for trips that they could not possibly arrange on their own, such as covering a two-week naval exercise aboard a ship.

Some media organizations address the issue of impropriety by acknowledging favours. Many quiz shows say that "promotional consideration" has been provided to companies that give them travel, lodging, and prizes. Just as forthright are publications that state that reviews are made possible through season passes or free samples. Acknowledging favours does not remove the questions but at least it is up-front.

ACCEPTED PRACTICES

Just as there is not a reliable correlation between law and ethics, neither is there one between accepted media practices and ethics. What is acceptable at one advertising agency to make a product look good in photographs might be unacceptable at another. Even universally accepted practices should not go unexamined, for unless accepted practices are examined and reconsidered on a continuing basis, media practitioners can come to rely more on habit than on principles in their work.

PRUDENCE AND ETHICS

Prudence is the application of wisdom in a practical situation. It can be a levelling factor in moral questions. Consider the case of Irvin Lieberman, who had built his *Main Line Chronicle* and several other weeklies in the Philadelphia suburbs into aggressive, journalistically excellent newspapers. After being hit with nine libel suits, all costly to defend, Lieberman abandoned the editorial thrust of his newspapers. "I decided not to do any investigative work," he said. "It was a matter of either feeding my family or spending my whole life in court." Out of prudence, Lieberman decided to abandon his commitment to hard-hitting, effective journalism.

Courageous pursuit of morally lofty ends can, as a practical matter, be foolish. Whether Irvin Lieberman was exhibiting a moral weakness by bending to the chilling factor of libel suits, which are costly to fight, or being prudent is an issue that could be debated forever. The point, however, is that prudence cannot be ignored as a factor in moral decisions.

CHAPTER WRAP-UP

The mass media enjoy great freedom under the Canadian Charter of Rights and Freedoms, which forbids the government from impinging on expression. Even so, the freedom has limits. Major restrictions on the mass media involve publication bans, censorship, commercial exploitation, invasion of privacy, libel, fair trials, and obscenity.

Mass media people also need to be concerned about ethics because they can have powerful effects. But answers do not come easily. Personal information can embarrass a person inexcusably. However, it can be argued that privacy is less important, for example, with candidates for high office.

QUESTIONS FOR REVIEW

1. Why cannot ethics codes anticipate all moral questions? And does this limit the value of codes for mass media people?

2. List and explain moral principles that mass media people can use to sort through ethics questions.

3. How can mass media people come to different conclusions depending on whether they use process-based or outcome-based ethics?

4. Is ethics the same as law? As prudence? As accepted practices?

5. What is the role of the CRTC to broadcasting in Canada?

6. Review the various Canadian ethics codes. How useful are such codes and the presence of the CBSC?

7. What is defamation?

8. What is copyright?

9. How is pornography different from obscenity?

QUESTIONS FOR CRITICAL THINKING

1. Can you identify the ethics principle or system most associated with Aristotle? Immanuel Kant? John Stuart Mill? John Dewey? John Rawls? Ralph Potter?

2. How can codes of ethics help mass media people make the right decisions? Do codes always work? Why or why not?

3. A candidate for mayor tells a news reporter that the incumbent mayor is in cahoots with organized crime. What should the reporter do before going on the air with this bombshell accusation? Why?

4. Can media people ever defend breaking the law as ethical?

5. What did Avery Haines do wrong?

6. Comment on Ron Cohen's observations in this chapter on self-regulation of the media in Canada.

7. View *The Valour and the Horror*. Defend the McKennas' representation of the war.

FOR KEEPING UP TO DATE

Ethicists sort through moral dilemmas involving mass communication in the scholarly *Journal of Mass Med* Many trade and professional journals also deal with media ethics, including the *Columbia Journalism Review* and *Broadcaster*.

FOR FURTHER LEARNING

Brian Bergman. "The Battle over Censorship." *Maclean's* (October 24, 1994).

Christie Blatchford. "This is CTV. You Will Not Be Funny." *National Post* (January 18, 2000).

Clifford G. Christians, Kim B. Rotzoll, and Mark Fackler. *Media Ethics*, 2nd ed. (Longman, 1987).

Roy Peter Clark. "The Original Sin: How Plagiarism Poisons the Press." *Washington Journalism Review* (March 1983), 43–47.

Ron Cohen. "Self-Regulation: A Canadian Success Story." *Broadcast Dialogue* (November 1999).

Michael G. Crawford. *The Journalist's Legal Guide* (Carswell, 1996).

Timothy Findlay. "Point–Counterpoint: Ethics in the Media." *Journal of Canadian Studies* (Volume 27, Number 4).

Matthew Fraser. "Time to Change Channels." *National Post* (March 7, 2001).

Brian Green. *Broadcast News Essentials* (Harcourt Brace, 2001).

Jeff Gray. "Jarring: Why Avery Haines Losing it On Air Stunned Us." *Press Review* (First Quarter 2000).

Sally Harris and David Potts. "Important Elements of the Internet Applicable to Cyber Libel." **www.cyberlibel.com/elements.html** (July 31, 2001).

Carl Hausman. *The Decision-Making Process in Journalism* (Nelson-Hall, 1990).

Walter B. Jaehnig. "Harrison Cochran—The Publisher with a Past." *Journal of Mass Media Ethics 2* (Fall/Winter 1986–87): 1, 80–88.

Paul Kaihla. "Sex and the Law." *Maclean's* (October 24, 1994).

Donna Soble Kaufman. *Broadcasting Law in Canada: Fairness in the Administrative Process* (Carswell, 1987).

Aonghus Kealy. "Defying the YOA." *Press Review* (First Quarter 2001).

Wilfred H. Kesterton. *The Law and the Press in Canada* (MacLelland and Stewart, 1976).

Janet Malcolm. *The Journalist and the Murderer* (Knopf, 1990).

John C. Merrill. *The Dialectic in Journalism: Toward a Responsible Use of Press Freedom* (Louisiana State University Press, 1990).

Stuart Robertson. *The Media Law Handbook* (Self-Counsel Press, 1983).

Stuart Robertson. *Pocket Guide to Media Law* (Hallion Press, 1994).

Nick Russell. *Morals and the Media: Ethics in Canadian Journalism* (University of British Columbia Press, 1994).

Jim Slotek. "Gaffing the Anchor." *Toronto Sun* (January 19, 2000).

Phillip Weiss. "Bad Rap for TV Tabs." *Columbia Journalism Review 28* (May/June 1989): 1, 39–42.

Marie Dunn White. "Plagiarism and the News Media." *Journal of Mass Media Ethics 4* (1989): 2, 265–280.

Antonia Zerbisias. "Ready or Not, CRTC Takes on Media Convergence." *Toronto Star* (April 14, 2001).

Orson Welles. Young Orson Welles scared the living daylights out of several million radio listeners with the 1938 radio drama *War of the Worlds*. Most of the fright was short-lived, though. All but the most naïve listeners quickly realized that Martians really had not devastated the New Jersey militia as they marched toward the Hudson River to destroy Manhattan.

Media Effects

Chapter 12

MEDIA TIMELINE
Understanding Mass Media Effects

1922	Walter Lippmann attributes powerful effects to the mass media.
1938	Hadley Cantril concludes that the *War of the Worlds* panic was drastically overstated.
1940S	Mass communication scholars shift from studying effects to uses and gratification.
1948	Paul Lazarsfeld challenges powerful effects theory in voter studies.
1967	George Gerbner launches his television violence index.
1970S	Mass communication scholars shift to cumulative effects theory.
1972	Maxwell McCombs and Don Shaw conclude that media create public agendas, not opinion.
1992	Virginie Lariviere presents Prime Minister Brian Mulroney with a petition urging the government to do something about violence on TV.
1993	A new violence code is introduced by Canada's AGVOT.

Media in Theory

Aggressive Reaction

Has your stomach ever tightened at a scary moment during a movie? Your skin tingled? These are the responses that the moviemaker, an expert at effective storytelling, had intended. They work, however, only if the moviemaker has succeeded at sweeping you into the story line. This process of getting "into" the story requires suspending disbelief. It is not unique to movies. In all fiction, no matter what the medium, the storyteller needs to move the audience from knowing the story is fictitious, which is disbelief, to going along with it and being affected, which is the suspending of disbelief. In a movie, you have suspended disbelief if you grab the arm of the person next to you to survive a frightening turn of events on the screen, or if you scream, or gasp, or cry.

There is no question that the media affect people, but there is considerable debate about whether these effects are momentary or long term and whether these effects can prompt people into antisocial behaviour. Some outspoken media critics charge that media-depicted male violence against women leads to rape on the streets and at home. There is wide concern that children are especially susceptible to violence on television and the movies and they imitate media violence in their own lives. What are your own experiences with the effects of media depictions of antisocial behaviour?

■ Have you ever been inspired to an antisocial act because you saw it on the screen?

■ Do you know anyone who has?
■ Do you worry that children might be affected by media depictions of violence in ways that you never were?
■ Does concern for your own safety increase after seeing violence depicted in the media?

These are the kinds of questions addressed in this chapter.

Effects Studies

MEDIA EFFECTS: THE CASE OF *WAR OF THE WORLDS*

The boy genius **Orson Welles** was on a roll. By 1938, at age 23, Welles's dramatic flair had landed him a network radio show, *Mercury Theater on the Air*, at prime time on CBS on Sunday nights. The program featured adaptations of well-known literature. For their October 30 program, Welles and his colleagues decided on a scary 1898 British novel, H.G. Wells's *War of the Worlds.*

Orson Welles opened with the voice of a wizened chronicler from some future time, intoning an unsettling monologue. That was followed by an innocuous weather forecast, then hotel dance music. Then the music was interrupted by a news bulletin. An astronomer reported several explosions on Mars, propelling something at enormous velocity toward Earth. The bulletin over, listeners were transported back to the hotel orchestra. After applause the orchestra started up again, only to be interrupted: Seismologists had picked up an earthquake-like shock in New Jersey. Then it was one bulletin after another.

The story line accelerated. Giant Martians moved across the countryside spewing fatal gas. One at a time, reporters at remote sites vanished off the air. The Martians decimated the Army and were wading across the Hudson River. Amid sirens and other sounds of emergency, a reporter on a Manhattan rooftop described the monsters advancing through the streets. From his vantage, he described the Martians felling people by the thousands and moving in on him, the gas crossing Sixth Avenue, then Fifth Avenue, then 100 yards away, then 50 feet. Then silence.

To the surprise of Orson Welles and his crew, the drama triggered widespread mayhem. Neighbours gathered in streets all over the country, wet towels to their faces to slow the gas. In Newark, New Jersey, people, many undressed, fled their apartments. Said a New York woman, "I never hugged my radio so closely . . . I held a crucifix in my hand and prayed while looking out my open window to get a faint whiff of gas so that I would know when to close my window and hermetically seal my room with waterproof cement or anything else I could get a hold of. My plan was to stay in the room and hope that I would not suffocate before the gas blew away."

War of the Worlds: Information and links to information regarding every version of *War of the Worlds* ever released, including books, performances, music, movies, television shows, models, and games.

www.war-of-the-worlds.org

Researchers estimate that one out of six people who heard the program, more than one million in all, suspended disbelief and braced for the worst.

The effects were especially amazing considering that:

- An announcer identified the program as fiction at four points.
- Almost 10 times as many people were tuned to a popular comedy show on another network.
- The program ran only one hour, an impossibly short time for the sequence that began with the blastoffs on Mars, included a major military battle in New Jersey, and ended with New York's destruction.

Unwittingly, Orson Welles and his Mercury Theater crew had created an evening of infamy and raised questions about media effects to new intensity. In this chapter, you will learn what scholars have found out about the effects of the mass media on individuals.

Effects Theory

POWERFUL EFFECTS THEORY

Media Effects Theory: UK website providing a particular perspective on straightforward media effects theory.

www.theory.org.uk/ ctr-eff.htm

The first generation of mass communication scholars thought the mass media had a profound, direct effect on people. Their idea, called **powerful effects theory,** drew heavily on social commentator **Walter Lippmann**'s influential 1922 book, *Public Opinion*. Lippmann argued that we see the world not as it really is but as "pictures in our heads." The "pictures" of things we have not experienced personally, he said, are shaped by the mass media. The powerful impact that Lippmann ascribed to the media was a precursor of the effects theory that evolved among scholars over the next few years.

Yale psychologist **Harold Lasswell**, who studied World War II propaganda, embodied the effects theory in his famous model of mass communication: *Who, Says what, In which channel, To whom, With what effect.* At their extreme, effects theory devotees assumed that the media could inject information, ideas, and even propaganda hypodermically into the public. The theory was explained in terms of a hypodermic needle model or bullet model. Early effects scholars would agree that newspaper coverage and endorsements of political candidates decided elections.

The early scholars did not see that the hypodermic metaphor was hopelessly simplistic. They assumed wrongly that individuals are passive and absorb uncritically and unconditionally whatever the media spew forth. The fact is that individuals read, hear, and see the same things differently. Even if they did not, people are exposed to many, many media—hardly a single, monolithic voice. Also, there is a scepticism among media consumers that is manifested at its extreme in the saying, "You can't believe a thing you read in the paper." People are not mindless, uncritical blotters.

MINIMALIST EFFECTS THEORY

Scholarly enthusiasm for the hypodermic needle model dwindled after two massive studies of voter behaviour. The studies, led by sociologist **Paul Lazarsfeld** were the first rigorous tests of media effects on an election. Lazarsfeld's researchers went back to 600 people several times to discover how they developed their campaign opinions. Rather than citing particular newspapers, magazines, or radio stations, as had been expected, these people generally mentioned friends and acquaintances. The media had hardly any direct effect. Clearly, the hypodermic needle model was off base, and the effects theory needed rethinking. From that rethinking emerged the **minimalist effects theory**, which included:

TWO-STEP MODEL. Minimalist scholars devised the **two-step flow** model to show that voters are motivated less by the mass media than by people they know personally and respect. These people, called **opinion leaders**, include many clergy, teachers, and neighbourhood merchants, although it is impossible to list categorically all those who comprise opinion leaders. Not all clergy, for example, are influential, and opinion leaders are not necessarily in an authority role. The minimalist scholars' point is that personal contact is more important than media contact. The two-step flow model, which replaced the hypodermic needle model, showed that whatever effect the media have with the majority of the population is through opinion leaders. Later, as mass communication research became more sophisticated, the two-step model was expanded into a **multistep flow** model to capture the complex web of social relationships that affects individuals.

STATUS CONFERRAL. Minimalist scholars acknowledge that the media create prominence for issues and people by giving them coverage. Conversely, neglect relegates issues and personalities to obscurity. Related to this **status conferral** phenomenon is **agenda-setting**. Professors **Maxwell McCombs** and **Don Shaw**, describing the agenda-setting phenomenon in 1972, said the media do not tell people what to think but tell them what to think about. This is a profound distinction. In covering a political campaign, explain McCombs and Shaw, the media choose which issues or topics to emphasize, thereby setting the campaign's agenda. "This ability to affect cognitive change among individuals," say McCombs and Shaw, "is one of the most important aspects of the power of mass communication."

NARCOTICIZING DYSFUNCTION. Some minimalists claim that the media rarely energize people into action, such as getting them to go out to vote for a candidate. Rather, they say, the media lull people into passivity. This effect, called **narcoticizing dysfunction**, is supported by studies that find that many people are so overwhelmed by the volume of news and information available to them that they tend to withdraw from involvement in public issues. Narcoticizing dysfunction occurs also when people pick up a great deal of information from the media on a particular subject—poverty, for example—and believe that they are doing something about a problem when they are really only smugly well-informed. Intellectual involvement becomes a substitute for active involvement.

CUMULATIVE EFFECTS THEORY

In recent years some mass communication scholars have parted from the minimalists and resurrected the powerful effects theory, although with a twist that avoids the simplistic hypodermic needle model. German scholar **Elisabeth Noelle-Neumann**, a leader of this school, conceded that the media do not have powerful immediate effects but argues that effects over time are profound. Her **cumulative effects theory** notes that nobody can escape either the media, which are ubiquitous, or the media's messages, which are driven home with redundancy. To support her point, Noelle-Neumann cites multimedia advertising campaigns that hammer away with the same message over and over. There's no missing the point. Even in news reports there is a redundancy, with the media all focusing on the same events.

Noelle-Neumann's cumulative effects theory has troubling implications. She says that the media, despite surface appearances, work against diverse, robust public consideration of issues. Noelle-Neumann bases her observation on human psychology, which she says encourages people who feel they hold majority viewpoints to speak out confidently. Those views gain credibility in their claim to be dominant when they are carried by the media, whether they are really dominant or not. Meanwhile, says Noelle-Neumann, people who perceive that they are in a minority are inclined to speak out less, perhaps not at all. The result is that dominant views can snowball through the media and become consensus views without being sufficiently challenged. To demonstrate her intriguing theory, Noelle-Neumann has devised the ominously labelled **spiral of silence** model, in which minority views are intimidated into silence and obscurity. Noelle-Neumann's model raises doubts about the libertarian concept that the media provide a marketplace in which conflicting ideas fight it out fairly, each receiving a full hearing.

FUTURE THEORIES

Scholar Melvin DeFleur, who has chronicled developments in mass communication theory, is pessimistic about what's happening now in mass communication studies. DeFleur, of Boston University, says recent years have lacked milestones, seminal studies on mass communication, after a rich history of significant studies from the 1930s to the early 1980s. Writing in the scholarly journal *Mass Communication and Society* in 1998, DeFleur said, "When asked by my publisher to revise a book summarizing the existing milestones and adding new ones, I could not identify even one that fit the same criteria as the earlier investigations."

The Golden Age of masscom research, as DeFleur calls it, yielded "important concepts, generalizations and theories that are now part of the accumulated knowledge of how the media function and the kinds of influence that they have on individuals and society." Among those seminal projects:

- *Payne Fund Studies*. These studies, in the 1930s, established theoretical fundamentals on movies' effects on children.
- *"War of the Worlds" Study*. This 1940 study, by Hadley Cantril, questioned whether the mass media have a bullet effect on audiences. It helped to usher in more sophisticated ways of understanding mass communication.
- *Lazarsfeld Studies*. These studies, in 1940 and 1948, created a new understanding of how mass communication influences people.

Is mass communication research dead in the water? DeFleur says that one factor has been a brain drain from universities, where such research took place in earlier times. Big corporations now offer much higher salaries than universities—sometimes double and triple—to attract people with doctoral degrees who can do research for their marketing and other corporate pursuits. Scholars are drawn to more practical and lucrative work that may help a detergent manufacturer to choose the right colour for packaging the soap but fails to further our understanding of how the mass communication process works.

Uses and Gratifications Studies

CHALLENGES TO AUDIENCE PASSIVITY

As disillusionment with the powerful effects theory set in after the Lazarsfeld studies of the 1940s, scholars re-evaluated many of their assumptions, including the idea that people are merely passive consumers of the mass media. From the re-evaluation came research questions about why individuals tap into the mass media. This research, called **uses and gratifications** studies, explored how individuals choose certain media outlets. One vein of research said people seek certain media to gratify certain needs.

These scholars worked with social science theories about people being motivated to do certain things by human needs and wants, such as seeking water, food, and shelter as necessities and wanting to be socially accepted and loved. These scholars identified dozens of reasons that people use the media, among them surveillance, socialization, and diversion.

SURVEILLANCE FUNCTION

With their acute sense of smell and sound, deer scan their environment constantly for approaching danger. In modern human society, surveillance is provided for individuals by the mass media, which scan local and global environments for information that helps individuals make decisions to live better, even survive.

News coverage is the most evident form through which the mass media serve this **surveillance function.** From a weather report, people decide whether to wear a raincoat; from the Bay Street averages, whether to invest; from the news, whether the prime minister will have their support. Although most people don't obsess about

Preparing for Y2K Crashes. Extensive media coverage of pending computer problems with the date conversion from 1999 to 2000 alerted everybody to prepare for a possible crisis. The coverage, which was in the news daily for months, prompted software changes and code writing to head off a disaster. Thanks to media surveillance, enough concern was generated at all levels in society to avert the crisis. Almost all computers rolled over seamlessly at midnight from 12311999 to 01012000.

being on top of all that's happening in the world, there is a touch of the "news junkie" in everybody. All people need reliable information on their immediate environment. Is snow expected? Is the bridge fixed? Are vegetable prices coming down? Most of us are curious about developments in politics, economics, science, and other fields. The news media provide a surveillance function for their audiences, surveying the world for information that people want and need to know.

It is not only news that provides surveillance. From drama and literature, people learn about great human issues that give them a better feel for the human condition. Popular music and entertainment, conveyed by the mass media, give people a feel for the emotional reactions of other human beings, many very far away, and for things going on in their world.

SOCIALIZATION FUNCTION

Except for recluses, people are always seeking information that helps them fit in with other people. This **socialization function,** a lifelong process, is greatly assisted by the mass media. Without paying attention to the media, for example, it is hard to participate in conversations about how the Ottawa Senators did last night or Atom Egoyan's latest movie. Mike Bullard's monologues give late-night television watchers a common experience with their friends and associates the next day, as do the latest movie and the evening news.

Using the media can be a social activity, bringing people together. Going to the movies or watching the NHL playoffs on CBC with friends is a group activity.

The media also contribute to togetherness by creating commonality. Friends who subscribe to *Maclean's* have a shared experience in reading the weekly cover story, even though they do it separately. The magazine helps individuals maintain social relationships by giving them something in common. In this sense, the media are important in creating community, even nationhood, and perhaps, with global communication, a fellowship of humankind.

Less positive as a social function of the mass media is **parasocial interaction.** When a television anchor looks directly into the camera, as if talking with individual viewers, it is not a true social relationship that is being created. The communication is one-way without audience feedback. However, because many people enjoy the sense of interaction, no matter how false it is, many local stations encourage on-camera members of the news team to chat among themselves, which furthers the impression of an ongoing conversation with an extended peer group that includes the individual viewer.

This same false sense of reciprocal dialogue exists also among individuals and their favourite political columnists, lovelorn and other advice writers, and humorists. Some people have the illusion that the friends David Letterman interviews on his program are their friends, and so are Mike Bullard's and Pamela Wallin's. It is also illusory parasocial interaction when someone has the television set on for companionship.

DIVERSION FUNCTION

Through the mass media, people can escape everyday drudgery, immersing themselves in a soap opera, a murder mystery, or pop music. This is the **diversion function.** The result can be stimulation, relaxation, or emotional release.

Stimulation. Everybody is bored occasionally. When our senses—sight, hearing, smell, taste, and touch—are without sufficient external stimuli, a sensory vacuum results. Following the physicist's law that a vacuum must be filled, we seek new stimuli to correct our sensory deprivation. In modern society the mass media are almost always handy as boredom-offsetting stimulants. It's not only in boring situations that the mass media can be a stimulant. To accelerate the pace of an already lively party, for example, someone can put on quicker music and turn up the volume.

Relaxation. When someone's sensory abilities are overloaded, the media can be relaxing. Slower, softer music sometimes can help. Relaxation, in fact, can come through any change of pace. In some situations, a high-tension movie or book can be as effective as a lullaby.

Release. People can use the mass media to blow off steam. Somehow a Friday night horror movie dissipates the frustration pent up all week. As can a good cry over a tear-jerking book.

Using the mass media as a stimulant, relaxant, or release is quick, healthy escapism. Escapism, however, can go further, as when soap-opera fans so enmesh themselves in the programs that they perceive themselves as characters in the story line. Carried too far, escapism becomes withdrawal. When people build on media portrayals to the point that their existence revolves on living out the lives of, say, Elvis Presley or Marilyn Monroe, the withdrawal from reality has become a serious psychological disorder.

CONSISTENCY THEORY

Gratifications scholars learned that people generally are conservative in choosing media, looking for media that reinforce their personal views. Faced with messages consistent with their own views and ones that are radically different, people pay attention to the one they're comfortable with and have slight recall of contrary views. These phenomena—selective exposure, selective perception, selective retention, and selective recall—came to be called **consistency theory.**

Consistency theory does a lot to explain media habits. People read, watch, and listen to media with messages that don't jar them. The theory raised serious questions about how well the media can meet the democratic ideal that the media be a forum for the robust exchange of divergent ideas. The media can't fulfill their role as a forum if people hear only what they want to hear.

Individual Selectivity

SELECTIVE EXPOSURE

People make deliberate decisions in choosing media. For example, outdoors enthusiasts choose *Field & Stream* at the newsrack. Academics subscribe to *Saturday Night.* Young rock fans watch MuchMusic, while country fans will tune in to Country Music Television. People expose themselves to media whose content relates to their interests. In this sense, individuals exercise control over the media's effects on them. Nobody forces these selections on anybody.

This process of choosing media, called **selective exposure**, continues once an individual is involved in a publication or a broadcast. A hunter who seldom fishes will gravitate to the hunting articles in *Field & Stream*, perhaps even skipping the fishing pieces entirely. On MuchMusic, a hard-rock aficionado will be attentive to wild music and tune in during "The Power Hour," but will take a break when the video jockey announces that a mellow piece will follow the commercial.

SELECTIVE PERCEPTION

The selectivity that occurs in actually reading, watching, and listening is less conscious than in selective exposure. No matter how clear a message is, people see and hear egocentrically. This phenomenon, known as **selective perception** or **autistic perception**, was demonstrated in the 1950s by researcher Roy Carter, who found that physicians concerned about socialized medicine at the time would hear "social aspects of medicine" as "socialized medicine." Rural folks on the Prairies, anxious for news about farming, thought they heard the words "farm news" on the radio when the announcer said "foreign news."

Scholars Eugene Webb and Jerry Salancik explain it this way: "Exposure to information is hedonistic." People pick up what they want to pick up. Webb and Salancik state that nonsmokers who read an article about smoking focus subconsciously on passages that link smoking with cancer, being secure and content, even joyful, in the information that reinforces the wisdom of their decision not to smoke. In contrast, smokers are more attentive to passages that hedge the smoking–cancer link. In using the mass media for information, people tend to perceive what they want. As social commentator Walter Lippmann put it, "For the most part we do not first see and then define, we define first and then see." Sometimes the human mind distorts facts to square with predispositions and preconceptions.

SELECTIVE RETENTION AND RECALL

Experts say that the brain records forever everything to which it is exposed. The problem is recall. While people remember many things that were extremely pleasurable or that coincided with their beliefs, they have a harder time calling up the memory's file on other things.

Selective retention happens to mothers when they tend to de-emphasize or even forget the illnesses or disturbances of pregnancy and the pain of birth. This phenomenon works the opposite way when individuals encounter things that reinforce their beliefs.

Nostalgia also can affect recall. For example, many mothers grossly predate when undesirable behaviour like thumb sucking was abandoned. Mothers tend also to suggest precocity about the age at which Suzy or José first walked or cut the first tooth. In the same way, people often use rose-coloured lenses, not 20/20 vision, in recalling information and ideas from the media. This is known as **selective recall**.

In summary, individuals have a large degree of control over how the mass media affect them. Not only do individuals make conscious choices in exposing themselves to particular media, but also their beliefs and values subconsciously shape how their minds pick up and store information and ideas. The phenomena of selective exposure, selective perception, and selective retention and recall are overlooked by people who portray the mass media as omnipotent and individuals as helpless and manipulated pawns.

Selective Retention. The influence of the mass media is a function of both media and audience. The success of nostalgia magazines like Memories, which was introduced in 1989 and whose circulation soared to 650 000, is a result of the rose-coloured lenses through which most people view the past. This is an example of selective retention at work.

The 1938 *War of the Worlds* scare demonstrates this point. The immediate response was to heap blame on the media, particularly Orson Welles and CBS, but panic-stricken listeners bore responsibility too. A Princeton University team led by psychologist **Hadley Cantril**, which studied the panic, noted that radio listeners brought to their radio sets predispositions and preconceptions that contributed to what happened. Among their subconscious baggage:

- A preconception, almost a reverence, about radio, especially CBS, as a reliable medium for major breaking news.
- A predisposition to expect bad news, created by a decade of disastrous global economic developments and another war imminent in Europe.
- Selective perception, which caused them to miss announcements that the program was a dramatization. While many listeners tuned in late and missed the initial announcement, others listened straight through the announcements without registering them.
- An awe about scientific discoveries, technological progress, and new weapons, which contributed to gullibility.
- Memories from World War I about the horror of gas warfare.
- An inability to test the radio story with their own common sense. How, for example, could the Army mobilize for a battle against the Martians within 20 minutes of the invasion?

Socialization

MEDIA'S INITIATING ROLE

Nobody is born knowing how to fit into society. This is learned through a process that begins at home. Children imitate their parents and brothers and sisters. From listening and observing, children learn values. Some behaviour is applauded; some is scolded. Gradually this culturization and **socialization** process expands to include friends, neighbours, school, and at some point the mass media.

In earlier times, the role of the mass media came late because books, magazines, and newspapers required reading skills that were learned in school. The media were only a modest part of early childhood socialization. Today, however, television is omnipresent from the cradle. A young person turning 18 will have spent more time watching television than in any other activity except sleep. Television, which requires no special skills to use, has displaced much of the socializing influence that once came from parents. *Sesame Street* imparts more information on the value of nutrition than Mom's admonition to eat spinach.

By definition, socialization is **prosocial**. Children learn that motherhood, baseball, and apple pie are valued; that buddies frown on tattling; that honesty is virtuous; and that hard work is rewarded. The stability of a society is assured through the transmission of such values to the next generation.

ROLE MODELS

The extent of media influence on individuals may never be sorted out with any precision, in part because every individual is a distinct person and because media exposure varies from person to person. Even so, some media influence is undeniable. Consider the effect of entertainment idols as they come across through the media. Remember all the Spice Girls look-alikes some years ago? This imitation, called **role modelling**, even includes speech mannerisms from whoever is hip at the moment—"Show me the money," "Hasta la vista, baby," and "I'm the king of the world." Let's not forget "yadda-yadda-yadda" from *Seinfeld*.

No matter how quirky, fashion fads are not terribly consequential, but serious questions can be raised about whether role modelling extends to behaviour. Many people who produce media messages recognize a responsibility for role modelling. Whenever Batman and Robin leaped into their Batmobile in the campy 1960s television series, the camera always managed to show them fastening their seat belts. Many newspapers have a policy to mention in accident stories whether seat belts were in use. In the 1980s, as concern about AIDS mounted, moviemakers went out of their way to show condoms as a precaution in social situations. For example, in the movie *Broadcast News*, the producer character slips a condom into her purse before leaving the house on the night of the awards dinner.

If role modelling can work for good purposes, such as promoting safety consciousness and disease prevention, it would seem that it could also have a negative effect. Some people linked the Columbine High School massacre in Littleton, Colorado, to a scene in the Leonardo DiCaprio movie *The Basketball Diaries*, where a student in a black trench coat executes fellow classmates. An outbreak of shootings followed other 1990s films that glorified thug life, including *New Jack City, Juice,* and *Boyz N the Hood.*

STEREOTYPING

Close your eyes. Think "professor." What image forms in your mind? Before 1973 most people would have envisioned a harmless, absent-minded eccentric. Today, the image is more likely to be the brilliant, sometimes brutal Professor Kingsfield portrayed by John Houseman in the 1973 movie and subsequent television series *The Paper Chase*. Both the absent-minded pre-1973 professor and the steel-trap post-1973

Kingsfield are images known as stereotypes. Both flow from the mass media. While neither is an accurate generalization about professors, both have long-term impact.

Stereotyping is a kind of shorthand that can facilitate communication. Putting a cowboy in a black hat allows a movie director to sidestep complex character explanation and move quickly into a story line, because moviegoers hold a generalization about cowboys in black hats. They are the bad guys—a stereotype. Newspaper editors pack lots of information into headlines by drawing on stereotypes held by the readers. Consider the extra meanings implicit in headlines that refer to a "Separatist," a "Mountie," or a "college jock." Stereotypes paint broad strokes that help create impact in media messages, but they are also a problem. A generalization, no matter how useful, is inaccurate. Not all Scots are cheap, nor are all Bay Street brokers crooked, nor are all college jocks dumb—not even a majority.

By using stereotypes, the mass media perpetuate them. With benign stereotypes, there is no problem, but the media can perpetuate social injustice with stereotypes. In the late 1970s, the U.S. Civil Rights Commission found that blacks on network television were portrayed disproportionately in immature, demeaning, or comic roles. By using a stereotype, television was not only perpetuating false generalizations but also being racist. Worse, network thoughtlessness was robbing black people of strong role models.

Feminists have levelled objections that women are both underrepresented and misrepresented in the media. One study by sociologist Eve Simson found that most female television parts were decorative, played by pretty California women in their 20s. Worse were the occupations represented by women, said Simson. Most frequent were prostitutes, at 16 percent. Traditional female occupations—secretaries, nurses, flight attendants, and receptionists—represented 17 percent. Career women tended to be man-haters or domestic failures. Said Simson, "With nearly every family, regardless of socioeconomic class, having at least one TV set and the average set being turned on 6.3 hours per day, TV has emerged as an important source for promulgating attitudes, values and customs. For some viewers, it is the only major contact with outside 'reality,' including how to relate to women. Thus, not only is TV's sexism insulting, but it is also detrimental to the status of women."

Media critics like Simson call for the media to become activists to revise demeaning stereotypes. While often right-minded, such calls can interfere with accurate portrayals. In the 1970s, Italian-American activists, for example, lobbied successfully against Mafia characters being identified as Italian.

SOCIALIZATION VIA EAVESDROPPING

The mass media, especially television, have eroded the boundaries that people once respected between the generations, genders, and other social institutions. Once adults whispered when they wanted to discuss certain subjects, like sex, when children were around. Today, children eavesdrop on all kinds of adult topics by seeing them depicted on television. Though meant as a joke, these lines ring true today to many squirming parents:

> **Father to Friend:** My son and I had that father-and-son talk about the birds and the bees yesterday.
>
> **Friend:** Did you learn anything?

Joshua Meyrowitz, a communication scholar, brought the new socialization effects of intergenerational eavesdropping to wide attention with his 1985 book, *No*

Media Awareness Network: A Canadian organization dedicated to media education and media issues affecting children and youth.

www.media-awareness.ca

Parents Television Council: This U.S. organization lobbies for positive, family-oriented television programming.

www.parentstv.org

Canada Deals with Media Violence: This essay at the Canadian Broadcast Standards Council's website traces the history of Canadian regulation of media violence and provides links to many of the primary documents in the debate.

www.cbsc.ca/english/canada.htm

Approaches to Television Violence: The CRTC's site about violence on Canadian television. Includes information about Canadian approaches to television, a bibliography, and source materials.

www.crtc.gc.ca/eng/social/tv.htm

Sense of Place. In effect, the old socially recognized institution of childhood, which long had been protected from "big-people issues" like money, divorce, and sex, was disappearing. From television sitcoms, kids today learn that adults fight and goof up and sometimes are just plain silly. These are things kids may always have been aware of in a vague sense, but now they have front-row seats.

Television also cracked other protected societal institutions, such as the "man's world." Through television, many women entered the man's world of the locker room, the fishing trip, and the workplace beyond the home. Older mass media, including books, had dealt with a diversity of topics and allowed people in on the "secrets" of other groups, but the ubiquity of television and the ease of access to it accelerated the breakdown of traditional institutional barriers.

Media-Depicted Violence

TELEVISION VIOLENCE AND CANADIAN CHILDREN

Consider the following:

- The average Canadian child spends about the same amount of time watching television as he or she does in school.
- By the time a Canadian child reaches 12 years of age, she or he has seen an average of 12 000 violent deaths on television.
- According to a University of Laval study, children's programs contain 68 percent more violence than programs for adults.

Violence and its effect on children has been an important political issue for Canadians in recent years. In 1990, a group of school-age children presented a petition with over 150 000 names to the Federal Minister of Communications, urging the government to "enact rules to eliminate violent and war programming for children on television." The issue became more meaningful in 1992, when Virginie Lariviere presented Prime Minister Brian Mulroney with a petition with 1.3 million names asking him to initiate legislation that would require broadcasters to reduce the level of violent programming on television, and asking Canadians to boycott violent TV shows. Lariviere's sister, Marie-Eve, was robbed, sexually assaulted, and murdered. Virginie Lariviere believed that violence on television was a factor in influencing her sister's murderer.

LEARNING ABOUT VIOLENCE

The mass media help bring young people into society's mainstream by demonstrating dominant behaviours and norms. This prosocial process, called **observational learning,** turns dark, however, when children learn deviant behaviours from the media. In Manteca, California, two teenagers, one only 13, lay in wait for a friend's father in his own house and attacked him. They beat him with a fireplace poker, kicked him and stabbed him, and choked him to death with a dog chain. Then they poured salt in his wounds. Why the final act of violence, the salt in the wounds? The 13-year-old explained that he had seen it on television. While there is no question that people can learn about violent behaviour from the media, a major issue of our time is whether the mass media are the cause of aberrant behaviour.

Individuals on trial for criminal acts occasionally plead that "the media made me do it." That was the defence in a 1974 California case in which two young girls

Wow, Pow, Zap. The notion that media-depicted violence triggers real-life violence gained currency in the 1960s after researcher Albert Bandura wrote a *Look* magazine article about his Bobo doll research. Kids in a laboratory began really whacking Bobos after seeing people doing the same thing in a film. There is a continuing debate, however, about whether people were accurate in inferring that media violence directly causes real violence. Bandura himself has been dismayed at some of the simplistic conclusions that have been drawn from the *Look* article.

playing on a beach were raped with a beer bottle by four teenagers. The rapists told police they had picked up the idea from a television movie they had seen four days earlier. In the movie, a young woman was raped with a broom handle, and in court, the youths' lawyers blamed the movie. The judge, as is typical in such cases, threw out media-projected violence as an unacceptable scapegoating defence and held the young perpetrators responsible.

Although the courts have never accepted transfer of responsibility as a legal defence, it is clear that violent behaviour can be imitated from the media. Some experts, however, say that the negative effect of media-depicted violence is too often overstated and that media violence actually has a positive side.

MEDIA VIOLENCE AS POSITIVE

People who downplay the effect of media portrayals of blood, guts, and violence often refer to a **cathartic effect**. This theory, which dates to ancient Greece and the philosopher **Aristotle,** suggests that watching violence allows individuals vicariously to release pent-up everyday frustration that might otherwise explode dangerously. By seeing violence, so goes the theory, people let off steam. Most advocates of the cathartic effect claim that individuals who see violent activity are stimulated to fantasy violence, which drains off latent tendencies toward real-life violence.

In more recent times, scholar **Seymour Feshbach** has conducted studies that lend support to the cathartic effect theory. In one study, Feshbach lined up 625 junior high school boys at seven California boarding schools and showed half of them a steady diet of violent television programs for six weeks. The other half were shown nonviolent fare. Every day during the study, teachers and supervisors reported on each boy's behaviour in and out of class. Feshbach found no difference in aggressive behaviour between the two groups. Further, there was a decline in aggression among boys watching violence who were determined by personality tests to be more inclined toward aggressive behaviour.

Opponents of the cathartic effect theory, who include both respected researchers as well as reflexive media bashers, were quick to point out flaws in Feshbach's research methods. Nonetheless, his conclusions carried considerable weight because of the study's unprecedented massiveness—625 individuals. Also, the study was conducted in a real-life environment rather than in a laboratory, and there was a consistency in the findings.

PRODDING SOCIALLY POSITIVE ACTION

Besides the cathartic effects theory, an argument for portraying violence is that it prompts people to socially positive action. This happened after NBC aired *The Burning Bed*, a television movie about an abused woman who could not take it any more and set fire to her sleeping husband. The night the movie was shown, battered-spouse centres were overwhelmed with calls from women who had been putting off doing anything to extricate themselves from relationships with abusive mates.

On the negative side, one man set his estranged wife afire and explained that he was inspired by *The Burning Bed*. Another man who beat his wife senseless gave the same explanation.

MEDIA VIOLENCE AS NEGATIVE

The preponderance of evidence is that media-depicted violence has the potential to cue real-life violence—even in Canadian cities and towns like Orleans, Ontario, and Taber, Alberta—and most catharsis theorists concede that this is a possibility. The **aggressive stimulation** theory, however, is often overstated to the point that it comes across smacking of the now generally discredited bullet, or hypodermic needle, theory of mass communication. The fact is that few people act out media violence in their own lives.

Albert Bandura: Further information about Albert Bandura and his controversial Bobo doll studies.

www.criminology.fsu.edu/ crimtheory/bandura.htm

An exaggerated reading of the aggressive stimulation theory became impressed in the public mind, indelibly it seems, after a 1963 *Look* magazine article by Stanford University researcher **Albert Bandura**. In his research, Bandura had found that there was an increase in aggressive responses by children shown films of people aggressively punching and beating on large inflated clowns called Bobos. After the film, the children's toys were taken away except for a Bobo doll, which, Bandura reported, was given a beating—just like in the film. The inference was that the children modelled their behaviour in the film violence. Bandura also conducted other experiments that all pointed in the same direction.

The **Bobo doll studies** gained wide attention, but, as with most research on the contentious media-triggered violence issue, other scholars eventually became critical of Bandura's research methodologies. One criticism is that he mistook child playfulness with the Bobo dolls for aggressiveness. Even so, everyone who has been stirred

Theodore Tugboat. Canadian programs like *Theodore Tugboat* don't resort to the violence of other popular children's shows like *Sailor Moon*. Psychologists such as Wendy Josephson argue that children's programming doesn't need violence or rapid editing to be effective.

to excitement by a violent movie knows from personal experience that there is an effect, and the early publicity on the Bobo studies seemed to verify that growing societal violence was caused by the media.

CANADIAN RESEARCH

A media researcher from the University of Winnipeg, **Wendy Josephson**, challenges some of the most common criticisms about the links between violence on television and increased levels of aggression in children. For example, while some may argue that there is no conclusive proof that watching violence on television will cause violent behaviour in children, Josephson says we should simply look at recent research studies: the vast majority of reports, including studies by the CRTC, the House of Commons Standing Committee on Communications and Culture, and the Royal Commission on Violence in the Communications Industry, claim there is a link between television viewing and violence. She claims that although earlier studies from the 1950s and 1960s might have been methodologically flawed, recent studies have improved research designs and, as a result, provide more reliable data.

Some of the other assumptions Josephson challenges include these:

- *The effect is too small to make a difference.* While television is only one agent of socialization that will influence how aggressive a child is, it is probably just as important as other variables like social class and gender, while being easier to control.

- *There is no clear definition of violence.* Different researchers may have used various definitions of what violent behaviour is, but they have a common theme—one person deliberately hurting another. When Canadians talk about violence, we refer to a set of shared experiences and examples.
- *Violence on television only reflects the violent society we live in.* This is absolutely untrue, says Josephson. Television crime is about 10 times more violent than crime in real life. Saturday morning cartoons are particularly violent. The average cartoon has about 20 to 25 violent acts per hour; in prime time, there are about five violent acts per hour.
- *Violence is on TV because that's what people want to watch.* Some research indicates that while violence may be a selling feature of both children's and adults' programs, there are other conventions of television, such as fast-paced editing, which make programs popular among children. Josephson says that it's the producers of television who use violence to their own advantage. The story lines of many children's shows are similar—simple conflict that can be communicated visually, fast-paced action, the building of suspense, and action that is easy to break up by commercials. In short, producers use violence as a hook to keep kids tuned in to their programs.

Josephson also asks Canadian television producers to try to avoid this kind of hook. She urges producers of children's shows to reduce the amount of violence and to contextualize the violence that is still included. Violence should not be used simply as comic relief or as an easy way to solve problems. The consequences of these acts need to be addressed, especially in programming for older children and teens. As for networks and television stations, she suggests they be careful when scheduling programs early in the day or late in the afternoon as this is prime time for many Canadian children, especially for "latch-key" kids who get home before their parents.

CATALYTIC THEORY

Simplistic readings of both cathartic and aggressive stimulation effects research can yield extreme conclusions. A careful reading, however, points more to the media having a role in real-life violence but not necessarily triggering it and doing so only infrequently—and only if several non-media factors are also present. For example, evidence suggests that television and movie violence, even in cartoons, is arousing and can excite some children to violence, especially hyperactive and easily excitable children. These children, like unstable adults, become wrapped up psychologically with the portrayals and are stirred to the point of acting out. However, this happens only when a combination of other influences is also present. Among these other influences are:

- *Whether violence portrayed in the media is rewarded.* In 1984 researcher David Phillips found that the murder rate increases after publicized prizefights, in which the victor is rewarded, and decreases after publicized murder trials and executions, in which, of course, violence is punished.

- *Whether media exposure is heavy.* A lesson from Monroe Lefkowitz's research and dozens of other studies is that aggressive behavioural tendencies are strongest among people who see a lot of media-depicted violence. This suggests a cumulative media effect rather than a single hypodermic injection leading to violence.

■ *Whether a violent person fits other profiles.* Studies have found correlations between aggressive behaviour and many variables besides violence viewing. These include income, education, intelligence, and parental child-rearing practices. This is not to say that any of these third variables cause violent behaviour. The suggestion, rather, is that violence is far too complex to be explained by a single factor.

Most researchers note too that screen-triggered violence is increased if the aggression:

■ Is realistic and exciting, like a chase or suspense sequence that sends adrenalin levels surging.
■ Succeeds in righting a wrong, like helping an abused or ridiculed character get even.
■ Includes situations or characters similar to those in the viewer's own experience.

All these things would prompt a scientist to call media violence a catalyst. Just as the presence of a certain element will allow other elements to react explosively but itself not be part of the explosion, the presence of media violence can be a factor in real-life violence but not a cause by itself. This **catalytic theory** was articulated by scholars **Wilbur Schramm**, Jack Lyle, and Edwin Parker, who investigated the effects of television on children and came up with this statement in their 1961 book *Television in the Lives of Our Children*, which has become a classic on the effects of media-depicted violence on individuals: "For *some* children under *some* conditions, *some* television is harmful. For *other* children under the same conditions, or for the same children under *other* conditions, it may be beneficial. For *most* children, under *most* conditions, *most* television is probably neither particularly harmful nor particularly beneficial."

SOCIETALLY DEBILITATING EFFECTS

Media-depicted violence scares far more people than it inspires to violence, and this, according to **George Gerbner**, a leading researcher on screen violence, leads some people to believe the world is more dangerous than it really is. Gerbner calculates that 1 in 10 television characters is involved in violence in any given week. In real life, the chances are only about 1 in 100 per year. People who watch a lot of television, Gerbner found, see their own chances of being involved in violence nearer the distorted television level than their local crime statistics or even their own experience would suggest. It seems that television violence leads people to think they are in far greater real-life jeopardy than they really are.

The implications of Gerbner's findings go to the heart of a free and democratic society. With exaggerated fears about their safety, Gerbner says, people will demand greater police protection. They are also likelier, he says, to submit to established authority and even to accept police violence as a trade-off for their own security.

TOLERANCE OF VIOLENCE

An especially serious concern about media-depicted violence is that it has a numbing, callusing effect on people. This **desensitizing theory**, which is widely held, says not only that individuals are becoming hardened by media violence but also that society's tolerance for such antisocial behaviour is increasing.

Media People

George Gerbner

George Gerbner

George Gerbner worries a lot about media violence. And he's been doing this longer than just about anybody else. In 1967 Gerbner and colleagues at the University of Pennsylvania created a television violence index and began counting acts of violence. Today, more than three decades later, the numbers are startling. Gerbner calculates the typical American 18-year-old has seen 32 000 murders and 40 000 attempted murders at home on television.

In a dubious sense, there may be good news for those who fear the effects of media violence. Gerbner's index has found no significant change in the volume of violence since the mid-1970s. It may be maxed out.

Gerbner theorizes that the media violence has negative effects on society. It's what he calls "the mean-world syndrome." As he sees it, people exposed to so much violence come to perceive the world as a far more dangerous place than it really is. One of his concerns is that people become overly concerned for their own safety and, in time, may become willing to accept a police state to ensure their personal security. That, he says, has dire consequences for the free and open society that has been a valued hallmark of the North American lifestyle.

Are there answers? Gerbner notes that the global conglomeration of mass media companies works against any kind of media self-policing. These companies are seeking worldwide outlets for their products, whether movies, television programs, or music, and violence doesn't require any kind of costly translations. "Violence travels well," he says. Also, violence has low production costs.

Gerbner notes that violence is an easy fill for weak spots in a television story line. Also, in television, violence is an effective cliff-hanger before a commercial break.

While Gerbner's stats are unsettling, he has critics who say his numbers make the situation seem worse than it really is. The Gerbner index scores acts of violence without considering their context. That means when Bugs Bunny is bopped on the head, it counts the same as Rambo doing the same thing to a vile villain in a skull-crushing, blood-spurting scene. A poke in the eye on *The Three Stooges* also scores as a violent act.

Despite his critics, Gerbner has provided a baseline for measuring changes in the quantity of television violence. Virtually every scholar cites him in the ongoing struggle to figure out whether media violence is something that should worry us all.

Media critics say the media are responsible for this desensitization, but many media people, particularly movie and television directors, respond that it is the desensitization that has forced them to make the violence in their shows even more graphic. They explain that they have run out of alternatives to get the point across when the story line requires that the audience be repulsed. Some movie critics, of course, find this explanation a little too convenient for gore-inclined moviemakers and television directors, but even directors not inclined to gratuitous violence feel their options for stirring the audience have become scarcer. The critics respond that this is a chicken-or-egg question and that the media are in no position to use the desensitization theory to excuse increasing violence in their products if they themselves contributed to the desensitization. And so the argument goes on about who is to blame.

Desensitization is apparent in news also. The absolute ban on showing the bodies of crime and accident victims in newspapers and on television newscasts, almost universal a few years ago, is becoming a thing of the past. No longer do newsroom practices forbid showing body bags or even bodies. During the 1991 Persian Gulf war, U.S. television had no reluctance about airing videos of allied troops picking up the bodies of hundreds of strafed Iraqi soldiers and hurling them, like sacks of flour, onto flatbed trucks for hauling to deep trenches, where the cameras recorded the heaped bodies being unceremoniously bulldozed over with sand.

In summary, we know far less about media violence than we need to. Various theories explain some phenomena, but the theories themselves do not dovetail. The desensitizing theory, for example, explains audience acceptance of more violence, but it hardly explains research findings that people who watch a lot of television actually have heightened anxiety about their personal safety. People fretting about their own safety hardly are desensitized.

CANADA'S BROADCASTERS RESPOND TO THE ISSUE OF VIOLENCE ON TV

Canadian broadcasters have had a violence code since 1987. However, with the social and political developments brought about by the Lariviere petition in 1992, the Canadian Association of Broadcasters and the CRTC took a hard look at the issue. In 1993, Lariviere's petition was the subject of a Standing Committee on Communications and Culture. This, in combination with two conferences on the effects of violence on children, led to the creation of the **AGVOT**: the Action Group on Violence on Television. Members included the CAB, the CBC, the Canadian Cable Television Association, the Association of Canadian Advertisers, and the Canadian Film and Television Producers Association.

A new violence code was introduced by AGVOT in late 1993. Some of the main elements of the code's rules for programming aimed at children under 12 years of age involve the following criteria:

- Only violence essential to the plot is allowed.
- Violence can't be the central theme in cartoons.
- Violence can't be seen as the only way to resolve conflict.
- Realistic scenes of violence that downgrade the effects of violent behaviour are not allowed.
- Programming can't invite imitation of violent or perilous acts.

For children over 12 years of age, the hour of 9 p.m. has become what AGVOT refers to as the "watershed" hour. In addition, a viewer advisory must accompany any program with violence, nudity, or strong language.

THE V-CHIP

The next step towards solving the problem was to be a piece of technology developed in Canada. That technology was a device that has become known as the **V-chip**. One Canadian concerned about the effects of television violence on his children is Tim Collings, who teaches engineering at Simon Fraser University. His solution: the violence-chip, or V-chip for short. Once installed inside the television, the chip will allow parents to predetermine what level of violence is acceptable.

Shows are rated on the following scale of acceptable levels of sex, language, and violence:

This rating is embedded into the signal in much the same way as is closed-captioning. Parents and caregivers simply take their remote control and enter the

Mediascope: U.S.-based nonprofit organization promoting issues of social relevance within the entertainment industry.

www.mediascope.org

V-Chip: An essay by Brian Burke, Director of the U.S. Center for Educational Priorities, opposing the implementation of the V-chip.

www.cep.org/vchip.html

Desensitization. Critics of media violence say movies like *The Exorcist* desensitize people, especially teenagers, to the horrors of violence. That concern extends to video games. In one, Carmaggedon, kids are encouraged on the packaging blurb, "Don't slow down to avoid hitting that pedestrian crossing the street—aim, rev up and rack up those points." In one sequence in the Mortal Kombat video game, a crowd shouts encouragement for Kano to rip the heart out of Scorpion, his downed protagonist. Kano waves the dismembered heart to the crowd, which roars approvingly. Although scholars disagree about whether media violence begets real-life violence, most do agree that media violence leaves people more accepting of violence around them in their everyday lives.

violence level that is appropriate, depending on the time of day and who's watching. If the level of violence coded into a program exceeds the pre-set level, the TV will block out the show.

Viewing Level	Violence	Language	Sexuality
0	None	None	None
1	Comedic	Suggestive	Mature themes
2	Mild	Mild	Brief nudity
3	Brief	Coarse	Mild sexuality
4	Violence	Strong	Full nudity
5	Graphic	Explicit	Explicit sexual nudity

Agenda-Setting by the Media

MEDIA SELECTION OF ISSUES

When the New York police wanted more subway patrols, their union public relations person asked officers to call him with every subway crime. He passed the accounts, all of them, on to newspapers and television and radio stations. He could not have been more pleased with his media blitz. News coverage of subway crime, he later boasted, increased several thousand percent, although there had been no appreciable change in the crime rate itself. Suddenly, for no reason other than dramatically stepped-up coverage, people were alarmed. Their personal agendas of what to think about—and worry about—had changed. The sudden new concern, which made it easier for the union to argue for more subway patrols, was an example of media agenda-setting at work. The police's PR person lured news media decision makers into putting subway crime higher on their lists of issues to be covered, and individuals moved it up on their lists of personal concerns.

The agenda-setting phenomenon has been recognized for a long time. Sociologist **Robert Park,** writing in the 1920s, articulated the theory in rejecting the once-popular notion that the media tell people what to think. As Park saw it, the media create awareness of issues more than they create knowledge or attitudes. Today, agenda-setting theorists put it this way: The media do not tell people what to think but what to think about. Agenda-setting occurs at several levels:

CREATING AWARENESS.   Only if individuals are aware of an issue can they be concerned about it. Concern about parents who kill their children becomes a major issue with media coverage of spectacular cases. In 1994 Susan Smith, a South Carolina woman, attracted wide attention with her horrific report that her sons, ages three and one, had been kidnapped. The story darkened later when the woman confessed to driving the family car into the lake and drowning the boys herself. Over several days of intense media attention, the public learned not only the morbid details of what happened but also became better informed about a wide range of parental, family, and legal issues that the coverage brought to the fore.

ESTABLISHING PRIORITIES.   People trust the news media to sort through the events of the day and make order of them. Lead-off stories on a newscast or on page one are expected to be the most significant. Not only does how a story is played affect people's agendas, but so do the time and space afforded it. Lavish graphics can propel an item higher.

PERPETUATING ISSUES.   Continuing coverage lends importance to an issue. A single story on a bribed senator might soon be forgotten, but day-after-day follow-ups can fuel ethics reforms. Conversely, if gatekeepers are diverted to other stories, a hot issue can cool overnight—out of sight, out of mind.

INTRAMEDIA AGENDA-SETTING

Agenda-setting also is a phenomenon that affects media people, who constantly monitor one another. Reporters and editors are often more concerned with how their peers are handling a story than with what their audience wants. Sometimes the media harp on one topic, making it seem more important than it really is, until it becomes tedious.

The media's agenda-setting role extends beyond news. Over time, lifestyles and values portrayed in the media can influence not just what people think about but what they do. Hugh Hefner's *Playboy* magazine of the 1950s helped to usher in the sexual revolution. Advertising has created a redefinition of our values by whetting an appetite for possessions and glamorizing immediate gratification.

Even so, individuals exercise a high degree of control in their personal agendas. For decades, William Randolph Hearst campaigned with front-page editorials in all his newspapers against using animals in research, but animal rights did not become a pressing public issue. Even with the extensive media coverage of the Constitutional debate, polls found that many Canadians were still apathetic about the state of the nation. For the most part, these were people who chose to tune out the coverage. The fact is that journalists and other creators of media messages cannot automatically impose their agendas on individuals. If people are not interested, an issue won't become part of their agendas. The individual values at work in the processes of selective exposure, perception, and retention can thwart media leadership in agenda-setting.

Also, media agendas are not decided in a vacuum. Dependent as they are on having mass audiences, the media take cues for their coverage from their audiences. Penny press editors in the 1830s looked over the shoulders of newspaper readers on the street to see what stories attracted them and then shaped their coverage accordingly. Today, news organizations tap the public pulse through scientific sampling to deliver what people want. The mass media both exert leadership in agenda-setting and mirror the agendas of their audiences.

Media-Induced Anxiety and Apathy

INFORMATION ANXIETY

While educated people traditionally have thirsted for information, the quantity has become such that many people feel overwhelmed by what is called **information pollution**. We are awash in it and drowning, and the mass media are a factor in this. Consider college students on campus:

- They pass newspaper vending machines and racks with a dozen different papers—dailies, weeklies, freebies—en route to class.
- On the radio, they have access to 40 stations.
- In their mailbox, they find a solicitation for discount subscriptions to 240 magazines. Plus, there is "spam" in their e-mail box.
- They turn on their television during a study break and need to choose from over 200 TV and music channels on satellite. Plus there are thousands of MP3 files to choose from online.
- At lunch, they notice advertisements everywhere—on the placemat, on the milk carton, on table stand-ups, on the butter pat, on the walls, on the radio coming over the public-address system, on the pen used to write a cheque.
- At the library, they have almost instant online access through computer systems to more information than any human being could possibly deal with.

Compounding the quantity of information available is the accelerating rate at which it is available. Trend analyst John Naisbitt has made the point with this example: When President Lincoln was shot in 1865, people in London learned about it five days later. When President Reagan was shot in 1981, journalist Henry Fairlie, in his office one block away, heard about the assassination attempt from his London editor who had seen it on television and phoned Fairlie to get him to go to the scene. Databases to which almost every college student today has access are updated day by day, hour by hour, even second by second. Even a relatively slender weekday edition of the *New York Times* contains more information than the average person in the 17th century was likely to come across in a lifetime, according to Richard Saul Wurman in his book *Information Anxiety*.

The solution is knowing how to locate relevant information and tune out the rest, but even this is increasingly difficult. Naisbitt reported in *Megatrends* that scientists planning an experiment are spending more time figuring out whether someone somewhere already has done the experiment than conducting the experiment itself.

On some matters, many people do not even try to sort through all the information that they have available. Their solution to information anxiety is to give up. Other people have a false sense of being on top of things, especially public issues, because so much information is available.

MEDIA-INDUCED PASSIVITY

One effect of the mass media is embodied in the stereotypical couch potato, whose greatest physical and mental exercise is heading to the refrigerator during commercials. Studies indicate that the typical North American spends four to six hours a day with the mass media, mostly with television. The experience is primarily passive, and such **media-induced passivity** has been blamed, along with greater mobility and access to more leisure activities, for major changes in how people live their lives. For example, the role of church auxiliaries and lodges, once central in community social life with weekly activities, has diminished. Neighbourhood taverns were the centre of political discussion in many areas, but this is less true today. Despite the fitness and wellness craze, more people than ever are overweight and out of shape, which can be partly attributed to physical passivity induced by television and media-based homebound activities.

While these phenomena may be explained in part by people's increased use of the mass media and the attendant passivity, it would be a mistake not to recognize that social forces besides the media have contributed to them.

WELL-INFORMED FUTILITY

The news media take pride in purveying information to help people be active and involved in public matters, but, ironically, the media contribute insidiously to passivity by lulling people into accepting news reports as the last word on a subject. To attract and impress audiences, reporters use techniques to enhance their credibility, coming across as more authoritative than they really are and making their stories seem comprehensive and complete. Consider the well-groomed, clear-spoken television reporter on Parliament Hill whose 40-second report seems to address all inherent questions. The slickness in presentation works against the journalistic ideal of promoting intelligent citizen involvement in the political and social process by seeming to be so complete that nothing more can be said. The result is called the syndrome of well-informed futility. Readers, listeners, and viewers feel satisfied that they're fully informed, which becomes an end in itself rather than actual involvement. This phenomenon works against democracy, which is predicated on citizen involvement, not apathy.

As agenda-setters, the mass media may also be working against the democratic ideal. The greater the role of the media in choosing the society's issues and fashions and even setting the values, the lesser the role of the people at a grassroots level.

CHAPTER WRAP-UP

The mass media influence us, but scholars are divided about how much. There is agreement that the media help initiate children into society by portraying social and cultural values. This is a serious responsibility because portrayals of aberrant behaviour, like violence, have effects, although we are not sure about their extent. This is not to say that individuals are unwitting pawns of the mass media. People choose what they read and what they tune in to, and they generally filter the information and images to conform with their preconceived notions and personal values.

In other respects too, the mass media are a stabilizing influence. The media try to fit into the lives of their audiences. An example is children's television programs on weekend mornings when kids are home from school but still on an early-rising schedule. The media not only react to audience lifestyles but also contribute to the patterns by which people live their lives, like going to bed after the late news. In short, the media have effects on individuals and on society, but it is a two-way street. Society is a shaper of media content, but individuals make the ultimate decisions about subscribing, listening, and watching. The influence issue is a complex problem that merits further research and thought.

QUESTIONS FOR REVIEW

1. Why have most media scholars abandoned the powerful and minimalist effect theories for the cumulative theory?

2. What is the uses and gratifications approach to mass media studies?

3. Do individuals have any control over mass media effects on them?

4. What role do the mass media have in socializing children?

5. How do scholars differ on whether media-depicted violence triggers aggressive behaviour? How does the work of Wendy Josephson deal with the issue?

6. What is meant when someone says: "The mass media don't tell people what to think as much as tell them what to think about"?

7. Does being informed by mass media necessarily improve citizen involvement in political processes?

8. What is AGVOT's role in the issue of media violence?

9. How does the V-chip work?

QUESTIONS FOR CRITICAL THINKING

1. Although generally discredited by scholars now, the powerful effects theory once had many adherents. How do you explain the lingering popularity of this thinking among many people?

2. Name at least three opinion leaders who influence you on issues that you do not follow closely in the media. On what issues are you yourself an opinion leader?

3. Give specific examples of each of the seven primary mass media contributing to the lifelong socialization process. For starters, consider a current nonfiction best-selling book.

4. Explain how selective exposure, selective perception, and selective retention would work in the imaginary case of a devout Muslim who was studying English literature at Harvard University

at the time Salman Rushdie's book *The Satanic Verses* was published. You may want to check newsmagazines in February and March 1989 for background.

5. Discuss the human needs that the mass media help satisfy in terms of the news and entertainment media.

6. Among the functions that the mass media serve for individuals are diversion and escape. Is this healthy?

7. Explain the prosocial potential of the mass media in culturization and socialization. What about the media as an antisocial force in observational learning?

8. Cite at least three contemporary role models who you can argue are positive. Explain how they might also be viewed as negative. Cite three role models who you can argue are negative.

9. What stereotype comes to your mind with the term *Uncle Remus*? Is your image of Uncle Remus one that would be held universally? Why or why not?

10. How can serious scholars of mass communication hold such diverse ideas as the cathartic, aggressive stimulation, and catalytic theories? Which camp is right?

11. Compare American programming to Canadian programming. Which is more violent? Why?

12. What problems can you foresee with the V-chip?

FOR KEEPING UP TO DATE

Among numerous scholarly journals that publish research on media effects are the *Journal of Communication*, *Journalism Quarterly*, *Journal of Broadcasting &; Electronic Media*, *The Canadian Journal of Communication*, and *Mass Communication Review*.

Also valuable is *Mass Communication Review Yearbook*, which is published annually by Sage.

FOR FURTHER LEARNING

Joe Chidley. "Toxic TV." *Maclean's* (June 17, 1996).

George Comstock. *Television in America* (Sage, 1980).

Diana Coulter. "A Kid's Eye View of TV." *Toronto Star* (May 31, 1996).

Tanya Davis. "The Ratings Game." *Maclean's* (June 17, 1996).

Cham Eyal, Jim Winter, and Maxwell McCombs. "The Agenda-Setting Role in Mass Communication." In Michael Emery and Ted Curtis Smythe, *Reading in Mass Communication: Concepts and Issues in the Mass Media*, 6th ed. (Wm. C. Brown, 1986), 169–174.

Leo W. Jeffres. *Mass Media: Processes and Effects* (Waveland, 1986).

Michael Jenkinson. "How to Clean Up the Wasteland." *Western Report* (March 18, 1996).

Wendy L. Josephson, Ph. D. *Television Violence: A Review of the Effects on Children of Different Ages* (Department of Canadian Heritage, 1995).

Robert M. Liebert, Joyce N. Spafkin, and Emily S. Davidson. *The Early Window: Effects of Television on Children and Youth*, 2nd ed. (Pergamon, 1985).

Joshua Meyrowitz. *No Sense of Place: The Impact of Electronic Media on Social Behaviour* (Oxford, 1985).

John Naisbitt. *Megatrends: Ten New Directions Transforming Our Lives* (Warner, 1982).

Williard D. Rowland, Jr. *The Politics of TV Violence: Policy Uses of Communication Research* (Sage, 1983).

Richard Saul Wurman. *Information Anxiety* (Doubleday, 1989).

Marshall McLuhan. The controversial Canadian theorist blamed Gutenberg for social alienation, but not all was lost. He also foresaw a transforming global village.

Mass Media and Society

Media in Theory

The Global Village

An intriguing, contrarian assessment of the media's effects on human society was laid out by Canadian theorist **Marshall McLuhan** in the 1960s. McLuhan argued that the print media had **alienated** human beings from their natural state. In pre-mass media times, McLuhan said, people acquired their awareness about their world through their own observation and experience and through their fellow human beings, whom they saw face to face and with whom they communicated orally. As McLuhan saw it, this was a pristine communal existence—rich in that it involved all the senses, sight, sound, smell, taste, and touch. This communal, tribal state was eroded by the written word, which involved the insular, meditative act of reading. The printing press, he said, compounded this alienation from humankind's tribal roots. The written word, by engaging the mind, not the senses, begat **detribalization**, and the printing press accelerated it.

According to McLuhan, the printed word even changed human thought processes. In their tribal state, he said, human beings responded spontaneously to everything that was happening around them. The written word, in contrast, required people to concentrate on an author's relatively narrow, contrived set of data that led from Point A to Point B to Point C. Following the linear serial order of the written word was a lonely, cerebral activity, unlike participatory tribal communication, which had an undirected, helter-skelter spontaneity.

McLuhan saw television bringing back tribalization. While books, magazines, and newspapers engaged the mind, television engaged the senses. In fact, the television screen could be so loaded with data that it could approximate the high level of sensual stimuli that people found in their environments back in the tribal period of human history. Retribalization, he said, was at hand because of the new, intensely sensual communication that television could facilitate. Because television could far exceed the reach of any previous interpersonal communication, McLuhan called the new tribal village a global village.

With retribalization, McLuhan said, people will abandon the print media's linear intrusions on human nature. Was McLuhan right? His disciples claim that certain earmarks of written communication—complex story lines, logical progression, and causality—are less important to today's young people, who grew up with sense-intensive television. They point to music videos, which excite the senses but make no linear sense. Many teachers say children are having a harder time finding significance in the totality of a lesson. Instead, children fasten on to details.

As fascinating as McLuhan was, he left himself vulnerable to critics who point out that, in a true nonlinear spirit, he was selective with evidence and never put his ideas to rigorous scholarly examination. McLuhan died in 1980. Today the jury remains divided, agreeing that he was a provocative thinker.

McLuhan Global Research Network: The online hub for an international McLuhan research network.

www.mcluhan.ca

Mass Media Role in Culture

ELITIST VERSUS POPULIST VALUES

The mass media can enrich society by disseminating the best of human creativity, including great literature, music, and art. The media also carry a lot of lesser things that reflect the culture and, for better or worse, contribute to it. Over time, a continuum has been devised that covers this vast range of artistic material that requires sophisticated and cultivated tastes to appreciate. This is called **high art.** At the other extreme is **low art,** which requires little sophistication to enjoy.

One strain of traditional media criticism has been that the media underplay great works and concentrate on low art. This **elitist** view argues that the mass media do society a disservice by pandering to low tastes. To describe low art, elitists sometimes use the German word **kitsch,** which translates roughly as "garish" or "trashy." The word captures their disdain. In contrast, the **populist** view is that there is nothing unbecoming in the mass media's catering to mass tastes in a democratic, capitalist society.

In a widely cited 1960 essay, "Masscult and Midcult," social commentator **Dwight Macdonald** made a virulent case that all popular art is kitsch. The mass media, which depend on finding large audiences for their economic base, can hardly ever come out at the higher reaches of Macdonald's spectrum.

Assessing Newspapers. The level of intellectual interest that is necessary to enjoy and appreciate high-end news coverage, like that in the *National Post*, is different from that needed to enjoy tabloids, like the *Toronto Sun*. The audiences of such diverse publications correlate with educational background, professional accomplishment, income, and social status.

This kind of elitist analysis was given a larger framework in 1976 when sociologist **Herbert Gans** categorized cultural work along socioeconomic and intellectual lines. Gans said that classical music, as an example, appealed by and large to people of academic and professional accomplishments and higher incomes. These were **high-culture audiences,** which enjoyed complexities and subtleties in their art and entertainment. Next came **middle-culture audiences,** which were less abstract in their interests and liked prime-time television. **Low-culture audiences** were factory and service workers whose interests were more basic; whose educational accomplishments, incomes, and social status were lower; and whose media tastes leaned toward kung fu movies, comic books, and supermarket tabloids.

Gans was applying his contemporary observations to flesh out the distinctions that had been taking form in art criticism for centuries—the distinctions between high art and low art.

HIGHBROW. The high art favoured by elitists generally can be identified by its technical and thematic complexity and originality. High art often is highly individualistic because the creator, whether a novelist or a television producer, has explored issues in fresh ways and often with new and different methods. Even when a collaborative effort, a piece of high art is distinctive. High art requires a sophisticated audience to appreciate it fully. Often it has enduring value, surviving time's test as to its significance and worth.

The sophistication that permits an opera aficionado to appreciate the intricacies of a composer's score, the poetry of the lyricist, and the excellence of the performance sometimes is called **highbrow**. The label has grim origins in the idea that a person must have great intelligence to have refined tastes, and a high "brow" is necessary to accommodate such a big brain. Generally, the term is used by people who disdain those who have not developed the sophistication to enjoy, for example, the abstractions of a Fellini film, a Matisse sculpture, or a Picasso painting. Highbrows generally are people who, as Gans noted, are interested in issues by which society is defining itself and look in literature and drama for stories on conflicts inherent in the human condition and between the individual and society.

MIDDLEBROW. **Middlebrow** tastes recognize some artistic merit but without a high level of sophistication. There is more interest in action than abstractions, in Captain Kirk aboard the Starship *Enterprise* than in the childhood struggles of Ingmar Bergman that shaped his films. In socioeconomic terms, middlebrow appeals to people who take comfort in media portrayals that support their status quo orientation and values.

LOWBROW. Someone once made this often-repeated distinction: highbrows talk about ideas, middlebrows talk about things, and **lowbrows** talk about people. Judging from the success of the *National Enquirer* and other supermarket tabloids, there must be a lot of lowbrows in contemporary North America. Hardly any sophistication is needed to recognize the villainy of Darth Vader, the heroism of Superman, or the sexiness of Catherine Zeta-Jones.

THE CASE AGAINST POP ART

Pop art is of the moment, including things like mood rings, hula-hoops, and grunge garb—and trendy media fare. Even elitists may have fun with pop, but they traditionally have drawn the line at anyone who mistakes it as having serious artistic merit. Pop art is low art that has immense although generally short-lived popularity.

Elitists see pop art as contrived and artificial. In their view, the people who create **popular art** are masters at identifying what will succeed in the marketplace and then providing it. Pop art, according to this view, succeeds by conning people into liking it. When Nehru jackets were the fashion rage in the late 1960s, it was not because they were superior in comfort or utility or aesthetics, but because promoters sensed profits could be made in touting them via the mass media as new and cashing in on easily manipulated mass tastes. It was the same with pet rocks, Tickle Me Elmo, and countless other faddy products.

The mass media, according to the critics, are obsessed with pop art. Partly this is because the media are the carriers of the promotional campaigns that create popular followings but also because competition within the media creates pressure to be first, to be ahead, to be on top of things. The result, say elitists, is that junk takes precedence over quality.

Much is to be said for this criticism of pop art. The promotion of the screwball 1960s sitcom *Beverly Hillbillies*, for example, created an eager audience that otherwise might have been reading Steinbeck's critically respected *Grapes of Wrath*. An elitist might chortle, even laugh at the unbelievable antics and travails of the Beverly Hillbillies, who had their own charm and attractions, but an elitist would be concerned all the while that low art was displacing high art in the marketplace and that the society was the poorer for it.

POP ART REVISIONISM

Pop art has always had a few champions among intellectuals, although the voices of **pop art revisionism** were usually drowned out in the din of elitist pooh-poohing. In 1965, however, essayist **Susan Sontag** wrote an influential piece, "One Culture and the New Sensibility," which prompted many elitists to take a fresh look at pop art.

POP ART AS EVOCATIVE. Sontag made the case that pop art could raise serious issues, just as could high art. She wrote: "The feeling given off by a Ruschenberg painting might be like that of a song by the Supremes." Sontag soon was being called the high priestess of pop intellectualism. More significantly, the Supremes were being taken more seriously, as were a great number of Sontag's avant-garde and obscure pop artist friends.

POPULARIZATION OF HIGH ART. Sontag's argument noted that the mass appeal of pop artists meant that they could convey high art to the masses. A pop pianist like Liberace might omit the trills and other intricacies in performing a sonata, but he nonetheless gave a mass audience an access to Mozart that otherwise would never occur. Sontag saw a valuable service being performed by artists who both understood high art and could "translate" it for unsophisticated audiences, a process known as **popularization.**

As Sontag saw it, the mass media were at the fulcrum in a process that brings diverse kinds of cultural products and audiences together in exciting, enriching ways. The result of popularization, Sontag said, was an elevation of the cultural sensitivity of the whole society.

POP ART AS A SOCIETAL UNIFIER. In effect, Sontag encouraged people not to look at art on the traditional divisive, class-conscious, elitist-populist continuum. Artistic value, she said, could be found almost anywhere. The word "camp" gained circulation among 1960s elitists who were influenced by Sontag. These highbrows began finding a perversely sophisticated appeal in pop art as diverse as Andy Warhol's banal soup cans and the outrageous TV program *Batman*. The mass media, through which most people experienced Warhol and all people experienced *Batman*, became recognized more broadly than ever as a societal unifier.

The Sontag-inspired revisionist look at pop art coincides with the view of many mass media historians that the media have helped bind the society rather than divide it. Radio united Canada effectively in the 1940s. Later, so did network television. In short, the mass media are purveyors of cultural production that contributes to social cohesion, whether it is high art or low art.

HIGH ART AS POPULAR. While kitsch may be prominent in media programming, it hardly elbows out all substantive content. In 1991, for example, Ken Burns's public television documentary *The Civil War* outdrew low-art prime-time network programs five nights in a row. It was a glaring example that high art can appeal to people across almost the whole range of socioeconomic levels and is not necessarily driven out by low art. Burns's documentary was hardly a lone example. Another, also from 1991, was Franco Zeffirelli's movie *Hamlet*, starring pop movie star Mel Gibson, which was marketed to a mass audience and yet could hardly be dismissed by elitists as kitsch.

Social Stability

MEDIA-INDUCED RITUAL

Northwest Airlines pilots, flying their Stratocruisers over the Dakotas in the 1950s, could tell when the late-night news ended on WCCO, the powerful Minneapolis radio station. They could see lights at ranches and towns all across the Dakotas going off as people, having heard the news, went to bed. The 10 o'clock WCCO news had become embedded as a ritual. Today, when most television stations run their late local news at 11 p.m., the commonest time to go to bed is 11:30, after the news. Like other rituals that mark a society, media-induced rituals contribute order and structure to the lives of individuals.

The effect of media-induced rituals extends even further. Collectively, the lifestyles of individuals have broad social effect. Consider just these two effects of evening newspapers, an 1878 media innovation:

EVENING NEWS. E.W. Scripps changed people's habits with his evening newspapers, first in Cleveland and 1878, then elsewhere. Soon evening papers outnumbered morning papers. The new habit, however, was not so much for evening newspapers as for evening news, as newspaper publishers discovered a hundred years later when television siphoned readers away with evening newscasts. The evening ritual persists, even though the medium is changing as evening newspapers go out of business or retreat to mornings.

COMPETITIVE SHOPPING. In the era before refrigeration and packaged foods, household shopping was a daily necessity. When evening newspapers appeared, housewives, who were the primary shoppers of the period, adjusted their routines to read

Cultural Impact. Eddie McGee is overjoyed at being the last person to exit the *Big Brother* house in one of a series of voyeur reality shows that made it big in television in 2000. Many of these shows were spawned from concepts honed by Dutch producer John de Mol. For many, watching *Big Brother* became a ritual. Other recent reality shows have included *Survivor*, *Popstars*, and the History Channel's *Pioneer Quest*.

Demanding a Better Life. Muscovites rioted against their government in 1993 when it became clear that the first-wave, post-Communist reformers could not deliver the Western-style prosperity that the Russian people had learned about through the mass media. They were acting out a process called "diffusion of innovation." Through media coverage of Western consumer economies, the people knew there was a better way, and they wanted their leaders to adopt the innovations that would make them prosperous also.

the paper the evening before their morning trips to the market. The new ritual allowed time for more methodical bargain hunting, which sharpened retail competition.

Besides shaping routines, ritual contributes to the mass media's influence as a shaper of culture. At 8:15 a.m. every Sunday, half the television sets in Japan are tuned to *Serial Novel*, a tear-jerking series that began in the 1950s. Because so many people watch, it is a common experience that is one element in the identification of contemporary Japanese society. A more recent ritual in North American society is watching *Survivor*, and a longstanding Canadian ritual is watching *Hockey Night in Canada* on Saturday nights.

THE MEDIA AND THE STATUS QUO

In their quest for profits through large audiences, the mass media need to tap into their audience's common knowledge and widely felt feelings. Writers for network sitcoms avoid obscure, arcane language. Heroes and villains reflect current morals. Catering this way to a mass audience, the media reinforce existing cultural beliefs and values. People take comfort in learning through the media that they fit into their community and society, which furthers social cohesion. This is socialization continued beyond the formative years. It also is socialization in reverse, with the media taking cues from the society and playing them back.

The media's role in social cohesion has a negative side. Critics say that the media pander to the lowest common denominator by dealing only with things that fit the status quo easily. The result, the critics note, is a thwarting of artistic exploration beyond the mainstream. Critics are especially disparaging of predictable, wooden characters in movies and television and of predictability in the subjects chosen for the news.

Cognitive Dissonance. Many white Americans from racist backgrounds found themselves challenging their own values when the U.S. federal government adopted proactive civil rights policies in the 1950s and 1960s. This dissonance escalated as these people followed news coverage of the long-overdue demands of blacks for fair treatment, as in this 1963 march. Some white racists resolved the discrepancy by abandoning racism. Many others simply retreated from discussion on the issue.

A related negative aspect of the media's role as a contributor to social cohesion is that dominant values too often go unchallenged, which means that some wrong values and practices persist. Dudley Clendinen, a newspaper editor who grew up in the U.S. South, faults journalists for, in effect, defending racism by not covering it:

> The news columns of Southern papers weren't very curious or deep or original in the late 1940s and 1950s. They followed sports and politics actively enough, but the whole rational thrust of Southern culture from the time of John C. Calhoun on had been self-defensive and maintaining. It had to be, to justify the unjustifiable in a society dedicated first to slavery and then to segregation and subservience. Tradition was everything, and the news pages were simply not in the habit of examining the traditions of the South.

THE MEDIA AND COGNITIVE DISSONANCE

The media are not always complacent. Beginning in the late 1950s, after the period to which Clendinen was referring, media attention turned to racial segregation. News coverage, literary comment, and dramatic and comedy portrayals began to point out flaws in the status quo. Consider the effect, through the mass media, of these individuals on racism:

- *John Howard Griffin.* In 1959 Griffin, a white journalist, dyed his skin black for a six-week odyssey through the American South. His book, *Black Like Me*, was an inside look at being black in America. It had special credibility for the white majority because Griffin was white.
- *George Wallace.* The mass audience saw the issue of segregation personified in news coverage of Governor George Wallace physically blocking black students from attending the University of Alabama. The indelible impression was that segregation could be defended only by a clenched fist and not by reason.

- *Martin Luther King Jr.* News photographers captured the courage and conviction of Martin Luther King Jr. and other civil rights activists, black and white, taking great risks through civil disobedience to object to racist public policies.
- *Archie Bunker.* The television sitcom character made a laughingstock of bigots.

To some people, the media coverage and portrayals seemed to exacerbate racial tensions. In the longer run, however, media attention contributed to a new consensus through a phenomenon that psychologists call **cognitive dissonance**. Imagine white racists as they saw George Wallace giving way to U.S. federal troops under orders from the White House. The situation pitted against each other two values held by individual racists—segregation as a value and an ordered society as symbolized by the presidency. Suddenly aware that their personal values were in terrible disharmony, or dissonance, many of these racists avoided the issue. Instead of continuing to express racism among family and friends, many tended to be silent. They may have been as racist as ever, but they were quiet, or watched their words carefully. Gradually their untenable view is fading into social unacceptability. This is not to say that racism does not persist. It does, and continues to manifest itself in North American life although, in many ways, in forms much muted since the media focused on the experiment of John Howard Griffin, the clenched fist of George Wallace, and the crusade of Martin Luther King Jr.

When the media go beyond pap and the predictable, they are examining the cutting-edge issues by which the society defines its values. Newsmagazines, newspapers, and television, utilizing new printing, photography, and video technology in the late 1960s, put war graphically into American living rooms, pointing out all kinds of discrepancies between Pentagon claims and the Vietnam reality. Even the glamorized, heroic view of war, which had persisted through history, was countered by media depictions of the blood and death. Unable to resolve the discrepancies, some people withdrew into silence. Others reassessed their views and then, with changed positions or more confident in their original positions, they engaged in a dialogue from which a consensus emerged. And the United States began a militarily humiliating withdrawal. It was democracy at work, slowly and painfully, but at work.

AGENDA-SETTING AND STATUS CONFERRAL

Media attention lends a legitimacy to events, individuals, and issues that does not extend to things that go uncovered. This conferring of status occurs through the media's role as agenda-setters. It puts everybody on the same wavelength, or at least a similar one, which contributes to social cohesion by focusing our collective attention on issues we can address together. Otherwise, each of us could be going in separate directions, which would make collective action difficult if not impossible.

MEDIA AND MORALITY

A small-town wag once noted that people read the local newspaper not to find out what is going on, which everybody already knows, but to find out who got caught. The observation was profound. The mass media, by reporting deviant behaviour, help enforce society's moral order. When someone is arrested for burglary and sentenced, it reaffirms for everybody that human beings have property rights.

Beyond police blotter news, the mass media are agents for reconciling discrepancies between **private actions** and **public morality**. Individually, people tolerate minor infractions of public morality, like taking pencils home from work. Some people even let life-threatening behaviour go unreported, like child abuse. When the deviant behaviour is publicly exposed, however, toleration ceases and social processes come into action that reconcile the deviance with public morality. The reconciling process maintains public norms and values. Consider Douglas Ginsburg. In the 1970s, Ginsburg, a young law professor, smoked marijuana at a few parties. It was a misdemeanour, but Ginsburg's friends tolerated it, and not a word was said publicly. In 1988, however, when President Reagan nominated Ginsburg to the U.S. Supreme Court, reporter Nina Totenberg of National Public Radio reported Ginsburg's transgressions. Exposed, he withdrew his name. There was no choice. His private action, publicly exposed, could not be tolerated, and his withdrawal maintained public norms and values, without which a society cannot exist.

This same phenomenon occurred in the 1980s when homelessness became a public issue. For years, homeless people in every major city had slept in doorways and alleys and, during winter, at steam vents. The homeless were seen but invisible. When social policies and economic factors in the 1980s sent the numbers skyrocketing, homelessness became a media issue that could not be ignored, and society had to do something. Under the glare of media attention, people brought their private behaviour, which had been to overlook the problem, into conformity with the tenet of public morality that says we are all our brothers' keepers.

Electronic Frontier Canada: Founded to ensure that the principles embodied in the Canadian Charter of Rights and Freedoms remain protected as new computing, communications, and information technologies are introduced into Canadian society.

insight.mcmaster.ca/ org/efc/

Cultural Transmission

HISTORICAL TRANSMISSION

Human beings have a compulsion to leave the wisdom they have accumulated for future generations. There is a compulsion, too, to learn from the past. In olden times, people gathered around campfires and in temples to hear storytellers. It was a ritual through which people learned the values that governed their community. This is a form of **historical transmission**.

Five thousand years ago, the oral tradition was augmented when Middle Eastern traders devised an alphabet to keep track of inventories, transactions, and rates of exchange. When paper was invented, clay tablets gave way to scrolls and eventually books, which became the primary vehicle for storytelling. Religious values were passed on in holy books. Military chronicles laid out the lessons of war. Literature provided lessons by exploring the nooks and crannies of the human condition.

Books remain the primary repository of our culture. For several centuries, it has been between hard covers, in black ink on paper, that the experiences, lessons, and wisdom of our forebears have been recorded for posterity. Other mass media today share in the preservation and transmission of culture over time. For example, the CBC archives include hundreds of hours of radio and TV programs, while the Canadian Science and Technology Museum in Ottawa features a look at the role radio and TV have played in Canadian history.

Friends of Canadian Broadcasting: An organization supporting public broadcasting.

friendscb.org

CONTEMPORARY TRANSMISSION

The mass media also transmit values among contemporary communities and societies, sometimes causing changes that otherwise would not occur. This is known as **contemporary transmission**. Anthropologists have documented that mass communication can change society. When Edmund Carpenter introduced movies in an

Media People

Linda and Robert Lichter

The Lichters and Stanley Rothman

It was love over the statistics. Linda and Robert Lichter met while working on a massive study of major media decision-makers and married. Later, they formed the Center for Media and Public Affairs in Washington, which today is a leading research organization on the mass media and social change. One of the most troubling findings of the Lichters and coresearcher Stanley Rothman is that major media are out of touch with the North American people. This conclusion comes out of massive studies of the people who run the entertainment media.

The Lichter-Rothman studies say that television executives and key creative people are overwhelmingly liberal on the great social issues of our time. More significantly, the studies have found that the programming these people produce reflects their political and social agenda. For example:

- Television scripts favour feminist positions in 71 percent of the shows, far more than public-opinion surveys find among the general population.
- Three percent of television murders are committed by blacks, compared with half in real life.
- Two out of three people are portrayed in positive occupations on television, but only one out of three businesspeople is depicted in a positive role.

These examples, according to the Lichters and Rothman, indicate a bias toward feminism and minority people and against businesspeople. The Lichter-Rothman work documents a dramatic turnaround in television entertainment fare. Two generations ago, leading programs, ranging from sitcoms like *Leave It to Beaver* to dramatic programs like *Wagon Train*, extolled traditional values. In the 1970s came programs like *Mary Tyler Moore* and *All in the Family* that questioned some values. Today, network schedules make plenty of room for programs like *The Simpsons* and *Ally McBeal* that examine nontraditional views and exhibit a dramatically different social orientation than, say, *Leave It to Beaver*.

It is hazardous, of course, to paint too broad a picture of contemporary television, where a sitcom such as *The King of Queens* is much in the 1950s mode, but the Lichters and Rothman, by analyzing 620 shows over a 30-year period, argue persuasively that there has been a dramatic shift. The same might be true of Canadian television. Consider how racial and gender stereotypes have changed from earlier Canadian programs such as *The King of Kensington* to the racial and gender equality seen in shows like *DaVinci's Inquest* and *The Associates*.

Stanley Rothman

isolated New Guinea village, the men adjusted their clothing toward the Western style and even remodelled their houses. This phenomenon, which scholars call **diffusion of innovations,** occurs when ideas move through the mass media. Consider the following:

- *Music, fashion, and pop culture.* In modern-day pop culture, the cues come through the American media, mostly from New York, Hollywood, and Nashville.
- *Developing world innovation.* The United Nations creates instructional films and radio programs to promote agricultural reform in less developed parts of the world. Overpopulated areas have been targets of birth control campaigns.
- *Democracy in China.* As China opened itself to Western tourists, commerce, and mass media in the 1980s, the people glimpsed Western democracy, government, and prosperity, which precipitated pressure on the Communist government to westernize and resulted in the 1989 Tiananmen Square confrontation. A similar phenomenon was a factor in the *glasnost* relaxations in the Soviet Union in the late 1980s.
- *Demise of Main Street.* Small-town businesses are boarding up as rural people see advertisements from regional shopping malls, which are farther away but offer greater variety and lower prices than Main Street Canada.

Scholars note that the mass media can be given too much credit for the diffusion of innovations. Diffusion almost always needs reinforcement through interpersonal communication. Also, the diffusion hardly ever is a one-shot hypodermic injection but a process that requires redundancy in messages over an extended period. The 1989 outburst for democracy in China did not happen because one Chinese person read Thomas Paine one afternoon, nor do rural people suddenly abandon their local Main Street for a Wal-Mart 40 kilometres away. The diffusion of innovations typically involves three initial steps in which the mass media can be pivotal:

Values Transmission. If not for mass media attention to the sexy attire and antics of pop stars such as Britney Spears, not so many young kids would be dressing and acting the way they do. In trivial ways, as with Spears, and in significant ways, as with fundamental social change, the mass media are a factor in diffusing "innovations" that lead eventually to change.

Responding to the *Kursk* Tragedy. Russians demonstrated their dissatisfaction with their government's bungling when the submarine *Kursk* sank off Murmansk, losing all hands. Huge bulletin boards posted with newspapers kept people up to date. At work too was a mass communication process—diffusion of innovation—that Western-style demonstrations against government policy are acceptable, an unthinkable option in earlier periods.

- *Awareness.* Individuals and groups learn about alternatives, new options, and possibilities.
- *Interest.* Once aware, people need to have their interest further whetted.
- *Evaluation.* By considering the experience of other people, as relayed by the mass media, individuals evaluate whether they wish to adopt an innovation.

CHAPTER WRAP-UP

The adoption process has two additional steps in which the media play a small role: the trial stage, in which an innovation is given a try, and the final stage, in which the innovation is either adopted or rejected.

The media contribute both to social stability and to change. A lot of media content gives comfort to audiences by reinforcing existing social values. At the same time, media attention to non-mainstream ideas, in both news and fiction forms, requires people to reassess their values and, over time, contributes to social change.

QUESTIONS FOR REVIEW

1. Why are mass media more interested in reaching large audiences than in contributing to cultural sensitivity?

2. How do the mass media contribute to stability in the society?

3. What are historical and cultural transmission?

4. How did scholar Marshall McLuhan foresee that television would ease the human alienation that he said was created by the mass-produced written word?

QUESTIONS FOR CRITICAL THINKING

1. Why do the mass media find little room for great works that could elevate the cultural sensitivity of the society?

2. Explain essayist Susan Sontag's point that the mass media bring culturally significant works to mass audiences through the popularization process.

3. Give examples of how people shape their everyday lives around rituals created by the mass media. Also, give examples of how the mass media respond to social rituals in deciding what to present and how and when to do it.

4. Why would a radical social reformer object to most mass media content?

5. How has cognitive dissonance created through the mass media worked against racial separatism in American society since the 1950s?

6. How do the mass media help determine the issues that society sees as important?

7. How do the media contribute to social order and cohesion by reporting private acts that deviate from public morality? You might want to consider the coverage given Monica Lewinsky or Chandra Levy in recent years. From a Canadian standpoint, what about "Shawinigate"?

8. Explain Marshall McLuhan's theory that the mass-produced written word has contributed to an alienation of human beings from their true nature. How did McLuhan think television could reverse this alienation?

FOR KEEPING UP TO DATE

Recommended are the *Canadian Journal of Communication, Critical Studies in Mass Communication, Journal of Popular Culture, Journal of American Culture,* and *Journal of International Popular Culture,* all scholarly publications.

FOR FURTHER LEARNING

Richard Gruneau. "Why TVTV?" *Canadian Journal of Communication* (Winter 1996).

Howard Hampton. "Out of Our Heads." *Gannett Center Journal* (Volume 1): 133–147.

S. Robert Lichter, Linda S. Lichter, and Stanley Rothman. *Watching America: What Television Tells Us About Our Lives* (Prentice Hall, 1991).

Marshall McLuhan. *The Gutenberg Galaxy: The Making of Typographic Man* (University of Toronto Press, 1967).

Herbert Schiller. *Mass Communications and American Empire* (Kelley, 1969).

Susan Sontag. "One Culture and New Sensibility." *Against Interpretation* (Farrar Straus & Giroux, 1966).

Michael Tracey. "The Poisoned Chalice: International Television and the Idea of Dominance." *Daedalus* 114 (Fall 1985): 4, 17–56.

Chapter 14

Transglobal Transplant. Indian movie star Amitabh Bachchan welcomes participants to the television quiz show *Kaun Banega Crorepati*, Hindi for *Who Wants to Be a Millionaire*, in Bombay. The Indian version of the successful British show drew the highest viewership in Indian television, with millions of viewers glued to their television sets from Mondays to Thursdays after its 2000 launch. The U.S. variation, with Regis Philbin, and the Canadian version, with Pamela Wallin, were also both prime-time leaders.

MEDIA TIMELINE

Globalization of Mass Media

1974	Change model is developed by Ray Hiebert, Don Ungurait, and Tom Bohn.
1988	APTN buys Worldwide Television News.
1993	NBC buys European Super Channel.
1995	MTV is marketed to Asia.
1995	Disney buys ABC.
1998	The World Trade Organization adopts the Canadian model of media regulation.

Global Mass Media

Media in Theory

New Media Models

As you will remember from Chapter 1, models help us visualize different media systems. Models have different levels of sophistication, such as going from a bipolar model for political systems to a more complex continuum to an even more complex compass. Besides political systems, models can demonstrate media cultural environments, developmental state, and other characterizing criteria.

Bipolar Model

To compare media systems, some scholars use a **bipolar model** with two extremes: authoritarianism at one end and libertarianism at the other. The model demonstrates opposites in an extreme way. Just as east is opposite from west, so is freedom from control. Bipolar models are useful beginning points to separate political systems.

Continuum Model

More sophisticated than a simple bipolar model is a variation called the **continuum model**. The basics of the continuum political system model are bipolar, with the extremes being authoritarianism and libertarianism, but there is an added element of sophistication. The media system of each country is placed not at an extreme but at points along the line. Canada and the U.S. would be near the libertarian end, although not quite at the extreme because North American media operate within limitations, such as libel and intellectual property law, and broadcast regulation. On the other end would be dictatorships and other repressive countries with tight controls on the mass media.

The continuum model recognizes the uniqueness of media systems in different countries. By assessing variables, scholars can plant individual countries on the continuum, which facilitates grouping countries for comparison.

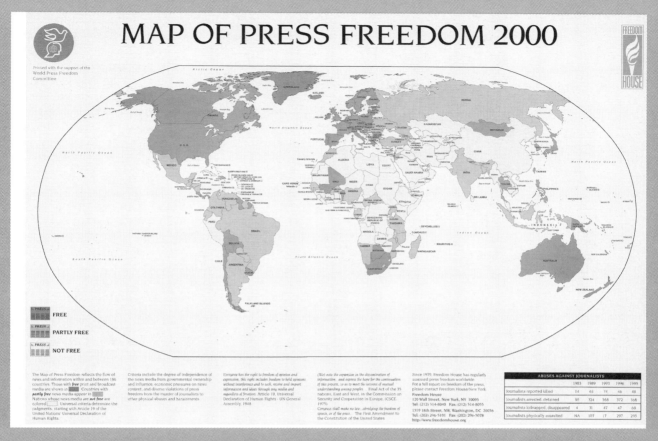

MAP OF PRESS FREEDOM 2000

Printed with the support of the
World Press Freedom
Committee

FREE

PARTLY FREE

NOT FREE

The Map of Press Freedom reflects the flow of news and information within and between 186 countries. Those with *free* print and broadcast media are shown in ▓▓. Countries with *partly free* news media appear in ▓▓. Nations whose news media are *not free* are colored [   ]. Universal criteria determine the judgments, starting with Article 19 of the United Nations' Universal Declaration of Human Rights.

Criteria include the degree of independence of the news media from governmental ownership and influence; economic pressures on news content; and diverse violations of press freedom from the murder of journalists to other physical abuses and harassments.

Everyone has the right to freedom of opinion and expression; this right includes freedom to hold opinions without interference and to seek, receive and impart information and ideas through any media and regardless of frontiers. Article 19, Universal Declaration of Human Rights - UN General Assembly, 1948

(We) note the expansion in the dissemination of information, and express the hope for the continuation of this process, so as to meet the interests of mutual understanding among peoples. Final Act of the 35 nations, East and West, in the Commission on Security and Cooperation in Europe, (CSCE 1975)
Congress shall make no law...abridging the freedom of speech, or of the press. The First Amendment to the Constitution of the United States

Since 1979, Freedom House has regularly assessed press freedom worldwide. For a full report on freedom of the press, please contact Freedom House/New York.
Freedom House
120 Wall Street, New York, NY 10005
Tel: (212) 514-8040 Fax: (212) 514-8055
1319 18th Street, NW, Washington, DC 20036
Tel: (202) 296-5101 Fax: (202) 296-5078
http://www.freedomhouse.org

ABUSES AGAINST JOURNALISTS					
	1983	1989	1993	1996	1999
Journalists reported killed	14	61	74	46	48
Journalists arrested, detained	80	324	368	372	368
Journalists kidnapped, disappeared	4	31	47	47	60
Journalists physically assaulted	NA	107	17	297	295

Press Freedom. The Freedom House, which tracks press freedom worldwide, reports relatively few countries where news and information flow freely within and across their borders. Massive sections of Africa and Asia, plus Cuba and scattered small European countries, do not have free flows and exchanges. In making its determinations, Freedom House considered media independence from government ownership and economic pressure.

Compass Model

In his book *The Imperative of Freedom,* scholar **John Merrill** looped the libertarian–authoritarian continuum around so that its ends meet themselves. On the loop Merrill marked the four major philosophical underpinnings as compass points that define the major media systems and their underlying political systems.

Among Merrill's points with the **compass model** is that a social responsibility system might not be just a variation on libertarianism but actually authoritarian. Merrill's compass addresses the troubling question that plagues the media: Who ensures responsibility? If it's government, then we have introduced shades of authoritarianism. If not government, then who? Broadcasters can't always be trusted to do the socially responsible thing.

Change Model

The effects of culture and geography on media systems are taken into account in the **change model,** which shows the interaction of many variables on media and systems and performance. One of the best of these models,

Press Freedom: The Freedom House website provides information and links in support of freedom and democracy across the world. Take a look at their annual survey of press freedom.
www.freedomhouse.org

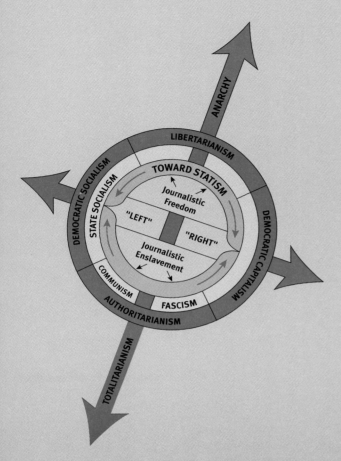

Compass Model. Scholar John Merrill rethought the libertarian–authoritarian continuum and folded in the four theories model to develop the compass model. The result: a graphic representation that a responsible press, if responsibility is by government mandate, is frighteningly close to traditional authoritarianism.

introduced in 1974 by scholars Ray Hiebert, Don Ungurait, and Tom Bohn, asks for an assessment of a country's political philosophy, as had Siebert, Peterson, and Schramm with their four theories model, but the Hiebert, Ungurait, and Bohn model goes much further by taking into account other variables:

- *Economics.* In impoverished parts of the world, such as Chad, few people can afford access to the mass media. There is no advertising. This lack of an economic base means a weak media system that is generally subservient to political leadership. A wealthy elite, of course, may have access to all kinds of media, often from other countries, which helps to maintain its advantage and privilege.

- *Culture.* A country's mass media reflect cultural values. The media of Iran, run by religious fundamentalists, are far different from the media of India, a democracy that accommodates a diversity of religions. Social norms, mores, and values vary from country to country, all with an effect on the mass media. So do language and traditions.

- *Technology.* Outdated equipment can undermine the service that media provide. For print media, poor roads can limit distribution. In much of the Third World, presses are hand-me-downs from more developed countries, not only outdated but also prone to breakdowns.

- *Climate.* In tropical climates, where trees used for pulp to make paper can't grow, the print media have extraordinary production expenses for importing paper. Mexico is an example.

- *Geography.* Broadcasters in a mountainous country like Nepal have a hard time getting signals to people living in narrow valleys shielded by steep terrain. This is a factor in the economics of broadcasting and also a station's influence.

- *Literacy.* If people can't read, the print media are handicapped. In Cameroon, for example, compulsory education goes only to age 12. Even then, one third of Cameroon's children don't attend school. The literacy rate is only 63 percent.

- *Media.* A country's media infrastructure can be an indicator of other realities. If the primary mass medium is radio, for example, it may be an indicator that low literacy has stunted growth of the print media. A country wired well for the web has a basis for sophisticated delivery of messages of all sorts.

Subsystem Model

The mass media have grown in complexity, especially in economically advanced countries. Some scholars are making a case that it doesn't make sense any more to evaluate media in the traditional broad terms of major media, like television, magazines, and newspapers. Instead, they advocate classifying media by subsystems to understand what's happening. The following are among the elements in a **subsystem model**:

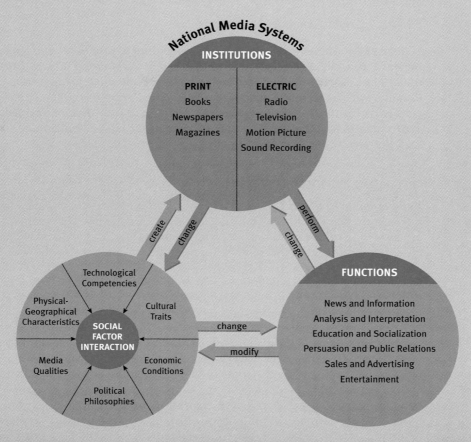

Change Model. A 1974 model developed by scholars Ray Hiebert, Donald Ungurait, and Thomas Bohn expanded the four theories model to recognize other factors in media systems, including economic conditions, technological competence, and even geography. The model also attempts to show how media systems and performance are affected by many variables.

- *Commercial media.* These are the profit-seeking media that have traditionally been the focus of comparative studies.
- *Government media.* Controlled by the government, these media may coexist with commercial media.
- *Public media.* Financed by citizens and government money to further the public good, like the CBC in Canada.
- *Organizational media.* Aimed at serving non-government bodies, such as professional groups, tribes, religions, and corporations.
- *Individualized media.* Media customized to an individual's needs and interests, as is possible through the web.
- *Political media.* Used by political parties.

The subsystem model recognizes the folly in describing a nation's mass media system in broad, singular terms. The divisions that the advocates of the subsystem model favour are well suited to today's media fragmentation and decentralization.

The subsystem model also distinguishes between the motivation that media owners have for their products, the range of content they offer, the audience they seek, the results that occur, and how their audiences provide feedback.

From Canadian content regulations to U.S. ownership of Canadian movie houses, Canadian concerns about foreign control and ownership have been well documented in this text. This chapter addresses what others, including the U.S., have to say about the influence of foreign media in their countries.

Effects of Globalization

Globalization of the media is made possible through a series of mergers, acquisitions, buyouts, and alliances. Only this time, it's not on a national level, but an international level. It's this foreign ownership that worries some media critics, not only in Canada, but also abroad. At stake, as these critics see it, is control of the direction of cultural advancement—something they believe should not be farmed out. Other experts say that global media companies are neutral as to content and have no ideological preferences except making money.

CULTURAL SUBVERSIVENESS

Experts disagree about the effect of globalization. Some critics, including respected media critic Ben Bagdikian, fret that "anonymous superpowers" such as Bertelsmann (a worldwide media conglomerate, whose media interests include BMG and Random House) are a potential threat to cultural autonomy and the free flow of information and ideas. In his book *The Media Monopoly*, Bagdikian said, "The highest levels of world finance have become intertwined with the highest levels of mass media ownership, with the result of tighter control over the systems on which most of the public depends for its news and information."

Other observers, such as Toni Heinzl and Robert Stevenson at the University of North Carolina, note that many global media companies, including Bertelsmann, have learned to let their local operating companies adapt to local cultures: "Following a global strategy, it is the company's policy to respect the national characteristics and cultural traditions in each of the more than two dozen countries in which it operates. It is impossible to detect even hints of German culture from the product lineup of Bertelsmann's companies abroad. Targeting specific preference of a national public or audience, the company has custom-tailored its products for each country: French culture in France, Spanish culture in Spain, American culture in the United States, and so on." The target is growth.

CORPORATE IDEOLOGY

By and large, the agenda of media conglomerates is profits and nothing more. They do not promote ideology. North American movie-goers did not see Japanese overtones in Columbia movies or CBS records after the Sony takeover or in MCA products after the Matsushita takeover. At the same time, it cannot be ignored that Bertelsmann tried to transplant its successful German geographic magazine *Geo* in the United States in 1979, only to give it up two years and US$50 million later when it realized that *National Geographic*'s following was unshakable. In the same vein, media mogul **Rupert Murdoch** imported British tabloid editors to reshape some of the U.S. newspapers he bought. What can be said with certainty about media globalization is that it is occurring and that observers are divided about its consequences.

WEB AND GLOBALIZATION

New web technologies open the way for more companies to seek global audiences directly at relatively low cost. E-books, for example, don't require expensive presses to produce. Nor do they need massive warehouses or require expensive shipping.

Producers of radio and television programs can use streaming instead of having to negotiate complex deals with networks or individual stations for distribution. In short, the web can eliminate middlemen.

Easy access to the web opens opportunities for upstarts to reach global audiences. Whether new companies can establish web followings that compete with the majors, which also have created presences on the web, isn't clear. With the massiveness of their repertoires, the major players certainly have a leg up.

The question for media critics, concerned about conglomeration on a global scale, is whether the web will level the playing field to give little guys a chance. The resulting diversity would ease concerns about the media becoming concentrated in only a few hands. If the majors continue to dominate the creation of content, as well as delivery, the critics of conglomeration will have added cause for alarm.

Cultural Intrusion

Some experts claim that the export of American pop culture is latter-day imperialism motivated by profit and without concern for its effect on other societies. This is one of the reasons that the CRTC and the Canadian government have always had some form of content regulations for most Canadian-owned media. But this fear is not unique to Canada; other countries feel the same way. In fact, many countries look to the CRTC for guidance in how to deal with cultural intrusion. In 1998, the World Trade Organization adopted the so-called "Canadian model of regulation." What this means, according to the CRTC, is that other countries want to "understand how Canada meets public interest goals while encouraging the growth of the public sector."

LATTER-DAY IMPERIALISM

The great concern about media globalization has been about the flow of values not among developed countries but to developing countries. Critics use the term **cultural imperialism** for this dark side of international communication. Their view is that the media are like the 19th-century European colonial powers, exporting Western values, often uninvited, to other cultures. At stake, these critics say, is the cultural sovereignty of non-Western nations. These critics note that the international communication media have their headquarters in the United States and in the former European colonial powers. The communication flow, they claim, is one way, from the powerful nations to the weak ones. The result, as they see it, is that Western values are imposed in an impossible-to-resist way. A Third World television station, for example, can buy a recycled American television program for far less than it costs to produce an indigenous program.

Scholar Herbert Schiller, who wrote Mass Communications and American Empire, argued that the one-way communication flow is especially insidious because the Western productions, especially movies and television, are so slick that they easily outdraw locally produced programs. As a result, says Schiller, the Western-controlled

U.S. Media Imperialism: Herbert Schiller is one of many media theorists who are concerned about the influence of American culture on smaller nations.

Murdoch Everywhere. In 2000 media mogul Rupert Murdoch consolidated his content delivery and satellite delivery system under a new banner: Sky Global. It was the largest distribution platform in the world—an outlet for Murdoch products from 20th Century Fox, News Corporation, and other media enterprises.

international mass media pre-empt native culture, a situation he sees as robbery, just like the earlier colonial tapping of natural resources to enrich the home countries.

India is a fascinating recent example of cultural intrusion, if not cultural imperialism. Until 1991 this nation had only one television network, which ran programs that originated in India almost exclusively. Then came StarTV, global media mogul Rupert Murdoch's satellite service from Hong Kong, which carried lots of U.S.-originated programming. Writing in *Media Studies Journal*, India media critic Shailaja Bajpai offered these observations:

■ Many Indians were dressing like the Americans they saw on *Baywatch*.

■ While Indian boys once wanted to grow up to be great cricket players, they now wanted to shoot baskets like Michael Jordan.

Other anecdotal evidence of U.S. culture rubbing off elsewhere is in South Africa. According to Sebiletso Mokone-Matabane, an executive with the Independent Broadcasting authority there, robbers were shouting "freeze," a word that had no roots in Afrikaans or the indigenous languages, when they stormed into a bank. The robbers had been watching too much U.S. television.

NON-DOWNWARD MEDIA EXCHANGE

In some ways, cultural imperialism is in the eyes of the beholder. Some Latin American countries, for example, scream "cultural imperialism" at the United States but don't object when Mexico exports soap operas to the rest of Latin America, as do Brazil and Argentina. Although they are exercising a form of cultural imperialism, nobody puts the label on them. Media observer Larry Lorenz, who has studied this phenomenon, explains it this way: "What is occurring is simply internationalism brought on by the ever more sophisticated media of mass communication."

The cultural imperialism theory has other doubters among scholars. The doubters note that the theory is a simplistic application of the now-discredited hypodermic needle model of mass communication. Media messages do not have immediate direct effects.

Also overstated are charges that news from Europe and the United States dominates coverage in other parts of the world. One study found that 60 to 75 percent of the foreign news in the Third World is about other Third World countries, mostly those nearby. While the giant Western news services—AP, Agence France-Presse, and Reuters—are the main purveyors of foreign news, the coverage that reaches Third World audiences is extremely parochial.

EMERGING GLOBAL MEDIA

Concern about Western cultural imperialism is slowly changing as two related things occur. First, the number of international media players, many in neither Europe nor the United States, is increasing. Second, rather than merely recycling domestic products abroad, American-based media companies are creating new, local-oriented content in the countries where they do business.

Prime-time U.S. television soap operas *Dallas* and *Dynasty* were once prime-time fare throughout the world, either with subtitles or dubbed awkwardly into local languages. Today, local media people who have mastered Western production techniques are producing local media content. Their programs go over big, attracting viewers and advertisers better than imported programs. Allan Ng, a Far East investment analyst, has seen the change at the giant Hong Kong satellite television service TVB. To *Business Week* reporter Joyce Barnathan, Ng said, "TVB dares not show *Dynasty* until 11 at night."

Indigenous local programming not only is taking hold in other countries, especially those with a developing middle class, but also many of these emerging media are exporting their material. Throughout Latin America, for example, people watch soap operas produced by TV Globo in Brazil and Televisa in Mexico. The Belgian broadcast company RTL, which once spent most of its programming dollars on imports like *Dallas* and *Dynasty*, now produces most of its own shows. The French TF-1 and Italian Rai Uno television services have cut back substantially on U.S. programs. The turnaround in Europe has been fuelled not only by audience preferences for local material but also by a European Union policy that half of each nation's broadcast programming must originate within the union.

There is also new competition, much of it well financed. In Europe the television service Canal One has teamed up with Bertelsmann of Germany to create a formidable competitor for the whole European audience. TVB in Hong Kong has its eye on dominating media fare to China, Southeast Asia, and the Subcontinent. What once were easy pickings for U.S. media companies are now tough markets.

To compete, U.S. media companies are investing in other countries to develop local programming. MTV and ESPN both have built advanced production studios in Singapore. In 1995 Viacom relaunched its MTV service to Asia with local hosts. In Europe, U.S. companies are forming local partnerships. NBC, for example, which bought the European Super Channel cable network in 1993, has added business news from the *Financial Times*, a London newspaper. NBC has teamed up with TV Azteca in Mexico to tap into local programming and marketing savvy. Time Warner's HBO is in partnership with Omnivision, a Venezuelan cable company, for the HBO Olé pay-television service in Latin America.

While many countries are developing significant local media powerhouses, some countries are decades away from having their own media production facilities, financing, and know-how. Their complaint today is not about cultural imperialism solely from the United States but also from Bonn, Caracas, Hong Kong, London, Mexico City, Paris, and Sao Paolo.

WESTERN INFLUENCE ON MEDIA FORM AND CONTENT

Although more media content is being originated in home countries, some critics say don't be fooled. Shailaja Bajpai, editor of an Indian television magazine, says that Indian TV producers clone U.S. television: "The American talk show has inspired Indian imitations. Never have so many Indians revealed so much about their private lives to such a wide audience. Every day a new show is planned. If nothing else, American television has loosened tongues (to say nothing of our morals). Subjects long taboo are receiving a good airing." Those Indian programs may be produced in India, but the concept is hardly Indian.

TRANSNATIONAL CULTURAL ENRICHMENT

Some scholars see transnational cultural flow in more benign terms than Herbert Schiller and his fellow cultural imperialism theorists. George Steiner has noted that European and American culture have been enriched, not corrupted, by the continuing presence of Greek mythology over 2000 years.

In a homey way, sociologist Michael Tracey makes a similar point:

> I was born in a working-class neighborhood called Oldham in the north of England. Before the First World War, Oldham produced most of the world's spun cotton. It is a place of mills and chimneys, and I was born and raised in one of the areas of housing— called St. Mary's—built to serve those mills. I recently heard a record by a local group of folk singers called the Oldham Tinkers, and one track was about Charlie Chaplin. This song was apparently very popular with local children in the years immediately after the First World War. Was that evidence of the cultural influences of Hollywood, a primeval moment of the imperialism of one culture, the subjugation of another? It seems almost boorish to think of it that way. Was the little man not a deep well of pleasure through laughter, a pleasure that was simply universal in appeal? Was it not Chaplin's real genius to strike some common chord, uniting the whole of humanity? Is that not, in fact, the real genius of American popular culture, to bind together, better than anything, common humanity?

Global Media Players

The first media companies to extend their operations abroad significantly were news agencies such as the Associated Press, Reuters, and United Press International. Today, companies that produce all kinds of media messages, not just news, are engaged in finding global markets.

NEWS AGENCIES

Hundreds of agencies cover news around the world and sell their accounts to subscribing media organizations. Most of these are national and regional services. In addition to CP and BN here in Canada, the primary global players are Associated Press, Reuters, Agence France-Presse, Interfax, Worldwide Television News and, to a lesser extent, United Press International.

ASSOCIATED PRESS. The **Associated Press** is the largest news-gathering organization in the world. There are 8500 subscribers in 112 countries. The AP is a nonprofit cooperative organization owned by daily newspapers. Each newspaper is obligated to furnish its local stories to the AP for distribution to other AP member newspapers and clients. Each member newspaper owns a share of the company based on its circulation and numerous other factors. Periodically the expenses are tallied, and member newspapers are billed for their share. Policies are set by member newspapers, which meet regularly.

REUTERS. **Reuters** serves 6500 media organizations worldwide, including 290 in the United States. Altogether, counting subscribers to its financial and business news services, Reuters has 27 000 subscribers worldwide. The service is offered in 11 languages. There are 120 bureaus in 80 countries. U.S. video clients include CNN and NBC.

Associated Press:

www.ap.org

Reuters:

www.reuters.com

AGENCE FRANCE-PRESSE. Paris-based **Agence France-Presse** was founded by Charles Havas in 1835. Using carrier pigeons, Havas supplied Paris newspapers by noon with news that had happened that same morning in London and Brussels. Today AFP is the third largest global agency. AFP has 2000 people in 150 bureaus worldwide, including 850 full-time journalists. Text, photo, audio, and video services are transmitted in Arabic, English, French, German, Spanish, and Portuguese to 500 newspapers, 350 radio, and 200 television clients and to 99 national news agencies that pass AFB stories on to more media outlets. AFP has more than 50 U.S. media clients.

INTERFAX. This Moscow-based news agency was founded as TASS in 1925. Today, reconstituted and renamed **Interfax**, the agency supplies reports in Russian, English, German, Spanish, and Arabic. At its peak, the agency claimed 5500 media and non-media subscribers, but the disintegration of communism and the shrivelling of Russian influence has meant inevitable declines.

UNITED PRESS INTERNATIONAL. Newspaper magnate E.W. Scripps, who founded one successful afternoon paper after another beginning in the 1880s, was frustrated that he couldn't run Associated Press stories. Older morning newspapers had exclusive AP franchises. In 1907, Scripps countered by founding United Press. The service became a formidable competitor but never caught up with AP, even after a 1958 merger with Hearst's International News Service.

A perennial money loser, **United Press International** eventually was sold by Scripps's successors. It passed through a series of owners. All of them scaled back to cut losses. Nothing worked. Today UPI has a few bureaus in only a few key cities. UPI has given up U.S. regional coverage.

The latest owner, News World, operated by the Unification Church, took over in 2000. There were assurances that the Reverend Sun Myung Moon, head of the church, would not interfere with content. Among doubters was Helen Thomas, UPI's most visible reporter as a 39-year veteran on the White House beat. She quit. Other parts of the Unification Church media empire, including the *Washington Times,* have a conservative thrust that is consistent with Reverend Moon's politics.

Agence France-Presse:
www.afp.com

Interfax:
www.interfax-news.com

VIDEO NEWS SERVICES

The major U.S. news networks—ABC, CBS, CNN, and NBC—prefer to cover foreign stories with their own crews, but they also subscribe to global video services for stories and pictures that they miss. The largest news video suppliers are, not surprisingly, the world's two largest news services: New York-based Associated Press and London-based Reuters.

APTV, a subsidiary of the Associated Press, cemented its leadership by buying Worldwide Television News, WTN for short, in 1998. WTN's owners, including the ABC television network, cashed in for US$44 million. The deal left only London-based Reuters as a major AP competitor in the business of providing video feeds for television.

SYNDICATES

After recruiters swept through Baraboo, Wisconsin, and signed up the local boys for the U.S. Civil War, **Ansell Kellogg** lacked the staff to get out his four-page *Baraboo Republic,* so he took to borrowing the inside pages of another newspaper. The practice not only saw Kellogg through a staffing crisis, but also sparked an idea to save

Mediachannel: A global network of media issues groups.

www.mediachannel.org

Global Media Giants: A look at the global conglomeration of media from the Fairness and Accuracy in Reporting website.

www.fair.org/extra/9711/gmg.html

The New Global Media: An article about media conglomeration by University of Illinois associate professor Robert W. McChesney.

past.thenation.com/issue/991129/1129mcchesney.shtml

AOL Time Warner: The world's first fully integrated media and communications company.

www.aoltimewarner.com

Viacom:

www.viacom.com

Newscorp: News Corporation is the world's leading publisher of English-language newspapers, with operations in the United Kingdom, Australia, New Zealand, Fiji, Papua New Guinea, and the United States.

www.newscorp.com

costs by supplying inside pages at a fee to other short-handed publishers. By 1865 Kellogg was in Chicago providing ready-to-print material for newspapers throughout the United States. In journalism history, Kellogg is remembered as the father of the newspaper **syndicate.**

In the 1880s **S.S. McClure** had a thriving syndicate, putting out 50 000 words a week in timeless features on fashion, homemaking, manners, and literature. McClure and other syndicators charged subscribing newspapers a fraction of what each would have to pay to generate such material with its own staff. Features, poetry, opinion, and serialized stories by the period's great literary figures, including Jack London, Rudyard Kipling, George Bernard Shaw, Robert Louis Stevenson, and Mark Twain, became standard fare in many newspapers through syndication.

Today syndicates seek international audiences, spreading expenses among more subscribers and building new revenue. Some syndicate material doesn't travel easily, like sophisticated humour columns and comic strips that flow from a particular culture. It's hard to imagine that "Family Circus" or "Beetle Bailey" would go over in South Asia, for example. But other syndicated material, like "Dear Abby" and medical advice columns, is easily adapted to many overseas audiences.

GLOBAL MEDIA COMPANIES

National origins of companies in the media business are blurring. In 2000 the French media giant Vivendi bought Seagram's of Canada, thus acquiring the Universal-MCA movie and music empire in the United States. Sony of Japan owned a share of United States-based AOL Time Warner. Bertelsmann of Germany was everywhere, it seemed, and looking to expand through internal growth and mergers and acquisitions.

U.S.-BASED COMPANIES. Four U.S. media rivals have established themselves as major players in other countries:

- *AOL Time Warner.* AOL Time Warner, which operates in 70-plus countries, is among the world's largest media companies—a position strengthened by the 2000 merger of America Online and Time Warner. Worldwide, the company is valued at US$183 billion. In Latin America the company has adapted its HBO pay-television service and calls it HBO Olé. It's the most widely distributed cable network in Latin America. Elsewhere, the company has alliances with Itochu and Toshiba.

- *Disney-ABC.* Disney became one of the world's largest media companies in 1995 when it acquired Cap Cities/ABC. The new company has annual revenues estimated at more than US$19 billion. The consolidation included major assets in movies, television, newspapers, and cable. Since 1995 the company has sold off some major properties, including several metro newspapers and also magazines to narrow its focus.

- *Viacom.* Viacom's MTV has been an entree into foreign markets. The music-video network reaches 240 million households in 63 countries, which is a model for Viacom to expand its VH-1 music and Nickelodeon satellite networks into other countries. There is a lot more that Viacom can market abroad. It holds 50 000 hours of television shows that it first sold to U.S. networks and now is recycling abroad.

- *News Corporation.* Australian-born Rupert Murdoch owns News Corporation, the interests of which go far beyond his 20th Century Fox movie studio, the Fox television network, and U.S. newspapers and magazines. In Asia his satellite television service, Star TV, beams signals to China, India, Taiwan, and Southeast

Asia. Through Star TV, two-thirds of the world's population, 3 billion people, have access to programming that Murdoch's company creates or buys from other sources, including MTV, ESPN, and Bart Simpson. Murdoch owns half of Sky Broadcasting, which sends signals by satellite to all of Europe. He also owns newspapers in Australia, Britain, and the United States.

NON-U.S. COMPANIES. Once U.S. media companies held the commanding lead for overseas markets, but home-grown companies are pumping out more content all the time. Some of these companies have become global players themselves:

- *Bertelsmann.* The German company Bertelsmann established itself globally as a book and magazine company. It has 200 subsidiaries in 25 countries, many of them operating under the name they had when Bertelsmann acquired them. In the United States these include Random House, Bantam, Dell, and Doubleday books. The company's U.S. interests include RCA records.
- *Hachette Filipacchi.* The French-Italian company Hachette Filipacchi publishes 74 magazines in 10 countries. This includes the 4.5 million circulation *Woman's Day,* which Hachette acquired when it bought the CBS magazine empire in 1988. Another Hachette magazine in the United States is the fashion magazine *Elle.*
- *Televisa.* Throughout Latin America, people watch soap operas, called *telenovelas.* Most of these originate from Televisa, a Mexican media giant.
- *TVB.* Hong Kong-based TVB has started an Asian television-satellite service. This company has plenty to put on the satellite. Its production runs about 6000 hours a year in both Cantonese and Mandarin.
- *TV Globo.* A Brazilian media company, TV Globo, true to its name, has developed a global audience. Its telenovelas air in all the Spanish-speaking and Portuguese-speaking countries and beyond, including China.

Bertelsmann:
www.bertelsmann.com

Hachette Filipacchi:
www.hfnm.com

Televisa:
www.esmas.com/televisa

TVB:
www.tvb.com

TV Globo:
redeglobo.globo.com/glo bointernacional

Media Pressure Points

The struggle between a free media and a controlled, suppressed, or badgered media plays and replays around the world. Case studies include Russia, where old ways die hard, and Colombia, where drug lords have strong sway.

RUSSIA

Optimists expected the dust of the imploding Soviet empire in 1989 would yield a robust, prosperous free society. In Russia, however, despite occasional signs of new media independence, old ways die hard.

The **NTV** network, part of the country's largest media chain, gained respect as an independent voice for its critical reports on Kremlin policies in the early **perestroika** period. Then in 2000, NTV owner Vladimir Gusinsky was arrested after months of harassment by the Kremlin. Gusinsky was dumped in one of Moscow's filthiest jails. It all smacked of authoritarianism. Embarrassed at the worldwide media attention on the heavy-handedness, the president of Russia, Vladimir Putin, distanced himself from the arrest and called it excessive. Still, it was Putin's administration that had gone after Gusinsky.

Meanwhile, NTV's coverage of the latest Russian military campaign against Chechnya separatists was toned down. From 1994 to 1996 the network had gained respect for fearless frontline reporting on stalled Russian tactics. Video showed frightened teenage Russian troops in over their heads against grizzled Chechens. When Russian troops destroyed Grozny, the coverage was not pretty and hardly heroic. As Russian public pressure shifted against the war, the Kremlin opted to act in old ways. NTV was told its broadcast licence was in jeopardy.

The Kremlin underscored its seriousness in 2000 when a Radio Free Europe correspondent from the first Chechnyan war, Andrei Babitsky, tried again to roam independently for balanced coverage. Suddenly Babitsky's reports stopped. He had been arrested by Russian forces, badly beaten up, and jailed for 40 days—a chilling effect that showed in all coverage, including NTV's.

It's not just government that has failed in the transition to a free mass media. In 1996 the president of Gusinsky's NTV managed the re-election campaign of President Boris Yeltsin. The infrastructure for independent media wasn't in place. At lower levels, too, many career media people, rewarded for years as loyal Leninists, found themselves suddenly in a strange transitional environment and couldn't deal with it. In many cities local media were beholden to town mayors for office space, equipment, and supplies—just as in the old days.

Organized crime and corruption also work against a free media. According to the Committee to Protect Journalists, 34 journalists died doing their work in Russia in the 1990s, mostly in war zones but some murdered elsewhere. Hundreds have reported being attacked.

COLOMBIA

High drama is popular on Colombia radio stations, but it is hardly theatrical. In Colombia thousands of people, both wealthy and ordinary, are kidnap captives. Families go on the air to express love and support in the hope that their kidnapped kin are listening. It makes for powerful radio. Tragically, it's real.

Drug lords and petty criminals alike have found kidnapping lucrative in a country where anarchy is close to an everyday reality. The mass media are hardly immune. In the 1990s, according to the U.S.-based Committee to Protect Journalists, 31 journalists were killed because of their work. Sixteen others have died in incidents that may or may not be related to their work. In a typical year, six to 10 journalists are kidnapped in a country whose population is under 40 million.

A political satirist, Jamie Garzón, was gunned to death in 1999 after a television show. *El Espectador*, a leading newspaper, has armed guards at every entrance and around the perimeter, as do most media operations. Many reporters are assigned bodyguards, usually two, both armed. Two *El Espectador* reporters have fled the country under threat. The editor of another daily, *El Tiempo*, fled in 2000 after supporting a peace movement.

Beset with corruption fuelled by the powerful cocaine industry, the government has no handle on assaults against the media. Although hypersensitive to negative coverage, the drug industry is not the only threat to the Colombian media. The Committee to Protect Journalists, Human Rights Watch, Amnesty International, and other watchdogs blame renegade paramilitary units and guerrillas, some of whom are ideologically inspired. Also, the Colombian military itself and some government agencies have been implicated.

Media People

Jineth Bedoya Lima

Jineth Bedoya Lima

After Jineth Bedoya Lima wrote about executions during a Bogotá prison riot, she got word that a paramilitary leader inside the prison wanted to give her his side. "Come alone," she was told. Like all Colombian journalists, Bedoya, 25 at the time, was aware of the dangers of reporting news, especially on subjects sensitive to warring factions. Her editor and a photographer went with her.

As they waited outside the prison, the photographer left to buy sodas, then the editor followed him. When they came back, Bedoya was gone. Guards at the prison gate said they had seen nothing.

Many hours later, a taxi driver found Bedoya at a roadside garbage dump. She said that two men had grabbed her and forced a drugged cloth over her face. She regained consciousness in a nearby house, where her captors taped her mouth, blindfolded her, and bound her hands and feet. They then drove her three hours to another city. They said they were going to kill her, as well as several other journalists they named. Then they beat and raped her and threw her off at the dump.

Her story, typical of violence against media people in Colombia, was disseminated widely by the Committee to Protect Journalists. It's a cautionary tale. Bedoya, who believed that she was being trailed months later, was assigned two government bodyguards. Even so, she feels at risk. Why does she still do it? Frank Smyth of CPJ, writing in *Quill* magazine, quoted her: "I love my work, and I want to keep doing it. The worst thing that could happen has already happened."

media future

GLOBALIZATION

For better or worse, globalization of the mass media can be expected to accelerate. Technology is improving all the time to support the delivery of mass messages globally, and companies are finding new ways to score profits from audiences in other countries.

The prospect of there someday being only a few major media companies in the world is worrying. Governments have been a traditional check on unbridled business growth and monopolies, but most governments in countries with major media production centres have been reluctant to slow the expansion of home-based companies for fear that their industries will lose a competitive edge. In countries whose own media are being subsumed by imported products, governments are stymied about what to do. It's almost impossible to prohibit people from picking up satellite signals, though China has tried with limited success to regulate direct-from-satellite reception. The fact is that imported media products are popular in the Third World. Stopping the flow is not a realistic option.

Some developing countries have objected through the United Nations about news coverage that they claim is slanted to favour the major powers. These calls, however, have been overstated if not hysterical. Hard data do not support claims that indigenous media are the pawns of the media of former colonial powers. The fact is that local media outlets, in developing countries as elsewhere, tend to be parochial in their news coverage. The foreign items that they pick up from global news agencies are, by and large, detached and neutral—hardly propagandist.

The technology that facilitates easy access to the web may diversify the sources of media sources around the world, but still upstarts are disadvantaged Davids against multinational Goliaths like AOL Time Warner, News Corporation, Bertelsmann, and Vivendi.

CHAPTER WRAP-UP

Models to help explain the world's great variety of mass media systems are important in this fast-changing era of globalization. The most useful model focuses on change—how economics, culture, technology, and other factors influence media infrastructures and content in an interactive way. Models alone, however, are insufficient to explain media policy in a global context. Economic imperatives are at the heart of understanding why mass media companies behave as they do. The implications are important in explaining media effects on different cultures, both positive and negative. It's also interesting to see how other cultures deal with the same issues that Canadians do.

QUESTIONS FOR REVIEW

1. What kind of ideology are global media companies interested in exporting?

2. Assess the negative connotation of Herbert Schiller's term *cultural imperialism*.

3. How does the continuum model bypass the bipolar model in sophistication?

4. How have global news agencies affected nations they cover for the rest of the world?

5. Where are the major global media companies based?

6. What problems beset media people in countries without independent media?

QUESTIONS FOR CRITICAL THINKING

1. Describe the globalization of the mass media in terms of content generation and distribution.

2. What impediments face global media companies in authoritarian countries with controlled economies?

3. Assess the view that *cultural imperialism* is a loaded term that misses an enriching aspect of transnational communication.

4. Use the subsystems model to explain the mass media in a particular developing nation.

5. Some Third World leaders argue that news agencies like AP and Reuters are lackeys of government policy in their home nations. Can these arguments be sustained?

6. Global media companies have subsidiary operations. List and organize these subsidiaries by their location, then analyze the implications.

7. What trends can you ascertain about media-government relations worldwide?

8. How are the concerns of some counties similar to Canada's?

FOR KEEPING UP TO DATE

Index on Censorship, published in London, provides monthly country-by-country status reports.

Scholarly journals that carry articles on foreign media systems, international communication, and media responsibility include the *International Communication Bulletin, Journal of Broadcasting and Electronic Media, Journal of Communication,* and *Journal and Mass Communication Quarterly.*

Professional journals that carry articles on foreign media systems and on media responsibility include *Columbia Journalism Review, Quill,* and *American Journalism Review.*

Ongoing discussions on media responsibility also appear in the *Journal of Mass Media Ethics.*

FOR FURTHER LEARNING

Herbert J. Altschull. *Agents of Power.* Longman, 1984.

Stephen P. Banks. *Multicultural Public Relations: A Social-Interpretive Approach,* second edition. Iowa State University Press, 2000.

Chris Barker. *Television, Globalization and Cultural Identities.* Open Universities, 1999.

Carl L, Becker. *Freedom and Responsibility in the American Way of Life.* Vintage, 1945.

Isaiah Berlin. *Karl Marx: His Life and Environment.* Oxford University Press, 1939.

J. Augment, P. Bross, R. Hiebert, O.V. Johnson and D. Mills. *Eastern European Journalism Before, During and After Communism.* Hampton, 1999.

David Buckingham, Hannah Davies, Ken Jones and Peter Kelley. *Children's Television in Britain.*

Bernard Cohen. *The Press and Foreign Policy.* Princeton University Press. 1963.

Commission on Freedom of the Press. *A Free and Responsible Press.* University of Chicago Press, 1947.

James Curran, editor. *Media Organizations in Society.* Oxford University Press, 2000.

Frank Ellis. *From Glasnost to the Internet: Russia's New Infosphere.* St. Martins, 1999.

Donna Evleth. *The Authorized Press in Vichy and German-Occupied France, 1940–1944: A Bibliography.* Greenwood, 1999.

Howard H. Frederick. *Global Communication and International Relations.* Wadsworth, 1993.

Urs E. Gattiker. *The Internet as a Diverse Community: Cultural, Organizational and Political Issues.* Earlbaum, 2001.

Leo A. Gher and Hussein Y. Amin, editors. *Civic Discourse and Digital Age Communication in the Middle East.* Greenwood, 2000.

Joseph Gibbs. *The Soviet Media in the First Phase of Perestroika.* Texas A&M University Press, 1999.

Emma Gray. "Glasnost Betrayed," *Media Studies Journal* (Spring-Summer 2000), Pages 94–99.

Shelton A. Gunaratne, editor. *Handbook of the Media in Asia.* Sage, 2000.

William A. Hachten and Harva Hachten. *The World News Prism,* fifth edition. Iowa State University press, 1999.

Edward S. Herman and Robert W. McChesney. *The Global Media: The New Missionaries of Global Capitalism.* Cassell, 1997.

Wolfgang Hoffmann-Riem. *Regulating Media: The Licensing and Supervision of Broadcasting in Six Countries.* Guilford, 1996.

William E. Hocking. *Freedom of the Press: A Framework of Principle.* University of Chicago Press, 1947.

Frank Hughes. *Prejudice and the Press.* Devin-Adair, 1950.

L. Martin John and Anju Grover Chaudhary. *Comparative Mass Media Systems.* Longman, 1983.

Carla Brooks Johnston. *Winning the Global TV News Game.* Focal Press, 1995.

Jerry W. Knudson. "Licensing Journalists in Latin America: An Appraisal." *Journalism and Mass Communication Quarterly* (Winter 1996), Pages 878–889.

Abbas Malek and Anandam P. Kavoori, editors. *The Global Dynamics of News: Studies in International News Coverage and News Agenda.* Ablex, 2000.

Marilyn Matelski. *Vatican Radio.* Praeger, 1995.

Robert W. McChesney. *Corporate Media and the Threat to Democracy.* Seven Stories Press, 1997.

John Merrill. *Global Journalism: Survey of International Communication.* Longman. 1995.

John C. Merrill. *An Imperative of Freedom: A Philosophy of Journalistic Autonomy.* Hastings House, 1974.

Ellen Mickiewicz. *Changing Channels: Television and the Struggle for Power in Russia,* second edition. Duke University Press, 1999.

John C. Nerone, editor. *Last Rites: Revisiting Four Theories of the Press.* University of Illinois Press, 1995.

David D. Perlmutter. *Photojournalism and Foreign Policy: Icons of Outrage in International Crises.* Praeger, 1998.

Frank Rose. "Vivendi's High Wireless Act," *Wired* (December 2000), Pages 318–333.

Fred Siebert, Theodore Peterson and Wilbur Schramm. *Four Theories of the Press.* University of Illinois Press, 1956.

Tony Silva, editor. *Global News: Perspectives on tile Information Age.* Iowa State University Press, 2001.

Frank Smyth. "Danger Zone: When the Press Becomes the Target," *Quill* (December 2000) Pages 58–59.

Colin Sparks with Anna Reading. *Communism, Capitalism and the Mass Media.* Sage, 1999.

Joseph Robson Tanner. *English Constitutional Conflicts of the Seventeenth Century. 1603–1689.* Cambridge University Press, 1928.

Daya Kishan Thussu. *International Communication: Continuity and Change.* Arnold, 2000.

Daya Kishan Thussu, editor. *Electronic Empires: Global Media and Local Resistance.* Arnold, 1999.

Sun Xupei. *An Orchestra of Voices: Making the Argument for Greater Speech and Press Freedom in the People's Republic of China.* Greenwood, 2000.

GLOSSARY

Chapter 1

advertisements Messages intended to persuade people to buy.

amplification Spreading messages through the media.

Bagdikian, Ben Critic of media consolidation.

Barthes, Roland Developed the semiotic school of communication.

bias in communication Theory proposed by Harold Innis, who claimed that media can have bias for either time or space.

Bohn, Thomas Devised the concentric circle model with Ray Hiebert and Donald Ungurait.

books One-time, bound publications of enduring value on single topic.

CBC Canada's national public television network. Began broadcasting in 1952.

channel noise Interference during the transmission of a message.

circulation Number of copies of a publication that circulate.

communication Exchange of ideas, information.

concentric circle model Useful radiating model of the mass communication process.

conglomeration Combining of companies into larger companies.

connotation Deeper level meaning of word or image. Carrier of cultural mythology according to Barthes.

content-distribution model Divides functions of media companies into a creation category, like producing a television program, to a distribution function, like delivering the program on a cable system.

convergence Early 21st century model of cross media ownership. Converged companies typically own print, broadcast and Internet holdings.

cool media Media, like television, that McLuhan says can be used passively.

decoding Translating a symbolic message to be understood.

demassification Media focus on narrower audience segments. Sometimes referred to as narrowcasting or niche marketing.

denotation Common, everyday meaning of word or image.

digitization Converting on–off coding for storage and for transmission.

effect Result of mass communication. Last step in the concentric circle model.

electronic media Recordings, radio, television, or web, whose messages are stored electronically for transmission and retrieval.

elitists People who focus on media responsibility to society.

encoding Putting something into symbols to be communicated.

environmental noise Interference at reception site.

feedback Recipient's response to the sender, which can be positive or negative.

filter Receiver factor that impedes communication.

gatekeepers Media people who influence messages en route to the receiver.

group communication More than two people; in person.

homophyly A coding oneness that makes communication possible.

hot media Print media, which require intimate audience involvement, according to McLuhan.

informational filter Receiver's knowledge limits impede deciphering symbols.

infotainment Melding of media role as purveyor of information and entertainment.

internalization Making sense of a decoded message. Part of Shannon and Weaver model.

interpersonal communication Usually two people face to face.

intrapersonal communication Talking to oneself, usually internally.

Lasswell, Harold Devised the narrative model.

magazines Ongoing bound publications of continuing value with diverse topics.

mass audiences Recipients of mass messages. Sometimes passive, sometimes active.

mass communication Many recipients; not face to face; a process.

mass communicators Craft media messages for communication through mass media.

mass media Vehicles that carry messages crafted by mass communicators.

mass message What is communicated through the mass media.

Maxwell, Robert Global media mogul who expanded too quickly.

melding Conversion of all media to a common digital technology.

narrative model Describes process in words; not schematic.

news Nonfiction reports on what people want or need to know.

newspapers Unbound publications, generally weekly or daily, with diverse, timely content.

noise Impedes communication before message reaches receiver.

physical filter Receiver's alertness impedes deciphering.

populists Applaud media that attract a large popular culture following.

print media Books, magazines, and newspapers.

psychological filter Receiver's state of mind impedes deciphering.

public relations Messages intended to win support.

regulators Non-media people (such as the CRTC in Canada) who influence messages.

semantic noise Sloppy message-crafting on the part of mass communicators which causes miscommunication.

Shannon, Claude Devised a basic communication model, with Warren Weaver.

status conferral Credence that a topic or issue receives because of media attention.

stimulation Idea that influences someone to communicate. Part of Shannon and Weaver model.

transmission Sending a message using media channels. Part of Shannon and Weaver model.

Weaver, Warren Devised a basic communication model, with Claude Shannon.

Chapter 2

alternative press Generally antiestablishment publication for a young alienated audience.

Black, Conrad Founder of the *National Post*.

Brown, George Founder of Canada's *Globe and Mail*.

classified advertising Want ads that make up a significant portion of a newspaper's revenue.

consolidation Retail mergers reduce number of major newspaper advertisers.

consumer magazines Sold on newsracks.

counterculture newspapers Challenge and defy mainstream values.

Davey Commission Royal Commission held in 1970 into newspaper ownership in Canada.

direct mail Advertisements sent directly to consumers.

electronic delivery Sending news to readers' computer screens via the web.

Esquire First classy men's magazine.

Gannett A leading U.S. newspaper chain with 90 dailies.

Gilder, George Claims wordless society not on the horizon and that words do much to anchor meaning.

Harper's Weekly Pioneered magazine visuals.

Hearst, William Randolph Chain owner who dictated contents of all his newspapers.

highbrow slicks Cerebral magazines, edited for the intelligentsia.

hometown daily Edited primarily for readers in a defined region.

Kent Commission Royal Commission held in 1981 into newspaper ownership in Canada.

Luce, Henry Founder of *Time* and later *Life*.

Maclean's First Canadian newsmagazine.

Mailer, Norman Among the founders of *Village Voice*, the counter culture newspaper.

muckraking Term for investigative reporting; often used during the turn of the last century.

National Geographic Introduced photography and photo journalism in magazines.

National Post National daily owned by CanWest Global. Launched in 1998 by Lord Conrad Black.

national representative Newspaper's agency to solicit national advertisers.

news hole Space for news in a newspaper after ads are inserted; time in a newscast for news after ads.

newspaper chain Company that owns several newspapers.

penetration Percentage of persons or households that a newspaper reaches in its circulation area.

personality profile In-depth, balanced biographical article.

Playboy Widely imitated girlie/lifestyle men's magazine.

Postal Assistance Program (PAP) Discounted magazine mail rates for Canadian magazines.

Reader's Digest Largest circulation newsrack magazine.

Roosevelt, Theodore Coined the term *muckraking* to describe investigative journalism.

shopper An advertising paper without news. It primarily features ads for local businesses.

sponsored magazine Generally non-newsrack magazine, often member supported.

tabloid Newspaper with half-size pages that are easy to hold. Not necessarily sensationalistic as popular mythology believes. The Toronto Sun is a tabloid.

telephone book journalism Practice by community newspapers to mention local people and places.

Toronto Star Most successful Canadian daily. With convergence is also interested in TV broadcasting.

trade journal Keeps members of profession, trade informed.

USA Today Newspaper with one of the first nonlinear computer editions.

Village Voice Model for contemporary alternative press.

Chapter 3

airplay When a record receives free time on radio or a video channel.

analogue recording Sound waves physically engraved in the record.

bandwidth Capacity of a medium, such as a cable, to carry messages. The greater the bandwidth, the greater the capacity.

Berliner, Emile Canadian inventor whose machine played discs that could be mass-produced.

Big Five The five main companies in the recording industry.

Billboard Weekly music trade journal.

black music Folk genre from American black slave experience.

Brenston, Jackie Recorded "Rocket 88," the first rock 'n' roll record, in 1951.

Canadian Recording Industry Association Record industry trade organization.

CanCon Short for "Canadian Content." CRTC regulation requiring that Canadian radio stations play a certain amount of Canadian material.

CD Short for compact disc.

compact disc Digital record format; now dominant.

compression Compacting audio and video messages to reduce transmission time over the web.

demassification Focusing of music at subgroups within the mass audience.

digital recording Recording and playback system using on-off binary code for sound.

Edison, Thomas Built the first audio recorder-playback machine.

Freed, Alan Disc jockey who integrated black music and rock into playlists.

garage bands Low-budget, aspiring groups.

Gold Seal Award for sales of 50 000 copies of a recording in Canada.

Goldmark, Peter Devised successful long-play records.

hillbilly music Folk genre from rural Appalachian, Southern white experience.

home dubbing Recording music from a purchased record onto a blank tape or CD for personal use.

Juno Awards Annual Canadian record industry recognition for artists and technicians; it's the Canadian equivalent to the Grammy Awards.

LP Long-play record, 33-1/3-rpm, plastic, larger disc than 78s.

magnetic tape German invention that allowed sound editing.

Maxwell, Joseph Introduced electrical recording in the 1920s.

microgrooves 240 grooves per inch, 25 minutes per side at 33-1/3-rpm.

mini-studios Use consumer-quality, not professional-quality, equipment.

MP3 Format in which digitized music is condensed for web transmission and smaller file size.

Parents Music Resource Center Crusaded for labels on "objectionable" music.

payola Bribes to radio people to promote new records.

Phillips, Sam Pioneered rockabilly, rock 'n' roll; discovered Elvis Presley.

Phonograph First recorder-playback machine.

piracy Manufacturing recorded music for sale without permission from record company and artists.

Platinum Seal Award for sales of 100 000 copies of a recording in Canada.

Presley, Elvis Artist who melded black and white genres into rockabilly in the 1950s.

rockabilly Black-hillbilly hybrid that emerged in the 1950s.

78-rpm Shellac records, rotated 78 times per minute, up to four minutes per side.

stereo Left and right audio tracks.

streaming Allows a user to begin seeing or hearing a web message while parts of the message are still being transmitted.

Chapter 4

Aird Commission First Royal Commission into Canadian Broadcasting in 1929.

amplitude modulation AM radio.

Armstrong, Edwin Invented FM as an alternative transmission method.

audion tube Made voice transmission possible.

Canadian National Railway One of Canada's first radio broadcasters.

Conrad, Frank Pioneer whose work led to KDKA.

Crissell, Andrew Devised the theory of the four signs of radio: words, music, silence, and sounds.

DAB Digital audio broadcasting; radio's "next big thing."

De Forest, Lee Inventor whose projects included the audion tube.

Diamond Jubilee Broadcast A national radio event, held in 1927. It helped unite Canada from coast to coast.

electromagnetic spectrum Energy waves on which radio messages are piggybacked.

Fessenden, Reginald Canadian who broadcast the first radio program, in 1906. The "father of radio."

Freed, Alan Pioneer rock 'n' roll disc jockey.

frequency modulation FM radio.

KDKA First licensed commercial radio station in the U.S.

Marconi, Guglielmo Produced the first wireless transmission. The "father of telegraphy."

McLendon, Gordon Program innovator; devised Top 40, all-news, and beautiful-music formats.

potted-palm music Popular, inoffensive early radio programming.

shock jock Announcer whose style includes vulgarities and taboos.

Stern, Howard Controversial New York radio host.

Top 40 Format that replays pop records in a strict rotation.

WEAF New York station that carried the first commercial.

XWA First radio station in North America. It began broadcasting in 1919 from Montreal.

Chapter 5

ABC American Broadcasting Company. Built from ABC radio network. One of the "Big Three" over-air networks.

Board of Broadcast Governors (BBG) The predecessor to the CRTC.

Broadcasting Act Federal Act that governs radio and television broadcasting in Canada.

CanCon Short for "Canadian content." Currently, Canadian television stations need to program 50 percent CanCon in prime time and 60 percent CanCon overall.

CanWest Global Canada's newest private television network. Also owns Hollinger newspapers and the *National Post.*

CATV Short for community antenna television. An early name for cable systems. Began in London, Ontario.

CBC Canadian Broadcasting Corporation. Canada's national public television network. Began broadcasting in 1952.

CBFT Canada's first TV station; began broadcasting in Montreal in 1952.

CBS Columbia Broadcasting System. Built from CBS radio network under William Paley. One of the "Big Three" over-air networks.

coaxial cable Heavy-duty landline for video signals.

CTV Canada's first private television network. Owned by Bell Canada Enterprises.

DTH Short for "direct to home" systems. Bell ExpressVu and Star Choice are the two leading DTH systems in Canada.

Farnsworth, Philo Invented technology that uses electrons to transmit moving images live.

fibre-optic cable High-capacity glass filament for video signals.

Fowler Commission First Royal Commission into television broadcasting in Canada. Took place in 1955.

Gemini Awards Recognize excellence in Canadian TV; Canadian equivalent of the Emmy Awards.

Harcourt, Peter Claims that American movies differ from Canadian movies. Canadian films reflect Canada's social uncertainties.

iconoscope Name given to Zworykin's television vacuum tube.

image dissector Name given to Farnsworth's television vacuum tube.

interactive television A television-web hybrid that allows viewers to send and receive web messages on television sets.

Jowett, Garth Claims that Canada has always been dependent on the U.S. for movies.

Lichter, Linda and Robert Scholars who claim TV is reformist.

microwave relays Towers re-angle over-air signals to match the earth's curvature.

Murdoch, Rupert Created Fox network.

National Film Board of Canada (NFB) Organization established in 1939 to help "explain Canada to Canadians."

NBC National Broadcast Company. Built from NBC radio network under David Sarnoff. One of the "Big Three" over-air networks.

Novak, Michael Believes TV is broad shaper of issues and society.

pay-per-view (PPV) Cable companies charge subscribers for each program they watch.

persistence of vision Retina's capability to retain an image briefly, allowing brain to fill in gaps between successive images.

pilot Prototype show for a series.

radio with pictures Simplistic definition of TV.

Rothman, Stanley Scholars who claim TV is reformist.

Smith, Steve Canadian TV personality and entrepreneur who feels passionate about Canadian TV.

standards and practices Network offices to review programs for suitability.

streaming Downloading video and audio from the web in advance of playing.

syndicators Independent program producers and distributors.

Turner, Ted Cable pioneer with WTBS superstation, CNN, and other program services to cable systems.

United Paramount Theaters Strengthened ABC in 1953 merger.

UPN United Paramount Network. New network for over-air affiliates; started in 1995.

WB Television Network New network for over-air affiliates; started in 1995.

Zworykin, Vladimir RCA engineer who claimed to have invented television.

Chapter 6

ARPAnet Military network that preceded Internet.

B2B Short for business-to-business advertising. More focused than most consumer advertising.

bandwidth Space available in a medium, such as cable or the electromagnetic spectrum, to carry messages.

Bardeen, Jack Codeveloper of the transistor.

Bell Labs AT&T facility where transistor invented.

Berners-Lee, Tim Devised protocols, codes for the World Wide Web.

Brattain, Walter Codeveloper of the transistor.

Bush, Vannevar Proposed a machine for relational information retrieval.

CERN European particle physics research facility in Geneva, Switzerland.

compression Technology that makes a message more compact by deleting nonessential underlying code.

Corning Glass Company that developed fibre-optic cable.

cost per thousand (CPM) Advertising measure of an ad's reach.

CRTC Canadian Radio Television Communications Commission. It determined in 1999 that it would not regulate the Internet "at this time."

cyber- Prefix for human connection via computers.

Daily Me Experimental computer newspaper with reader-determined content.

digitization Converting on-off coding for storage and for transmission.

fibre-optic cable Glass strands capable of carrying data as light.

giant magneto-resistance (GMR) Allows superminiaturization.

Gibson, William Sci-fi writer who coined the term *cyberspace.*

hit Tallied every time someone goes to a web page.

hyperfiction Nonlinear novels, games, and other fiction.

hypertext markup language (HTML) Language that is the coding for messages on the web.

hypertext transfer protocol (HTTP) The coding that allows web-linked computers to communicate with each other.

hypertext Method of interrelating messages so that users control their sequence.

Internet A network of computer networks.

linear communication Messages in a specified start-to-end sequence.

Media Lab Massachusetts Institute of Technology research facility.

memex Machine proposed by Vannevar Bush for nonlinear information access.

miniaturization Reducing the size of devices for data recording, storage, and retrieval.

multiplexing Technology to transmit numerous messages simultaneously.

National Science Foundation Developed current Internet to give scholars access to supercomputers.

Nelson, Ted Coined the term *hypertext* for nonlinear communication.

Nexis First online database with national news.

peer review A screening mechanism in which scholarly material is reviewed by leaders in a discipline for its merits, generally with neither the author nor the reviewers knowing each other's identity.

Personal Journal Wall Street Journal computer newspaper with reader-determined content.

point-of-purchase In-store advertising to influence buyers.

semiconductor Tiny sand-based transistor that responds to weak on-off charges.

Shockley, William Codeveloper of the transistor.

shovelware Computer-delivered products without modification from the linear original.

streaming Technology that allows playback of a message to begin before all the components have arrived.

technological convergence Melding of print, electronic, and photographic media into digitized form.

transistor Sometimes referred to as a semiconductor. The silicon inside responds to electrical impulses.

universal access Giving everyone the means to use the web.

universal resource locator (URL) The address assigned to a page on the web.

USA Today Newspaper with one of the first nonlinear computer editions.

visit Tallied for every person who visits a website.

W3 consortium Organizations that use the web work through the W3 consortium (World Wide Web, 3Ws, get it?) to update web coding.

Webby A major award of excellence for websites.

World Wide Web System that allows global linking of information modules in user-determined sequences.

Chapter 7

Adams, John Federalist U.S. president.

Alien and Sedition Acts Discouraged criticism of government in the U.S.

Associated Press Co-op to gather and distribute news.

Bernstein, Carl *Washington Post* reporter who dug up Watergate.

Bly, Nellie Pioneering woman reporter during the Yellow Press Period.

Broadcast News (BN) Canadian-based news agency for radio.

Canadian Press (CP) Canadian-based news agency for print journalists.

consensible nature of news News organization second-guesses competition in deciding coverage.

CRTC Canadian Radio Television Communications Commission. It was concerned about the effects of convergence on the news, and ordered BCE and CanWest Global to keep editorial control for each medium separate.

Day, Benjamin Published the *New YorkSun*.

exploratory reporting Proactive news-gathering.

Federalist Papers Essays with diverse views on the form the new U.S. nation should take.

flow Significance of events worth covering varies from day to day.

Gans, Herbert Concluded that journalists have mainstream values.

gatekeeper Person who decides whether to shorten, drop, or change a story en route to the mass audience.

Green, Brian Canadian journalism professor who defines news as "the significant and that which affects us."

growth period Kesterton's second period in Canadian journalism; marked by expansion due to immigration following the War of 1812.

Hamilton, Andrew Urged truth as defence for libel. Canada's Joseph Howe would also argue the "truth defence."

Harris, Benjamin Published *Publick Occurrences*.

Hearst, William Randolph Built circulation with sensationalism in a circulation war with Pulitzer.

inverted pyramid Classic media writing model in which the most important information is given first. Developed during the Civil War.

investigative journalism Seeking stories that would not surface on their own and that subjects would prefer not be told.

jazz journalism Common in the 1920s, similar to yellow journalism.

Jefferson, Thomas Anti-Federalist U.S. president.

Kesterton, Wilfred Writer whose work on journalism in Canada is among the best. He divides the history of news in Canada into periods.

Lyon, Matthew Member of U.S. Congress jailed for criticism of President Adams.

Morse, Samuel Invented the telegraph, which made "lightning news" possible during the Civil War.

New York Sun First penny newspaper; published in 1833.

news hole Space for news in a newspaper after ads are inserted; time in a newscast for news after ads.

objective reporting Writing news without bias.

Owens, Anne Marie Canadian journalist who covered the Bernado-Homolka trials in the 1990s.

partisan period Period in journalism from the American Revolution at least to the 1830s. Known for political debates in the media.

penny papers Newspapers that were affordable by almost everyone.

penny press period Time when one-cent newspapers were geared to mass audiences and mass advertising.

Prestedge, Sue Canadian journalist-teacher who helped launch WTSN, the first network in the world devoted to woman's sports.

Publick Occurrences First colonial newspaper; published in Boston in 1690.

Pulitzer, Joseph Emphasized human interest in newspapers; later sensationalized in a large circulation war with Hearst.

Rooney, David Canadian author who claims that journalists are like everyone else: they develop their own attitudes and biases over time.

soft news Geared to satisfying audience's information wants, not needs.

transplant period First period in Canadian journalism, in which journalists from Britain and the U.S. were "transplanted" to Canada.

Watergate Reporting of the Nixon administration scandal.

westward growth Third period in Canadian journalism: as Canadians moved west, so did the press.

Woodward, Bob Carl Bernstein's colleague in the Watergate revelations.

yellow press period Late 1800s; marked by sensationalistic reporting and "stunt" journalism.

Zenger, John Peter Defied authorities in New York *Journal*. Pioneer of the Colonial Period.

Chapter 8

adversarial public relations Attacking critics openly.

advertising Unlike public relations, advertising seeks to sell a product or service.

advertorials Paid advertisements that state an editorial position.

ambivalent media relations Mix of proactive, reactive, and inactive media contacts.

APR Indicates CPRS accreditation for Canadian public relations professionals.

Baer, George Epitomized offensive corporate paternalism in the 1890s.

Barnum, P.T. Known for exaggerated promotion.

Canadian Public Relations Society (CPRS) Professional public relations association.

contingency planning Developing programs in advance of an unscheduled but anticipated event.

crisis management Helping a client through an emergency.

Darwin, Charles Devised survival-of-the-fittest theory.

enlightened self-interest Mutually beneficial public relations.

Evans, Sarah Canadian public relations specialist who says that in times of crisis, PR should focus on the safety of people first.

external public relations Gearing messages to outside organizations, constituencies, and individuals.

flakkers Derisive word for public relations people.

Garrett, Paul Devised the notion of enlightened self-interest.

image consulting Coaching individuals for media contacts.

information boycott Severing ties with news media.

institutional advertising Paid space and time to promote an institution's image or position.

integrated marketing communication Comprehensive program that links public relations and advertising.

internal public relations Gearing messages to inside groups, constituencies, and individuals.

Lee, Ivy Laid out fundamentals of public relations.

Livesey, Bruce Canadian who claims that PR professionals are "flacks" for big business.

lobbying Influencing public policy, usually legislation or regulations.

Ludlow Massacre Colorado tragedy that Ivy Lee converted into a public relations victory.

media kit A packet provided to news reporters to tell the story in an advantageous way.

media relations Using mass media to convey messages by public relations people.

Nelson, Joyce Canadian researcher/writer whose writing is critical of PR's hidden agenda.

Page, Arthur Established the role of public relations as a top management tool.

Pennsylvania Railroad Took Ivy Lee's advice, which favourably changed railroad's approach to public relations.

political communication Advising candidates or groups on public policy issues, usually in elections.

proactive media relations Taking initiative to release information.

promotion Promoting a cause or idea.

public information One alternative word for public relations; others are public affairs, corporate communication.

public relations A management tool to establish beneficial relationships between constituents.

public relations agencies Companies that provide public relations services.

publicity Brings public attention to something deemed significant.

puffery Inflated claims by corporations. Not what PR professionals aim for..

Rockefeller, John D., Jr. Ivy Lee client who had been the target of public hatred.

Schmertz, Herb Pioneered advertorials as a stance against the media..

social Darwinism Application of Darwin's survival-of-the-fittest theory to society.

Vanderbilt, William Henry Embodied the bad corporate images of the 1880s, 1890s with "The public be damned."

whitewashing Covering up an issue by a person or corporation.

Chapter 9

account executives Agency reps to clients.

ad clutter So many competing ads that all lose impact. It's information overload.

advertising director Coordinates marketing and advertising.

Advertising Standards Canada (ASC) Reviews complaints about ads.

Audit Bureau of Circulations Verifies circulation claims.

Ayer, Wayland Founded the first American ad agency.

barrages Intensive repetition of ads usually done in flights or waves.

Bok, Edward Set media standards for ads.

brand image Image created for a brand name.

brand manager Coordinates marketing and advertising for a specific brand.

brand A non-generic product name designed to set the product apart from the competition.

bunching Short-term ad campaign, usually seasonal, such as "back to school" sales.

caveat emptor Buyer beware. Was the dominant ideology for many years.

caveat venditor Seller beware. This is the current ideology for advertisers and they must be careful about what is said in commercials.

Caxton, William Printed the first advertisement.

commission system Agencies bill clients 15 percent more than media charge for time and space.

Competition Act The federal statute that regulates advertising in Canada.

CPM Cost per thousand; a tool to determine the cost effectiveness of different media.

creative director Key person in ad campaigns. In charge of creative (copy writing, etc) aspects of the ad.

Dichter, Ernest Pioneered motivational research.

fee system Agencies bill clients for expenses plus add-on percentage as profit.

flights Intensive repetition of ads.

Goodis, Jerry Canadian advertising guru who is a big believer in brand image.

infomercial Program-length broadcast commercial.

Key, Wilson Bryan Sees subliminal advertising widely used. His classic work is Subliminal Seduction.

lowest common denominator Messages for broadest audience possible.

McKim, Anson Founded the first Canadian ad agency.

media buyers Decide what media to use and where to place ads.

media plan Lays out where ads are placed and what media are used.

MediaWatch Critical, volunteer Canadian organization that often researches the content of advertising.

motivational research Seeks subconscious appeals that can be used in advertising.

Ogilvy, David Championed brand imaging for advertisers.

online advertising Provides messages to computer users based at web sites.

pass-along circulation All the people who see a periodical or publication.

Pollock, Griselda Cultural theorist, whose classic work is a study on sex roles in advertising.

positioning Targeting ads for specific consumer groups.

Reeves, Rosser Devised unique selling proposition (USP).

shelf life How long a periodical remains in use. Magazines have the longest shelf life.

stealth ads Advertisements, often subtle, in nontraditional, unexpected places such as a sitcom.

subception Receiving subconscious messages that trigger behaviour.

subliminal advertising Ads that cannot be consciously perceived.

trailing Shorter, smaller ads after larger media campaign is introduced.

Trout, Jack Devised positioning.

unique selling proposition (USP) Emphasizing a single feature.

Vicary, Jim Made dubious subliminal advertising claims.

waves Intensive repetition of ads.

'zine Magazine whose entire content, articles and ads, pitches a single product or product line.

Chapter 10

applied research Usefulness, usually economic, is apparent.

Audit Bureau of Circulations Checks newspaper and magazine circulation claims.

Baby Boomers Today's 40-something and 50-something generation.

Bureau of Measurement (BBM) Organization that has been surveying radio and television in Canada since 1956.

circulation Number of readers of a publication.

cohort analysis Demographic tool to identify marketing targets by common characteristics.

confidence level Degree of certainty that a survey is accurate.

content analysis Measuring media content to establish a database for analysis.

demographics Characteristics of groups within a population being sampled, including age, gender, and affiliations.

Depression Survivors Today's 80-something and 90-something generation.

diaries Sampling technique in which respondents keep their own records.

effects studies Impact of media on society, and of society on media.

flush factor Viewers leave during commercials to go to the refrigerator, bathroom, etc.

focus groups Small groups interviewed in loosely structured ways for opinion, reactions.

Gallup, George Introduced probability sampling.

galvanic skin checks Monitor pulse, skin responses to stimuli.

Generation X Today's 30-something generation.

geodemography Demographic characteristics by geographic area.

interviews Face-to-face, mail, and telephone survey technique.

margin of error Percentage points that a survey may be off mark.

Nielsen Media Research Surveys television viewership in Canada.

900 telephone numbers Used for call-in surveys; respondents select selves to participate and pay for the call.

opinion surveys Seek audience reaction and views.

passive meter Recognizes individuals by body mass to track viewing habits.

policy analysis Seeks implications of public policy and future effects.

population Group of people being studied, most often larger than the sample size.

Portable People Meter Monitor that tracks individual viewing habits.

Postwar Generation Today's 60-something generation.

Print Measurement Bureau (PMB) Company that measures magazine readership in Canada.

PRIZM Identifies population characteristics by zip code.

probability sampling Everyone in population being surveyed has an equal chance to be sampled.

process studies To understand the mass communication process.

prototype research Checks response to product still in development.

psychographics Breaking down a population by lifestyle characteristics.

quota sampling Demographics of the sample coincide with those of the whole population.

ratings Measurements of broadcast audience size.

Robbin, Jonathan Devised PRIZM geodemography system.

sample selection Process for drawing individuals to be interviewed.

sample size Number of people included in a survey. The larger the number, the better the results.

statistical extrapolation Drawing conclusions from a segment of the whole.

straw poll Respondents select themselves to be polled; unreliable indicator of public opinion.

sweeps Times during the year when broadcast ratings are conducted.

technological research To improve technology and find new technology.

theoretical research Goal to advance knowledge.

384 Number of people in a properly selected sample for results to provide 95 percent confidence that results have less than 5 percent margin error.

uses and gratifications studies To explain why people choose their media outlets.

VALS Psychographic analysis by values, lifestyle, and life stage.

World War II Veterans Today's 70-something and 80-something generation.

zapping Viewers record programs and eliminate commercial breaks.

zipping Viewers change television channels to avoid commercials.

Chapter 11

Aristotle Advocate of the golden mean.

Brass Check, The 1919 book that exposed newsroom corruption.

Broadcasting Act Federal statute governing radio and television broadcasting in Canada.

Butler ruling 1992 decision that helps define obscenity in Canada.

CAB Canadian Association of Broadcasters, a group of Canadian private broadcasters.

Canadian Charter of Rights and Freedoms Federal law that has guaranteed freedom of speech and freedom of the media in Canada since 1982.

categorical imperative Follow principles as if they had universal application.

CBSC Canadian Broadcast Standards Council, which offers guidelines for Canadian radio and TV.

Cherry Sisters Complainants in a U.S. case that barred performers from suing critics.

code of ethics Statement that defines acceptable and unacceptable behaviour.

Cooke, Janet Classic case of representing fiction as true.

copyright Protects intellectual property from theft.

CRTC Canadian Radio Television Communications Commission, the regulator of broadcasting in Canada.

defamation Comments made that ruin a person's reputation in the eyes of his/her colleagues.

Dewey, John Advocate of pragmatism.

"Do unto others" Judeo-Christian principle for ethical behaviour.

egalitarianism Philosophy that says we should treat everyone the same.

freebie Gift for which the giver may expect favours in return.

golden mean Moderation is the best course.

Haines, Avery Canadian journalist who, unintentionally, made controversial comments on CTV Newsnet in early 2000.

Hutchins Commission Advocated social responsibility as goal and result of media activities.

junket Trip with expenses paid by someone who may expect favours in return.

Kant, Immanuel Advocated the categorical imperative.

Mill, John Stuart Advocated utilitarianism.

misrepresentation Deception in gathering or telling information.

new journalism Mixing fiction techniques with nonfiction.

plagiarism Using someone else's work without permission or credit.

Potter, Ralph Ethicist who devised the Potter's Box.

Potter's Box Tool for sorting through the pros and cons of ethics questions.

pragmatic ethics Judge acts by their results.

principle of utility Best course bestows the most good for the most people.

public domain Intellectual property that may be used without permission of the creator or owner.

publication bans An exception to freedom of the press in Canada; primarily used in conjunction with the Young Offender's Act.

Radio Television News Directors Association of Canada (RTNDA) Organization that believes the broadcasting of factual, accurately reported, and timely news and public affairs is vital.

Rawls, John Advocated egalitarianism.

reality programs Broadcast shows with a nonfiction basis.

re-enactments Re-creating real events.

selective editing Misrepresentation through omission and juxtaposition.

Sinclair, Upton Author of *The Brass Check*.

SOCAN Licensing agency for media use of music in Canada.

social responsibility Making decisions that serve society responsibly.

staging news Creating an event to attract news media attention and coverage.

Valour and the Horror, The Three-part docudrama on World War II that sparked debate over how much artistic licence documentary makers could take.

veil of ignorance Making decisions with a blind eye to extraneous factors that could affect the decision.

Young Offender's Act Federal law that makes it illegal to broadcast the names of people under 18 years of age who are before the courts in Canada.

Chapter 12

agenda-setting Media tell people what to think about, not what to think.

aggressive stimulation Theory that people are inspired to violence from media depictions.

AGVOT Action Group on Violence on Television, an organization that helped develop programming codes for Canadian television.

Aristotle Defended portrayals of violence as positive and cathartic.

autistic perception Synonym for *selective perception*.

Bandura, Albert Found media violence stimulated aggression in children.

Bobo doll studies Kids seemed more violent after seeing violence in movies.

Cantril, Hadley Concluded that there is less media effect than had been thought.

catalytic theory Media violence is among factors that sometimes contribute to real-life violence.

cathartic effect People release violent inclinations by seeing them portrayed.

consistency theory People choose media messages consistent with their individual views and values.

cumulative effects theory Theory that media influence is gradual over time.

desensitizing theory Tolerance of real-life violence grows because of media-depicted violence.

diversion function Media used as an entertainment source.

Feshbach, Seymour Found evidence for media violence as a release.

Gerbner, George Speculated that democracy is endangered by media violence.

information pollution Media deluge people with information and no sense of order or priority.

Josephson, Wendy Canadian researcher who believes that violence on TV has an effect on children.

Lasswell, Harold His mass communication model assumed powerful effects.

Lazarsfeld, Paul Found voters more influenced by other people than by mass media.

Lippmann, Walter His *Public Opinion* assumed powerful media effects in the 1920s.

McCombs, Maxwell Along with Don Shaw, articulated agenda-setting theory.

media-induced passivity Media entice people away from social involvement.

Meyrowitz, Joshua Noted that media have reduced generational and gender barriers.

minimalist effects theory Theory that media effects are mostly indirect.

multistep flow Media effects on individuals come through complex interpersonal connections.

narcoticizing dysfunction People deceive themselves into believing they're involved when actually they're only informed.

Noelle-Neumann, Elisabeth Leading cumulative effects theorist.

observational learning Theory that people learn behaviour by seeing it in real life and in depictions.

opinion leaders People that influence friends, and acquaintances.

parasocial interaction A false sense of participating in dialogue.

Park, Robert Argued that media create awareness.

powerful effects theory Theory that media have immediate, direct influence.

prosocial Socialization perpetuates positive values.

role modelling Basis for imitative behaviour.

Schramm, Wilbur Concluded that television has minimal effects on children.

selective exposure People choose some media messages over others.

selective perception People tend to hear what they want or expect to hear.

selective recall People recollect some events and messages for long term but not others.

selective retention Subconsciously, people retain some events and messages, not others.

Shaw, Don Along with Maxwell McCombs, articulated agenda-setting theory.

socialization function Media help people fit into society.

socialization Learning to fit into society.

spiral of silence Vocal majority intimidates others into silence.

status conferral Credence that a topic or issue receives because of media attention.

stereotyping Using broad strokes to facilitate storytelling.

surveillance function Media provide information on what's going on.

two-step flow Media effects on individuals are through opinion leaders.

uses and gratifications Theory that people choose media that meet their needs, interests.

V-chip Invented by Canadian Tim Collings, this chip offers parents a way of monitoring what their children watch.

War of the Worlds Novel that inspired a radio drama that became the test bed of the media's ability to instil panic.

Welles, Orson His radio drama casts doubt on powerful effects theory.

Chapter 13

alienation Dissatisfaction with individual and cultural deviations from basic nature.

cognitive dissonance Occurs when people realize their values are inconsistent.

contemporary transmission Communication of cultural values to different cultures.

detribalization The removal of humankind from natural, tribal state.

diffusion of innovations Process through which news, ideas, values, and information spread.

elitism Mass media should gear to sophisticated audiences.

Gans, Herbert Said social, economic, and intellectual levels of audience coincide.

global village Instantaneous connection of every human being.

high art Requires sophisticated taste to be appreciated.

high-, middle-, and low-culture audiences Continuum identified by Herbert Gans.

highbrow, middlebrow, and lowbrow Levels of media content sophistication that coincide with audience tastes.

historical transmission Communication of cultural values to later generations.

kitschPejorative word for trendy, trashy, low art.

low art Can be appreciated by almost everybody.

Macdonald, Dwight Said all pop art is kitsch.

McLuhan, Marshall Blamed human alienation on mass-produced written word.

pop art revisionism Pop art has inherent value.

popular art Art that tries to succeed in the marketplace.

popularization Adjust media content to appeal to broader audience.

populism Mass media should seek largest possible audiences.

private actions versus public morality Dichotomy that exposes discrepancies between behaviour and values.

retribalization Restoring humankind to natural, tribal state.

Sontag, Susan Saw cultural and social value in pop art.

Znaimer, Moses Canadian media guru, successful entrepreneur, and media critic.

Chapter 14

Agence France-Presse Paris-based global news agency.

Associated Press U.S.-based global news service; largest news-gathering organization in the world.

bipolar model Portrays extremes as opposites, as libertarian and authoritarian political systems.

change model Shows the effect of mass media on numerous social variables and the effect of those variables on the media.

compass model A looped model that juxtaposes traditional authoritarian and social responsibility models.

continuum model A scale with authoritarianism at one end, libertarianism at the other, and media systems at varying points in between.

cultural imperialism One culture's dominance of another through mass media products.

Interfax Russian news agency.

Kellogg, Ansell Founded the first syndicate.

McClure, S.S. Expanded syndicate concept.

Merrill, John Introduced the compass model, which showed that social responsibility and authoritarianism could be bedmates.

Murdoch, Rupert Australian-born owner of the global company News Corporation.

NTV Privately owned Russian television network.

perestroika Russian policy to restructure institutions in the spirit of candour and openness.

Reuters British-based global news agency.

Schiller, Herbert Saw Western cultures subsuming others through the exporting of mass media.

subsystem model Examines media in terms of originator and intended audience.

syndicatesProvide low-cost, high-quality content to many news outlets.

United Press International Faded major news agency.

NAME INDEX

SUBJECT INDEX

PHOTO CREDITS

Chapter 1

p. 1 AP/Wide World Photos; p. 2 AP/Wide World Photos; p. 4 (top) AP/Wide World Photos; p. 4 (bottom) CRTC; p. 5 Warner Brothers Pictures, Inc. HARRY POTTER, characters, names and related indicia are trademarks of Warner Bros. 2001; p. 11 Canapress; p. 15 reprinted by permission of Autowraps.com; p. 17 Jacques Chenet/Woodfin Camp & Associates; p. 19 (left), Courtesy of AT&T Archives; p. 20 reprinted from the Columbia Journalism Review, January/February 2001; p. 22 The Everett Collection, Inc.; p. 23 (insert left), News and Publications Service, Stanford University; p. 24 John Barnett/Globe Photos, Inc.; p. 26 CBC Television

Chapter 2

p. 32 Brian W. Smith/TimePix; p. 34 North Wind Picture Archive; p. 35 reprinted courtesy of the Canadian Newspaper Association 1998 ad. p. 36; p. 39 Hulton Getty/Archive Photos; p. 40 USA Today; p. 41 National Post; p. 43 with permission: The Toronto Star Syndicate; p. 45 MetroValley Newspaper Group; p. 55 Bob Carroll; p 52 (top left) George Strock, Life Magazine 1944 Time Inc.; p 52 (bottom right) Joe Scherschel, Life Magazine 1958 Time Inc.; p. 53 Courtesy of Maclean's; p. 57 Watterson. Reprinted with permission of Universal Press Syndicate. All rights reserved; p. 58 Canoe.ca

Chapter 3

p. 65 Canadian Press; p. 69 Canpress; p. 71 from the collections of the Library of Congress; p. 74 AP/Wide World Photos; p. 77 (top right), UPI/Corbis; p. 77 (bottom left) UPI/Corbis-Bettman; p. 77 (bottom right) Corbis-Bettman; p. 78 Canapress/Andrew Wallace; p. 79 Canapress/Frank Gunn; p. 80 Ethan Miller/Reuters/TimePix; p. 83 AP/Wide World Photos; p. 84 (left) Forrest Anderson/TimePix; p. 84 (right), AP/Wide World Photos; p. 85 AP/Wide World Photos

Chapter 4

p. 90 Canapress/Curt Petrovich; p. 93 UPI/Corbis-Bettman; p. 94 The Granger Corbis; p. 95 (all)

AP/Wide World Photos; p. 98 (both) Bettmann; p. 101 Chip Hires/Gamma-Liaison; p. 102 ABC Radio, Chicago; p. 103 AP/Wide World Photos; p. 105 Jeff Slocomb/Outline

Chapter 5

p. 111 CBC; p. 115 UPI Corbis; p. 118 2000 TiVo, Inc.; p. 121 CBC Television; p. 123 AP/WideWorld Photos; p. 127 Everett Collection, Inc.; p. 130 Tundra Books; p. 132 Johnnie Eisen; p. 133 AP/Wide World Photos

Chapter 6

p. 136 Canapress; p. 137 Juno and the Juno logo are registered trademarks of Juno Online Services, Inc. YellowOnline banner is YellowOnline.comtm; p. 138 CERN Geneva; p. 144 Jeff Scheid/Liaison Agency, Inc.; p. 145 UPI/Corbis-Bettman; pp. 146–7 1998 Spaceshots/Living Earth Inc. Reprinted by permission; p. 149 Corbis; p. 151 The Daily News, Halifax; p. 153 David Young-Wolf/PhotoEdit

Chapter 7

p. 157 Canapress; p. 159 North Wind Picture Archives; p. 160 (left) Bettmann; p. 160 (right) North Wind Picture Archives; p. 161 (both right) Culver Pictures; p. 211 (left) Bettmann; p. 171 Canapress

Chapter 8

p. 179 AP/Wide World Photos; p. 181 (all) Naum Kazhdan/NYT Pictures; p. 184 Allen Tannenbaum/Sygma; p. 237 (top) Colorado Historical Society; p. 237 (bottom) AP/Wide World Photos; p. 188 NAC; p. 191 David Grossman; p. 193 (top) Kevin Horan; p. 193 (bottom) Sygma; p. 195 (top and middle) Canapress; p. 195 (bottom) AP/Wide World Photos; p. 197 (left) Van Bucher; p. 197 (right) Herb Smertz

Chapter 9

p. 203 (all) Wilson Bryan Key; p. 206 Actmedia; p. 209 Pizza Hut; p. 213 (left) United Colors of Benetton; p. 216 Alene M. McNeill; p. 217 Bamboo Inc.; p. 219 North Wind Picture Archives

Chapter 10

p. 329 Roger Huchins/Woodfin Camp & Associates; p. 229 AP/Wide World Photos; p. 232 (both) Nielsen Media Research; p. 233 The Arbitron Company, NY; p. 236 Douglass Burrows/Liaison Agency, Inc.; p.237 CNN; p.238 Time Inc. Magazine Company. Reprinted with permission. p. 241 (both) Reuters/John C. Hillary

Chapter 11

p. 244 Electronic Frontier Foundation; p. 248 Canapress; p. 250 Joel Veak; p. 251 (top left) David M. Grossman; p. 251 (bottom left) AP/Wide World Photos; p. 251 (top right) David M. Grossman; p. 251 (bottom right) Ed Lallo/Liaison Agency, Inc.; p. 255 Toronto Star; p. 259 Canapress; p. 261 (all) New York Daily News Photos; p. 263 Corbis; p. 264 (both) North Wind Picture Archive; p. 269 Charles Steiner/JB Pictures

Chapter 12

p. 274 Culver Pictures; p. 279 AP/Wide World Photos; p. 283 David Dempster; p. 287 (all) Dr. Albert Bandura; p. 289 Cochran Entertainment Inc.; p. 292 Hekki Saukkoma; p. 294 (left) Everett Collection, Inc.; p. 294(right) 1998 sCi (Sales Curve Interactive) Limited. All rights reserved.

Chapter 13

p. 300 Corbis; p. 302 (left) The Toronto Sun; p. 302 (right) The National Post; p. 305 Reuters/Jill Connelly/Archive Photos; p. 306 Gamma Liaison; p. 307 AP/Wide World Photos; p. 310 (left) Fredrich Cantor; p. 310 (right) Center for Media and Public Affairs; p. 311 Canapress; p. 312 (left) AP/Wide World Photos; p. 312 (right) AFP Photo/Sergey Chirikov/Corbis/Sygma

Chapter 14

p. 314 AP/Wide World Photos; p. 315 Freedom House; p. 319 USCD Photo; p. 320 Roslan/Rahman/AFP Photo/Corbis; p. 327 Reuters/Luis Ramirez/Colombia Press/Corbis/Sygma